HOW TO SAY IT

Choice Words, Phrases, Sentences, and Paragraphs for Every Situation

by Rosalie Maggio

PRENTICE HALL
Paramus, New Jersey 07652

Library of Congress Cataloging-in-Publication Data

Maggio, Rosalie.
   How to say it! : choice words, phrases, sentences, and
paragraphs for every situation / Rosalie Maggio.
     p. cm.
   Includes index.
   ISBN 0-13-424367-6 (case)—ISBN 0-13-424375-7 (pbk.)
   1. Letter-writing. I. Title.
PE1483.M26 1990   90-38681
808.6—dc20   CIP

Printed in the United States of America

20 19 18 17   *20*   *(pbk)*

ISBN 0-13-424367-6   ISBN 0-13-424375-7 (PBK)

PRENTICE HALL
Paramus, NJ 07652

A Simon & Schuster Company

On the World Wide Web at http://www.phdirect.com

Prentice-Hall International (UK) Limited, *London*
Prentice-Hall of Australia Pty. Limited, *Sydney*
Prentice-Hall Canada Inc., *Toronto*
Prentice-Hall Hispanoamericana, S.A., *Mexico*
Prentice-Hall of India Private Limited, *New Delhi*
Prentice-Hall of Japan, Inc., *Tokyo*
Simon & Schuster Asia Pte. Ltd., *Singapore*
Editora Prentice-Hall do Brasil, Ltda., *Rio de Janeiro*

To DAVID
Liz, Katie, Matt

Acknowledgments

Many thanks to such generous people as Steve Sikora of The Letter Exchange; H. Jack Lang, editor of *The Wolf Magazine of Letters*; Dr. Matt Maggio; Patrick Maggio, Esq.; Kevin Maggio, Esq.; Frank Maggio; Terry Hay Maggio; Mary Maggio; Dr. Paul T. Maggio; Mark Maggio; Irene Nash Maggio; Dr. Paul J. Maggio; Lt. Mike Maggio; Bonnie and Steven and Emily Goldsmith; John Wall; Patricia Yeager and the Denver Center for Independent Living; Esther Lilley; Nick Niemeyer; Andy Parr; Roseanne and Jerry DePalma; Larry Lilley; Sheila Hanley and The Dublin Walk; Maggie Parr; Cathryn and Keith Tonn; Dr. Greg Filice; Debbye Calhoun Spang; Irmiter Contractors and Builders Limited; Jeanne Goerss Novak; Garry D. Rooney and Unocal; Ronald Severson and the Newgate auto vocational school.

Contents

Introduction

letter\'let-ər\n. a direct or personal written or printed
message addressed to a person or organization.
(*Webster's Ninth New Collegiate Dictionary*)

Letterwriting sounds so simple. And perhaps it was, once upon a time. To-day, however, more and more letters are being written (over 79 *billion* per year), and they are more complex and more critical to our well-being. Jobs, sales, friendships, public relations, fundraising, and even our day-to-day satisfactions depend on our ability to communicate quickly, accurately, and succinctly.

Although an impressive amount of business and social interaction takes place over the telephone or in person today, oral communication has not yet begun to replace the written word. The well-written letter remains a staple of business success and one of the strongest connecting links between individuals.

Most of us are capable of writing an intelligible, convincing letter, but few of us have the time and mental energy to write the countless and diverse letters that life today seems to demand.

This practical, easy-to-use book contains everything you need to know to write an effective business or social letter in little more time than it takes to handwrite, type, or input it. The convenient, flexible approach presented here emphasizes letters that are not only quickly written but clear, compelling, and *personal*. Unique among letter-writing books, it features comprehensive, versatile lists of words, phrases, sentences, and paragraphs that allow you to express yourself immediately on any topic in your own "voice" and style. Based on the general principle of the thesaurus, these lists provide you with every expression relevant to your topic. Whether you want to sound formal or casual, traditional or contemporary, businesslike or lighthearted, distant or intimate, you will find the words for every letter-writing occasion in this one practical reference—from the most simple letters to the most sophisticated, from strong, cogent business letters to warm, sensitive personal letters. Using this method, you'll find yourself writing letters with increased speed, flexibility, and individuality.

Napoleon was probably the only individual in history who could not have made some use of this book. He was reputed to have written more than 50,000 letters in his lifetime.

1

How to Use This Book

Before writing your first letter, familiarize yourself with the appendixes. There you will find a treasury of sensible, concise, and logically arranged guidelines to help you produce the letters you want to write.

Appendix I deals with the *mechanics* of letterwriting: what kind of stationery to use, how to address an envelope, how to set up a letter on the page, when to write a memo, how to use postal service programs to reduce your mailing costs.

Appendix II deals with the *content* of your letter: writing tips, grammar and usage, names and titles, exclusive language, frequently misspelled words, redundant words and phrases, correct forms of address.

To write a specific letter, turn to the Table of Contents where you will find forty broad letter topics (for example, sales letters, thank you letters, letters of sympathy, letters dealing with employment) arranged alphabetically.

Each chapter includes a brief introduction, a list of occasions for writing that type of letter, what to include in each letter, what not to say, comments on special situations, and what format (for example, letterhead stationery, foldover notes, or memo paper) to use.

At the heart of each chapter are lists of appropriate words, phrases, sentences, and paragraphs that can be used to construct your letter. Sample letters are also given.

These lists serve three main purposes: (1) they "prime the pump"—get you thinking along the lines of that letter topic; (2) they provide those who want to compose their own letter with a number of appropriate words; (3) they allow those who are using the sample letters as guides to substitute words that fit the specific situation.

Some of the words in each list will not be appropriate for your particular letter. These words are chosen to cover all types of, for example, sales letters or invitations. Your needs will be narrower, and thus you will probably use only a few of the words in a list for each letter.

Some of the words will not sound like you, but a range of words is offered so that ones that *do* sound like you will be available.

The process of composing a letter is simple:

- ☐ Read through the "How to Say It" section, note the elements that your letter should include, and personalize them to reflect your situation.

2

- ☐ Choose from the lists of words, phrases, sentences, and paragraphs those terms that are useful to you.

- ☐ Study the sample letters to see if one of them can serve you as a model. If you tend to be logical and linear in your approach to life, you may want to choose a sample letter and combine your checked-off words, phrases, sentences, and even paragraphs until you have a letter that conveys your message. If you are more intuitive and spontaneous, you will weave together those words, phrases, sentences, and paragraphs that appeal to you without following any particular sample letter.

- ☐ Once you have a rough draft, check it against the list of what not to say. Have you inadvertently written something inappropriate? At this point, you may have a question about format or grammar or a social title. Check the index to quickly locate your question in one of the Appendixes.

Because your two most important tools are the lists of words, phrases, sentences, and paragraphs and the "How to Say It" list, the book's design allows you to locate these two sections in each chapter very quickly.

The index may be the most valuable section of all as it lists hundreds of references to letterwriting situations and issues.

After writing your first few letters using this book, you may feel that it is not so difficult or time-consuming after all to write your share of the 79 billion letters mailed each year.

1

Acceptances

"The oldest, shortest words—'yes' and 'no'—are those which require the most thought." (Pythagoras)

Once you have decided to accept an invitation or accede to a request, it is a simple matter to say so; this is one of the least difficult letters to write. The average person will write many more refusals (which are more difficult to write) than acceptances because of the rising numbers of requests and invitations generated by today's increasingly complex society.

Occasionally you may write an acceptance with less than a whole heart. You don't really want to attend or comply, but there is some feeling that you "ought to," that something is expected of you, that you owe someone the favor. This results in an unenthusiastic acceptance or, worse, reneging or canceling later on. Writing the acceptance is not as difficult as being sure you want to say "yes" in the first place.

Write Acceptances For

- admissions requests: schools/clubs/organizations
- advice/recommendations/suggestions
- changes requested
- franchise applications
- invitations: dinner/meeting/party/luncheon/hospitality
- job applications/offers
- membership: board/commission/organization/club
- office: political/business/social club
- proposals
- requests: contributions/favors/help
- speaking engagements: conference/workshop/banquet
- wedding invitations (see WEDDINGS)

How to Say It

❑ Express your pleasure in accepting the invitation/offer/proposal/bid or state your agreement to do what was asked.

❑ Repeat, confirm, or describe the details of what you are accepting (date and time of a meeting, amount of the bid or of the contribution you are sending, the precise nature of your assistance, the duties you are agreeing to assume).

❑ Mention special circumstances or needs (receipt for a tax-deductible contribution, directions to your host's home, special equipment for your speech, club handbook, list of other organizers, etc.).

❑ End with an expression of future pleasure (in seeing the person, working for the company, being part of the group) or future action (what you would like to accomplish, what actions you intend to take, a reciprocal invitation).

What Not to Say

❑ Avoid ungracious and unnecessary amplifications: you are very busy but you suppose you can manage it; you have two other events on the calendar that evening but you will try to stop by; you probably won't be a very good speaker but, sure, you'll try. Let your "yes" be a simple "yes." If you have reservations or difficulties with your acceptance, it may be better to decline.

Tips on Writing

❑ Acceptances are invariably brief and deal only with the acceptance; do not include other matters unless your letter is casual and your correspondent well known to you.

❑ Be enthusiastic. Although it is entirely proper to simply state your acceptance and repeat the details of the invitation, your hosts, employers, or friends will look forward to seeing you with greater pleasure if you add at least one sentence containing something personal, cheerful, or lively.

❑ If your invitation is issued in the name of more than one person, mention all of them in your reply and mail your reply either to the person listed under the R.S.V.P. or to the first name given.

Special Situations

❑ In some situations (large weddings, for example), one of a couple may accept an invitation while the other person declines. In other cases (large dinner parties), check with your host to see if this is acceptable.

◻ All White House invitations include the phone number of the Social Office where you may telephone your acceptance or regret and where you can ask questions about protocol, where to park your car, what to wear, how to respond to the invitation. Otherwise, general guidelines are: send your reply within a day of receiving the invitation; write the reply yourself (do not have a secretary do it); handwrite your reply on plain or engraved personal stationery; use the same format and person (first person or third person) to reply but insert "have the honor of accepting"; if the invitation was sent to you from the President's or First Lady's secretary (in the case of an informal invitation), reply to that person ("Would you please tell/convey to . . ."); if the invitation is addressed to the woman in a married couple (as is sometimes the case in traditional, formal invitations), she writes the acceptance but says, "My husband and I will be delighted to accept . . ." When declining an invitation, specify the reason (there are only four generally accepted excuses for not accepting a White House invitation: a death in the family, a family wedding, prior travel plans, illness) by saying, "We regret that owing to the illness/recent death of . . ."

◻ Children can write their own brief acceptances for invitations: "Thank you for inviting me to your Halloween party. Wait 'til you see my costume!"

◻ Send acceptances as soon as possible. If you are late, apologize briefly and sincerely, but do not dwell on it.

Format

◻ The correct format for an acceptance is simple: model your reply after the invitation or letter. If it is handwritten, handwrite your reply. If letterhead stationery is used, reply using your own letterhead. If the language of the invitation is informal, your reply should also be informal. In the case of formal invitations, you will use nearly the same words, layout, and style as the invitation in your reply. For example, see the following invitation and acceptance.

Mr. and Mrs. Masterson Finsbury

request the pleasure of

Mr. and Mrs. Edward Bloomfield's company

at a dinner-dance

on Saturday, the seventh of February

at eight o'clock

Gideon Country Club

. . . .

Mr. and Mrs. Edward Bloomfield

accept with pleasure

the kind invitation of

Mr. and Mrs. Masterson Finsbury

to a dinner-dance

on Saturday, the seventh of February

at eight o'clock

Gideon Country Club

WORDS

accept	delighted	possible
acknowledge	favorable	probably
agree	feasible	reciprocate
approve	gratifying	satisfying
assent	likelihood	thoughtful
certainly	likely	welcome
compatible	pleased	willing
comply	pleasure	workable
confirm		

PHRASES

able to say yes	it is with great pleasure that
agree to	it was so thoughtful of you to
by all means	it will be a pleasure to
comply with	may/can count upon
conform to	thank you for asking me to
give consent	thank you for nominating me for
happy to commit ourselves to	to your satisfaction
happy to let you know	vote yes to
have no objection	we always enjoy
I'm pleased/happy to accept	we are delighted to accept
in all likelihood/probability	we have accepted your bid of
in response to your letter	your good offer/kind invitation

─────────────── **SENTENCES** ───────────────

After reviewing your request, we have decided we can offer you the assistance you need.

I accept with pleasure the position of senior research chemist.

I am happy to be able to do this.

I am pleased/happy/honored to accept your invitation.

I look forward to seeing you again.

I'm glad we can help.

In a word, absolutely!

In response to your letter asking for support for the Foscari Children's Home, I'm enclosing a check for $500.

I will be happy to meet with you in your office on Thursday, March 11, at 10:30 a.m. to begin planning for this year's All-City Science Fair.

Please extend my appreciation to the board for their confidence in me.

Thanks for asking me/for thinking of me.

There's nothing we'd rather do.

We accept your kind invitation with great pleasure.

We are pleased to tell you that your application for admission to the Emmet School has been approved.

We look forward to working with you.

You can count on us being there.

Your franchise application has been approved and accepted.

─────────────── **PARAGRAPHS** ───────────────

▷   I will be delighted to have dinner with you on Friday, the sixteenth of March, at seven o'clock. Thanks so much for asking me. I am looking forward to seeing you and Anders again.

▷   Thanks for telling me how much the children at St. Joseph's Home liked my storytelling the other night. I'm happy to accept your invitation to become a regular volunteer and tell stories every other Thursday evening. Do you have a record player or tape deck so that I could use music with some of the stories?

▷   I'm looking forward to your graduation and the reception afterwards. Thanks for including me.

─────────────── **SAMPLE LETTERS** ───────────────

Dear Selina,
    Vickers and I accept with pleasure your kind invitation to a celebration of your parents' fiftieth wedding anniversary on Saturday, July 16, at 7:30 p.m.
                              Cordially,

. . . .

Dear Dr. Cheesewright:

Thank you for inviting me to speak to your county dental society's dinner banquet on October 26 at 7:00. I am happy to accept and will, as you suggested, discuss new patient education methods.

I'm not sure how much time you have allotted me—will you let me know?

With best wishes,

. . . .

Dear Mr. Grandby:

We are pleased to accept for publication your self-help book, tentatively entitled *Don't Give Up.* All of us are very excited about its possibilities.

Enclosed are some guidelines from the production editor to help you prepare the final manuscript. Also enclosed is a preliminary draft of the book contract. Please look it over, and I will call next week to discuss it.

Sincerely yours,

. . . .

Dear Ms. Unwin:

Congratulations! Your franchise application has been approved. Welcome to the Sunshine family.

Enclosed is the contract, which we suggest you discuss with your attorney, and a packet of informational materials.

Please call this office to set up an appointment to discuss any questions and to finalize our agreement.

Sincerely,

. . . .

Dear Violet,

Yes! I will be delighted to come stay with the twins while you and Gordon take the horses to the state fair. A week is *not* too long for me. And thanks for the offer of the plane ticket—I accept with pleasure.

Love,

. . . .

Dear Francis,

I will be happy to write you a letter of reference, and I'm delighted that you thought to ask me. You were always one of my favorite students, and I'll enjoy explaining just why to Main Street Press.

Yours truly,

. . . .

Mr. Clarence Rochester

accepts with pleasure

William Portlaw and Alida Ascott's

kind invitation to dinner

on the sixteenth of June at 7:30 p.m.

but regrets that

Dr. Maggie Campion

will be absent at that time.

See also: REFUSALS, RESPONSES.

2

Acknowledgments

"Life is not so short but that there is always time enough for courtesy." (Ralph Waldo Emerson)

Although letters of acknowledgment do sometimes have a purpose of their own, more often they are hybrid letters. When a big order comes in, do you send a letter of acknowledgment, confirmation, or thanks—or a little of all three? When someone writes you a letter of sympathy, do you write a thank you letter or an acknowledgment letter? Sometimes, too, "acknowledgment" letters are really sales letters that use the excuse of acknowledging something (an order, a payment) to present an additional sales message. If you do not find the precise type of letter you want in this section, check the related sections.

In its narrow sense, a letter of acknowledgment has two purposes: (1) to let someone know that their letter, gift, package, merchandise, or shipment has been received by you; (2) to say that you will be responding more fully later. If someone mails you a report, you acknowledge its receipt and say that you will call and discuss it as soon as you've had time to read and digest it. Many newly married couples send acknowledgments of wedding gifts to let people know that their gifts have arrived and to say they'll write a thank you note very soon. When you receive a complaint, you acknowledge it to let the sender know you've received it but have not yet looked into the matter.

Most business transactions require no acknowledgment: payments are sent, orders are received, merchandise is mailed out on schedule. You would, however, acknowledge receipt when the situation is unusual—when, for example, the previous order went astray and you want the sender to know that this one arrived. Or perhaps you receive payment from someone to whom you've been sending collection letters, and you want the person to know that payment has been received (and, by implication, that there will be no more collection letters). You may want to acknowledge very large or important payments, orders, and shipments—or those from first-time customers or suppliers. You would also acknowledge receipt of an order that cannot be filled immediately.

Write a Letter of Acknowledgment For

- anniversary/birthday greetings
- apologies
- complaints
- condolences
- congratulations
- divorce announcements
- documents/reports/files received
- gifts (a "thank you" to come later)
- information received
- inquiries/requests (will respond as soon as possible)
- letters from constituents
- letters of introduction
- letters received (action underway, will let you know)
- manager's absence (secretary acknowledges receipt)
- manuscripts (under consideration, will give decision later)
- oral agreements (see also CONFIRMATION)
- orders (see also CONFIRMATION, ORDERS)
- payments
- sales
- sympathy messages
- telephone discussions/agreements (see also CONFIRMATION)
- wedding gifts (see WEDDINGS)

How to Say It

☐ Refer specifically to the letter or items you are acknowledging.

☐ Describe what action (if any) is being taken.

☐ Tell when the reader will hear further from you or from someone else.

☐ If indicated, explain why you are not able to respond fully to the letter/request/gift at the moment.

What Not to Say

☐ Acknowledgments are meant to be brief; do not belabor explanations (why you can't give an immediate response, for example).

Tips on Writing

▫   A letter of acknowledgment is, almost by definition, one sent immediately. If your acknowledgment is late, apologize briefly, but do not dwell on it. An exception to the "sent immediately" rule is the acknowledgment of expressions of sympathy; because of the hardships involved, responses may acceptably be sent up to six weeks later.

Special Situations

▫   If a friend writes to announce a divorce, it is best to avoid any response (congratulations or sympathy) that presumes to judge the situation. Simply acknowledging the information is adequate.

▫   In some instances, printed or engraved cards or foldovers may be sent in response to expressions of sympathy. When someone well-known dies, many people who knew the person only superficially send sympathy cards and notes to the family. A personal response is unnecessary in this case, although everyone who writes should receive an acknowledgment. A handwritten line or two is added for those people who sent more than the traditional card or message. (Formal acknowledgments—with or without black borders—usually carry the printed message on the top sheet, leaving you the undersheet for any personal message.) The use of printed or engraved acknowledgments of sympathy should be restricted to special instances, however.

▫   When someone apologizes to you, you may want to acknowledge it. Your letter is not so much a thank you (although you may begin your letter with "thank you") as an acknowledgment that the apology was received and accepted.

▫   Organizations that receive memorial donations must acknowledge receipt of the contribution and must also notify the family so that they can thank the donor themselves.

Format

▫   For acknowledgments of reports, orders, documents, payments, and other business items, use letterhead stationery, memo paper, or form letters.

▫   Personal acknowledgments on formal or informal personal stationery should, almost without exception, be handwritten.

▫   Printed acknowledgment cards may be sent when you must delay a response. You can thus let a number of people know that you have received their gifts/manuscripts/expressions of sympathy, and that you will respond personally as soon as you can.

▫   If you routinely acknowledge orders, you may want to have printed postcards made up. You could also simply send the customer a copy of the form on which you enter the order. Be sure to identify the particular order by invoice number, date, and description.

▫   Printed forms with fill-in blanks may be used to acknowledge routine transactions.

_____ WORDS _____

accept	corroborate	received
acknowledge	endorse	reply
affirm	indicate	respond
agreed-upon	meet	satisfaction
appreciate	notice	settle
approve	receipt	willing
confirm		

_____ PHRASES _____

abide by	in compliance with
acknowledge receipt of	in fulfillment of
arrived today	in response to your letter
as we agreed yesterday	I sincerely appreciated
bring to my/your notice	point out
by all means	show appreciation for
comply with	subscribe to
conform to	take into account/consideration
express gratitude for	take note of
give consent	to fulfill
go along with	to your satisfaction
have no objection	your kind message of sympathy

_____ SENTENCES _____

I enjoyed speaking with you on the telephone this morning.
I have received your letter of June 10.
Just a note to let you know that the printer ribbons finally arrived.
Thank you for taking the time and effort to write me about your views on socialized medicine.

Thank you for the wallpaper samples, which arrived this morning.

Thank you for your kind letter.

The family of Annis Gething gratefully acknowledges your kind and comforting expressions of sympathy.

The members of the Board of Directors and I are grateful for the presentation you gave yesterday and want you to know that we are taking your concerns under serious advisement.

This is to acknowledge receipt of the rerouted shipment of Doncastle tennis rackets, catalog number AE-78573.

We hereby acknowledge that an inspection of the storm drain and street construction installed by the Bagshaw Company in the Rockingham subdivision has been completed.

Your thoughtfulness and sympathy were much/greatly appreciated.

PARAGRAPHS

▷   Your letter of July 16 has been referred for review and appropriate action. We value you as a customer and ask your patience while a response to your communication is being prepared.

▷   Thank you for the update on the preparation of the Price-Stables contract. I appreciate knowing what progress you're making.

▷   Thank you for your workshop proposal, which we have just received. Ms. Bramber is out of the office for the next two weeks but will contact you soon after she returns.

▷   Thanks for the samples. As soon as we've had a chance to get them under the microscope and run some tests, we'll let you know what we find.

▷   I've just received your invitation to join the Friends of the Library committee and am flattered that you asked me. I need to look at several other commitments to be sure that I can devote as much time to this organization as I'd like. I will be in touch with you in a week or so. In the meantime, thanks again for thinking of me.

▷   The information you sent was exactly what I needed. It's going to take me several weeks to reach a decision, but I will call you as soon as I do. In the meantime, thanks for the prompt and complete information.

▷   Thanks for the call this morning, Janet. I'll see you on May 23 at 10:00 a.m. and will bring the spring lists with me.

▷   I wanted you to know that I received your letter this morning, but as I'm leaving for Dallas later today I won't have time to look into the billing problem with the contractor for another week or so. If you need action sooner than that, give Agnes Laiter a call.

▷   This is to acknowledge receipt of the Dakers contracts. As soon as I have had a chance to look them over, I'll let you know my opinion. In the meantime, thanks for getting them here so promptly.

▷   I'm so glad we were able to reach some agreement on the telephone this morning. I will have the contracts retyped, inserting the new delivery date of March 16, 1993, and the new metric ton rate of $55, and sent to you by the end of the week.

▷   Thank you for telling me about the divorce. It's been too long since I've seen you. Can we get together sometime? How about breakfast Saturday morning? That used to work for us.

▷   Thank you for your letter of June 9, describing the employee behavior you encountered on three different visits to our store. We are looking into the situation and will let you know what we find. In the meantime, please accept our most sincere apologies for any embarrassment or unpleasantness you may have experienced.

▷   Thank you for your letter of application and your résumé. We have received numerous responses to our advertisement, which means you may not hear from us immediately. We will be calling qualified applicants to arrange interviews beginning March 1.

―――――――――――――― SAMPLE LETTERS ――――――――――――――

Dear Edna Bunthorne:
   This will acknowledge your letter of August 6 addressed to Francis Moulton. Mr. Moulton is on a six-month medical leave of absence, and his interim replacement has not yet been named.
   I am enclosing materials that will answer some of your questions, and I will refer the others to the new director as soon as possible.
   If the delay is unacceptable to you, I wonder if you wouldn't like to contact Kate Croy at the Lowder Foundation. She may be able to help you.
                                        Sincerely,

. . . .

The family of Philip Hipplewayne
wishes to acknowledge with gratitude
your kind expression of sympathy.

. . . .

Dear Eleanor,
   Thanks for the letter and all the latest news. As for your colleague's visit to the Windy City, I'm sure I would find him interesting, particularly because of the work he's currently doing on alkanes. I will call him, but can't promise too much as I'm booked solid the next two weeks and his free time may not coincide with the little I have. However, I am looking forward to meeting him and will do all I can to show him around, time permitting.
                                        With best wishes,

. . . .

Dear Professor Erlin:

Thank you for your paper, "The Rise and the Fall of the Supercomputer," which we received this week. Because of an overwhelming response to our call for symposium papers, our editorial staff will not be able to respond within the usual two to three weeks. It may be five to six weeks before we can let you know if we're able to publish your work. Thanks for your understanding.

Yours truly,

. . . .

Dear Member,

Thank you for your order.

Unfortunately, we're temporarily out of stock on the item below. We've reordered it and expect to have a new supply in a few weeks. We'll send it to you as soon as it arrives.

Please excuse the delay.

Sincerely,

See also: APPOINTMENTS, CONFIRMATION, RESPONSES, SALES, THANK YOU.

3

Letters of Adjustment

> "Always do right. This will gratify some people, and
> astonish the rest." (Mark Twain)

Business inadequacies—incorrect bills, damaged merchandise, late payments—are unfortunately not as rare as we all might wish. Adjustments are commonly and routinely dealt with in most instances. Overly apologetic letters are not necessary, nor are any remedies beyond a quid pro quo replacement, refund, repair, or other resolution of the problem. However, good customer relations demand that you not treat the problem too lightly either—assume responsibility for the error, express your regrets, and make amends in a straightforward and fair manner.

(Note: If you are writing to request an adjustment, see COMPLAINTS; this chapter deals with making adjustments.)

Kinds of Adjustment Letters

- billing errors
- corrected bills/invoices
- credit
- damages
- exchanges
- explanations: oversight/error
- newspaper corrections
- refunds/discounts
- refusing to make (see CREDIT, REFUSALS)
- repairing damages
- replacements
- time extensions

19

How to Say It

□   Refer to the error, specifying dates, amounts, invoice numbers.

□   If the customer was correct, say so.

□   State your regret about the confusion, mix-up, or error.

□   Describe clearly how you propose to resolve the problem or what you have already done. Sometimes you will give customers a choice: do they want a replacement, a refund, or a credit to their account?

□   Mention a date by which you expect the problem to be resolved, even if it is only "immediately," "at once," or "as soon as possible."

□   Assure the customer that you do not expect a repeat occurrence of this problem.

□   Thank the person for their patience, and ask for continued customer loyalty.

What Not to Say

□   Long explanations are unnecessary and possibly counterproductive. The customer doesn't really care about your problems. The important thing is whether an adjustment will be made. An explanation of several words ("due to a delayed shipment from our suppliers" or "because of the recent switch-over to a new accounting system") may be included, however.

□   Avoid an excessively apologetic tone. "We regret the error" or something equally simple is adequate for most small slip-ups. Grand-scale errors may need something more, but most competent businesses don't make too many of these.

□   Even if it's true, don't try to place some of the responsibility for the problem on the customer. Only if the trouble arises entirely from the customer's ineptness would you be justified in phrasing your adjustment letter so that you both share in the responsibility.

□   Never indicate in writing that the company was negligent. If negligence was involved, consult with your lawyer who can suggest the best approach to take in your letter.

□   Don't blame a computer for the error—most people won't buy this excuse. Also avoid saying that these things are bound to happen from time to time. This makes your company appear lackadaisical and careless.

□   Don't overemphasize the problem. One simple factual reference to it is sufficient.

☐   Do not imply that you are doing the reader a big favor; this may not be correct if the customer has a legitimate complaint, and it will cancel out any feeling of goodwill that your letter could otherwise carry.

Tips on Writing

☐   A brief, perhaps conventional, apology is necessary in all cases, but when the customer has obviously suffered a good deal of inconvenience, do not be afraid to be generous with your sympathy for their plight. Sometimes out of fear that the customer will "take advantage" of such openness, businesses fail to give customers their due—and pay for it in reduced customer satisfaction.

☐   The tone of your letter should be upbeat. If you are going to grant an adjustment, do it cheerfully. A grudging attitude may negate the goodwill effect of the adjustment and leave you with a customer who still feels disgruntled.

☐   Be specific: about the problem, about the steps you are taking, about what the customer can expect in the future. Vagueness leaves the customer expecting more than is offered and unhappy when it doesn't eventuate.

☐   Restore confidence in the customer by stating that this error is rare and that the company works very hard to satisfy customers.

Special Situations

☐   In the case of a product recall consult your attorney first, since the wording of your notice may be important. Most recalls are announced in a form letter that describes the recalled product in complete detail, tells what the problem is, and explains where and how the consumer can receive an adjustment, replacement, or refund.

Format

☐   Most adjustments can be dealt with in a brief paragraph or two, which means that full-size letterhead stationery is often unnecessary. In a large operation with many routine adjustment matters, use a half-sheet size memo or form letter, perhaps with blanks to fill in the details.

☐   For problems outside the ordinary, a typewritten personal letter of adjustment on letterhead stationery is appropriate.

□   Some small companies may return the customer's letter with a hand-written notice resolving the problem: "We apologize for the error. Enclosed is a check for the difference."

_____ WORDS _____

accommodate	fix	reimburse
adjust	guaranteed	remedy
adjustment	mend	remunerate
alter	modify	repair
amend	reassure	replace
apologize	rebate	return
arrange	recompense	satisfaction
compensate	rectify	satisfy
correct	redress	settle
credit	refund	solution
discount	regulate	sorry
explanation		

_____ PHRASES _____

appreciate your pointing out	set right
clear up	shipping error
corrected invoice/statement/bill	sincerely sorry to hear that
greatly regret your dissatisfaction	sorry for the inconvenience/ misunderstanding
I'm sorry to learn that	sorry to learn that
make amends for	square it with you
make good	try harder next time
make up for	unfortunate error
our apologies	until you are completely satisfied
please disregard	will receive immediate credit
prevent a recurrence	you are correct in stating that
reduce the price	you certainly have a right to
remiss of us	

_____ SENTENCES _____

If we can be of further service, please let us know.
I hope you know how sorry we are for the problems you've experienced with this order.
Thank you for your patience and understanding.
We appreciate your business and look forward to serving you again.

We are pleased to grant you the six-week extension you requested to complete your work.

We're sorry you had to write; this should have been taken care of some time ago.

We hope to continue to serve your banking needs.

We regret the inconvenience to you.

We would like to adjust this to your satisfaction.

Your business and goodwill are very important to us.

PARAGRAPHS

▷   Thank you for responding to our recall notices and returning the Small World farm set to us for a refund. Small World has been making quality toys for children since 1976, and we very much regret the design error that made this set potentially dangerous to young children.

▷   Thank you for calling to our attention the pricing error on our Bluewater automatic pool cleaners. Enclosed is a check for the difference. We look forward to serving you again.

▷   Thank you for your telephone call. You are correct in thinking that you should not have been charged interest this past month. We have credited $2.85 to your account.

▷   I am sorry that your order was filled incorrectly. Enclosed are the back issues that you ordered. Please keep the others with our apologies.

▷   We regret the difficulties you have had with your Backwoods chain saw. From the description you sent us, it is evidently defective. Please return it to us parcel post and insured (we will reimburse you your costs) and we will send you a replacement immediately.

SAMPLE LETTERS

Dear Mr. Stefanopoulos:

Thank you for your letter requesting a correction of several statements that appeared about you and your company in the most recent issue of *Small Business Today*. The information we were given was not double-checked; we apologize.

The correction appears on page 4 of this month's issue.

Sincerely,

. . . .

Dear Eva Steer:

I am sorry that the Irish linens you purchased from us proved to be flawed. Your photograph was most explicit.

Please return the entire order to us, complete with packaging. We will replace it at once and also refund your mailing costs.

I notice that you have been a loyal customer for the past eight years, so you know that our quality control people don't let something like this happen very often. I'm enclosing a discount good for 10% off your next order as our way of apologizing for your inconvenience.

Best regards,

· · · · · · · · · · ·

Dear Mr. Steinmetz,

No, the motor on your vacuum should not have "worn out" six months after you purchased it. We can't be sure what the problem is, but this is very unusual for our top-of-the-line Costello vacuum.

Please take the vacuum to one of our repair shops (see attached list to find the one closest to you). They will examine the machine and if they can repair it, they will do so and bill us. If they find that the machine is defective, we will arrange to have a replacement shipped to you.

Please accept our apologies for the inconvenience this has caused you.

· · · · · · · · · · ·

Dear Mr. Ramsdell:
Re: Claim 02018-1134 WB 753

Enclosed is a check in full settlement of your claim.

Because Shipper's Transit Insurance was not purchased, the carrier's liability is limited to $1.25 per pound times the weight of the load. This conforms with tariff regulations.

To obtain full reimbursement for damages or loss you must file a claim with your corporation traffic department or their insurance carrier. Please check with them about this.

Thank you for your patience and cooperation during the necessary delays in processing your claim.

Sincerely,

See also: ACKNOWLEDGMENTS, COMPLAINTS, CREDIT, REFUSALS, RESPONSES.

4

Letters of Advice

"The true secret of giving advice is, after you have honestly given it, to be perfectly indifferent whether it is taken or not, and never persist in trying to set people right." (Hannah Whitall Smith)

The giving and getting of advice can be very helpful and constructive. It can also be counterproductive and destructive. Choose carefully those people you consult for advice, and give advice only when you have been formally and sincerely asked to do so.

Kinds of Letters Dealing with Advice

- asking for/requesting
- giving unsolicited
- offering suggestions
- rejecting
- responding to request for
- thanking for

How to Say It

□   Explain why you are writing (you were asked to do so by your addressee or by someone else, something came to your attention, you noticed something, you thought the person would like to know this).

□   Give your opinion, advice, or suggestions.

□   Offer reasons or explanations for your stand.

□   State what, if any, action you think the person should take.

□   Include a disclaimer of some sort: "this is only my opinion," "use your own judgment," "just something for you to think about."

□   End with an encouraging sentence that tells your reader you are sure they will make the best decision, manage the situation, be successful.

What Not to Say

□   Don't ask for advice when you already know the "advice" you want to receive. It isn't fair to the person who spends time trying to put together a response, it is mildly dishonest, and you may be unpleasantly surprised. There should be no hidden agenda in a letter of advice; ask for it only when you really want it.

□   Do not over-explain your advice. It is sufficient to state in a few sentences why you are suggesting a particular course of action.

□   Avoid the word "should" as in "I think you should . . ." Many people today are conscious of the damage done by the words "should" and "ought to." Find a softer way of phrasing your suggestion.

Tips on Writing

□   When giving advice, you must use tact, tact, and more tact. Read your letter as though you were receiving it to see how it feels. You might even ask another person to read it to make sure it isn't abrasive or patronizing.

□   Start with a compliment or upbeat remark so that your advice or suggestions fit into a positive context.

□   When possible, attribute the advice to someone else. In fact, consider the possibility of getting another person to offer the advice you want to give. The advice that is so unwelcome from a parent is often considered thoughtfully if it comes from a third party, or the advice from a superior may be better received from a colleague—or vice versa.

Special Situations

□   Letters giving professional advice (a lawyer advising a client, a doctor outlining a suggested program of patient health care, a teacher suggesting special testing for a child) will be treated much less casually than most advice letters. The advice must be professionally defensible and should perhaps include references or sources for the advice. Copies of the letter must be kept (and sometimes sent to third parties). On occasion, another person's opinion should be sought to reinforce the advice and protect yourself. Ours is a very litigious society; even good Samaritans often enjoy no protection under the law for their altruistic works and intentions.

Format

▫   Use letterhead stationery when writing a business associate outside the firm, memo paper or letterhead when writing someone inside the firm, and informal stationery for social relationships.

▫   The choice of a handwritten or typewritten letter of advice can be critical in setting the desired tone for your letter. A handwritten note to an employee might be perceived as being too personal and a bit apologetic, where a typewritten message might seem more matter of fact and detached. On the other hand, writing a personal note in some sensitive situations indicates that you are writing as a friend as well as a customer, client, or supervisor.

───────────────── WORDS ─────────────────

advantageous	dissuade	precaution
advisable	encourage	prescribe
advocate	expedient	principle
appropriate	fitting	prudent
apt	forethought	rational
befitting	forewarn	reasonable
beneficial	guidance	recommend
best	guidelines	refer
beware	help	resource
careful	hint	sensible
caution	insight	suggest
caveat	instructions	suitable
consider	judicious	tip
consult	monitor	urge
contemplate	open-minded	useful
counsel	opinion	warn
debate	persuade	wisdom
desirable	politic	worthwhile
direction	practical	

_____ PHRASES _____

after full consideration
alert you to the possibility
appeal to your sense of
as I understand it
backseat driver
be advised by
clue you in
compare notes
follow advice
give advice/hints/tips/suggestions
give careful consideration to
guard against
handwriting on the wall
high time
I am convinced that
I don't like to interfere, but
I feel/assume/presume/think
if you don't mind
I have no doubt
I have the impression that
in my estimation/judgment/opinion/view
I noticed that
inside information
I take it that
it seems to me
it strikes me that

just wanted to suggest/recommend
keep a lookout for/an eye on
look into
my information is
offer an opinion
open to/ready for advice
piece of advice
put on your guard
so far as I know
sound the alarm
speak for
stand up for
take care of
take it amiss/the wrong way
take to heart
tell someone what to do
think through
to my way of thinking
to the best of my knowledge
watch out for
weigh both courses of action
what you should do
whether you take my advice or not
word to the wise
you've probably already thought of this, but

_____ SENTENCES _____

Ever since you asked my opinion about the Middlemarch line, I've been mulling over the situation, weighing the benefits against the rather considerable cost.

I don't usually give unsolicited advice, but this seems to me to be a special case.

I hope this is the sort of advice you wanted.

I'm writing to you for advice.

I thought I should mention this.

I will appreciate any comments or advice you'd care to give.

I wouldn't like to presume to tell you your business.

Thank you for your excellent advice about our hot rolling equipment—we're back on schedule.

There is one thing you might want to consider.

We are unable to take your advice just now, but we're grateful to you for thinking of us.

Would you be able to spare a few minutes to advise me about a career change I am considering?

You must, of course, use your own judgment, but I would suggest this.

Your counsel and advice have meant a great deal.

Your idea is excellent and I may regret not going that route, but I'm going to try something else first.

You were kind enough to ask my advice about the Hexam-Riderhood merger, so here it is.

PARAGRAPHS

▷   I think perhaps you should hire an investment banking firm to help with your financial restructuring. They can assist you in exploring strategic alternatives to rebuild your liquidity and improve value for shareholders.

▷   I'm flattered that you want my advice on choosing a college. But I know from talking to your parents that you are interested in the eastern colleges, and I know very little about them. I wonder if you wouldn't want to talk to Ling Ch'ung, who in fact knows quite a bit about them.

▷   Thanks so much for your advice on the hip roof and preparing for the building inspector. I doubt if she would have given me the building permit the way I was going about things!

▷   The newsletter is not carrying its own weight, and I wonder if we ought to continue to subsidize it. I suggest we put it on a subscription basis. This will also oblige it to become more responsive to readers—one of the current complaints being that it isn't. If it can't survive on the income from subscriptions, I question its necessity.

▷   I would like to suggest that you examine the issue of cooperation versus competition in the school environment. Since we moved here three years ago, I've noticed that the school is oriented quite strongly toward competition, with little value assigned to cooperative learning, cooperative sports, and cooperative activities. I'm enclosing several reports and studies on this important issue. May I stop in and speak to you about this next week?

▷   You asked what I thought of the new store hours. They are certainly more convenient for customers and will bring us the early evening business that will make a big difference in our year-end numbers. However, I wonder if it is profitable to stay open so late on Saturday evenings. It's my impression that it's not going to pay. Let's keep a record of Saturday evening sales for a month and then we'll discuss it.

▷   We suggest that, instead of external motors and vacuum seals around the drive-shafts, you install internal, pancake motors to handle the required tension ranges. Let us know if this takes care of the problem.

▷   I'm grateful to you for the time you took to outline a solution to our current problem. We are very interested in your ideas. However, we just started working on another approach last Thursday and I'm going to wait and see how that develops. I'll let you know if we are later able to consider your plan. In the meantime, thanks for your helpful suggestions.

_____ SAMPLE LETTERS _____

Dear Hazel,

I appreciate your concern, and I am sure you have good reasons for feeling that we ought to move as soon as possible. However, after careful consideration of your proposal, I have decided that the situation is fairly stable at present and we should stay put.

Do let me know if you have any further information that would affect this decision.

Yours truly,

. . . .

Dear Mr. Pendennis,

You asked me how to become a writer. I know of no better advice than Epictetus': "If you wish to be a writer, write."

You tell me you "want" to write, you "know" you could write, people "love it" when you tell stories.

When you have actually written something, when you are writing day in and day out, week in and week out, contact me again and we can talk about fine tuning what you are doing.

Sincerely,

. . . .

Dear Mrs. Ruyslaender,

Our parish is planning to publish a cookbook next year, and I'm wondering if you could spare some time—either over the phone or at a meeting time and place of your convenience—to give us some tips on how you and your committee produced your wonderful parish cookbook, *Heavenly Creations.* We will be grateful for any advice you can give us.

Yours truly,

. . . .

Dear Tony,

As one of our most aggressive sales representatives, you have an enviable record and I expect you will be up for an award at the end of the year. The flip side of this aggressiveness is, unfortunately, a certain abrasive attitude that has been reported to me by several customers lately.

I'd like to suggest two things. One, come in and talk this over with me. I can give you some idea of how people are responding to you and why it's a problem over the long term if not the short term. Two, spend a day or two with Tom Jerningham. He's very good with words and has a manner that is effective without being too insistent.

Let me hear from you.

Sincerely,

. . . .

TO: Mildred Bluewater-Dutton

I understand from several of the Wychecombe production editors that you have proved to be a valuable copyeditor over the past six months. You have handled a number of different manuscripts, met all your deadlines, come in under budget, and dealt successfully with your authors. Because you have such potential and because we are always on the lookout for especially competent editors, I would like to suggest that you maximize your skills in the following ways:

1. Become more familiar with *The Chicago Manual of Style* by the University of Chicago Press. We depend heavily on this style book to achieve consistency in our publications.

2. Be more careful about allowing sexist language to slip through. You might want to get a copy of *The Nonsexist Word Finder*, an inexpensive handbook that will quickly give you alternatives for exclusive words and phrases.

3. Review the use of "that" and "which."

I hope you will see this letter as the compliment it really is. We are impressed with your abilities and expect you to become one of our top copyeditors.

Best wishes.

. . . .

Dear Mr. Brimblecombe:

I was present at the Music Educators' Conference when your elementary school jazz band performed. I was very much impressed to hear that out of a school population of 640, you have 580 students in your instrumental music program. This is, as I'm sure you know, rather unusual.

Do you have any advice for other elementary music directors trying to increase the number of student musicians? If you do not have the time to respond by letter, perhaps you could indicate on the enclosed postcard a time and date when I could call you long-distance. I would appreciate any tips you might have.

Gratefully,

. . . .

Dear Walter,

I hope you will forgive this unasked-for intrusion into your business affairs, but I felt I would be less than a friend if I didn't tell you my thoughts after visiting one of your gift shops last week (the one on Lewis Street). I was surprised to see the china all jumbled together on the shelves, the collector's dolls covered with dust and wrinkles, and some of the figurines chipped and dirty. This hasn't seemed to hurt business—customers were lined up at both counters when I was there—but I couldn't help thinking that over the long term it might be unfortunate.

With best wishes,

. . . .

Dear Shreve,

We are both proud of how well you're doing in college—your grades, your job, your friends. I think we've told you often how much we love you and admire the way you handle things. BUT . . . (did you know there was a "but" coming?) we are extremely concerned about one new thing in your life: cigarettes. You're more or less independent now, so we can't and wouldn't tell you what to do, but will you please think about what it will mean if you let this habit take hold?

I'm enclosing some literature on the subject. We won't nag you about this, but we had to speak up strongly at least once and say that based on our experience, knowledge, and love for you, this is not a good choice.

You know, I'm sure, that this letter is written with your best interests at heart.
Love,

· · · · · · · · · · ·

Dear Marion and Leopold,

Thanks so much for driving all the way into the city just to look over the situation with the house. The decision whether to repaint or put on all new siding was really getting us down. Your advice was excellent, and we feel good about our decision now. It was also great to see you again. Let us know when you want our advice about anything!
Love,

· · · · · · · · · · ·

Dear Uncle Thorkell,

Thank you for your letter. I appreciated your advice about my earrings. I know it doesn't seem very "manly" to you, but my friends and I like earrings. I'm coming home at the end of the month for a visit, and I didn't want you to be disappointed when you saw that I still have them. Although I am grateful for your concern, I am going to keep wearing earrings. I hope this won't hurt our good relationship.
Love,

See also: EMPLOYMENT, REFUSALS, REQUESTS, THANK YOU.

5

Announcements

"It is good news, worthy of all acceptation! and yet
not too good to be true." (Matthew Henry)

Announcements are little more than a listing of the essential facts in the
fewest words possible. Because some of them are formal, however, they
appear difficult to compose. This is not the case, as you will see after writing
several of them.

If you want to combine an announcement with another message (seasonal greetings, sales letter, cover letter, or goodwill, for example) see also
the chapter on that topic.

Announcements Are Made For

- acquisitions
- anniversaries: business/wedding
- baby birth or adoption
- changes in benefits (reduced/increased/additional), policies
  (purchasing/hiring), regulations, procedures (billing dates)
- changes of address
- collection actions on overdue account (see COLLECTION)
- company mergers/reorganizations
- deaths
- divorces
- employee resignations/retirements (see EMPLOYMENT)
- engagements
- graduations
- introduction of new partners/employees
- layoffs (see EMPLOYMENT)
- marital separations

- meetings/workshops/conferences
- new acquisitions/divisions/subsidiaries
- new company policies/directions/administrations/management
- new home/house/apartment/condominium
- new office/business/professional practice/service
- open houses: schools/businesses
- price increases/reductions
- product recalls
- promotions
- raises/salary increases
- weddings (see WEDDINGS)

How to Say It

□   The form of the announcement of a directors' meeting is often fixed by corporate by-laws or by state or federal laws. You will want to follow these guidelines, but in general the announcement must include the date, time, and place of meeting; the reason for the meeting (annual meeting/election of directors); and who is invited to attend. A waiver of notice or a proxy card is often enclosed along with a postage-paid reply envelope.

□   When a family member dies, there are four possible types of announcements to be made: (1) a (usually paid) death notice is published in the obituary section of the newspaper; (2) a news article describes the person's contributions to the community or achievements in business, the arts, etc.; (3) printed announcements (sometimes black-banded) are sent to out-of-town friends and acquaintances; (4) handwritten notes are sent to close family and friends who live out of town. Since you may not know all the deceased person's friends, you may want to go through their address book and send either printed announcements or handwritten notes to people listed there. The obituary should include the following information: complete name of deceased including birth name of woman if she was not already using it; address; date of death; age at time of death; names, relationships, and hometowns of survivors; affiliations; personal or career information; date and place of services and interment; whether services are private or open to friends and relatives; if flowers are not wanted a notice stating "Please omit flowers" or "Memorial contributions to (name of organization) preferred"; name, address, and telephone number of funeral home. Since the death announcement must go in the newspaper almost immediately you should hand deliver it or you can read it over the phone.

□   After a divorce it is helpful to announce the changed circumstances, addresses, and even perhaps names to family, friends, acquaintances, and businesses where separate accounts and responsibilities are now necessary. Include a simple statement of where each person (and the children) will be living. If the woman has taken back her birth name, mention that. It appears less like a bald announcement if you can combine the news with seasonal greetings (Easter, Thanksgiving, New Year) or if you use a commercial change of address card that makes the address change the primary reason for writing. Depending on circumstances, you can handle a marital separation similarly. When sending the announcement to close friends, you may want to add a personal note at the bottom. You are not obliged to explain everything, and if people sense from your announcement that you are retaining some privacy, it will be easier to deal with them the next time you see them.

□   A name change (woman taking back her own name after a divorce, the adoption of a pen name, married woman resuming use of her birth name, person changing undesired name in court) is announced simply by saying that the person will be known by the new name as of a certain date. No reasons are necessary, especially in business, but you may add a handwritten note to friends and relatives if you like.

□   When announcing changes in company policies/procedures/regulations to employees or customers include: an expression of pleasure in announcing the change, a specific description of the change, an explanation of what the change will mean for employees or customers, the reason for the change and why it is an improvement, appreciation for people's help in implementing the change.

□   When sending adoption or birth announcements include: the baby's full name and, if not obvious from the name or if still unnamed, whether it is a boy or girl; birthdate (and time, if you wish) or age (if the baby is adopted); parents' full names; siblings' names (optional); some expression of happiness ("pleased to announce"). Baby announcements used to be solely of the "Mr. and Mrs. Jeremy Small announce . . ." variety. Today you will see announcements by unmarried parents ("Julia Norman and Basil Fane announce the birth of their son Alec Norman-Fane"), by single parents ("Jean Emerson announces the birth of her son Howard Thede Emerson"), and by married couples where each uses their own name. There are no longer hard and fast rules; your announcement will reflect your own situation, values, and interests.

□   Newspaper birth announcements include: the date of birth, sex of child and name if known; parents' names and hometowns; grandparents' names. Some newspapers will allow weight and height information, such sentiments as "welcome with love," and mentions of "many aunts, uncles, and cousins" in listing the baby's relatives. Check with your newspaper well before the baby is born to ask about its guidelines.

□   When announcing your engagement in a personal, handwritten note to friends and relatives, include: your fiancée/fiancé's name; the wedding date (if known); how you met and how long you've known the person (this is optional, and you needn't go into much detail); some expression of your happiness; a personal comment to the person you're writing (that they are the first to know, that you can't wait for them to meet your fiancé/fiancée).

□   When placing an engagement announcement in the newspaper, generally include: both your full names; hometowns; both sets of parents' names and hometowns; education backgrounds and places of employment for both; date of wedding or general plans ("a spring wedding is planned"). Begin the announcement with the names of whoever is making the announcement. Traditionally, and sexistly, this was always the bride-to-be's parents ("Mr. and Mrs. Alexander Holder announce the engagement of their daughter Mary . . ."). If only one parent is living, you can add, "Mary Holder is also the daughter of the late Alexander Holder." If the parents are divorced, the announcement can read either "Mr. Alexander Holder of Stevenson, Illinois, and Mrs. Esther Hobson of Middletown, Arizona, announce the engagement of their daughter . . ." or "Mr. Alexander Holder announces . . . Mary Holder is also the daughter of Mrs. Esther Hobson of Middletown, Arizona." Today, many engaged couples make their own announcement: "Thérèse Espinal and Henry Maitland announce their engagement and forthcoming marriage on December 16." Some newspapers have rigid requirements and deadlines for engagement announcements, and some will run either an engagement or a wedding announcement, but not both, so check with an editor before planning your announcement.

□   Sometimes a broken engagement needs no announcement as no formal announcement was made and not many people were aware of it. However, if you have written family and friends of the engagement, you should write the same type of personal note telling them simply that you have canceled your plans. There is no need to explain why except very vaguely ("thought it better to go our separate ways," "for a number of reasons decided not to marry"). If formal wedding invitations have already been sent, however, you will need to send a formal cancellation. It can be in a much plainer style, but it should not be of a completely different quality from the original invitation. The cancellation should be very simple: "Leila Yorke and Percy Potter announce that their marriage on the sixteenth of October, nineteen hundred ninety-three, will not take place."

□   If your address has changed because you are going to live as a couple with someone, send a printed change-of-address card with a simple statement saying that you and the other person (give name) are now living at that address.

What Not to Say

❑   Leave out extraneous information or news. Although there are some exceptions (changes in company policy, for example), an announcement is generally not the place to go into lengthy explanations, instructions, or descriptions. When you choose to combine an announcement with a sales message, your letter is still very narrowly focused. The problem arises when a simple announcement turns into a one-page letter and the important information becomes lost or diluted.

Tips on Writing

❑   When announcing changes (company policies or benefits, for example), you may sometimes need to include a brief explanation.

❑   You may take advantage of some routine announcement (new type of billing statement/new address/meeting notice) to develop a goodwill letter (thanking customer for business/employee for good year) or a sales letter.

Special Situations

❑   Timely events or news of interest to the general public (product recall, quarterly financial status, important anniversary celebration, fundraiser, new programs/policies/managers, company achievements) are often sent to newspaper editors and to radio and television station news directors. Include your organization's name and address along with the name and telephone number of a contact person. Double or triple space your material, leaving wide margins, and answer the who-what-when-where-why-how questions in the first paragraph or two. News releases traditionally have "more" typed at the bottom of each page except the last, which has "- 30 -" or " # # # " to indicate the end.

❑   Announcements of a new business opening are often handled as invitations to an open house or special sales event.

❑   If you are divorced, you may want to write a special letter to your ex-spouse announcing your intention to remarry. In some cases, this will be a matter of simple courtesy. In others, it may involve future financial or custodial arrangements. A simple "I thought you would like to know" is sufficient.

Format

□   Announcements can be made in a traditional letter format typed on letterhead or bond stationery. Since business announcements are always aimed at a number of people, form letters are the vehicle of choice.

□   Formal announcements are usually printed or engraved in black on a white or cream-colored card (with matching envelopes). Stationery stores and printers can show you sample announcements ranging from traditional to modern in a variety of type styles, papers, inks, and formats.

□   Many announcements made to close friends and family are handwritten on foldovers or personal stationery.

□   Announcements submitted to the newspaper are typed, double-spaced, with roomy margins. Check with the paper about guidelines and policies.

□   For interoffice announcements (new benefits package, change in flex-hours procedures), memo paper can be used.

□   Postcards are especially appropriate for announcing changes of address, meetings, and special sales.

□   Baby announcements can be engraved, printed, hand-lettered, or specially designed by you. Also, commercial baby announcement cards are available in styles to please almost everyone. A printer can help you choose from a variety of typefaces, colors, and messages. If you are making your own announcements, libraries usually have books on the subject, such as *We Are Proud to Announce* from the editors of *Redbook*. Pink stationery, ribbons, or attachments for girls and blue for boys used to be standard; people are making much wider and less sex-specific choices now.

□   In very formal situations, an engagement announcement can be printed or engraved on white or off-white cards or formal notes. Often an announcement can be made in the form of an invitation to celebrate the engagement at a dinner party or other event.

_____ WORDS _____

advise	inform	present
announce	introduce	report
celebration	joyfully	reveal
delighted	mention	share
gratified	notice	signal
happy	pleased	well-pleased
honor		

───────────────── **PHRASES** ─────────────────

announces the appointment of

are happy to announce the opening of

are pleased/proud and happy to announce

give notice that

happily announce the merger of/a new
subsidiary

have the honor of announcing

it is with great happiness that we
announce

joyfully announce the birth/adoption/
arrival of

make known/public

notice is hereby given that

pleased to announce

public announcement

take pleasure in announcing

wish to announce/inform/advise you

───────────────── **SENTENCES** ─────────────────

A beautiful baby girl, Katherine Helen Pettigrew, born August 12, weighing 8
pounds, 5 ounces, measuring 21 inches long, is welcomed with love and pride by
her mother, Anne Pettigrew.

Although we have maintained our prices for many years, we find ourselves obliged
to respond to increased prices from our suppliers.

A meeting of the Broadway-Aldine Community Council will be held October 3 at
7:00 p.m. in the NewBank boardroom to elect board members and officers for the
coming year.

Annabel and Maurice Malherb take pleasure in announcing the adoption of Grace
Ann Malherb, age six months.

Ben Bowser announces that by permission of the court of Ramsey County, New
Jersey, April 18, 1992, he will now be known as Benjamin Middleton.

Dolores Haze (formerly Mrs. Richard F. Schiller) has changed her address to 155
Carol Avenue, Gilberts, IL 60136.

Isabel Wahrfield and Frank Goodwin announce the dissolution of their marriage,
effective July 15.

Jhansi Slane announces that she will be known as Jhansi McKenna as of September 1,
1993.

Mrs. Rachel Dean announces the engagement of her daughter Susan to Richard Tebben.

NGUYEN Van Truy and TRAN Huong Lang are proud and happy to announce the
birth of their son NGUYEN Van Tuân on March 11, 1992.

Please be advised that your payment due date has been changed to the sixteenth day
of each month.

Please note our new address and telephone number.

Rachael Jordan and Jeremiah Beaumont are living at 1950 Penn Warren Road, Rob-
bins, CA 95676.

We are pleased to announce the formation of a new sector/company/division.

With great sadness we announce the death of our husband and father, Leon Gonsalez.

——————————————— PARAGRAPHS ———————————————

▷   Fairford Corporation, Cooper City, announces that it has reached a distributor-ship agreement with Antoine-Lettice, based in Paris, France, granting them exclu-sive marketing rights for its Superbe! ultra-high-pressure waterjet equipment in France and Italy, with nonexclusive rights for the rest of Europe.

▷   Wattie Gillespie, age 89, of Urquhart. Preceded in death by wife Mirren. Sur-vived by sons Thomas, Arnold, and Walter, daughters Meg Ashe, Grace Wilson, Bella Anderson, and Kate Gillespie.

▷   Edith and William Harcourt and big sister Mary welcome with love their new little daughter and sister, Lucy Marie, born September 3 at 10:04 a.m., 6 pounds, 3 ounces. The proud grandparents are Mr. and Mrs. Robert Graham and Mrs. Alithea Harcourt.

▷   Susan Harding and Theophilus Grantly plan to marry on October 3, 1992, at Divine Redeemer Church in Center City. The couple's parents are the Reverend and Mrs. Septimus Harding, Center City, and Mr. and Mrs. Henry Grantley, Barchester Towers, England. Ms. Harding is a graduate of Charleston University and is em-ployed by Arabin Paperworks. Mr. Grantly is also a graduate of Charleston Univer-sity and is in private law practice.

▷   Miles and I have decided that we would make better friends than spouses, so as of last week, we have canceled our engagement. We are both, I think, quite relieved, although we still think the world of each other. I know how happy you were for me when I wrote about our engagement, so I wanted to let you know right away that you can still be happy for me—but not because I'm engaged.

▷   Medwin Associates is pleased to announce the acquisition of the Boothby Lease Group, Inc., a Wilfred-area company with eighty-six employees that specializes in public-sector lease financing.

▷   Averill Airlines will now serve Paris's Charles de Gaulle Airport (previously Orly). Airport transfers included in any of our vacation packages will provide conve-nient motorcoach transportation between Charles de Gaulle Airport and Port Mail-lot Station in Paris (formerly Mortparnasse Station).

▷   Carrie and Frederick Josser, New London, celebrated their twenty-fifth wed-ding anniversary on March 2. An open house was hosted by Cynthia and Ted Josser of Collins. Eight proud children and many friends and relatives were there.

▷   I'm sorry to tell you that Mother died on July 11 of a heart attack. I know how much your friendship and your lively letters meant to her over the years. She spoke of you often.

▷   We regret to announce that our Davy Jones Aquarium Pump, Model no. 686, has been found to be defective. It is possible that it could deliver a fatal shock. Please return your pump as soon as possible to the store where you purchased it or call the toll-free number below for instructions.

▷   Eggerson Power Equipment Company is proud to announce the opening of a new store on County Road B and Highway 47. One of the largest power equipment sources in the state, the new store specializes in an exhaustive in-store stock and a forty-eight-hour "we can get it" guarantee.

▷ Cornelia (Kay) Motford, George and Gladys are now living at 1941 Knowles Avenue, Centralia, KY 42330 (502/555-4590). Henry Moulton Pulham is living at 332 Riverside Drive, Lexington, KY 40507 (606/555-2441).

▷ If you've insured your automobile with us continuously for five years or more, a discount has been applied to your current premium. An even higher discount applies if you've been with us continuously for ten years or more.

▷ Montford Estates is pleased to announce the expansion of its commercial construction division. The division offers cost-efficient, high-quality commercial construction with emphasis on interior detailing.

▷ Georgina Gardner was promoted to director of retail leasing for Pelham Development Properties. She will be responsible for leasing Pelham Mall in downtown Brandon.

▷ Due to the rapid rise in labor and operating costs, Ames Fast Maintenance finds it necessary to increase service charges as of September 1. Service charge increases will vary, depending upon the type of service your company uses: on call, when needed, monthly preventive maintenance, etc.

▷ The Board of Directors of the Fiske Corporation will meet on Wednesday, December 3, at 10:00 a.m. at the Company's central office in Harrington. New contracts for executives will be discussed, and such other business as may come before the meeting will be acted upon. If you cannot attend, please sign the enclosed waiver of notice.

▷ Phyllis Bligh and Stephen Newmark announce the forthcoming marriage of their daughter Phyllis to Clarence Rochester, son of Mr. and Mrs. Barney Rochester of North Fortress, Michigan. A spring wedding is planned in Paris, where both Ms. Bligh and Mr. Rochester are employed by Newmark International.

▷ Thanks to you, and the orders that have been pouring in for our special line of children's clothing, we are able to make greater bulk purchases of raw materials and thus manufacture at a lower cost. We are proud to announce that we are passing on these savings to you. Enclosed is our current catalog, but please note the new low prices printed in red.

▷ Francis Getliffe, age 44, of Cambridge. Survived by wife, Katherine March Getliffe; son, Francis, Jr.; brother Herbert; also nieces and nephews and good friends from C.P. Snow, Inc. Special thanks to the staff at Cambridge Lutheran Hospital. Memorial service Sunday at 2:00 p.m. at the Hillside Memorium Funeral Home. Family will receive friends one hour prior to service. Interment Hillside, with reception following in the Hillside Community Room. Memorials preferred. Hillside Memorium, 555-1216.

SAMPLE LETTERS

FOR: Immediate Release

Boorman, Inc. of Menzies announces the recall of its fresh and frozen sandwiches because of the discovery of bacterial contamination during a recent Food and Drug Administration (FDA) test. Some of the sandwiches were found to contain *Listeria monocytogenes*, a bacterium that can endanger fetuses, infants, pregnant women, the elderly, and people with weakened immune systems.

No illnesses have been reported.

Please destroy all Boorman QuickWich sandwiches from lot 480032 or return them to Boorman for a refund.

. . . .

Brangwen International
is pleased to announce
that Lydia Lensky
has joined the firm
as a partner.
She will direct the
Southeast Asia Operations.

. . . .

NOTICE

If you have not previously carried Sewer or Drain Back-Up Coverage, that protection in the amount of $5,000 has now been added to your policy. This coverage protects you from direct loss caused by water that backs up through sewers or drains, and from direct loss caused by water that enters into and overflows from within a sump pump, sump pump well, or other system designed to remove subsurface water drained from the foundation area.

Please read the attached endorsement for complete information. You may purchase increased coverage limits for an additional premium.

If you have questions about this change, please contact your agent.

. . . .

Paul J. Maggio, D.D.S.
and Matthew J. Maggio, D.D.S.
Announce the Opening
of Their New Office
at 1099 Kenyon Road
Fort Dodge, Iowa 50501
(515/576-1981)
and an Open House
on July 15, 1986.

Dear Bondholder:

This letter is to inform you that a portion of the July 1, 1992 debt service payment for the above-referenced bond issue was made with monies transfered from the Reserve Fund established pursuant to Section 4.09 of the Indenture of Trust dated December 1, 1987, between Simmons International and Herbert Banking & Trust, as Trustee. Use of such monies in the Reserve Fund does *not* constitute an Event of Default under the indenture. However, the Trustee considers this information may be of interest to bondholders and potential bondholders.

Sincerely,

. . . .

We are pleased to announce

and welcome to our firm

Edward Hugh Bloomfield

as Manager of

Fixed Income Securities

Stevenson & Osbourne

1889 Forsyth Boulevard

Robertstown, Ohio 45042

513/555-0012

. . . .

TO: All City of Sinclair Citizens
RE: Proposed increase to property taxes for 1993

The City of Sinclair City Council is proposing to increase total property taxes for 1993 by $960,190 over 1992 taxes. Of this amount, $900,440 will replace state aid shifted from the city to the Sinclair School Districts. This results in an increase of 22.5% in property tax collections for the city. If state aid had not been shifted, the increase would have been 1.6 percent. The total amount proposed is $4,612,642. This increase is a proposal only. All citizens of Sinclair are invited to attend a public hearing at which the City Council will discuss the proposed increase. The Council will have a first reading of the ordinance to pass the budget at the hearing. A second reading and passage of the budget ordinance will take place on December 15, 1992. Please come and give the members of the Council your opinions on this proposal.

Public Hearing: November 20, 1992 at 7:30 p.m. in the City Council Chambers. If additional time is needed, the hearing will be reconvened on December 7 at 7:30 p.m. in the same place. Summaries of the City's proposed 1993 budget are available for review in the City Manager's office. Persons unable to attend this hearing may send written comments to the Council. For more information call the Sinclair City Manager's office between 9:00 a.m. and 5:00 p.m. weekdays.

. . . .

Dear Customer:

As of May 1 of this year, your garbage hauling fee will be increased by $1.45 per month. We are always reluctant to raise prices, but are obliged to do so in this case by a recent ruling of the Silvius County Board of Commissioners.

In order to conserve landfill space, all garbage collected in Silvius County since July of 1989 has been required to be taken to the new recovery facility in Shepard rather than to landfills. However, it costs more to "tip" a load of garbage at Shepard than at a landfill, so the County agreed to subsidize haulers until April 30 of this year.

Although other haulers may be raising the householder's portion of the bill more than $1.45 (due to inflation and haulers' additional operating expenses), we are going to try to keep the price increase as low as possible.

It is only fair to warn you, however, that there may be more increases in sight. The current legislature is considering raising landfill surcharges and putting a sales tax on hauling fees, which could further increase garbage bills.

There are several ways you can lower your garbage bills. Enclosed are flyers with information on using a volume-based garbage hauler, recycling, composting yard waste at home or at one of the County composting sites, and disposing properly of household hazardous waste.

For further information, call 555-1567.

Sincerely,

. . . .

Bonnie and Steven Goldsmith

are most happy to announce

the arrival of their daughter

Emily Virginia

born in Korea May 23, 1989

welcomed home October 11, 1989

. . . .

Dear Friend,

We have moved! During the past fifteen years we were so crowded in our old location that sometimes customers had to stand shoulder to shoulder or squeeze through the aisles. Nowadays you'll find it much easier to call on Taylor & Company.

Easy parking facilities in our parking lot and pleasant offices will make it simple for you to meet all your printing needs.

Enclosed is a map showing the new location, along with a one-time 10% discount coupon. Come in and see us while the paint's still fresh!

Sincerely yours,

. . . .

Notice of Annual Meeting of Shareholders

The Annual Meeting of Shareholders of the Sinclair-Highland Railroad Company will be held at the Scott Motor Inn, U.S. Highway 41 West, in Sinclair, Michigan, on Monday, April 28, 1993, at 10:00 a.m., local time, for the following purposes:

1. To elect a full board of eight (8) directors of the Company.

2. To consider and act upon the appointment of independent auditors for 1994. The Board of Directors recommends the employment of Magnus Troil Associates.

3. To transact such other business as may properly come before the meeting.

An oral report on the affairs of the Company will be presented at the meeting, and an audited report of the Company's financial affairs will be available for inspection by any qualified shareholder.

If you do not expect to attend the meeting, please date, sign, and return your proxy as soon as possible. If you attend the meeting, you may withdraw your proxy.

By order of the Board of Directors,

See also: COVER, GOODWILL, SALES.

6

Apologies

"Things could be worse. Suppose your errors were
counted and published every day, like those
of a baseball player." (Anon.)

Although some apologies can be made in person or over the telephone, most need to be written—and written quickly. Procrastination turns writing an apology into a major chore and may mean that we have to apologize twice, once for the infraction and once for the delay. Whether you think of apologies as etiquette, as ethics, as justice, even as "good business," they are an inevitable by-product of being alive and human. Because we all make mistakes, people are a lot less bothered by your errors than you are; write your apology with dignity and self-respect.

Occasions That Call for Apologies

- belated response to a gift, favor, invitation, or major event in someone's life
- billing or financial errors: failure to give appropriate credit, collection letters sent in error
- business errors: incorrect information given, order mix-ups, contract misunderstandings, merchandise that is defective, dangerous, ineffective, damaged, delayed, or that is missing parts, instructions, or warranties
- children's misbehavior, damage to property or pet
- damage to another's property
- employee problems: rudeness, ineptness, dishonesty, poor service, unsatisfactory work
- failure to keep an appointment, deadline, shipping date, payment schedule, or promise
- insulting or insensitive remarks

- personal errors: giving someone's name and phone number to a third party without permission, forgetting to include someone in an invitation, betraying a secret
- pets that bite, bark, damage property, or are otherwise nuisances
- sexual harassment
- tactless, inappropriate, rude, or drunken behavior

How to Say It

□ State that you regret a specific offense ("I am sorry for/that . . ."). In the case of a customer complaint, summarize the person's problem ("I understand that . . .").

□ Offer to make amends or, if amends seem definitely called for, announce your intention of making amends, indicating how you will do this. If you're not sure how best to redress the situation, describe several possible solutions and ask which the person prefers.

□ Assure the person that this will not happen again.

□ If it concerns a problem you were unaware of, thank the writer or caller for bringing it to your attention.

□ In a business context, finish the letter by asking for continued patronage.

What Not to Say

□ Do not be overly dramatic ("You will probably never want to see me again after what I did." "I wish I were dead after the way I behaved last night." "I am very, very, very sorry.").

□ Keep your letter free of guilt-inspired soul searchings and agonizing; it is uncomfortable and unappealing for the reader. State your apology clearly and briefly; don't belabor it or end up apologizing many times in different ways.

□ Reread your apology to make sure you aren't inadvertently implying that the other person is at fault; some people's "apology" sounds more like an accusation. Especially in a business context, it is better not to write at all than to imply the customer is at fault. With a little ingenuity, it is possible to express regret about a situation without accepting responsibility for it if it's not your fault.

□ Don't blame clerical errors on computers ("A computer error/mishap was responsible for the delay in payments."). Most people are irritated by this weak and patently untrue excuse. In the same way, avoid saying that these things are bound to happen from time to time. Although this may be true, saying so indicates that company policy may be more inclined to shrugs than vigorous action.

□   Avoid a grudging attitude; if you are going to apologize, do so cheerfully and wholeheartedly.

□   Do not acknowledge that the company was negligent. If negligence is a factor, consult with your attorney, who will suggest the best approach to take in your letter.

Tips on Writing

□   Write as soon as possible after the incident.

□   Be brief, straightforward, and sincere. Admit the fault straight away, apologize, and sign off.

□   Apologize only for the specific issue. Do not generalize about how this always seems to happen, what a klutz you are, and so forth.

□   Avoid trying to justify or defend the error or behavior, although in some cases, an explanation could accompany your apology. When a shipment is delayed, for example, you may want to mention the dockworkers' strike or that half the employees in the shipping department were out that week with the flu. At other times, however, an explanation may weaken or invalidate your apology. The French say that "justifying a fault doubles it." This is especially true when you try to explain why you were rude, for example, or why a child said something tactless but undeniably true. In certain circumstances, a brief and sincere apology (accompanied perhaps by flowers) is better than any explanation.

□   When apologizing for a business problem, the goal is to right the wrong (or the perceived wrong) while turning a dissatisfied customer into one who will continue to deal happily with you. Most customers will respect an honest, generous, and tactful response.

□   Mentally put yourself in the other person's place when determining the type of apology, restitution, damages, or other actions that would be appropriate if your positions were reversed.

□   Ethicist Jeremy Iggers says an apology has to be made unilaterally. When we begin to stray into the area of what the other person did to us, we lose the ethical base of making an apology. Whatever anyone else did to us is a separate matter from whatever mistake we made.

Special Situations

□   The apology may have a special place in customer relations. Ron Graham, executive director of the St. Paul, Minnesota, Better Business Bureau, says that in the strategies for achieving customer satisfaction, the apology is "one of the prerequisites to creating the environment for mediation, and it's a necessary prerequisite when either the customer or the business believes that the other side has something to apologize for. It's a way of removing the emotion, or neutralizing the emotion so that the substance of a dispute can be laid on a table for settlement." He adds that sometimes apologies are necessary on both sides of a dispute.

□   The problem of sexual harassment has become increasingly visible, and employers and employees no longer categorize certain behavior as "just fooling around," "having a good sense of humor," or "feeling one's oats." Making sexual remarks, threats, innuendoes, or passes is illegal. Anything that can be construed as sexual harassment requires a heartfelt apology that lets the recipient know that the offender has some real (as opposed to expedient) understanding of what was done. Facile apologies won't do it. The apology may not avert a company reprimand or even legal action, but then again it might. In any case, an apology is owed to anyone who has been sexually harassed. In addition to exhibiting sincere contrition, the trespasser should promise never to repeat the behavior. Those who are being sued in sexual harassment cases are generally repeat offenders who still don't understand how offensive their actions were. Few people will go after a one-time offender who didn't fully realize the original harm done and who is now contrite and reformed.

□   If the situation is serious (for example, an attack by your dog requiring significant medical attention), you may want to consult an attorney before writing your apology in case it affects your liability.

□   When you are late with a thank you note, a gift, congratulations, or greetings of any kind, it's best to keep your apology for the delay brief and unadorned. There are not many good excuses for being late with a thank you note, for example, so don't offer one—it's bound to appear feeble. It's better to say that you have no good excuse and that you're sorry.

□   Sometimes you will be able to offer customers a refund, discount, free pass, or some other material "apology" for their inconvenience. At other times, there may be nothing you can do in addition to the written apology. Be clear about this from the beginning so that there is no misunderstanding later on.

□   When a child annoys or hurts others or damages their property, an apology should be sent by a parent or guardian. However, the child should also be held responsible for some form of apology, depending on age, and it might be mentioned in the adult's note that "of course, Drusilla will want to apologize for herself."

□   In the case of a misunderstanding or disagreement, apologize for your share of it, even if the other person contributed as much or more to the problem.

Format

□   Use personal stationery or notecards for all apologies dealing with personal situations. There are a few contemporary cards that charmingly or amusingly say "I'm sorry," but you still need to add a handwritten message.

□   Use business stationery for all apologies to customers, clients, suppliers, and other businesses. If, however, the situation has personal overtones (a manager has publicly slighted someone or a supervisor has unjustly docked someone's pay) the apology might be handwritten on business-personal stationery.

□   Routine apologies (shipping delays, out-of-stock merchandise) can be handled with a form letter. However, a form letter is intended only for commonplace matters. It should not be used, for example, to apologize for a major mix-up with a longtime customer.

_____ WORDS _____

absentmindedly	fault	mend
accidental	faulty	miscalculation
acknowledge	flaw	misconception
admit	forgive	misconstrued
amends	heavyhearted	misdirected
apologize	howler	misinformed
awkward	ill-advised	misinterpreted
blame	imperfect	misjudged
blooper	imprudent	misleading
blunder	impulsive	mismanaged
boner	inaccurate	misprint
botched	inadequate	misquote
careless	inadvertent	misrepresented
compensate	incomplete	misspell
defect	inconsiderate	misstatement
deplorable	inconvenient	mistaken
disconcerting	incorrect	misunderstanding
distressed	ineffective	muddle
disturbed	inexact	negligence
embarrassed	inferior	offended
erroneous	inoperative	omitted
error	insufficient	overlooked
excuse	irresponsible	oversight
explanation	lamentable	pardon
failure	lax	recompense

rectify
red-faced
redo
redress
regret
regrettable
reimburse
remiss
repair
repay
responsible

restitution
restore
sheepish
short-sighted
slip
sorry
tactless
thoughtless
troubled
troublesome
unaware

undesirable
unfortunate
unhappy
unintentional
unjust
unsatisfactory
unsound
unwarranted
unwise
violation
wrong

─────────────── PHRASES ───────────────

accept the blame for
admit myself in the wrong
angry with myself
an unexpected complication
appreciate your calling our attention to
asleep at the wheel/on the job/at the
  switch
avoid this in the future
blotted my copybook with you
breach of good manners
correct the situation
didn't mean in the least to
eat humble pie
express my regret
false/hasty conclusion
feel sorry/terrible/bad about
greatly regret your dissatisfaction
how can I apologize for
I am most upset about
I am not excusing our/my errors, but
I am so sorry for
I certainly do apologize for
I don't know how it happened that
I have thoroughly investigated/looked
  into the matter, and
I'm sorry you were dissatisfied with the
inattention to detail
in full restitution
it was most embarrassing to discover that

it was most understanding of you to
I was distressed to
  hear/read/discover/learn that
I was distressed to receive your letter
  about
make allowances for
make amends/restitution
make right with you
much to my regret
my apologies for any inconvenience
owe you an apology for
own up to
please accept my/our apology/apologies
  for
please forgive my delay in
presumed where I shouldn't have
  presumed
prevent a recurrence
processing error
put a false construction on
out to rights
remiss of me
reproach myself
second thoughts
shipping error
sick at heart
sincerely regret/apologize
slip of the tongue
sorely regret

sorry for the inconvenience/confusion/
  mix-up/misunderstanding
sorry to hear that you were not satisfied
  with
taking steps to avoid this kind of error
  in the future
the least I can do is to
there is absolutely no excuse for my not
there was no intention to deceive you as
  to the
to compensate for

try harder next time
under the mistaken impression that
until you are completely satisfied
very rash on my part
very sorry about the error in
weight on my mind
we regret to inform our customers that
we were distressed to learn
will receive immediate credit
you were entirely right about

_____ SENTENCES _____

As you rightly pointed out, a mistake has been made on your July bill.
I am extremely embarrassed about my behavior last night.
I am sincerely/very sorry.
I apologize for Jimmy's behavior.
I can only hope you will forgive this serious lapse of good taste on my part.
I can understand why you are angry.
I don't blame you for being upset.
I don't know why I acted so badly.
I don't like being on the outs with you, particularly since it was my own fault.
If you choose not to deal with me in the future I will certainly understand.
I have taken steps to ensure that it doesn't happen again.
I hope this situation can be mended to everyone's satisfaction.
I'm sorry you were treated in so disparaging a manner by the salesclerk.
I only realized later how insulting my remarks might appear.
I shouldn't have done what I did.
I understand how disappointed you must have been to receive only half your order.
My face gets red every time I remember that night.
Please accept my apology for this unfortunate oversight.
Please disregard your previous bill; it was sent in error.
Please excuse my inattention/shortsightedness/thoughtlessness.
Please forgive me this once.
Thank you for advising us of this error/for bringing the matter to my attention.
Thank you for your patience and understanding.
The problem is being corrected.
The situation has now been rectified, and a check has been sent.
This will not, of course, happen again.
We apologize for the delay—it is unfortunately unavoidable.
We apologize for the error that resulted in the overcharge.
We are sorry/apologize for any embarrassment and inconvenience this may have
  caused you.

We are unfortunately unable to deliver your order on time.
We are very concerned about this situation.
We look forward to continuing to serve you.
We value your patronage and your friendship.
We were caught napping on this one.
We will make certain this doesn't happen again.
You have every right to be annoyed/irritated/upset/unhappy with us.

PARAGRAPHS

▷ We are unable to deliver the spring fabric samples by the date promised. The product supervisor promises me that you will have them by January 5. If this is unsatisfactory, please telephone me. It isn't often we have to renege on a delivery date, and we're not very happy about it. Please accept our sincere apologies for the delay.

▷ My behavior yesterday was inexcusable, and I must tell you how sorry I am. If you are unable to forgive me, I will understand completely, but I did want you to know how much I regret the incident. You have shown nothing but kindness to me and certainly did not deserve such a tirade.

▷ Please accept our sincere apologies for what's recently happened at your house. We are all working very hard to find other homes for the litter of bunnies. When Hillel assured you that both bunnies were female, he was relying on the green-striped ribbons they wore around their necks. None of us knew that a four-year-old neighbor had switched one green-striped ribbon for a yellow polka-dotted ribbon that the male rabbits were wearing. I know this explanation doesn't make up to you for what you've been through, but I thought you should know that our intentions were good. Again, we're very sorry and we'll let you know as soon as we've found ten good homes.

▷ We were sorry to hear that the track lighting fixture you ordered was defective, as described in your letter of April 29. Please return it to us using its original mailing box and the enclosed label, and we will send you a replacement by return mail. All Midlothian merchandise is inspected twice before leaving the factory, but with a recent 45% increase in production, we have a few rough spots to work out yet. I'm sorry that you were inconvenienced, and hope that you will continue to use our fine Midlothian products—products that we proudly back with our full-service Midlothian guarantee.

▷ It occurred to me in a dream, or maybe it was in the shower, that you had asked for the return of your baby books some time ago. I suppose the friend's child has gone off to college by now. I'm sorry for the tardiness—they're in today's mail.

▷ We erroneously mailed you the same order you placed last month. This month's order has been sent this morning, and we've marked the box plainly with AUGUST written in large red letters. If you will please refuse acceptance of the first box, the carrier will simply bring it back to us. We apologize for the error.

▷ We were very sorry to hear that the last neon tetras you bought from us were infected with ich and subsequently infected your entire aquarium. As tropical fish enthusiasts ourselves, we appreciate how devastating this has been. I immediately spoke to our supplier about the problem, and they have assured me this was an isolated slip-up. In the meantime, please feel free to restock your aquarium at our expense. Thank you for your understanding, and I hope you will continue to be one of our most valued customers.

_____ SAMPLE LETTERS _____

Dear Dorothea,

I feel dreadful about ruining your lovely luncheon yesterday by arguing with Celia about Will Ladislaw. You certainly did everything you could to save the situation, and I apologize most humbly for ignoring good taste, old friendship, and common sense in pursuing a "discussion" that was completely inappropriate.

I talked to Celia first thing this morning and attempted to mend my fences there, but I feel a great deal worse about what I did to you. The luncheon was delicious, and the first two hours were delightful. I hope you will someday be able to forgive me for blighting the last half-hour.

Your friend,

. . . .

Dear Mr. Ravenal:

As editor of the Cotton Blossom newsletter, I want to apologize for omitting your name in the last issue. Captain Hawks asked me how I could have possibly forgotten to include our hottest new actor! In proofreading the copy, my eyes failed to notice that your name wasn't where my brain expected it to be. I'm sorry. A correction will appear in the next issue.

Regretfully,

. . . .

Dear Sir,

We are sorry to hear that the Irving snooze-alarm clock you ordered from us was defective. Unfortunately, since the model you purchased was under warranty for only one year we are unable to offer a replacement. We are pleased, however, to enclose a coupon good for 25% off on your next purchase of any Irving snooze-alarm clock. We think you will be impressed and pleased with the improvements in this product since your last purchase.

With best wishes,

. . . .

Dear Hsiao-Wei,

I completely forgot the meeting scheduled for this morning. Although there is truly no excuse for such a thing, I will say that I was involved in an automobile accident on the way to work and had to fill out forms, notify my insurance company, and arrange for a rental car.

Can we reschedule the meeting for this Thursday, same time? Thanks—and again, I'm sorry.

Regards,

. . . .

Dear Merton Denscher,

Thank you for your letter of March 19. I am sorry that the background research I submitted was unusable. A careful re-reading of your instructions showed me at once where I'd gone wrong. I do apologize.

With your permission, I would like to resubmit the work—this time correctly. I believe I can get it to you by the end of next week since I am already familiar with the relevant sources for your topic.

Please let me know at once if you prefer me not to go ahead.

Sincerely,

. . . .

TO: Cecelia Shute
FROM: First Bank of Somerville
RE: Account # 445-421-00

Please accept our apologies for the errors on your last two bank statements. One of the interns in the bookkeeping department confused your account with one bearing a very similar number and name. We sincerely regret any inconvenience or embarrassment this may have caused you.

Enclosed are corrected copies of the last two statements. If you have any further questions, please call me directly.

Thank you for alerting us to the problem and for being so understanding.

Sincerely yours,

. . . .

Dear Annette,

I must beg your forgiveness for my outspoken and insensitive remarks last night about your religious convictions. I am afraid I got carried away in the heat of the discussion. I certainly feel that each of us has a right to our own beliefs, and I in no way meant to belittle yours.

I would be very happy if you would accept an invitation to dinner at my house on Saturday, August 3, at 7:00 p.m. I'm just having a few friends, most of whom you know.

Hoping to see you then, I am

Yours truly,

See also: ACKNOWLEDGMENTS, ADJUSTMENTS, COMPLAINTS, RESPONSES.

7

Letters About Appointments and Interviews

"Showing up is 80% of life." (Woody Allen)

Many appointments and interviews are arranged by telephone today, although they are often confirmed in writing.

Sometimes writing about an appointment is simplicity itself. This is the case when you are confirming or changing an appointment made earlier, reminding someone of an appointment, or refusing or canceling an appointment.

The difficult appointment/interview letters involve appealing to someone for their time—time that they may not want to give you. When you want the meeting in order to make a sales pitch, your letter must be a sales letter itself, persuading the person that it is in their interest to see you. When you want a job interview, you will be sending some combination of a résumé, cover letter, and letter of application (see RÉSUMÉS).

Letters About Appointments Include

- accepting
- asking for/requesting
- canceling
- changing/postponing/delaying
- confirming/following up
- making/setting up
- missing
- refusing
- thanking for

How to Say It

□   When asking for an appointment, state your request, explain why you want to meet with the person, offer some possible dates, times, and places, give your phone number and address, and express your appreciation for the person's attention to your request.

□   When agreeing to meet with someone, say "yes" to the meeting, express your pleasure or thanks, and repeat the date, time, and place as confirmation (see also ACCEPTANCES, CONFIRMATIONS).

□   When confirming arrangements made over the phone, indicate the date of the phone call and repeat the meeting specifics: date, time, place, purpose.

□   When changing an appointment, mention the original time and date, give your alternative, apologize for any inconvenience, and ask for confirmation of the new time.

□   When refusing a request for an appointment, thank the person for their letter, say "no" politely, and (if appropriate) offer an alternative or indicate why you cannot accept.

□   When postponing or delaying an appointment, mention the time and date previously set, state that you are obliged to postpone the meeting, offer another date or state that you will call to set up another appointment, and apologize for any inconvenience.

□   When canceling arrangements, repeat the specifics (time, date, place), state that you must cancel (briefly explaining why), and apologize for the inconvenience.

□   When sending a follow-up letter after an appointment, mention the date of the meeting and your pleasure at all that was accomplished. Enclose any promised information or materials. End with a reference to your hopes for future meetings/contacts/business.

□   If you fail to record a scheduled meeting or simply forget it, you need to write an immediate, sincere apology. Ask what you can do to make amends. If you are the stood-up party, you may want to contact the person. Consider first the possibility that the error was yours, that you mistook the date. If you are sure of the date, and especially if others were involved, you may want to write a gentle letter of complaint.

What Not to Say

□   Don't turn a letter canceling or changing an appointment into a lengthy apology unless the situation is a special one (you have requested the meeting and the company has gone all out inviting their upper-level management, arranging for refreshments and video equipment). Usually all you need to say is a brief "I'm sorry to have to cancel/change/postpone . . ." For more complex situations, see APOLOGIES.

☐   Don't "postpone" or "delay" a meeting that you are actually canceling. If you have no intention of ever meeting with the person, use the word "cancel" and do not refer to the possibility of a later meeting.

Tips on Writing

☐   When requesting a sales or job interview, use your letter to pique the person's curiosity—make them want to see you. Sell your product or yourself, but don't tell so much that the person thinks nothing more will be gained by an interview.

☐   Sound happy about the prospect of meeting the person.

☐   Be firm and assertive about making an appointment; if you leave it to the person ("I'd appreciate hearing from you") you may not get a response.

☐   When pressed for time, ask for a telephone confirmation.

Special Situations

☐   Sometimes people are extremely persistent about wanting some of your time—from the neighbor who is determined to learn everything you know about genealogy (or playing bridge or writing poetry or gardening) to the sales rep who won't take no for an answer. When it's someone you will continue to deal with (the neighbor), equal doses of tact and firmness are called for: "I know you will understand, but I must say no." For the sales rep, it's better to err on the side of firmness. You will get the best results with very persistent people by *not* giving any explanation. The moment you tell why you are unable to meet with them ("I'm really busy just now"), they will have a response ("It will only take a minute"). When you offer another reason, they will have another rebuttal. Engaging you in wearying debate is part of the strategy; you wouldn't be the first person to say "yes" just to avoid being harangued. A simple "I'm sorry, but no" repeated many times is most effective.

Format

☐   All correspondence about business appointments should be typewritten on either business letterhead or personal-business stationery.

☐   Interoffice communications are ideally handled by memo, which may be handwritten.

▫   Letters regarding personal appointments can be either typed or handwritten. The more formal or personal the appointment is, the stronger the indication for a handwritten message.

───────────────── WORDS ─────────────────

able	confer	meeting
accept	consult	notify
agree	contact	postpone
arrange	interview	session
call	join	unable
cancel		

───────────────── PHRASES ─────────────────

already committed/have plans
another engagement
an unexpected complication
can't keep our original date
convenient time
get together
hear from you
hope you can
introduce you to
looking forward to seeing/meeting you

may I suggest
meet with you
move up the date to
of interest to you
otherwise engaged
previous commitments
set a time and date
unfortunately obliged to
won't be free
would be convenient for me

───────────────── SENTENCES ─────────────────

Can we change our meeting on July 15 from 2:00 p.m. to 4:30 p.m.?

I am unfortunately obliged to change the date we set earlier.

I do not believe a meeting would benefit either of us.

If you are unable to make the meeting on the tenth, please let my secretary know as soon as possible.

I'll give you a call in a couple of days to see if you can schedule a meeting with me.

I'm not able to meet with you for several months—please contact me again in late January.

I will be happy to meet with you in my office on Friday, November 8 at two o'clock to discuss your invention.

I would appreciate twenty minutes of your time this week.

Let me know as soon as possible if this is convenient for you.

May I stop by your office for a few minutes next week to drop off our latest samples and catalog and to explain how our new service contract works?

Mr. Patterne is seriously ill and will be unable to keep his appointment with you on June 23 at 1:30.

Thank you for your time yesterday—I enjoyed meeting with you.

Thank you for your letter asking for an appointment.

This will confirm your appointment with Ms. Tucker on Tuesday, December 18 at 3:00 p.m.

PARAGRAPHS

▷   Thanks for your call this morning. I'm looking forward to our meeting next week—Tuesday, April 24, 3:00 p.m., your office. By the way, have you read Thurber's book on his adventures in Paris? It reminded me of you.

▷   After you have evaluated my application and résumé, I hope we can arrange an interview at a mutually convenient time. I note several areas where the company's areas of emphasis and my areas of expertise overlap, and I would like to discuss these aspects of the position. You will no doubt have questions for me as well. I look forward to hearing from you.

▷   Charlotte Moulin, managing director of Hardy's Cycle Supply, will be in Alberta the week of August 4, and would like to tour Wheels Unlimited while she is there. Please let me know if something can be arranged.

▷   I understand you are looking for acreage east of town. May I come in and speak with you sometime this week about the property I have for sale?

▷   Did I have the date wrong? I thought we had a meeting scheduled for 1:30 yesterday. I'm afraid I won't be free again until late next week, but maybe we can arrange something then. Please let me hear from you.

▷   May I have fifteen minutes of your time next week to show you some large color photographs of what Office Greenery has done for other area businesses? Offices that use our services report increased customer and employee satisfaction, and I think you will be glad you investigated our unique, effective, and cost-efficient program. I will call your secretary on Monday to see if you are available for a brief meeting.

SAMPLE LETTERS

Dear Ms. Green,

According to the article about you in last Sunday's paper, you are researching the Arapaho peoples for your new book. My great-grandmother was an Arapaho, and I have a number of papers, mementos, and other belongings that might be of interest to you. I am at home most evenings if you would like to call for an appointment to see if I have anything that interests you.

Congratulations on your most recent book, which I read with great pleasure.

With best wishes,

. . . .

Dear Lionel,

I have to cancel the meeting we set up for Friday, September 3, at 2:30 p.m., as we've got a little trouble at the Valliscourt plant. I should be back on September 6 and will call you then to set up another appointment.

Thanks for understanding.

Sincerely,

. . . .

Dear Mr. Stobbs:

I've received your letter of June 16 requesting an appointment to see me about your Handley Cross computer software.

We have been using the Surtees line of software for all our business needs for the past three years, and we are very satisfied with it. I don't see a meeting benefiting either of us.

Thanks anyway.

Yours truly,

. . . .

Dear Ms. Vulliamy:

People with disabilities get hired for one very special reason: they're qualified.

I would like to tell you about some of the highly qualified people listed with the Ogilvy Employment Agency who could make a positive and energetic contribution to your organization.

May I meet with you sometime next week?

Sincerely,

See also: ACCEPTANCES, ACKNOWLEDGMENTS, CONFIRMATION, EMPLOYMENT, FOLLOW-UP, INVITATIONS, REFUSALS, REQUESTS, THANK YOU.

8

Letters of Appreciation

"Wise sayings often fall on barren ground; but a kind word is never thrown away." (Sir Arthur Helps)

Letters of appreciation build goodwill for you in both the personal and professional spheres. They are easy to write and appeal to common courtesy and to good public relations.

Letters of appreciation are sometimes interchangeable with letters of acknowledgment, congratulations, or thanks. In many instances, however, an acknowledgment is too matter-of-fact, congratulations might appear patronizing, or a "thank you" ignores the mutuality of your exchange.

For example, it is, strictly speaking, inappropriate to thank someone for prompt payment, for turning in a report, for giving you a bonus based on performance, or for returning your lost wallet intact. In all these cases people are doing the generally expected thing. However, it is entirely appropriate to show your appreciation.

You don't thank a colleague for having a lunch with you, but you might want to express your pleasure and appreciation at how much you accomplished during the lunch.

If someone gives a particularly fine speech at a workshop, thanks are not called for—the person was presumably fulfilling an agreement to speak and was compensated. Congratulations may sound patronizing, as though giving a fine talk were something out of the ordinary. However, expressing your appreciation for what you learned and how it was presented would be welcome.

Write Letters of Appreciation For

- awards/honors
- bonuses
- complimentary letters about your company/employees/services/products

- congratulations/commendations/compliments/encouragement/praise: employees/colleagues/teachers/family/friends
- customer referrals
- customers whose business, orders, or contracts you want to acknowledge
- customers to whom you extend privileges in appreciation of their business/prompt payments/new accounts
- employees you want to compliment/encourage/praise
- employers for a bonus/raise/promotion
- favorable mentions in a book/article/talk
- financial contributions
- group efforts
- introductions
- invitations to speak
- jobs well done
- helpful advice/suggestions/tips
- lunches/meetings/dinners with associates/colleagues/co-workers
- personal favors
- prompt payments
- recommendations
- references
- refusals with thanks
- speeches/workshops/conferences
- sympathy (see also ACKNOWLEDGMENTS, THANK YOU)
- visits/tours/open houses
- volunteers

How to Say It

□   State what you appreciate (a talent, the business lunch, the plans for the new building).

□   Explain briefly why you feel appreciative.

□   Make some mention of future action, theirs or yours: you would be willing to reciprocate, you hope the two of you can get together again, you hope the person will contribute further.

What Not to Say

☐   Do not tack other news, information, or a sales message onto a letter of appreciation; for maximum impact your upbeat message should stand alone.

Tips on Writing

☐   Be brief, warm, and sincere. The "brief" part is easy enough, but if you have trouble being warm and sincere, you might want to take a second look at why you are writing. Perhaps it is not a letter of appreciation that you need to send.

Special Situations

☐   Letters of appreciation sent to customers, present and potential, are more sales letters than letters of appreciation (see SALES).

☐   Sometimes you may need to turn down something—a gift, an invitation, a membership—but you are flattered and pleased at the thought behind it, so you write a letter that is part appreciation, part refusal (see also REFUSALS).

☐   Letters of appreciation can be written to several employees at once— teams, divisions, branch offices, sectors, and other groups that have performed particularly well or solved a problem.

Format

☐   Consider using postcards for sending one- or two-sentence notes of appreciation. This will allow you to dash off notes rich in public relations potential in very little time. Consider postcards featuring scenery from your area for people outside it, art postcards, reprints from old movies that might relate to your business or your interests, or even an especially attractive picture of your factory, office, building, or other installation.

☐   Personal notes of appreciation should be handwritten on foldovers or personal stationery.

☐   Business letters of appreciation are typed on letterhead stationery if you have a somewhat formal, distant, or "official" relationship with the person. In more casual contexts, you could jot an appreciative message on memo paper.

_____ WORDS _____

admire	honor	refreshing
appreciate	impressed	remarkable
approve	indebted	respect
artistic	inspired	satisfying
attractive	interesting	sensational
captivating	inviting	sincere
charming	kindness	special
commendable	knowledgeable	stunned
credit	large-hearted	superb
delightful	lavish	surprised
elegant	lovely	tasteful
enchanting	marvelous	terrific
encourage	memorable	thanks
engaging	one-of-a-kind	thoughtfulness
enjoyable	overwhelmed	thrilled
esteem	pleased	touched
fascinating	pleasure	treasure
favorite	praise	treat
generous	prize	triumph
gracious	prompt	unique
gratifying	recognize	valuable
happy	recommend	welcome
heartily		

_____ PHRASES _____

appreciate the good/complimentary words

appreciate your contributions to this project

as a token of our gratitude/appreciation

big success

congratulate you on

delighted to learn about

for future consideration

generous contributions

grateful to you for

hand it to you

held in high regard

hope I can return the favor someday

I am impressed by/with

I appreciate the time and effort you expended on

important contribution

it's a pleasure to know

it was thoughtful of you to

I want you to know how much we/I appreciate

job well done

let me tell you how much I liked

offer my compliments

practical/helpful/constructive suggestion

realize the worth of

set great store by

think highly of

thoughtful/helpful letter

to your credit

we can point with pride

wish you well

without your dedication and expertise

would like to compliment you on

your recent success

---------------------------------- SENTENCES ----------------------------------

Customers like you are the reason we stay in business.

I don't know how I would have managed without your help.

If I can reciprocate/repay your kindness, let me know.

I greatly appreciated your help.

I hope someone writes you such a nice letter when the occasion arises.

I just read Frank Goodwin's syndicated column, and I want to convey my deepest admiration to you for your stand on the Barker honorary degree.

I sincerely appreciate your time and attention.

I want you to know how much I appreciate the photo album.

I would be most happy to return the favor.

Many thanks for your helpful letter.

Thanks again for your clever and useful suggestion.

Thank you for offering.

We appreciate your taking the time to write us.

We are all happy for you.

What would I do without you?

You make my job so much easier.

Your efforts have made this possible.

Your support is greatly appreciated.

---------------------------------- PARAGRAPHS ----------------------------------

▷   You've been a valued cardmember with Stuyvesant Bank since 1975, and we thank you for the exceptional manner in which you've handled your account. To show our appreciation, we've pre-approved you for our premier bankcard, the Gold 100. We think you will find it to be the ultimate in credit card performance.

▷   Please accept the enclosed token of our appreciation for your five years as one of our most dependable and delightful volunteers. We don't know what we would do without you!

▷   Thank you for your timely and excellent solution to the problem of tangled hoses. Only those of us who have struggled with this annoying and time-consuming inconvenience can appreciate what a delight the new boom system will be. You will be receiving an Outstanding Contribution award in May, but I didn't want to wait that long before telling you how pleased and impressed we all are.

▷   Although I appreciate very much your offer of the cabin, I'm afraid we won't be able to get away at all this month. Can we take a raincheck?

▷   All of us here at Legson, Ltd. enjoyed your enthusiastic letter about the quality of our lace goods. We are proud to offer such a wide selection of fine handiwork from all four corners of the globe. Please accept with our appreciation the enclosed 20% discount coupon good on your next order.

▷   Thank you for returning the signed contracts. We appreciate the opportunity of doing business with you again.

_____ SAMPLE LETTERS _____

Dear Dr. Rowlands,

Your suggestions for next year's technical forum are much appreciated. I've turned them over to the steering committee, although I suspect you'll be invited to join them. I hope you will accept—your ideas are very workable and useful.

Sincerely yours,

. . . .

Dear Ms. Lees-Noel:

I'm told that you were the good-hearted soul who kept my desk from overflowing during my sick leave (while still keeping up with your own work).

Instead of the chaos I expected to return to, I was able to start back with a clear slate. I am most appreciative of everything you did. I don't know whether this is a compliment or not, but you did things just the way I would have!

Do call on me if I can ever return the favor.

Sincerely,

. . . .

Dear Mr. Fitzmarshall:

We were pleased to learn that you received such outstanding service from one of our employees. Be assured that we have passed on your compliments to Ms. Stretton. You will perhaps enjoy knowing that in recognition of her talent and managerial skills, Ms. Stretton has just been promoted to floor supervisor.

We appreciate your taking the time to write us.

Yours truly,

. . . .

Dear Mr. Loomis,

I wanted you to know how much I appreciate the letter you sent me thanking me for my vote on the Hartshorn and Montjoy matter. I appreciated all your hard work and the information you provided on the subject.

If I can be of assistance to you on any other matter, feel free to call.

Sincerely,

. . . .

Dear Mrs. Sixsmith,

Thank you for accompanying the fifth and sixth graders to Language Camp last weekend. I understand you chaperoned the group on your own time. Since Ronald arrived home, I've heard dozens of stories of your helpfulness, good humor, and ability to make the camp a home-away-from-home for these youngsters.

We felt a lot better knowing you would be with the group, and we appreciate Ronald's opportunity to spend time with a dynamic adult who's a good role model.

With best wishes,

. . . .

Dear Pritchard Van Lines:

Pritchard Van Lines recently moved us from Chicago to San Francisco, and I would like to tell you that it was a pleasant experience from start to finish. I thought the odds were against having so many efficient people in one company.

I chose Pritchard in the first place because the woman who answered the phone was extremely knowledgeable, helpful, and agreeable. I decided that if the company had the sense to put someone like her in the front office, they probably knew what they were doing. And they did! The estimator, the packers, loaders, drivers, unpackers, warehouse people—all did a great job.

Some 8,000 pounds of household goods were moved with the care and know-how I would have given had I been able to do it myself. A one-hundred-year-old stained glass window, my collections of Christmas plates and Occupied Japan porcelain, and several other treasures arrived intact.

Thank you for a professional and positive moving experience!
Sincerely,

See also: ACKNOWLEDGMENTS, CONGRATULATIONS, THANK YOU.

9

Collection Letters

"Creditors have better memories than debtors."
(Benjamin Franklin)

Collection letters are difficult to write because you have two goals that tend to work against each other: you want the customer to pay the overdue account and you want to keep the customer's goodwill and business. Well-written, effective collection letters pay off handsomely, not only because of the retrieved income but also because of the delinquent accounts that eventually become dependable accounts.

Collection attempts start out most often as past-due reminders from a company's billing office, accounting department, or credit division. When the account is thirty, sixty, or ninety days overdue, depending on company policy, the first of a series of collection letters will be sent. Only when the company's series of increasingly aggressive collection letters is ignored is the account turned over to a collection agency. Many large firms use statistical models to predict which accounts need more aggressive action early on. Remember, too, that given a large population of overdue accounts, the single most effective collection method may be a pleasant telephone reminder.

Collection Letters Include

- announcements that the account is being turned over to lawyer/collection agency
- letters to lawyer/collection agency
- personal collection letters: friend/relative
- reminders
- series of increasingly insistent letters
- thank you for payment

How to Say It

□   Collection letters are generally sent in a series. Each letter in the series should summarize the relevant information: customer's order number, date of purchase, items purchased, seller's invoice number and date, reference to previous reminders sent, dollar amount past due, and the original due date. Each letter in the series should also name a specific date by which payment must be received and allow enough time to give the customer a chance to pay. You may also suggest a special payment plan. End your letters with a strong, definite request as well as a statement that if payment has already been sent this letter should be ignored. Include a postage-paid reply envelope to encourage a prompt response. A suggested plan featuring six collection letters is given below. Your own needs may be better met by a series of four, or ten, or you may prefer to vary the message.

□   Collection letter 1: After you have sent several statements indicating the past-due status of the account (perhaps with a stamped message or reminder sticker that says "Past Due" or "Second Notice"), you send a gentle, friendly letter calling to the person's attention the overdue payment. Your letter is brief, saying little more than that a stated amount is so many weeks or months overdue. You pleasantly request payment.

□   Collection letter 2: You are a little more insistent and firmly remind the customer that payment still has not been received. In a second paragraph, you might ask for explanations or suggest several face-saving reasons why the person hasn't paid (bill was overlooked, was lost in the mail, customer was away). Close with an expression of your confidence that the payment will be sent at once.

□   Collection letter 3: Your tone becomes more urgent, your letter is longer, and you give the customer one or more good reasons to pay the bill: it will protect their credit rating and good reputation; it is a matter of fairness/justice/conscience; it is the responsible thing to do; it will make them feel good; it is a matter of their pride and self-respect; it is in their own best self-interest. (You can, of course, use these appeals in any of your letters.) In this or the next letter, you might want to propose two payment schedules that are acceptable to you, and offer the customer a choice of the one they prefer. Divide the past-due amount into weekly, semi-monthly, monthly, or two lump-sum payments.

□   Collection letter 4: Your message is increasingly stern, and you present additional arguments for payment: you have carried out your obligations by providing the service or shipping the goods and now they must carry out their obligations by sending payment; the amount is too small to risk losing their credit rating over; the customer would not wish to be placed on your delinquent list; they would certainly not wish to be reported to the trade credit bureau; they will not be able to place any future orders with you.

Then, for the first time, you mention the possibility of turning their account over to a collection agency or an attorney for collection.

☐   Collection letter 5: By now you assume the customer is aware of the problem and deliberately choosing not to pay. In a very strong message, you announce that you are obliged to take other action—turning the account over either to a collection agency for collection or to a lawyer for legal action. (If you opt for legal action, you will be wording your letter with your attorney's advice.) Even now, however, state that you will give the customer ten days in which to make arrangements to settle the account before taking action. Be clear that the action can be avoided if the customer responds at once.

☐   Collection letter 6: This final letter represents your belief that this particular customer is going to pay only if forced to do so. You announce that the account is being transferred to a stated collection agency or to a stated law firm as of a stated date. This letter is a simple announcement of the action you are taking; you no longer attempt to get the customer to pay.

☐   When you write to the collection agency, give complete information: name, address, telephone numbers, account number, copies of all correspondence, statements, data sheets.

What Not to Say

☐   Do not threaten the customer with a collection agency or legal action until you are actually ready to pursue these avenues. If you say you are turning the account over to a collection agency in ten days, do so.

☐   Some words act like red flags to many people, and they will not help you accomplish your purpose. Don't use "failure" ("failure to respond," "failure to pay"); "ignore" ("you have ignored our letters"); "insist" or "demand" ("we insist/demand that you send payment at once"). Avoid humiliating or demeaning the person.

☐   Avoid the arch, falsely helpful tone sometimes found in collection letters: "We simply cannot figure out why someone with such a good credit rating . . ." "We are at a loss to understand why we have not heard from you." "We've been scratching our heads . . ."

☐   Do not say anything that might be construed as libelous.

☐   Avoid bad language, insults, name-calling, bullying, sarcasm, arrogance, and verbal wrist-slapping. Such negative approaches most often bring negative results; debtors have an excuse to make you the bad guy and thus undeserving of settlement. It also does your company's reputation no good.

Tips on Writing

❑   Write each letter as though you expect it to be the last. You are optimistic, appreciative, confident.

❑   The tone of your letters is important. People with payment problems are often psychologically fragile; a poorly written collection letter can inspire feelings of anger, self-pity, or helplessness, none of which leads to the writing of a check. Reread your letters to see if they are respectful, businesslike, fair, and considerate. Give customers the benefit of the doubt; sometimes the missed payment is merely an oversight. In the beginning at least, assume goodwill on the part of the customer. While being friendly and courteous, you can also adopt a tone that ranges from firm to insistent to forceful.

❑   Space your collection letters properly. In the beginning send them out monthly, immediately after a payment date is missed. Allow enough time for the customer to respond or for delays caused by illness, excessively busy periods, or vacations. Later, you may want to send letters every ten days to two weeks. The more stubborn the account, the closer together you will space your letters. When the account has a good credit history, you will not send letters quite as often.

❑   When writing collection letters to an individual, do not send them to the person's place of business where others might open the mail. Postcards carrying collection information are risky for this reason too. You do not want to embarrass your customer or, worse, leave yourself open to complaint or legal action.

Special Situations

❑   Although most collection letters are written by businesses, occasionally you may need to call in an overdue loan from a friend or relative. It is especially important in this situation to help the other person save face. Include a ready-made excuse in your letter ("I know how busy you are . . ." "I wonder if you forgot about . . ." "Am I mistaken, or did we agree that you'd repay the loan September 1?" "I know what a procrastinator you are!") It will be helpful if you have drawn up a loan agreement—or, at the very least, a letter stating the terms.

❑   If you are trying to collect a past-due amount from a customer who reports adverse circumstances (illness, unemployment, financial reverses, bankruptcy), work out a feasible payment program even if it is an extremely generous one. A background check should give you a good sense of whether the person is actually experiencing difficulties that merit special attention. Reducing a bill by even a very small amount is a success for both creditor and debtor and is worthy of your best efforts.

Format

□   Collection letters are always typed on letterhead stationery.

□   Form letters are often useful, especially for the first few collection letters in a series. The first can be a simple reminder with spaces to fill in the amount and due date. The second and third letters in the series are worded more strongly.

--------------------------------- WORDS ---------------------------------

action	embarrass	policy
advise	explanation	propose
agreement	extend	regret
amount	immediately	reliable
appeal	invoice	remainder
arrangement	liability	reminder
arrears	misunderstanding	remit
balance	necessitate	remittance
circumstances	nonpayment	repayment
collect	notice	request
concerned	outstanding	require
cooperation	overdraft	satisfy
credit	overdue	settle
creditworthy	overlooked	statement
debt	oversight	terms
default	owe	unpaid
disappointed	past-due	urge
due	payment	urgent

--------------------------------- PHRASES ---------------------------------

account past due	balance due
accounts receivable	balance sheet
act upon	be good enough to/so good as to
additional costs	be in debt
a little behind with your payments	call/direct your attention to
amount due/owed	collection agency/proceedings
answerable for	credit rating/standing/record
appreciate hearing from you	current financial statement
at least a partial payment	damaging your credit
bad debt	record/standing/rating
balance accounts with	deferred payment

delinquent status of your account

despite our notice of a month ago

did not respond

discuss this with you

easy payment plan

entire amount/balance

escaped your attention

final opportunity

financial difficulties

friendly reminder

have heard nothing from you

have the goodness to

how can we work together to

immediately payable

important to resolve this matter

in arrears

insufficient funds

I regret to tell you that

it is our policy

I understand and appreciate your position, but

just a reminder

just to remind you

legal action/advice/steps

let us hear from you right away

made no effort to pay

mail today

make payment

must hear from you

mutually satisfactory solution

not made a payment since

now due on your account

official notice

only recourse

other action

outstanding balance

pay in full

perhaps you didn't realize

please give this matter your immediate attention

please let us hear from you by

please mail/remit/send us

pressing need for action

previous notices/claims for payment

prompt payment/remittance

reasonable payment arrangement

recourse to legal action

reduce your balance

regarding payment

resolve this matter

return mail

review of our files

review of your account shows

seriously delinquent

several statements and letters

should have been paid by

since you haven't replied to our last letter in which we suggested a payment plan solution

so that we may clear your account before the next statement period

so that you can maintain your credit standing with us

special appeal

strongly suggest

there has been no activity on your account

to avoid additional expenses, delays, and unpleasantness

unacceptable delay

valued customer

we haven't heard from you

we remind you once more

we would appreciate your sending us

will be obliged to withdraw credit privileges

without further delay

———————————————————— SENTENCES ————————————————————

After 120 days, we normally/routinely/automatically turn an account over to our attorneys for collection.

A postage-paid envelope is enclosed for your convenience.

Despite our last three monthly reminders, your account remains unpaid.

Enclosed is a copy of your last statement, showing a balance of $457.89 that is ninety days overdue.

I am sorry, but we are unable to extend you any more time for the payment of your outstanding balance of $896.78.

If there is a reason for the delay, please let us know.

If we do not hear from you at once/within the next ten days, we will be obliged to pursue other collection procedures/we will have no choice but to engage the services of a collection agency.

If you have already sent your check/paid your balance of $324.56, please ignore this notice.

If you haven't already mailed in your payment, won't you take a moment to send it today/won't you mail it today?

If your financial circumstances make it impossible to pay the full amount at this time, please let us know as I am sure that we can work out an acceptable schedule of installment payments.

If your payment is not received by June 1, we will be obliged to turn your account over to the Costello Collection Agency.

It is important that you take some action before this unpaid balance affects your credit rating.

It is our policy to turn over unpaid accounts of more than 90 days to our attorneys.

Just a reminder: your account balance of $106.87 is thirty days past due.

May we have your check for $89.43 by return mail?

Our records show your account to be seriously in arrears.

Please call or write to make arrangements.

Please forward payment in the amount of $269.89 promptly.

Please mail your check by May 5 so that no future action will be necessary.

Thank you for your cooperation/attention to this matter/for taking care of this at once.

There may be a good explanation for your lack of response to our requests for payment of your overdue account—won't you tell us about it?

This matter must be resolved without further delay.

Unfortunately your payment has not been received.

We are concerned that your payment of $1,466.59, due June 1, has not yet reached us.

We are unable to fill your order dated June 3 because your account is currently in arrears.

We ask for your cooperation in paying the balance due.

We expect to hear from you by July 15 without fail.

We have allowed nearly 120 days for payment, but cannot carry your account any longer.

We have been writing you about your past-due account for several months now.

We have had no response from you to our last three letters.

We have sent a number of friendly requests for payment but have had no response from you.

We hope that you will take advantage of this last invitation to settle your account and to avoid further damage to your credit rating as well as the costs of any possible legal action.

We look forward to hearing from you.

We must know your intentions immediately.

We provide prompt service, and we expect prompt payment.

We resort to legal action with the greatest reluctance.

We urge you to resolve this matter before we are obliged to take this serious step.

We were hoping to hear from you in response to our last letter.

We were pleased to hear from you regarding your account.

We would be happy to work with you to arrange an easy payment plan suitable to your circumstances.

We would like to work with you to resolve this matter.

Why not take care of this matter right now?

You are a much-appreciated customer, and we hope there is no problem.

You may not realize that your account is ninety days past due.

Your account has been turned over to Darley and Havison, our attorneys, for collection and, if necessary, legal action.

Your account is past due.

Your payment of $876.23 will be very much appreciated.

Your prompt payment will protect your good credit rating.

You still owe us $187.53 for goods received/services rendered.

You will be hearing from our attorneys shortly.

You will want to mail your check today so that you can continue using your credit privileges.

PARAGRAPHS

▷   Enclosed are copies of your statements, year to date. Please check them against your records, and let us know if they do not agree with ours. We show an outstanding balance of $1,236.90.

▷   The Locksley-Jones Collection Agency has been authorized by Elliot Lumber to collect the $980.54 past due amount on your account. According to information turned over to us by Elliot, you have not responded to requests for payment made over a period of eight months. This letter serves as your official notice that collection proceedings will begin ten days from the date of this letter unless you contact us to make some satisfactory arrangement for payment.

▷   Perhaps you are not able to pay the full amount all at once. If you would like to suggest an appropriate payment plan, we will be happy to accommodate you.

▷   Thank you for your payment of $763.21, received today. We are happy to be able to remove you from our collection system and to reestablish your line of credit. We do this with the understanding that you will keep your account current in the future. We hope to continue to serve you with all your plumbing and electrical needs.

▷   The nonpayment of your balance is expensive for both of us: it is costing you your excellent credit record as well as monthly service charges and it is costing us lost revenues and extra accounting expenses. We strongly urge you to make out a check right now for the balance due on your account (a self-addressed stamped envelope is enclosed for your convenience). If you wish to discuss some financial difficulty or arrange for a special payment schedule, please call 555-1331 today so that we can avoid reclassifying your account as delinquent.

_____ SAMPLE LETTERS _____

TO: Gombold Collection Agency
FROM: Van Allen Department Stores
DATE: February 3, 1992
    We would like to engage your services to collect a past-due account in the name of:
                            Hermione Roddice
                            1921 Lawrence Parkway
                            Sunnybrook, OH 45043
Enclosed are copies of statements sent, the data sheet on this account, and all correspondence between us and Ms. Roddice to date.
    Please let us know if we can be of further help.

. . . .

Dear Ms. Phippard:
    Your account is now ninety days overdue in the amount of $85.89. As you are one of our longtime customers with an excellent credit rating, we assume this is a simple oversight.
    Thank you for taking care of this matter promptly.
                                                        Sincerely,

. . . .

Dear Mr. Landauer,
    We would like to remind you once again that we have not yet received any payment on your account balance of $597.45. If you need additional time or would like to arrange a special payment schedule, please call the credit department today or tomorrow at extension 91. Otherwise, we will expect to receive a check in the mail.
    We will appreciate your prompt attention to this matter.
                                                        Sincerely,

. . . .

TO: Nolan Associates
FROM: Charney Office Supplies
DATE: March 6, 1992
RE: Past-Due Account
    We have alerted you several times (see our statements of November 4 and December 7 and our letters of January 6 and February 5) that your account has a balance of $1,059.32 outstanding. Because your credit rating could be adversely affected by continuing nonpayment, we hope that you will send us something on account immediately.

We need to hear from you this week concerning your plans for repayment. Thank you.

Sincerely yours,

. . . .

Dear Ms. Seebach:

We are very concerned about your past-due account of $473.23 and your lack of response to our inquiries about it. We would very much like to hear from you within the next ten days so that we are not obliged to seek other, more serious means of satisfying this debt.

Please consider protecting your credit rating by sending us a check promptly. You will be glad you did.

Sincerely,

. . . .

Dear Stephen Bracebridge:

Your account (# 8103-484-2329) is seriously in arrears. As we have had no response from you to our repeated reminders, we are obliged to consider the possibility of seeking help in collecting the past-due amount of $12,489.19 with the help of a collection agency.

If at all possible, we like to avoid this way of removing unpaid accounts from our books—both for your sake and ours. Your credit standing will be affected by such action, and we lose time and money trying to collect money that is, in all justice, owed to us.

We will be transferring this account to a collection agency on April 3. We would, however, be very happy to work out a payment schedule with you if you will call us before then.

Hoping to hear from you, I am

Sincerely,

. . . .

Dear Sarah Scally:

On September 15, your account (#3178-S) will be transferred to the Bowyer Collection Agency for collection of the past-due amount of $481.69. If we should hear from you before then, we would be glad to make other arrangements. Otherwise, however, you will be hearing from someone at Bowyer.

Sincerely,

. . . .

Dear Algy,

I dislike reminding you yet again, but it's now been six weeks since I lent you $200 "for just a few days." If I could just forget about it, I would, but as it happens I need that money myself—right away.

Shall I stop by after work to pick it up or do you want to drop it off at the house? Let me know.

Sincerely,

See also: CREDIT.

10

Complaints

If you are writing a letter of complaint, you are not alone. Millions write them every year. One multifoods corporation, for example, receives some three hundred thousand complaining phone calls and letters per year. The St. Paul, Minnesota, mayor's office receives more than two thousand complaints every month, ranging from international issues to the way people are treated at a local gas station. Residents complain about a man who painted stripes on his garage just to annoy the neighbors, speeding and disregard for traffic laws, poorly kept-up alleys, property-line disputes, and, of course, snow removal and car-eating potholes.

Because you are one of a crowd, you'll want your letter to stand out. Put yourself in the place of the person receiving your letter and remember that your goal is not to get revenge or to express your perhaps considerable anger, but to get results (unless, of course, your goal *is* simply to let off steam). If you want results the best way is to make your letter short, factual, and reasonable. A little good humor doesn't hurt either.

Write Letters of Complaint About

- billing/collection/financial/ordering errors
- children: misbehavior/damage by
- community or neighborhood problems: adult bookstores/unkempt property/noisy parties
- delays: late reply/shipment/refund/merchandise/supplies/payment
- employees: incompetent/rude/inappropriate behavior
- legislative problems: high taxes/unfair laws/pending bills
- merchandise: defective/damaged/dangerous/overpriced/missing parts, instructions, or warranties

- mistakes, misunderstandings, and personal errors
- pets: damage by/attacks by
- policies: unfavorable/restrictive/discriminatory
- schools: undeserved reprimands/undesirable programs
- suspected fraud, misleading advertising, bait-and-switch tactics, unfair practices, discrimination

How to Say It

☐ State the problem clearly, briefly, fairly: what it is, when you noticed it, how it has inconvenienced you, what you have done/what needs to be done to correct it.

☐ Give all important facts: date and place of purchase, sales slip number, detailed description of product or service, serial or model number, amount paid, name of person who performed the service/sold you the item/gave you the wrong information, your account number or charge card number, history of previous correspondence (include company filing number or reference number).

☐ Provide complete and accurate names and addresses—your own and the person to whom you are writing. Also include your home and work telephone numbers.

☐ Include appropriate documentation: sales slips, warranties or guarantees, previous correspondence, pictures of damaged item, repair or service orders, canceled checks, contracts, paid invoices. (Send only photocopies of your documents; retain originals.)

☐ Tell why you think it's important that the complaint be taken care of.

☐ State clearly what you expect from the person or company. Request a reasonable, possible solution.

☐ Suggest a deadline for the action requested.

☐ If your complaint involves an incident with an insolent sales clerk, another driver, a belligerent or threatening stranger, include the date and time of the incident, the name of person involved (if you know it), where it occurred, names of witnesses, and any other significant details.

☐ In closing, express your confidence that the matter will be taken care of to your satisfaction.

What Not to Say

☐ Avoid sarcasm, accusations, abuse, recriminations, blaming, smart remarks, and emotional outbursts. You will only antagonize the very person who is in the best position to help you. Negative letters are not only ineffective, they make you look foolish (and feel foolish later, when you think about it).

□ Do not threaten to sue. This is generally recognized as a bluff; people who are really going to sue leave this announcement to their lawyer. You might—if you mean this—say that you are going to take the case to small claims court. This is one possible way of achieving a quick, inexpensive resolution.

□ Do not hint for free products or "compensation" beyond what you are due.

Tips on Writing

□ Write your letter soon after the incident or problem; details will be fresher in your mind, and your chances of getting a good response are greater.

□ In the first line of your letter (or at least in the first paragraph) state clearly what you want from the company. Then state it again in the last line.

□ Write your letter with the assumption that the reader will be willing to resolve the problem. The positive approach is more effective than one that says, "I don't suppose you'll do anything about it, but . . ."

□ Stick to one issue whenever possible. Writing to your senator about the U.S. position in Central America, abortion, high taxes, and flag-burning all in the same letter almost certainly ensures a less-than-satisfactory response.

□ Place more emphasis on how the problem can be resolved and less emphasis on the details of the mix-up, your reactions and feelings, and what a disaster it has all been.

□ Keep track of the names and titles of individuals you have spoken with, the date, time, and outcome of each conversation, and include this information in your letter.

□ If your complaint has several components (list of ordered items missing, series of events, response requested about a number of issues), set off these items in a numbered or bulleted list to make it easier for the reader to see and respond to them.

□ Unless you know otherwise, assume that the person to whom you are writing is unaware of the problem. Say that you are sure someone would like to know what has occurred.

□ State facts and avoid emotion. Numbers, figures, objective facts, quotations, photographs, and charts all support a position effectively. Subjective phrases like "I want," "I feel," and "I need" are not persuasive.

□ In many cases the person who receives your letter is not the person who caused your problem, so be polite. Complaint departments read so many angry letters that they are glad to respond to a reasonable one.

◻   Include positive remarks: why you chose that product, how long you have used the company's services or products, that you think perhaps this incident is an aberration.

◻   Use a light touch when possible. A little humor (as long as it is benign) goes a long way to lightening the recipient's mood when faced with a problem.

◻   Express confidence in the recipient's ability to do something. Assume that the person is going to be helpful and let this show in your letter. Try to get the person on your side by pointing out something you have in common. Close on an optimistic note: "I am sure you will have a solution for this problem." "I am confident that you will want to replace this defective answering machine."

◻   There's nothing less effective than writing a great letter to the wrong person—or the wrong address. When writing to lawmakers or government officials, check in the reference department of your local library for listings in *U.S. Government Manual* (new edition every year), *Who's Who in American Politics*, and various state and federal handbooks and directories. *Federal Information Centers*, which lists centers across the country to contact when you need assistance from the federal government, is available free from: Consumer Information Center, Pueblo, CO 81009.

◻   When writing businesses, you can obtain names and titles of company officials from the publications listed below or by calling the company. You may want to direct your first letter to the owner, president, or manager; sometimes, however, you can get satisfaction by writing the person closest to the problem. If your first letter isn't productive, then write to higher-ups. If they are unable or unwilling to deal with it, you may want to contact your local Better Business Bureau or a local, county, or state consumer agency. If you are involved in a disagreement with a professional, write the state board that licenses the person. You can find the addresses of most companies in one of the following: *Consumer's Resource Handbook* (see below); *Standard & Poor's Register of Corporations, Directors and Executives* (in the reference section of your local library); *Standard Directory of Advertisers* (library); *Thomas Register of American Manufacturers* (library); *Trade Names Directory* (library).

◻   The *Consumer's Resource Handbook* (a 93-page publication available free from the Consumer Information Center, Pueblo, CO 81009) lists corporate consumer contacts, automobile manufacturers, better business bureaus throughout the country, trade associations, third-party dispute resolution programs, federal agencies as well as state, county, and city government consumer offices. Also included are lists of occupational and professional licensing boards—there are about fifteen hundred state agencies that license or register members of more than five hundred professions and service industries including doctors, lawyers, nurses, accountants, pharmacists, funeral directors, plumbers, electricians, auto repair shops, employment agencies, collection agencies, beauticians, and TV and radio repair shops. The booklet also lists state agencies on aging, insurance regulators, state banking authorities, state utility commissions, state vocational and rehabilitation agencies, and other groups that might be of help to the consumer with a complaint.

□   If your complaint is serious or involves a significant amount of money, do some homework. Get a copy of the company's annual report from the library or from a stockbroker. You may get a better response if you show some familiarity with the company.

□   Keep copies of all correspondence and documents.

□   Mention third parties with whom you have discussed the issue or from whom you have requested assistance in resolving the problem. Send copies of your letter to these third parties. (Indicate this on the copy line of your original letter.)

□   Help the other person save face. If you act as though only your threats and string-pulling are bringing about a settlement, you deny the other person their sense of themselves as decent, generous people.

□   When you have complaints about your child's school, assume nothing at the outset. It is best to begin your exchange of letters with questions: "Can you tell me . . . ?" "Is it true that . . . ?" "When was this announced?" Too often, misunderstandings crop up somewhere between the school and the home, so it is well to clarify the issues before giving your opinion or asking for changes, apologies, and so forth.

□   When schools have complaints about students, phone calls are usually the first avenue of communication, but sometimes letters spelling out the problems must eventually be sent. In writing parents about problems, school officials will do well to remember "tact" and "fact." State exactly what has happened without becoming emotional, subtly abusive, judgmental, or threatening. Suggest a date and time for a meeting or ask that the parent call you. Enclose a copy of the school regulations the child violated or refer the parent to the student handbook. Be clear about what action is being taken or may be taken by the school. The actions themselves must, of course, be consistent with School Board policy, be clearly stated in the student handbook, and be legally defensible.

Special Situations

□   A "claim" is another way of talking about a complaint. You assert that something is owed you and you want restitution. To register a claim, use the same rules and format as you would for a complaint letter. (If you are settling a claim, see ADJUSTMENTS.)

▫   In any disagreement with the airlines, give your flight number, dates of flight, points of origin and termination, description of problem or incident, where and when it occurred, what you want them to do about it.

▫   If you are one of a large group of people protesting an action, product, service, or corporate behavior, it is far better for you to write individual, personalized letters than to send form letters or group-generated complaints. Companies are much more likely to respond to one well-written, original letter than to hundreds of mimeographed postcards. In a few cases, the number of complainants may have a value in itself, but check to be sure you aren't wasting time and postage on mass-produced complaints.

▫   Sometimes apologies are necessary on both sides of a dispute. Even when you have a legitimate complaint, it's possible that you have in some small way aggravated the situation. Making your own apology is not only honest (if called for) but is often helpful in eliciting the response you want.

▫   In addition to writing the company responsible for the problem, you will want to write your credit card company if you have paid for the merchandise with the card. Ask them to withhold payment while the problem is being resolved (you must do this within a certain period—see the information on the back of your statement).

▫   When you receive damaged merchandise, notify the shipper first. Describe the problem and ask for a claims form. In some cases a claims adjuster will be sent to talk to you.

▫   When writing about a credit card billing error, give as much information as possible: name of the credit card holder, account number, reference number, amount, store where purchased, and description of the disputed item. Explain the error (that you did not make the purchase, that the amount is incorrect or the bill is a duplicate), and ask for a corrected statement or a credit to your account.

Format

▫   Business letterhead, business-personal stationery, or personal letterhead are all good choices for a complaint letter.

▫   Type the letter if at all possible. If you must handwrite it, be sure it is legible and neat.

────────────────── WORDS ──────────────────

action	incompetent	overlooked
adjustment	incomplete	oversight
agreed-upon	inconsiderate	protest
angry	inconsistent	rankled
annoyed	inconvenient	regrettable
botched	incorrect	reimburse
carelessness	indignant	remake
compensation	inept	repair
concerned	inexperienced	repay
controversial	inferior	replace
damaged	infuriating	resolve
deception	insufficient	restitution
defective	irritated	restore
difficulty	lackadaisical	return
disagreement	lax	rude
disappointed	lazy	second-rate
disconcerting	maddening	shoddy
displeased	misapprehension	short-sighted
dispute	miscalculation	slipshod
disrespectful	misconception	sloppy
dissatisfaction	misconstrued	slovenly
disservice	mishandled	thoughtless
disturbed	misinformed	trouble
drawback	misinterpreted	uncomfortable
embarrassing	misjudged	uncooperative
exasperated	misleading	unethical
exorbitant	mismanaged	unfit
failure	misprint	unfortunate
fake	misquote	unfounded
false	misrepresented	unfulfilled
fault	missing	unhappy
flaw	misstatement	unpleasant
fuming	mistake	unprofessional
furious	misunderstanding	unqualified
grievance	negotiate	unreasonable
ill-advised	nonfunctioning	unreliable
impolite	nuisance	unsatisfactory
imprudent	offended	unsound
inaccurate	off-putting	untidy
inadequate	omission	untrue
inappropriate	overcharged	unwarranted
inattentive	overestimated	upset
incident		

_____ PHRASES _____

am entitled to
a mix-up in my order
appealing to you for help
are you aware that
check on this problem
correct your records
defective product
delivery problems
direct your attention to
does not meet our performance
  standards
doing a slow burn
every reasonable effort should be made to
expecting to hear from you soon
fails to meet industry standards
fit to be tied
fly in the ointment
has not met my expectations
have the right to
hope to resolve this problem
I am concerned about
I feel certain you would want to know
  that
I feel let down by
I found it irritating in the extreme to
I must insist that/insist upon
inexcusable treatment
I strongly oppose your position on
it has come to my attention that

it is with great reluctance that I must
  inform you
it was somewhat disconcerting to find
  that
it was with indignation that I realized
I seldom write letters of complaint, but
I was displeased/distressed/disturbed/
  offended/disappointed by
I wish to be reimbursed for
I wish to register a complaint about
I would like to alert you to
laboring under a misapprehension/
  misconception
makes me see red
makes my blood boil
may not be aware that
not accustomed to dealing with
not up to your usual high standards
returning to you under separate cover
serious omission/problem
shipping error
under the mistaken impression that
unpleasant incident
unsatisfactory performance
we were very unhappy with
will look for some improvement
with all possible speed
would like credit for

_____ SENTENCES _____

Anything you can do to speed matters up/resolve this problem will be greatly appre-
  ciated.
Here are the facts.
I am expecting the courtesy of a prompt reply.
I am writing regarding my last bill, invoice # G4889, dated August 15, 1992.
I believe that an apology is due us.
I'd be interested in hearing from you within the next few days.
I expect an adjustment to be made as soon as possible.
I feel sure you will know how to solve this problem.
I feel you should know about/be aware of this.

I hope you will take this complaint in the helpful spirit in which it is meant.

I know you will want to see that such an incident does not occur again.

I like your product, but I object strongly to your advertising.

I'm confident that we can resolve this matter to our mutual satisfaction.

I regret/am sorry to inform you of the following unpleasant situation.

I strongly oppose your position on this weapons system.

It is my understanding that it will be repaired/replaced at your expense.

I will send a check for the balance as soon as I receive a corrected statement.

I wish to receive credit on my account for this item.

I would appreciate a telephone call from you about this situation.

I would like a refund in the amount of $49.99.

I would like to clear up this misunderstanding as soon as possible.

Let me know what is being done.

Maybe you'd like to hear my side of the story.

One expects more of a company with your fine reputation and long history.

Please call the principal's office to arrange a meeting with the principal, the school counselor, and myself regarding Christie's suspension.

Please let me hear from you at your earliest convenience.

Please let me know what options are available to me.

Please send a corrected invoice.

Thank you for your prompt assistance in this matter/with this problem.

The following situation has come to my attention.

The most satisfactory solution for us would be for you to send us a replacement lamp and reimburse us for the cost of mailing the defective lamp back to you.

There was far too little feedback to us during the design of the original #2 unit.

This has caused me a great deal of difficulty and embarrassment.

This product has been unsatisfactory in several respects.

This will not do.

We experienced the following problem in your store/restaurant/hotel last week.

We seem to be at cross purposes.

We would like to resolve this situation without delay/without having recourse to the Better Business Bureau or Small Claims Court.

Will you please check on this?

─────────────── **PARAGRAPHS** ───────────────

▷   I notice that you are now closing The Old Curiosity Shop at 5:00 p.m. instead of 7:00 p.m., and are no longer open weekends. Many of us who work find it difficult to shop during those hours, and we are wondering if you would reconsider your decision. It is possible, of course, that you are unable to keep the store open longer because of financial considerations, but the following signers of this letter would like you to know that we appreciated the more convenient hours.

▷   I received the leather patchwork travel bag today (copies of catalog page and invoice enclosed), but the matching billfold was not included. Please send me one as soon as possible, in burgundy to match the bag. Thank you.

▷ It has been five weeks since I mailed you my check for the first night of our stay at the Vörös Csillig in Budapest, and I have not yet received any confirmation of our reservations. As the rest of my itinerary depends on whether we are able to stay in Budapest, I would appreciate an immediate phone call from you to let me know what arrangements have been made.

▷ I wonder if you would look into the way requisitions are handled here at Darby & Winter. Again yesterday I had to tell the Bicket people that the lab results weren't ready yet. To complete the project for them I need certain materials—materials that were ordered two months ago. I particularly question the need for dealing with three different people and two sets of forms, the long delays for approval, and the necessity of waiting for material to be delivered instead of being able to pick it up myself at Central Supplies.

▷ Channel 12's insistence on running inappropriate programming between 5:00 p.m. and 7:00 p.m., when many young people are watching, means that this family at least will no longer turn to Channel 12 for any of its news, entertainment, or programs.

▷ Please find enclosed a bracelet, a necklace, and a pair of earrings. We would appreciate either repair or replacement of these items. The bracelet has a broken clasp, the gold on the earrings appears to be chipped, and the silver finish is overlaying the gemstone on the necklace. In each case, dissatisfied customers returned the items to us. Your immediate attention to this matter will be greatly appreciated.

▷ I'm enclosing a photocopy of a collection letter I received from your agency. This is approximately the tenth letter I have received about this account. Although my first initial and last name are the same as the person responsible for it, we have nothing else in common. I marked each of the earlier letters "incorrect address" and returned them to you—to no avail evidently. Please verify the correct address of your correspondent. I would appreciate a letter from you stating that my name and address have been removed from your files and that my credit rating has not been affected by this error.

▷ My order (#578942-E) for two dozen Shipley short wave radios, placed three weeks ago, has not yet been received. I was told to expect them within the week. Will you please check to see if the order has gone astray? We need them immediately.

▷ I object most vigorously to the tactic used in your telephone sales efforts. Today a caller identified herself as someone from the credit bureau. After hearing the words "credit bureau" I stayed attentively on the line. It was only after several minutes of trying to understand what was wrong with my credit rating that I realized I was actually being asked to buy life insurance. I think your approach is false and misleading; enclosed is a copy of the letter I have written to the Better Business Bureau complaining of it.

▷ We recently acquired a pole figure device from you. Since texture determination is the primary purpose of our X-ray diffractometer, we were pleased to finally receive this instrument and, on the whole, are happy with it. We also appreciate the source programs you provided us with; they appear to be well written and easy to follow. Unfortunately, we have had a number of problems with the pole figure software. Gustaf Sondelius suggested I document these problems in a letter to you.

▷ Thank you for your 56-page report on your department's activities over the past six months. The graphics are outstanding. However, while there is much to reflect on in the text itself, I find many questions unanswered and several important issues left unaddressed. I would like to discuss with you the kinds of information I need to see in a departmental semiannual report. Please phone my secretary to set up an appointment.

▷ I regret to inform you that the paperweights delivered today (see enclosed copies of our order and your invoice) arrived without a single paperweight intact. We will need a replacement order at once, as well as instructions for returning the damaged goods. You will want to conduct your own investigation, but it appears to us that the problem was due to improper packing. Please advise at once when we can expect the new shipment.

▷ Imagine our embarrassment when we served one of your Paramount Hams for Easter, and none of our guests were able to eat it because it was so excessively salty. I would like a refund for the inedible ham (label and store receipt enclosed). Also, can you give me any good reasons for ever buying another Trotter and Duff Paramount Ham? I don't like writing someone off on the basis of a single error, but one bad ham is one too many.

▷ The Abbeville Faxphone 200 that I ordered from you two weeks ago receives documents but will not transmit them. Several phone calls to your service department (I was, of course, unable to fax them) about this serious problem have been unhelpful. The only information I was given was that I was not to return the machine without prior approval. Please send such approval immediately.

─────────────── SAMPLE LETTERS ───────────────

Dear Mr. Tallant:

As you know, a great deal of our work must be coordinated with Harvey Crane Construction. They must complete their paving and other operations before the median work on Pearl Street can begin.

I have seen no progress on their part for about a month. Their delays mean that we incur such damages as loss of production, lower profits, winter protection costs, remobilization, accelerated schedules (overtime), and barricade rental—to name just a few items.

As these costs and damages will necessarily be passed on to you, you may want to check into the situation.

Sincerely,

· · · · · · · · · · ·

Dear Mr. Thornton,

This is the third time we have contacted you about your dog, Buck. The neighborhood children continue to be frightened of him, and refuse to play outdoors when he is in your yard. There have been several reports of him snapping at the children.

When would be a good time to discuss this situation with you? We would like to come to some agreement without going to the authorities.

Hoping to hear from you very soon, I am

Sincerely yours,

· · · · · · · · · · ·

dear cummings writing machine company,

i would like an immediate replacement for this typewriter. i bought it on june 3 of this year from 'tulips' in cambridge, massachusetts (sales slip enclosed), but, as you can see, it will not produce capital letters.

the 'tulips' people tell me that the manufacturer is responsible for all defects. please let me know at once how you plan to supply me with a typewriter that types capital letters.

yours truly,

. . . .

Dear Mr. Abednego,

When I bought my first insurance policy with the Independent W. Diddlesex Insurance Company, I was told that buying my auto, homeowners, and life insurances from you would guarantee me a 20% reduction over the rates I would normally pay separately. Now that I have switched my life insurance to Diddlesex to obtain this complete coverage, I find that I am paying substantially the same rates as before.

Will you please check to see why I am not getting the lower rates, and let me know as soon as possible?

Sincerely,

. . . .

Dear Harter & Benjamin Jewelers:

We, the undersigned members of the Eustace College staff, object most strongly to the recent ads for Harter & Benjamin Jewelers that have appeared in the college newspaper. All of them advertise your jewelry with the word *Intoxicating* and show a young man and young woman obviously drinking alcohol. The artwork features champagne glasses and wine and liquor bottles.

Why are you using alcohol to sell jewelry? There must be many other symbols, appeals, campaigns, graphics that would better sell your product. By associating alcohol with "the good life," you are selling college students on the "joys" of booze. We believe this is completely undesirable and indefensible.

We have spoken to the newspaper staff and advisor about the wisdom of accepting any more of these ads and have also suggested they write an article explaining why such ads are refused.

We sincerely hope you will consider dropping this particular angle in your advertising, especially in periodicals aimed at young audiences.

Sincerely,

. . . .

Dear Dean Higgs:

Last week the College hosted one of the most important international conferences on philosophy in many years—and virtually nobody knew about it.

The Public Affairs Office was briefed about the conference over a period of months: at a two-hour breakfast meeting in March, at three meetings in April, via ten pages of updated notes, details, and list of interview possibilities in May, and at a final one-hour meeting in June.

Despite this, no news releases were sent by the College's publicity department, no photographers were present at major events, the Nobel Prize-winning speakers were not interviewed, and neither of the metro area newspapers carried articles or features on what was surely an event of local and international significance.

I ask that this situation be investigated, an apology be tendered, and some guarantees for future College publicity be spelled out.

Yours truly,

. . . .

Dear Mr. Bellman:

We have come to expect a high degree of judgment and integrity from the Calcutta Tape and Sealing Wax Office. It was therefore as surprising as it was distressing when the last shipment turned out to be substandard.

Substitutions were made without our permission—invariably a substitution of an inferior product at the original price. In two instances, quantities were not the quantities ordered (they were smaller), with no equivalent adjustment made on the invoice.

I am enclosing a copy of our order, a copy of your invoice, and a list of what we actually received. I would appreciate hearing from you immediately on what we can do not only to remedy the current shipment but also to ensure that this doesn't happen again.

Sincerely,

. . . .

Dear Mr. Atterbury:

Before scheduling an appointment with you to discuss the incorporation of my business, I asked your secretary about your legal fees. He told me you charge $100 an hour. I was therefore very surprised to receive a bill for $350 when I spent no more than one hour with you.

I will appreciate an explanation of my bill. Thank you.

Sincerely,

. . . .

Dear Ms. Scanlon,

We have been renting Apartment 206 at 1935 Chicago Avenue for the past four years and have been very pleased with our situation until just recently, when new tenants moved into Apartment 306.

We have spoken to Mr. Longigan and Ms. Branahan about the frequent parties, arguments, and loud noises after 11:00 p.m., and we have also asked the building manager to do what she could. However, we think you need to look into this situation yourself.

Please let us know what we can expect. Hoping for an early response from you, we are

Sincerely yours,

. . . .

Dear Mrs. Tilford,

We all enjoyed Mary's visit with us last weekend. Because it was so pleasant, I'm sorry to be writing with this problem.

When I was a child, my father brought me back a small carved giraffe from Africa. As he died soon afterwards, I have always treasured this memento. I missed it Sunday evening and spent several days looking for it. Karen just told me that Mary now carries it around in her schoolbag and freely admits to "finding" it here. In her six-year-old way, Karen demanded it back, but Mary was evidently not ready to let it go. I trust that you will find some good way of convincing Mary to return it.

Thank you for taking care of this.

Sincerely,

. . . .

Dear Mr. Blowberry,

I would like to register a complaint about one of your employees, Albert Grope. When I was in your bookstore last week, Mr. Grope persisted in answering my questions in a very loud voice, using one-syllable words and enunciating in an exaggerated fashion. Although I have an accent, my English is correct enough to allow me to teach classics at the university level, and I feel his behavior was inappropriate. Between sentences he would archly eye the other clerk, obviously aware of how hilariously "funny" he was. Even if I had as little command of the English language as Mr. Grope assumed, and were dim-witted besides, I believe he owes every customer a certain respect.

I have spoken to you on several occasions and I felt you were the sort of person who would want to know about this.

Sincerely,

. . . .

Re: BankCard # 2378-54-8970

My statement dated August 28, 1993, shows an entry for $29 payable to NewFit Shoes, Murray Road and Converse Boulevard, Chicago, dated June 30, 1993.

This charge does not belong on my account. I was in California at the time and, in any case, have never been in that particular store.

Please remove this charge from my account. Enclosed is my check for the balance of my account, $148.53. This amount does not include the $29 for the shoes.

Thank you for taking care of this matter.

. . . .

Dear Wheatley Office Products:

On April 3, I purchased your four-drawer, self-locking EZ-Open File Cabinet, serial number 007800, from your Wheatley outlet on Broadway. I paid a sale price of $329.99 plus tax for the unit.

Unfortunately, the file cabinet does not function as claimed. It self-locks arbitrarily; half the time it does, half the time it doesn't, and no one is able to predict just when it will do which. The one-touch unlocking mechanism does not work at all, which means that usually the drawers have to be unlocked manually with the "emergency only" key. Even when the drawers are not locked, they are difficult to open because of a design problem with overlapping inside shelving.

Mr. Denny Swinton, who sold me the unit, informs me that because the unit is on sale I am unable to return it. I am certain, however, that, sale price or no, I have a right to expect that the unit will perform as promised.

I would like to hear within the next several days that a truck will be coming from Wheatley to pick up the defective unit and that my purchase price will be refunded.

Sincerely,

. . . .

Dear Dr. Blenkinsop,

As you know, we have been satisfied patients of yours for the past six years. However, I wonder if you are aware that the condition of your waiting room is very off-putting. The carpet rarely appears vacuumed, the plastic plants are thick with dust, and the magazines and children's playthings are strewn about, apparently untouched from one of our visits to the next. Hygiene seems particularly important in a healthcare environment, and, although I know what an excellent physician you are, I can't help worrying about how clean everything else is.

I hope you find this letter helpful rather than unpleasant—it was written with the best intentions.

Sincerely,

. . . .

Dear Governor Foyle:

RE: Susan Price

I am writing to protest most strongly and urgently the treatment of Susan Price, a pacifist prisoner, by the State—specifically for several assaults by prison guards that left her with bruises, lacerations, and possible head injuries.

This is unconscionable.

I urge you to have this situation investigated at once. Please let me know how you plan to handle it.

Sincerely yours,

See also: ACKNOWLEDGMENTS, ADJUSTMENTS, APOLOGIES, ORDERS, RESPONSES.

11

Letters of Confirmation

"Talk of nothing but business, and dispatch that business quickly." (Aldus Manutius, circa 1490)

Letters of confirmation fall somewhere between acknowledgments and acceptances. The letter of confirmation serves one main purpose: to let your correspondent know that you have "heard" them. It generally restates and agrees to something that has transpired earlier: a telephone conversation, an order, a letter, a memo.

Confirmation letters may have secondary purposes: thanks, appreciation, acceptance, or changing part of an earlier message.

Write Letters of Confirmation When

- acknowledging receipt: documents/materials/information (see also ACKNOWLEDGMENTS)
- supervisor is away (to let people know their messages/letters have been received/will be dealt with later)
- confirming receipt of orders/merchandise (see also ORDERS)
- confirming receipt of wedding gifts (see WEDDINGS)
- following up on an oral discussion, telephone call, or earlier agreement
- sending last-minute reminders: meetings/business dinners/events
- verifying reservations, speaking dates, invitation times

How to Say It

□ Refer reader to your last contact (telephone conversation, previous letter, in-person discussion). Mention the date or occasion.

□ Indicate the topic (order, proposal, scheduled meeting).

□   State (or repeat) all pertinent details: order number, time, place, amount, plan, title, and so forth.

□   Express your pleasure either for the previous contact or for some future meeting or business.

What Not to Say

□   Avoid a chiding tone ("just to help you remember" or "thought I'd make sure we were both talking about the same thing"). Your letter should be a factual repetition of the facts or items you are confirming.

□   Do not use a letter confirming a forthcoming meeting as an opportunity to begin or continue an argument or discussion that properly belongs to the meeting.

Writing Tips

□   Be brief and businesslike. Most confirmation letters need only several sentences to do the work.

□   Brief and businesslike doesn't have to be cold; a sentence at the end expressing some appreciation, pleasure, or cheerfulness about the order, meeting, proposal, or other mutual business is welcome.

□   There are exceptions to "brief": sometimes a confirmation letter may be turned into a sales letter. In other cases, when a letter is confirming an agreement, it really ought to spell out the terms and conditions of the agreement.

Special Situations

□   It is usually necessary to confirm that you have received an order only in atypical cases: perhaps the item must be back ordered, the price has been raised, the delivery date has to be delayed, or a substitution must be made. In this case, your "confirmation" has the secondary purpose of informing the customer about the other circumstance.

□   Domestic hotel and motel reservations are often made and confirmed entirely by phone. Occasionally, however, written confirmation is requested or necessary because of special conditions or changes of plans. Include the essential information: date, length of stay, kind of accommodation, price, extras requested (crib in a room, for example) and such additional information as handicapped accessibility, availability of pool, HBO, entertaining facilities. It is generally wise to request confirmation from foreign hotels or resorts. Include an International Reply Coupon (IRC) for their response.

❑   In the absence of a manager, co-worker, spouse, or family member, you may have to confirm receipt of a package, proposal, document, or letter. This is usually a two-sentence letter stating, first, that the material has arrived and, second, that the other person will respond as soon as possible.

Format

❑   Routine confirmations (receipt of applications, manuscripts, requests, payments) can be handled with a simple form letter, perhaps with blanks to indicate what was received and the date of receipt.

❑   Lengthier business confirmations require a typed message on letterhead stationery.

❑   In casual situations, especially for interoffice communications, a hand-written note on memo paper is acceptable.

WORDS

accept	assure	ensure
acknowledge	comply	notify
affirm	concur	reaffirm
agree	corroborate	reassure
agreed-upon	double-check	verify
approve	endorse	willing
assent		

PHRASES

agree to
as I mentioned on the phone yesterday
as per our telephone conversation
as we agreed yesterday
consent to
go along with
have no objection

I enjoyed our conversation of
in accord with
look forward to continuing our discussion
to confirm our recent telephone
  conversation
want to confirm in writing

SENTENCES

I enjoyed speaking with you this afternoon and look forward to our meeting next
  Thursday at 2:30 at your office.
I want to confirm that your vacation of 1902 Storks Avenue will be completed by
  September 1.
I will appreciate written confirmation of our reservations.

Please confirm the requested delivery date of May 24.

Thank you for your important order, which we received yesterday; it will be shipped to you this week.

This is to confirm our recent conversation about the identification and removal of several underground storage tanks on my property.

This is to confirm that you have asked us to represent you in the Lammiter bankruptcy.

This will confirm our revised delivery date of November 6.

We are proceeding with the work as requested by Jerome Searing in his May 3, 1992, telephone call.

PARAGRAPHS

▷   This is to confirm your telephone request to prepare a legal description of the property to be deannexed from Hornyold District. If this is not your understanding, please notify us immediately. You will be billed on a time and materials basis for work performed prior to notifying us of any change in this Agreement.

▷   This will confirm our telephone conversation of September 17 in which we arranged to photograph the interior of your home for the December issue of *Interiors/Exteriors*. We will supply a fourteen-foot tree, several large wreaths, and an assortment of holiday greenery. Thank you for agreeing to make available your famous collection of Christmas decorations. Every care will be taken to disturb you and your family as little as possible and to safeguard your home and possessions.

▷   I was so glad to run into you at the workshop Saturday. I am definitely interested in your "floating counselor" program and would appreciate a call from you when you have time.

▷   This is to confirm our telephone conversation of this morning. It looks as though August 20 will work—weather permitting. I've contacted a number of parents who can be on hand that day to help assemble the playground equipment. Thanks for being so flexible about the delivery date.

▷   We received your request for more information on estrogen replacement therapy and for a sample of the placebo skin patch. Because of an unexpectedly enthusiastic response to our advertisement, we have temporarily exhausted our supplies of the skin patch. I'm enclosing the literature you requested, and will send the skin patch in approximately two weeks. Thank you for your interest and patience.

▷   I am very pleased that you will be able to accommodate us in June. As I explained in my telephone call of March 1, we will need one room with three beds for June 9-18 (ten nights) at 180 francs per night, breakfast included. Enclosed is a check for the first night and an International Reply Coupon for your confirmation.

SAMPLE LETTERS

Dear Mr. Borkin:

   To confirm our telephone conversation, Barry Studio Supplies will be happy to provide you with all your photographic needs. We make deliveries in the metropolitan area within twenty-four hours of receiving an order.

Enclosed is a copy of our current catalog, a pad of order forms, and my card. As your personal representative, I will be happy to answer any of your questions or help you with special orders.

Sincerely yours,

· · · · · · · · · · · ·

Dear Dr. Breeve,

This is to confirm that you have permission to use the Great Organ of St. Luke's Church for an organ recital next March 30 at 7:30 p.m. As agreed, any organ repairs necessary for the recital will be carried out at your own expense.

Please call me to arrange for an extra key when you need to begin practicing and to work out further details for that evening.

We're delighted that someone of your talent is going to be using our wonderful old—but often forgotten—organ.

With best wishes,

· · · · · · · · · · · ·

Dear Geraldine Dabis:

We have received your loan application and will process it as quickly as possible. However, because of the complex nature of the application, it is being reviewed and evaluated by loan officers from two different divisions. This may delay our response somewhat.

If you have any questions about this delay or about our process, please call me at 555-1216.

Yours truly,

See also: ACCEPTANCES, ACKNOWLEDGMENTS, APPOINTMENTS, RE-SPONSES, THANK YOU.

12

Congratulations

"I can live for two months on a good compliment."
(Mark Twain)

In the appropriate situations, we are not surprised to receive thank you notes, sympathy cards, or letters of apology. The one message we don't expect—even when it is highly appropriate—is the congratulatory note. For this reason, you make twice the impact and give twice the pleasure when you take a moment to remember a friend's good news. And don't wait until the good news is big—small landmarks and successes have a sweetness all their own, and the recipient of your note will long remember your thoughtfulness.

Occasions That Call for Letters of Congratulations

- achievements/awards/honors/prizes/speeches/publications/recognition
- adoption or birth of child
- anniversaries: business/years of service/wedding
- birthdays
- business: good business year, opening of new store, new venture, obtaining new account or new contract, opening own business, securing a franchise, merging with another company, joining trade association, election to professional membership, other business successes
- changes: new car/home/job
- customers: good news and major life events
- election to office: public/organization or club/professional society/social group
- employees' work: compliments/congratulations/bonus
- graduation: high school/technical school/special programs/college/advanced degree programs

- jobs: new job or assignment/promotion/advancement/new title/ retirement
- loan payment (see CREDIT)
- religious milestones: baptism/christening/circumcision/bar or bat mitzvah/first communion/confirmation/ordination/taking of religious vows
- sales "congratulations": being selected to receive special offer/credit limit raised (see SALES)
- significant personal achievement or anniversary: quitting smoking or drinking
- wedding (see WEDDINGS)

How to Say It

☐   Use the word "congratulations" early in your note.

☐   Mention the specific occasion.

☐   Tell how happy you are for the person, and why (the person's struggles, hard work, talent).

☐   If appropriate, tell how you learned about the good news. If you read it in the newspaper, you might want to enclose the clipping or a photocopy of it.

☐   Relate an anecdote, shared memory, or reflection that has some bearing on the occasion.

☐   Close with your assurances of best wishes, affection, love, admiration, warmth, interest, delight, pleasure, continued business support, or good wishes for another anniversary period.

What Not to Say

☐   Avoid effusiveness, exaggerations, and excessive flattery.

☐   Don't make your congratulatory note do double duty: save for another day any questions, information, sales messages, or work matters that aren't relevant to the good news at hand. (Exception: personal letters accompanying birthday congratulations.)

☐   Be positive in the way you phrase your remarks: instead of "I never thought you could do it," say "You've shown us what a person can do with enough energy and determination." Reminding people of their humble beginnings at a time like this may not be well received; know your recipient before using this tack.

□ When congratulating an employee, colleague, or business associate, avoid exaggerating the closeness of a relationship that is primarily business. Your message can be warm and dignified without presuming an intimacy that does not exist.

□ In anniversary or birthday letters, omit any "joking" references to age, incapacity, passing years, or other negative aspects of the situation.

□ When congratulating someone on an adoption, do not write, "I'll bet you get pregnant now." People adopt for reasons other than fertility, and adoption is not a cure for infertility (pregnancies occur after adoption at approximately the same rates as they occur in couples dealing with problems of infertility). Do not ask prying questions about the child's background or biological/birth parents (never write "real parents"; you are writing to the real parents). Do not say that you "admire" your friends for adopting anymore than you would "admire" a biological parent for having a child. What *do* you write? Ask the parents to tell you all about the child and the great arrival day, say that you can't wait to come visit, and wish them all much happiness.

□ Your first response to news of an engagement should be pleasant and congratulatory. If you have reservations about the relationship (because of age, previous marriages, children who do not like the prospective stepparent, and so forth) deal with these separately, preferably in person. When you have serious reservations, do not write a congratulatory letter at all. Congratulations and cautions are not a good combination.

Tips on Writing

□ When congratulating or complimenting someone, be as specific as possible about the work, product, situation, talent, or award.

□ Even when you are close to the person you are writing, you may want to make your congratulatory letter brief and somewhat formal; this increases its impact.

□ Focus on the other person's good news; don't compare it to something you once did that was very like it or to somebody's achievements in the same field that you read about in the paper. Let the person enjoy their moment in the sun—alone.

□ A good rule in letterwriting is to never express more than you feel. People sense when your congratulations are insincere, so restrict yourself to expressions that feel genuine to you, that you're comfortable with.

□ It is good public relations to write notes of congratulations to customers, clients, colleagues, and other business associates when there is good news (births, weddings, promotions, new business). It is one of the few times you contact such individuals without requiring something in return and is thus effective in establishing business loyalty.

□   Be timely, but if you can't, write anyway; people are always happy to get this type of mail. Apologize only briefly for the delay.

□   Congratulating someone for abstaining from cigarettes, alcohol, or drugs for a certain number of years implies an intimate relationship where such a mention is welcome and both parties are comfortable with it. It is rarely appropriate in the case of business acquaintances or casual friendships.

Special Situations

□   Sometimes a personnel department will have a system for tracking service anniversaries and will automatically notify a supervisor of anniversaries coming up in that department. If such a system does not exist, you might ask the personnel department for a list of starting dates of the people working for and with you so that you can keep track of significant anniversaries. This is an excellent goodwill gesture. When congratulating an employee on a service anniversary, single out some aspect of the individual's work that you particularly appreciate. For colleagues, recall a shared experience.

□   The announcement of a divorce can elicit a simple acknowledgment, a letter of sympathy, or a letter of congratulations. The latter is sent rarely, and then only to someone you know very well. You might, however, want to congratulate a person not so much on the divorce per se as on surviving the upheaval, conflict, and distress of a very difficult period.

□   Sometimes a "congratulations" approach is used in sales letters, but this is more sales than congratulations since here the congratulations are generic, never personal (see SALES).

□   Birthday greetings are a type of congratulations. The use of commercial cards is so widespread that there are very few letters or notes written solely to commemorate a birthday. However, a card should include a handwritten message, even if—in the case of someone you don't know well—it is only one sentence. Letters that accompany cards can mention the birthday briefly and then revert to the usual news and reflections.

□   Many newspapers have columns for anniversary announcements where couples can make their own announcements, or family and friends can have their public congratulations printed.

□   In the case of a premature baby, send congratulations, gifts, and good wishes in the normal way. Do not hold off to see how the baby does.

□   Tradition always had it that one sent "congratulations" to the engaged man, and "best wishes" to the engaged woman; do not perpetuate this distinction based on old inequalities. You may properly use either expression for men or women.

Format

□   Most congratulations take the form of a note—on personal stationery, foldovers, note cards, or commercial cards with a handwritten message.

□   In some contexts (business, politics, clubs and organizations), the congratulations may be typed on business letterhead, business-personal paper, or even memo stationery, depending on the degree of closeness between sender and recipient and the importance of the good news.

□   Commercial cards are almost universal for birthday congratulations, and there are congratulatory cards that range from very specific (new job, promotion, graduation) to the generic. They are acceptable as long as a handwritten note is included.

WORDS

accomplishment	happy	resourceful
achievement	honor	salute
admire	impressed	satisfying
applaud	incomparable	sensational
appreciate	inspiring	skillful
award	invaluable	special
celebration	knack	success
champion	leadership	superb
commend	mile-marker	superior
compliment	milepost	superlative
contribution	milestone	talent
dazzling	occasion	thrilled
début	opportunity	tribute
delighted	outstanding	triumph
diligence	peerless	unique
distinguished	performance	unparalleled
enterprising	perseverance	unrivaled
excellent	pleased	valuable
exceptional	proficient	venture
feat	prolific	victory
genius	proud	well-deserved
gratifying		

PHRASES

accept my heartiest congratulations on

achieved your goals

achievements in the field

all possible joy and happiness

am pleased/delighted to know

an impressive record

beyond all expectations

cheerful/cheering news

continued health and happiness/success

couldn't let this happy occasion go by
    without

delighted/happy to hear/read in the
    newspaper/receive the news

did us good to hear

every happiness

feel very fortunate to know you

good fortune/luck

good/great/sensational/joyful/thrilling
    news

high quality of your work

how happy we were to hear

how nice of you to write me about

I especially liked the way you

in awe of all that you've done

in honor of

I was so impressed with/when I heard

joins me in sending best/good/warm
    wishes

know that you're held in high esteem

let us wish you

made your lifetime dream come true

many congratulations and much
    happiness

many happy years ahead

much happiness as the years go by

my warmest/sincerest/heartiest
    congratulations

no one deserves it more

offer my congratulations

on this joyful/festive occasion

permit me to congratulate you on

pleasantly surprised to hear

please add my warmest congratulations to

red letter day

rejoice with you

richly deserve

sharing in your happiness

sincere wishes for continued success

so happy/delighted/thrilled for you

so impressed with this latest award/
    honor/prize/achievement

take great pleasure in sending
    congratulations to you

take this opportunity to wish you every
    happiness

think much of/well of/highly of

to your credit

truly earned the respect of everyone in
    the company

very proud of you

were thrilled to hear about

wishing you all the best/much success/
    continued success

with all good wishes to you in your new
    venture

with flying colors

wonderful ability to get things
    done—and done well

won the recognition you so richly merit

your important contribution(s)

you've done a superb job of

SENTENCES

Baxter called this evening to tell us that the two of you are engaged to be married,
    and we wanted to tell you immediately how happy we are for you.

Best of luck to you, now and in the future.

Best wishes from all of us.

Congratulations not only on this latest accomplishment, but also on your consistently fine work of the past seven years.

Congratulations on surpassing this year's collection goal/securing the new account/your speedy inventory reduction/a new sales volume record/a smooth departmental reorganization.

Congratulations on the littlest Woodley—may she know health, happiness, and love all her life.

Every good wish to both of you for much health, happiness, prosperity, and many more years of togetherness.

Hear hear!

I am almost as delighted as you are with this recent turn of events.

I am so impressed!

I couldn't be happier if it had happened to me.

I hear wonderful things about you.

I hope we will enjoy many more years of doing business together.

I hope your birthday is especially happy; you deserve the best.

I just heard the news—congratulations!

It's a great pleasure to send you my congratulations on forty years of service.

It was a splendid performance/great triumph/brilliant speech.

I understand that congratulations are in order!

I very much admire your organizational skills/perseverance/many achievements/ingenuity/calm in the face of difficulties.

I wish I could be with you to share in this happy occasion.

Many happy returns of the day!

May these first twenty-five years of success serve as the inspiration for the next twenty-five.

May you enjoy many more anniversaries—each happier than the last.

My hat's off to you!

My heartiest congratulations to you both.

My thoughts are with you today as you celebrate.

This is the best news I've heard in a long time!

We are very pleased with your work on ethics-in-government legislation.

Well done!

We've all benefited from your expertise and creativity.

With best wishes for fair weather and smooth sailing in the years ahead.

You certainly haven't let the grass grow under your feet!

You must be delighted with your recent success.

Your report was complete, well-written, and highly convincing.

Your reputation had preceeded you, and I see you intend to live up to it.

You've done it again!

You've topped everyone in the store in sales this past month—congratulations!

---------- PARAGRAPHS ----------

▷   I was delighted (although not surprised!) to hear that you won the Schubert piano concerto competition this year. Congratulations! I have watched you develop as a fine pianist over the years, and it is a thrill to see you rewarded for your talent—and, above all, for your hard work.

▷   You certainly deserved this latest award. Your industry, your attention to detail, and your creative problem-solving have been an inspiration to all of us.

▷   Congratulations! You have been preapproved to receive the enclosed membership registered in your name. Respond now to activate your membership.

▷   I well remember your diffident début twenty-five years ago. Who would have guessed that your "awkward little offspring" would grow to be the successful business it is today?

▷   Best wishes for a happy anniversary to a couple we have long admired and loved. May your relationship continue to be a blessing to both of you as well as to all those who know you.

▷   This marks the fifth anniversary of our doing business together. In that time, we have come to appreciate your prompt service, reliable products, and knowledgeable staff. I'm sure the next five years of doing business with you will be equally happy and productive. Congratulations to all of you.

▷   In the past ten years, the company has grown beyond all recognition—a complete line of new products, computerization of all departments, financial growth beyond our wildest expectations—and wherever there has been innovation, development, progress, you've been in the front ranks. We wouldn't be the company we are today without you. Please accept the enclosed bonus as a sign of our gratitude and appreciation for ten wonderful years.

▷   Happy birthday, Andrea! Here are 7 balloons, 7 red-and-white striped pencils, 7 elephant stickers, and 7 packages of flower seeds. Now, how old did you say you are today?

▷   Barbara and Dick Siddal will celebrate their 50th wedding anniversary on February 14. They have four children, nine grandchildren, and many wonderful friends. Love and congratulations from your family.

---------- SAMPLE LETTERS ----------

Dear Professor Arronax,
    Heartiest congratulations on the recently published accounts of your discoveries. I have read them with the greatest fervor and admiration.
    With all best wishes, I am

                                    Faithfully yours,

          . . . .

Dear Briggs,
    I was happy to hear about your promotion. Let's celebrate!
                                    Your cousin,

          . . . .

Dear Mirandolina,

So you've gone and done the deed at last! Congratulations on opening your own country inn. Put us down for a double room the first weekend in October.

Although I am all admiration for your courage, I'm not sure your venture is as risky as it looks. You are uniquely suited by background, experience, and temperament to the role of successful innkeeper. I'll want to be one of the first to say, "I told you so!" when you're a great success.

Best,

. . . .

Dear Raoul,

Congratulations on being named this year's Outstanding Manager. Having recently visited one of your division branches, I know that you very much deserve this honor.

I'm looking forward to seeing you at the May banquet when you accept your plaque. Until then, best wishes.

Sincerely,

. . . .

Dear Governor Peck,

Congratulations on your landslide election. All of us who campaigned for you in this area are proud and pleased to have been part of your victory.

Please accept my very best wishes for a distinguished, productive, and happy term of office.

Respectfully yours,

. . . .

Dear Penrod,

Congratulations on your twelfth birthday! I hope you have a wonderful time and get everything you want (although, from what your father tells me, I hope you don't want another slingshot).

Your uncle and I are sorry we can't be there to celebrate with you, but I'm sending you a little something in a separate package. Have a good time and give everyone a hug for us.

Happy birthday!

. . . .

Dear Mr. Dodsworth:

Congratulations on the opening of your newest branch of the Revelation Motor Company. We have always appreciated doing business with you, and expect to enjoy it even more now that your new office is only two blocks from us.

Best wishes for happiness and success to all of you at Revelation!

Sincerely,

. . . .

Dear Synnöve,

Congratulations on receiving the Granliden award! That's terrific. I was so happy for you when I saw the announcement in the paper.

I hope everything else in your life is going as well!

Best,

. . . .

Dear William,

I've just heard from Katherine that you are finally a full-fledged chemical engineer—congratulations! I've admired you very much as I've watched your struggles these past few years to acquire an education. Katherine and I said some rather flattering things about you and concluded that you're going to go far in this world.

My best wishes to you for a bright and happy future.

Fondly,

. . . .

Dear Mr. Rochester,

Congratulations on your election to the Thornfield School Board. I hope that after running such a vigorous and inspiring campaign you still have enough energy to carry out some of your sound and needed ideas.

Be assured of our continued support, and do not hesitate to call on us if we can do anything to help.

With best wishes,

. . . .

Dear Martin,

All of us here at Eden Land Corporation congratulate you at Chuzzlewit Ltd. on your twenty-five years of solid contributions in the field of architecture.

We know that when we do business with you we can count on superior designs, reasonable costs, and dependable delivery dates.

May the success of these first twenty years lead to an even more successful second twenty.

With best wishes,

. . . .

Dear Dr. Arnold,

On behalf of the governing board, I would like to congratulate you on ten years of outstanding service as headmaster. Under your leadership the School has established itself among the premier ranks of such institutions.

Be assured of our continued admiration and support.

Very sincerely yours,

. . . .

Dear Debbye and Jeff,

Congratulations on your engagement! Although our record on marriage is not very good as a society, I am very optimistic about the two of you. Seldom have I seen such a hardworking, loving, sensible (yet wildly romantic!) pair. I like the way you respect and support each other. I like the way you make difficult decisions together. Offhand, I'd say you've struck gold!

I'm looking forward to your wedding!

Love,

. . . .

Dear Ms. Hubbard,

Congratulations on an outstanding first year at Grattan Public Relations, Inc. A growing company like ours needs and appreciates people with your energy, expertise, and intuition. We are all predicting a brilliant future for you.

Congratulations and best wishes!

Sincerely,

. . . .

Dear Helen and Arthur,

So little Laura has arrived at last! It has been such a long process, and I know it's been hard for you wondering if there would ever be an end to the red tape and waiting. But all that's over now, and the three of you can begin your life together.

From what I hear, this is definitely an adoption made in heaven! I know that Laura will add a great deal to the joy you two already find in each other.

With every good wish,

See also: APPRECIATION, EMPLOYMENT, FAMILY, RESPONSES, WEDDINGS.

13

Letters About Contracts

"A verbal contract isn't worth the paper it is written on."
(Sam Goldwyn)

Signing a legal contract may require writing back and forth a number of times before all clauses are written to everyone's satisfaction. And sometimes letters may actually serve as contracts. In the case of a straightforward contract, for example, letter format is often simpler and more efficient. Whether you need an attorney to check such letters depends on the complexity of the contract and the possible outcomes if it is poorly written.

Contract Letters Deal With

- agreements
- cancellations of agreements/contracts
- changes in terms
- contracts written as letters
- negotiations to arrive at acceptable contract
- questions about contracts

How to Say It

□   Give full names and addresses of both parties to the agreement or contract.
□   State what each party will give and receive.
□   Specify a time limit (if any) for the contract, and state whether and under what conditions it may be broken or canceled.

What Not to Say

□   Avoid legal terminology unless you are a lawyer. It is better to use plain, clear English, so that nobody can later argue that they didn't understand it.

Tips on Writing

□   If your letter is to serve as a contract, plan carefully before beginning to write, listing all factors that will protect your agreement (time limits, price ceilings, and so forth). Have someone familiar with the situation read it over with you.

□   Don't be afraid to write as though you were speaking. Just because it is a contract doesn't mean a letter has to sound like legislative statutes. Use personal pronouns ("I promise to . . . in exchange for . . .") and ordinary grammar and sentence structure. On the other hand, you will want to maintain a businesslike tone to inspire confidence and to strengthen the letter's use as a contract.

Special Situations

□   If timing is important to your contract (or to its cancellation), send your letter return receipt requested so that you can verify that the letter was received, and the date that it was received. For example, if your lease requires you to give thirty days' notice, you will want to be sure that the property owner cannot say that you violated the terms of the lease by giving only twenty days' notice.

Format

□   All contracts and letters dealing with contracts are typed on business letterhead, personal letterhead stationery, or good bond stationery.

_____ WORDS _____

agreement	conditions	pledge
allow	confirm	promise
arrangement	conform	provisions
assure	consent	settlement
bind	endorse	stipulation
certify	guarantee	terms
clauses	negotiation	transaction
complete	obligations	underwrite
conclude	pact	warrant

PHRASES

agreed-to arrangements
agree to terms
articles of the agreement
come to an understanding
come to terms
comply with
effective as of
financial arrangements

I agree to
in return, you agree to
mutual satisfaction
on condition that
reach an understanding
signed, sealed, and delivered
strike a bargain
this contract is effective until

SENTENCES

Clause 2b asks for a final inspection on October 1, 1993; we would prefer this to read "December 1, 1993."

Enclosed is a check for $500, which will serve as earnest money.

Paragraph N in your contract is irrelevant to the matter at hand; please delete it.

This agreement will be in effect from January 1, 1992, until January 1, 1993.

This letter will serve as an informal agreement between us.

PARAGRAPHS

▷   We refer you to the advance clause, where it is stipulated that one-half the advance is due on signing of the contract, one-half is due on publication of the work. Please change "publication" to "completion."

▷   Thank you for the copies of the contracts, which we received October 31. As we review them with our lawyer, a few questions occur to us. We would appreciate being able to sit down with you and your lawyer to discuss a few of them. When would this be possible?

▷   In response to your telex of June 3, I'm sending the three original contracts along with two copies of each, four pro forma invoices with two copies of each, and a bill of lading. Please let us know at once if everything is in order.

▷   I agree to translate your Moroccan contracts, letters, telexes, and other messages for the fee of $30 per hour. I further agree to complete the outstanding translations by February 10. You will pay messenger service fees between your office and mine, parking fees when I have to consult at your downtown offices, and postage for any mail services.

SAMPLE LETTERS

Dear Mr. Bowling,

    As required by our lease, we hereby give you thirty days' notice of our intention to move from Apartment 2 at 619 Fourth Street.

Please call any evening after 6:00 p.m. to let us know when you need to show the apartment.

Our rent deposit of $450 will need to be refunded to us as we have not damaged the apartment in any way during our tenancy.

We have enjoyed our two years here very much, and will be sorry to move.

Sincerely yours,

. . . .

Dear Ms. Hart:

Pryke Financial Services, Inc., will be happy to act as Investment Advisor to the Collins Foundation and, as such, will assist with cash management and investment of foundation funds with the exception of the initial investment of the bond issue proceeds from certain bond issues.

We agree to provide the following services:

1. A complete review and analysis of the Collins Foundation's financial structure and conditions.

2. The preparation of written investment objectives outlining preferable investments, portfolio goals, risk limits, and diversification possibilities.

3. The establishment of preferred depository or certificate arrangements with banks or savings and loans.

4. Soliciting bids for guaranteed investment agreements.

5. Monitoring fund transfers, verifying receipt of collateral, completing documentation.

6. Working with a governmental securities dealer to execute governmental security transactions.

7. Meeting with your treasurer and financial advisor periodically and with your board of directors as requested.

8. Providing monthly portfolio status reports with sufficient detail for accounting and recording purposes.

Pryke Financial Services, Inc., will submit quarterly statements for services. Our fees will be billed in advance and calculated by multiplying .000375 times the Collins Foundation's invested portfolio at the beginning of each calendar quarter (.0015 annually). Fees will be adjusted at the end of each quarter to reflect the rate times the average invested balance for the previous quarter. Adjustments will be included in the next billing.

Fees can be reviewed and adjusted annually on the anniversary date of this contract.

This agreement will run from June 1, 1993, through June 1, 1994, but may be cancelled by either party without cause with thirty days' written notice.

Sincerely,

Grace Bloom
President

The above agreement is accepted by the Collins Foundation (blanks for date, signatures, titles).

See also: ACCEPTANCES, ORDERS.

14

Cover Letters

A cover letter (also called a transmittal) usually accompanies, identifies, and explains anything you are sending someone. It may be as short as two sentences, telling what is enclosed and why, or as long as two pages, commenting on the enclosure or developing a sales message to accompany the report, sample, document, information, or package.

Cover Letters Usually Accompany

- application forms
- brochures/booklets/catalogs/pamphlets/product literature
- checks unaccompanied by statements or invoices
- complimentary or review copies of books
- contracts/agreements/proposals/reports
- contributions to charitable causes
- documents
- information/instructions
- manuscripts
- résumés
- samples

How to Say It

☐ State briefly what is enclosed, attached, or mailed under separate cover.

☐ If there are several items, list them. Or indicate the number of items of the same type: "brochures (3)."

☐ If appropriate, mention why you are sending the material (in response to

114

a request, an order, a third person's suggestion, or to introduce the person to the product).

□ If necessary, explain what the item is and how to read, interpret, or use it.

□ Indicate any response you are expecting or any future action you will be taking.

What Not to Say

□ Avoid duplicating the enclosed information. Summarizing a document or mentioning the salient points of a contract is helpful in orienting the reader, but repeating sentences and paragraphs from the enclosure may lead the reader to skip over those parts later while reading the material.

Tips on Writing

□ Be brief. Except when the cover letter is actually a sales letter accompanying a sample, product literature, or a catalog, it is only a side dish, not the main course. Its job is to point to the enclosure. A good cover letter will make the reader want to set it aside quickly in order to get to the enclosure.

Special Situations

□ Cover letters do not usually accompany routine orders, payments, shipments, recommendations, or letters of reference, but they may be necessary in special circumstances.

□ When your recipient has not requested or is not expecting your enclosure, a more detailed cover letter is necessary.

□ When sending a report to someone, begin by stating that it is enclosed (identifying it by title) and mentioning why it was prepared and who authorized it. Summarize the report (use its abstract, introduction, or summary) and name those who helped write it. Express your hope that the report will meet with the recipient's approval.

□ A cover letter accompanying a sample or product literature has a much bigger job than the usual cover letter. It is, in fact, more of a sales letter than a cover letter (see SALES).

□ When you send a cover letter with a résumé it should be brief but contain enough information to make the reader want to look at the attached résumé. See RÉSUMÉS for tips on writing this kind of cover letter.

□ Although they are not called cover letters, notes that accompany gifts have the same approximate purpose and format. Mention the enclosure ("just a small gift/a little something") and the occasion for the gift, and include your greetings and best wishes.

Format

❑   Except for notes accompanying gifts or the most informal transmittals, all cover letters should be typed on business letterhead or memo paper (the latter is used for in-house materials or for those outside people and firms with which you have a fairly high-volume and casual correspondence).

❑   Use a form letter when you are writing routine cover letters—for example, letters that accompany requested information. You seldom need the more expensive computer-generated "personal" form letter; a multi-purpose form stating what is enclosed is sufficient. When you want to give the form letter a more personal appearance, use good quality paper, address the person by name (instead of using "Dear Friend" or "Dear Subscriber"), and sign each letter individually. For potentially important customers, you may want to revert to the personal cover letter.

_____ WORDS _____

acquaint	message	prospectus
announce	notice	provisions
attached	outline	report
deliver	plan	statement
document	policy	summarize
draft	program	terms
enclosed	project	transfer
illustrate	proposal	transmittal

_____ PHRASES _____

acquaint you with
as promised
brochure that presents/details/describes/
   outlines/explains
come/agree to terms
complimentary copy
direct your attention to
enclosed are
for further information
here are/is the
I am sending you

if you need/want additional information
I'm also enclosing
inform of
planning stages
please note that
point out
rough draft
the enclosed booklet/brochure/pamphlet
   describes
will show you

_____ SENTENCES _____

After you have reviewed the enclosed documents, we would welcome the opportunity to discuss them with you.

Also enclosed is the initial application fee of $250.

Complete medical records from the office of Dr. Anna Lakington for Mr. Barnabas Holly are enclosed.

Enclosed are copies of the recorded deeds and easements for the above-referenced properties.

Enclosed is a quitclaim deed conveying the new Fort Road from Faulkland County to the City of Sheridan.

Enclosed is my check for $125.

Enclosed is the information you requested.

Enclosed is the requested report on the Heat Treatment Seminar, held July 14-17.

Here are the documents you requested in your letter of April 12.

Here is the report you requested.

If you want material on other topics, please let me know.

I hope this report proves useful/is acceptable/meets with your approval.

I'm sending you a copy of the article on the Minnesota twins study that we discussed last week.

I will call you next week to discuss this.

Ms. DeGroot has asked me to forward a copy of our latest findings to you.

Our company check for $1,896.87 is enclosed.

Please sign both copies of the enclosed letter of agreement and return them to us.

_____ PARAGRAPHS _____

▷   Enclosed is a sample (ref. #4467-AB) of the film that Alwyn Tower and I discussed with you last Thursday. Please keep in mind that the sample was produced under laboratory conditions. If you have any questions about this material or variations of it, please call Alwyn or me.

▷   Enclosed is an Agreement and Release between you and Lakely Associates, which gives the terms of the settlement for the redevelopment of your well. When you sign the Agreement and present written proof of the adjudication of the well to Lakely Associates, we will send you a check for the agreed-upon amount.

▷   Here is the check for the balance of my order. Thank you for all your help. Please keep my name and address on your mailing list.

▷   Enclosed are two short stories for your consideration and possible use in _Best Stories_. Also enclosed is an SASE for your reply. If you cannot use the stories, please just discard them instead of returning them. Thank you for your time and attention.

▷   This is the ring I described to you on the telephone last week. Please let me know as soon as possible what sort of replacement is available. Thank you.

▷   Enclosed is a Notice of Public Hearing on Petition for Exclusion of Real Property in the Corodale Water & Sanitation District and its attached Exhibit A. Please publish this Notice three times in the *Munro Daily Times*—on February 22, 1992, March 1, 1992, and March 8, 1992. Your invoice should be forwarded to this office.

▷   Today I am shipping approximately one square foot each of 0.090 to 0.100 inch thick sheets of Fe-3% Si (hot-rolled) and IF (niobium-containing interstitial-free; hot-rolled, one sheet, cold-rolled, one sheet). The rolling direction is marked on each sheet.

▷   Enclosed is the complete report on the foreign language survey conducted last fall. Vice-presidents and personnel directors of one hundred of the nation's largest corporations were asked which foreign language would be most important for a successful business career during the next twenty years. The results may surprise you!

▷   We enjoyed preparing this study for you, and we hope it is helpful. Please call if you need additional information.

▷   Enclosed please find a money order for $100 to cover the 50% deposit you have made for my order. I will look forward to hearing from you when the tea set has arrived.

▷   Thank you for your interest in Griffiths Collar and Shirt Company. I'm enclosing a packet of materials that will describe our range of products and services. I will call you next week to see if you have any questions and to discuss how we might be of help to you. You are, of course, always welcome to visit our offices and factory here in Lycurgus.

▷   You've been buying Ponderevo's Cough Lintus and our line of Mogg's soap for years. Now we proudly announce a new product that is sure to become a household word: Tono-Bungay! Enclosed are several samples. Try Tono-Bungay yourself and share some with friends. Our Order Line is available to you 24 hours a day, and orders are shipped within 48 hours.

▷   The attached set of project plans covers work through the end of 1994. The plans have been generated in consultation with each of the key people involved. We expect to review progress the first of each month and to adjust the work accordingly. You will note that we are dependent on the work of others in the office and that they are in turn dependent on us. Please review the scheduled work and give me your comments.

▷   Enclosed is a copy of my January bill for $198.73 and a check for payment in the amount of $178.73. There was an addition error of $20. Let me know if your findings do not agree with mine.

▷   I'm sending you a little gift under separate cover. I hope it takes you back to our stay in Hong Kong all those years ago and brings you much pleasure in the years ahead.

SAMPLE LETTERS

Dear Kurt,

Enclosed is a copy of the letter of recommendation I wrote for you. I've sent the original on to the academic dean in the envelope you provided. I thought you might like a copy for your files.

I am so pleased you asked me to do this. I just hope I was of some small help. Let me know as soon as you hear the good news!

With best wishes,

. . . .

Dear Ms. Hoenikker:

Re: General Forge and Foundry Company

Please find enclosed a copy of the Order issued by Judge Asa Breed on June 23. As the Order indicates, General Forge and Foundry Company, together with all its assets and accounts, has been placed under receivership. The Court's control of General Forge and Foundry Company has necessitated a change in the company's address. Please direct all future correspondence and payments on your account to their new address (see enclosed change of address announcement).

Please accept our apologies for any inconvenience resulting from this underlying litigation; we appreciate your patience. Be assured that the Court's decision will have no adverse repercussions on your account. We expect, in fact, that General Forge and Foundry Company's service should improve in the coming weeks.

I look forward to working with you until the company is ready for its return to private ownership. Please feel free to contact my office if you have any questions or comments regarding General Forge and Foundry's new business arrangement or if you have any advice as to how we can better serve your needs.

Sincerely,

. . . .

Dear Maria:

I received the film sample (#18-1A) from Julian Silvercross and am very impressed. We are excited about the performance improvement that we think this technology may offer us. As Nancy Sibley explained to you on the phone, we are interested in using it for our silicon detector assembly, which is an integral part of sensors used for various industrial purposes.

I'm enclosing three of these detector assemblies for your review. Feel free to dissect them to locate the detector assemblies.

We ask that you respect the confidentiality of our product and interest in your film.

Please give me a call after you have had a chance to look at the sensors.

Yours truly,

. . . .

Dear Mr. Oakley:

Enclosed is your copy of the contract between Sullivan Press and Eaglesham Publications. Several of the clauses are being revised, and I will see that you receive the amended version as soon as it is ready.

If you have any questions about your obligations under the contract, please check with our attorney Mary Jane Reed in the Legal Services Department.

Sincerely yours,

. . . .

Dear Ms. Kenealy,

Enclosed is the Ralph Kello denim dress you ordered six months ago. I can only apologize most sincerely for all the difficulties you have had placing this order.

I am pleased that you are still interested in obtaining the dress. To help compensate you for your troubles I am also enclosing a check for $40—half the amount you sent us six months ago. Thank you for your patience, and I hope we can serve you again soon.

Sincerely,

. . . .

Dear Customer,

Thank you for writing for your free sample of the "world's toughest disposable rubber gloves!" Please read through the enclosed flyer for the many ways you can use these gloves to save your hands from damaging liquids and abrasives. Then go ahead and try the last word in convenience, comfort . . . and toughness! You will never want to use any other glove again.

We would appreciate hearing your comments on the gloves after trying them. Enclosed is a postage-paid reply postcard.

. . . .

Dear Unocal Marketer:

Attached for your use is a VHS videotape on Unocal's exciting new "Thermally Stable MP Gear Lube—LS."

This short video talks about the difficult conditions automobile and truck gear boxes must operate under in today's world, where high heat, dusty conditions, and prolonged high speed are all normal operating environments.

The tape demonstrates how Unocal's unique thermally stable gear lube gives operators an edge in performance when compared to conventional products in the marketplace.

I am excited, as I hope you will be, about the endless opportunities to use video to demonstrate the benefits of a product, and assist in increasing sales volumes and margins. The professionalism of this type of presentation should give you a real advantage in your efforts to solicit and service large fleet and other commercial customers.

As the tape says, "THE HEAT IS ON." It is my sincere wish that this video lets you turn up the heat on your competition!

Sincerely,

. . . .

Dear Isabella and John,

Enclosed are photocopies of the original Last Wills and Testaments that I have drafted upon your request. Would you please examine these copies thoroughly and then phone or write my office. If the contents of the Wills meet with your approval, please make arrangements with my secretary, Judith Trevisa, to come to my office and formally execute the original Wills.

If there are any changes or corrections you wish to make to your Wills, please call or write me and I will be happy to discuss them with you.

Best regards,

See also: RÉSUMÉS, SALES.

15

Letters About Credit

"The size of sums of money appears to vary in a
remarkable way according as they are being
paid in or paid out." (Julian Huxley)

Consumer credit amounts to well over $700 billion annually. It takes a fair amount of paperwork, including letters, to support this mountain of debt. Although most credit-related letters are routine and governed by federal, state, or institutional rules and guidelines, each one must be carefully written. When dealing with someone's need for money, credit rating, or good character reference, it is essential to double-check the facts and to choose your words with care.

Letters About Credit Include

- approving loans
- canceling an account
- collecting past-due accounts (see COLLECTIONS)
- congratulations: fine record/payment (see also SALES)
- credit bureaus: letters to and from
- delinquent account
- denying/refusing credit or loan applications (see REFUSALS)
- errors in credit history
- explaining credit/loan refusals/conditions
- extending payment deadlines
- family members and friends: lending/borrowing
- information about credit
- inviting new accounts/reviving inactive accounts
- obtaining one's own credit history
- requesting credit/bankcard/loan

How to Say It

□   When approving a loan application or granting credit, state that you've approved the request, indicate the amount approved and the effective date, and explain credit or loan payoff procedures. If the customer is new, you could welcome them to your lending institution or business and suggest they bring all their credit needs to you.

□   When asking a credit bureau to run a check on yourself, give your name, address, social security number, and telephone number. Use letterhead stationery or enclose a business card to substantiate that you are the subject of the check. If you are asking a credit bureau to check on another person's credit history, you must supply the person's name, address, and social security number, and give a legitimate business reason for asking (you are renting property to the person, trying to sell them a car, cosigning a contract for deed with them).

□   When writing to ask for a correction of an inaccurate credit record, identify yourself fully, state the incorrect portions of the record, and explain why they are incorrect. Include copies of any documents (statements, loan papers, references, tax returns, paycheck stubs) that will substantiate your position. Ask them to correct your record immediately and send you a copy of the amended report. Do not write an angry letter; the person who receives it probably had nothing to do with the error and can, in fact, help you.

□   Most requests for credit today involve filling out a form rather than writing a letter to request it. However, you may want to write a cover letter to send with the form if you have additional information or if you wish to add a personal touch.

□   If you are unable to make a loan payment or installment credit payment on time, write the company at once. Apologize for being overdue, tell them that you intend to pay as soon as possible, and enclose whatever portion of the balance you can. If you have a particularly good reason for being overdue (illness, layoff), you could mention it. Otherwise, do not go into lengthy excuses; your creditor is more interested in knowing that you are taking responsibility for the account.

□   When you must deny credit to an applicant, you can take one of two approaches. The first is used when you think the situation calls for a personal, sales-type letter. In it, you express regret that you are unable to extend the loan, suggest some alternative courses of action, and encourage them to reapply to you later and to remember you for their other credit needs. You may want to include a disclaimer to the effect that the denial is based solely on the person's financial record and not on sex, race, religious affiliation, or other nonfinancial grounds. The second approach is used to respond to the great number of routine loan requests received by banks and savings and loan institutions. A form letter states simply "Your request for a a loan has been denied" and then includes a check-off list of possible reasons: length of employment, excessive credit obligations, garnishment/judgment, and so forth. You may want to leave a blank to fill in the name of the credit bureau where negative information was received so that the person knows where to correct inaccurate information.

☐   When you write an individual or a business to ask for a credit reference, give the name and address of the person under consideration, politely request any pertinent credit information they might have about the person, explain briefly why you want it ("we are discussing a partnership"), state that you will treat the information confidentially, express your appreciation for the information, and enclose a self-addressed stamped envelope for their reply. In some cases you might want to mention how you were referred to them (for example, by the person under consideration). Instead of asking for general credit information, you could ask specific questions: How long have they known the person? In what capacity? What kinds of credit have been extended? What is the current balance? The person's payment pattern? How long have they been employed there? What is their weekly/monthly/yearly income?

What Not to Say

☐   When discussing someone's credit history, never say anything that cannot be documented. Phrases like "misses payments" or "habitually late with payments" must be substantiated by records of such payment patterns. Double-check spellings of names and account numbers to be sure you are discussing the right person's credit history.

Tips on Writing

☐   All credit matters are confidential. Although confidentiality is sometimes more of a principle than a fact, you should still make every attempt to safeguard the credit information you give or receive.

☐   Accuracy is essential when providing information on someone's credit history. Check and double-check your facts.

☐   Be tactful. Even people with poor credit histories want to hear good of themselves and often feel they are doing a good job given their circumstances. It is never helpful to make people feel inadequate.

Special Situations

☐   If you decide to request a loan of a family member or friend (presumably because it is the only option available to you), choose the individual carefully (you may have to answer the question "Why me?"). Make your letter businesslike and factual; do not plead or try to play on their sympathies. Suggest a repayment plan and tell how much interest you plan to pay. For the sake of your future relations with the person, offer them a convenient excuse for not agreeing to the loan ("You may have financial problems of your own, for all I know," "This may not be a good time for you," or "You may disapprove on principle of loans between friends"). Thank the person for all previous support and express your appreciation for their accessibility. Let them know there is no reason for them to feel guilty or uncomfortable about turning you down. It may be difficult to be gracious; if you need a loan badly enough to approach a friend or family member, you may be desperate. However, pressuring someone who is unwilling to lend you money will not only not get you the money, but it will lose you a friend.

□   Letters beginning "Congratulations!" are sometimes sent by firms wishing to attract credit customers. Although they may congratulate someone on a fine credit record or a recent loan payoff, they are really sales letters. For example, "Congratulations! Because of your excellent credit record, you are eligible to apply for our preapproved Silver Bank Card."

□   If a person wants to know why a credit request or loan application was denied, explain your credit criteria, list the problems presented by the person's credit background, and tell what sources you used to determine creditworthiness.

Format

□   There are virtually no handwritten letters dealing with credit matters. Routine correspondence may be handled with form letters. Others will be typed on business letterhead.

─────────────────── WORDS ───────────────────

account	budget	due
accrue	capital	finance
advise	certificate	funds
application	client	guarantee
approval	collateral	insolvent
arrangement	collection	installment
arrears	creditor	IOU
assets	creditworthy	irregularities
balance	debt	ledger
bookkeeping	debtor	lender
borrow	default	lessor

liability   receipt   surety
lien   record   unpaid
loan   regretfully   urge
mortgage   reimbursement   vendor
nonpayment   repayment   verification
overdraft   request   voucher
overdue   requirements   warrant
owe   solvency
past-due   soundness

_____ PHRASES _____

accounts receivable

advance loan/cash payment

after careful consideration

although you have only occasional
    payment problems

apply for credit privileges

as much as we would like to extend you
    credit

cannot justify approval

cash basis only

collection agency

consistently timely credit payments

credit agency/bureau

credit application/history/record/
    standing/rating

credit customer

credit information

credit limit

current collection problems

current/up-to-date financial statement

deferred payment

down payment

due to a rise in the number of
    uncollectable past-due accounts

due to cash flow difficulties

embarrassed circumstances

entire balance

excellent credit rating

extending credit

financial difficulties/needs/services

in arrears

in checking your credit background

insufficient funds

it is our policy

I understand and appreciate your
    position, but

late payments

lend on security

letter of credit

line of credit

one of our credit requirements is

overdrawn account

overdue amount

past-due account

pattern of late payments

pay in advance/in full

pleased to be able to accommodate you

poor payment history

preferred customer

receipt in full

regret that we are unable to

responsible use of credit

review of our files

revolving line of credit

run up a bill/an account with

square the accounts

steady credit payments

straitened circumstances

subject only to normal credit
    requirements

unable to accommodate you at this time
    because

unpaid balance

we are happy/pleased to approve

will you please run a credit check on

your request for an account

―――――――――――――――――――――――――― SENTENCES ――――――――――――――――――――――――――

Because our inquiries disclosed a number of past-due and unpaid accounts, we are
   unable to extend the line of credit you requested.

Cressida Mary MacPhail, 1968 Taylor Avenue, Bretton, IN 47834, has applied to the
   Maxwell Credit Union for a loan, and gave us your name as a reference.

Eileen Schwartz has had an excellent credit history with this company, and we
   recommend her highly as a credit customer.

I appreciate your courtesy in allowing me to pay off the balance of my account in
   small installments.

If you require additional information, we will be happy to provide it.

It is a pleasure to increase the credit line on your Flex-Checks account.

Please keep us in mind for your other credit needs.

Thank you for applying for a charge account with Boylan & Gleeson.

The credit bureau cites repeated credit delinquencies.

We are pleased to extend credit to you at any of our nine metropolitan stores.

We are pleased to report that our credit dealings with Angela Crossby have been
   excellent.

We are pleased to welcome you as a preferred credit customer.

We are unable to furnish you with any current credit information on Emerson-
   Toller—they have not been a credit customer of ours for over ten years.

We expect to be making large purchases of office furniture from your firm as well as
   routine purchases of office supplies and would like to open a credit account with
   you.

We have carefully reviewed your loan application, and find that we are unable to
   extend you credit at this time.

We have run into some difficulties checking the references you supplied.

We note a persistent pattern of nonpayment in your credit history.

We suggest you reapply for the loan once you have resolved some of these problems.

We will appreciate any credit information you can give us about Walter Tillotson.

We will need a current financial statement from you.

Your credit references all supplied very complimentary reports.

―――――――――――――――――――――――――― PARAGRAPHS ――――――――――――――――――――――――――

▷   Enclosed please find a check for $457.32, which will bring my account up to
date. I am sorry that I let the account become past due. I expect to keep it current in
the future.

▷   I would like to see the credit record you currently have on me. I am applying for
a second mortgage on my home next month, and would not want to be unpleasantly
surprised by anything that may be on file. Thank you.

▷   I am pleased to report that we are able to approve your loan request in the
amount of $5,000. A check is enclosed, along with a payment booklet and a packet of
payment envelopes. Please read your repayment schedule carefully.

▷   Because of your excellent credit record, we are pleased to offer you a special holiday gift. The enclosed Holiday Charge Card entitles you to buy now (beginning December 1) and pay nothing—not even interest!—until February of next year.

▷   We are sorry to report that your loan application has not been approved. Our decision was based primarily on information received from the Carnaby Reporting Services credit bureau. You may want to look at their record on you to verify that it is correct. If it is, we suggest working with a financial counselor, something that has been helpful to several of our customers. We will be happy to review your loan application at a later date if your circumstances change.

▷   You have earned the rights and privileges of our most exclusive credit card. We created this card to reward customers like you who show exceptional responsibility with their credit purchases. Your card gives you a new level of buying power as well as exclusive invitations to Preferred Customer Sales. As a Preferred Customer you are now entitled to a number of special privileges, including free gift wrapping, a new higher credit limit, and special monthly discounts.

▷   Because of an electrical fire at our main plant three months ago, we have been experiencing some temporary financial difficulties and have fallen behind on our payments to you. We expect to rectify the situation by the end of the year. In the meantime, please accept the enclosed check on account. We thank you for your understanding.

▷   We must report that our business experiences with the Baroness de la Cruchecassée have been less than satisfactory. Over a period of eighteen months we have failed to collect anything on a fairly large outstanding balance. We trust you will keep this information confidential.

—————————————————— SAMPLE LETTERS ——————————————————

TO: Dudley Credit Data
FROM: Eustace Landor, Landor First Banks
DATE: September 3, 1992
RE: Edith Millbank
    Will you please run a credit check for us on:
              Edith Millbank
              1844 Coningsby
              Oswald, OH 45042
    Ms. Millbank is taking out a loan application with us, and we wish to verify the information she has given us with regard to her credit history.
    Thank you.

                    · · · · · · · · · · · ·

Dear Michael Dunne,
    We noticed that you have not used your Pearson Charge Card in some time now. If you do not use it before it expires in March of 1993, we will be unable to issue you a new card for the following year.
    We would be very sorry to lose you as a good charge customer, but we think that you would lose too—lose out on such benefits as the $250,000 flight insurance that

is yours every time you charge an airline ticket on your card . . . the twice-yearly newsletter that saves you money by offering discounts on motels, car rentals, and vacation packages . . . the low annual rate . . . the variable interest rate . . . and the flexibility of a card that can be used at over 15,000 places of businesses!

We hope that you will rediscover the many uses and benefits of the versatile Pearson Charge Card!

Sincerely yours,

See also: ANNOUNCEMENTS, APOLOGIES, COLLECTION, COMPLAINTS, ORDERS, REFUSALS, RESPONSES, THANK YOU.

16

Letters of Disagreement

> "Anyone who thinks there aren't two sides to every argument is probably in one." (*The Cockle Bur*)

There are people who thrive on conflict, and there are those who spend a great deal of energy avoiding it. If they live in the real world, both types will sooner or later have to write a letter of disagreement. Disagreement is neither good nor bad, but the way you handle it will greatly affect subsequent events, feelings, and actions. (See COMPLAINTS for additional ideas about letters of disagreement.)

Letters of Disagreement May Concern

- continuing arguments
- contracts
- decisions
- job descriptions
- oral agreements
- personnel problems
- policies/programs/procedures/regulations
- property lines

How to Say It

☐ Refer to the previous correspondence or to the event responsible for the present letter.

☐ Outline the two opposing views or actions.

☐ Give clear (perhaps numbered) reasons for your stand, using statistics, quotations from an employee handbook, supportive anecdotal material, and names of witnesses or others who agree with you (with their permission).

□   If appropriate, suggest an intermediate stage of negotiation: a reply to specific questions in your letter; further research; a meeting between the two of you or with third parties present; visits to a lawyer, accountant, or other appropriate expert.

□   If the disagreement has reached the stage where you can effectively do this, finish by stating clearly the outcome you desire.

□   End with your best wishes for a solution acceptable to both of you and a reference to good future relations.

What Not to Say

□   Do not put the person on the defensive. This is one instance in which you want to use more "I" phrases than "you" phrases. When you are in the midst of a conflict, "you" statements can all too often seem accusatory. Consider whether your letter is going to make the person feel bad, shamed, inept, or weak. If this is what you are aiming to do, that's fine. But if you want to negotiate or solve a problem, you are short-circuiting yourself; people who feel shamed are not apt to give you what you want.

□   Avoid emotional statements. Concentrate on facts instead of feelings. For example, saying, "I don't feel this is fair" does not carry as much weight as saying, "I believe it is unfair that only one out of seven secretaries is consistently asked to work overtime—and without overtime pay."

Tips on Writing

□   The tone of your letter can make all the difference between being "heard" and not being heard. Strive for a letter that is factual, dispassionate, considerate, and even-handed.

□   Be clear about your goal. It will help you write the letter if you finish this sentence: "I want them to . . ." Do you want a rebate, an exchange, repairs? Do you want an apology, a corrected statement, a credit? Do you want to convince the person that their facts, statistics, opinions are wrong? Do you want something redone?

□   Do everything you can to help the other person save face. Set up the situation so that the person can do what you want in a way that makes them feel generous, gracious, powerful, and *willing*.

□   Although active voice is almost always preferred to the passive voice, you may want to consider the more tactful passive voice when involved in a disagreement. Instead of saying, "You did this," say, "This was done."

□   Examine your own position for possible areas of negotiation. Can you trade one point for another? Can you accept anything less than what you originally wanted?

□   If you are writing to disapprove the passage of legislation, note whether the bill is state or federal and then write the appropriate lawmakers. Federal bills have numbers prefixed by HR (House Resolution) or SR (Senate Resolution) and there is usually a reference to their passage by Congress. State bills may also require house and senate passage but are usually denoted HF (House File) and SF (Senate File).

Special Situations

□   You can handle many disagreements yourself or with the help of others in your workplace or home. However, in situations like the following you may want to consult a lawyer: in marital separations where one or both parties are writing letters containing admissions, demands, or threats; where a question of property lines does not seem amenable to informal agreement or you need to reduce oral agreements to written agreements; when family disagreements about an estate become heated; when you are being accused of something; when the disagreement escalates to threats of lawsuits.

□   Sometimes groups band together to form letterwriting campaigns on controversial issues. A sample letter will be distributed for members or proponents to copy over their own signature. When representatives are interested in the number of people on each side of an issue, such letterwriting campaigns have value. Most often, however, form letters do not get much attention. One well-written original letter will carry more weight with a lawmaker than a hundred form letters. It is important to know when a group effort is effective and when it is not.

□   When you write to disagree with a lawmaker's support of a bill or other issue, you may want a response from the person. In other instances, however, your goal is simply to inform your representative of your opinion on an issue, and you would prefer not to receive a three-page letter outlining the person's views at great length—and taxpayer expense. Many members of Congress and of state houses automatically send form letters to any constituent who writes them, even though these letters are often of minimal value to the recipient. You may want to end your letter with, "Please do not respond to this letter with a letter giving me your views. I know your views; I wanted you to know mine."

Format

□   Letters dealing with business disagreements are typed on letterhead stationery. These letters should be particularly impressive—neatly typed, spaced, and signed.

▫   When writing about personal disagreements, your letter will appear friendlier and a little more open to negotiation if you handwrite it. If you wish to appear firm and *not* open to negotiation, typing is best.

────────────────────────── WORDS ──────────────────────────

argument	dissent	misunderstanding
awkwardness	disservice	nuisance
breach	disturbing	object
break	diverge	offense
conflict	estrangement	protest
contention	faction	quarrel
contradiction	feeler	rankle
controversy	feud	reconcile
deplorable	friction	regrettable
differ	fuming	rift
difficulty	furious	rupture
disagree	incompatible	sorry
disagreement	infelicitous	spat
disapprove	infuriated	squabble
discord	irate	tiff
disharmony	irritated	trouble
displeased	lawsuit	unfortunate
dispute	litigation	unhappy
dissatisfaction		

────────────────────────── PHRASES ──────────────────────────

agree to differ/disagree
as I understand it
at cross purposes
be at odds/variance with
beg to differ
believe you should know that
bone of contention
break off negotiations
bury the hatchet
come to terms
complicated situation
conduct an inquiry
difference of opinion
direct your attention to

disputed point
do a disservice to
fail to agree
fly in the ointment
I am convinced that
I assume/presume/think/have no doubt that
I have the impression that
in my estimation/judgment/opinion/ view
in the best interests of
I take it that
it seems to me
it strikes me that
matter/point in dispute/at issue/
    under discussion/in question

my information is
part company with
point of view
question at issue
register my opinion
so far as I know

strongly oppose
take into consideration
think differently
to my way of thinking
to the best of my knowledge
wonder if you are aware that

SENTENCES

Are we ready to put this to a vote?

Do you think it would help to call in an arbitrator?

Enclosed please find several abstracts that may be helpful.

I am convinced that the passage of this bill would do more harm than good/is not in the best interests of the state/would be a grave error.

I disagree with the store policy of filling prescriptions with generic drugs without notifying the customer.

I found the language and tone of your last letter completely unacceptable; please put us in touch with someone else in your organization who can handle this matter.

If you would like some background reading on this issue, I would be happy to furnish you with some.

I received your letter this morning and am sorry to hear that you cannot accept our terms.

Several of the points you mention are negotiable; some are not.

We are submitting this matter to an independent referee.

We still have one major area of disagreement.

What would make the situation more agreeable to you?

PARAGRAPHS

▷   It was my impression that we agreed upon a delivery date of May 15. The confirmation I have just received gives June 15. This will unfortunately be far too late for us. Please let me know at once if this was just a clerical error or if we have a serious problem on our hands.

▷   My lawyer requested the addition of the following clause to the contract: "Clause S. This agreement will expire ten years from the date of execution." It does not appear in the final contract. I am returning the unsigned contracts to you for correction.

▷   I realize that there is technically no more to be said about the Dillon-Reed merger, but I would like to state for the record that I strongly oppose the move. I refer you to the enclosed independent report that we commissioned from Elkus, Inc. This is the classic situation where one owns a dog but persists in barking oneself. The Elkus people, acknowledged experts in the field, advised us against the merger. Do we have strong enough grounds for rejecting their conclusions? I think not.

▷   I know we've talked about this until we're both sick of it, but I feel strongly that Great-Aunt Elsie is not yet ready for a nursing home. It would make her unhappy and shorten her life to be placed in one prematurely. What changes could be made that would allow her to keep living in her apartment?

───────────────────── SAMPLE LETTERS ─────────────────────

Dear Ms. Burling-Ward:
    I very much enjoy working for Stegner Publishing, and you in particular have been most helpful in introducing me to people and showing me around.
    When I was interviewed for the job, Mr. Oliver consistently used the term "production editor," and the job duties he listed were those generally associated with the position of production editor.
    In my three weeks on the job, I have done nothing but copyediting. After speaking to you yesterday and discovering that this was not just a training stage but my permanent position, I suspect there has been a misunderstanding.
    I would like to meet with you and Mr. Oliver sometime soon to see if we can clarify this situation.
                                        Sincerely,

· · · · · · · · · · ·

                                        Philadelphia, July 5, 1775
Mr. Strahan,
    You are a member of Parliament, and one of that majority which has doomed my country to destruction. You have begun to burn our towns and murder our people. Look upon your hands! they are stained with the blood of your relations! You and I were long friends : you are now my enemy and—I am yours,
                                        B. Franklin

· · · · · · · · · · ·

TO: Adrian Singleton
FROM: Herbert Fraide
DATE: November 3, 1992
RE: Reading for Young People Series
    I am concerned about the narrow scope of our new series. Of the fifty stories to be included, fifty feature middle-class, white protagonists. All fifty are set in the United States. All fifty are domestic fiction dealing with fairly trivial school and neighborhood themes. I find the series unacceptably homogeneous—and, yes, boring. It cannot begin to respond to the varied experiences of our prospective readers. It also fails to conform to the company's stated guidelines on inclusiveness and global awareness.
    Marianna Selby and I are 180 degrees apart on this issue, and find ourselves presently deadlocked. I told her I'd ask you to help us, either with a three-way discussion or by calling for a department meeting or with some other clarification procedure.
cc.: Marianna Selby

. . . .

Dear Senator Burrows,

I urge you to oppose the Television Soundtrack Copyright Reform Bill.

As you know, music performance rights for syndicated television programs are licensed in one of four ways: (1) a blanket license with a performing rights society; (2) a per program license; (3) a source license; or (4) a direct license. This bill would mandate that music performance rights for syndicated television programs be licensed in only one way, at the source in conjunction with all other broadcast rights for the program.

The current system has been used since the beginning of television and has been upheld in court challenges. It assures a fair return based on performance to composers and songwriters who create television music. The proponents of the bill have a heavy burden to demonstrate the need for Congress to interfere in the current system and mandate a single way of doing business.

They have not met their burden, and I oppose the legislation.

Sincerely,

See also: COMPLAINTS, REFUSALS.

17

Letters to the Editor

"I disapprove of what you say, but I will defend to the death your right to say it." (Voltaire)

Almost every newspaper and periodical prints letters to the editor, but not all the letters received are printed. A typical daily newspaper might publish 30% to 40% of the letters it receives. One of the big national weekly news-magazines, on the other hand, publishes only about 2% to 5% of the letters it receives, although it acknowledges (with a form postcard) that each letter was received and read. Fortunately there are ways of increasing the chances of your letter being chosen for publication.

Write a Letter to the Editor When

- You agree or disagree with a story, article, news item, editorial stance, or other letter writer.
- You need to correct published information.
- You want to reach a large number of people with additional information on a published topic or with information that you think most readers would be interested in.
- You have an opinion about a topic that is currently of strong national or local interest.

How to Say It

☐   In the first sentence, refer to the issue that prompted your letter, so that the reader knows immediately what you're talking about.

☐   State your position clearly ("I agree with," "I oppose," "I question").

☐   Briefly support, defend, or explain your position.

☐   Include facts (statistics, items of record, quotes) rather than feelings and impressions.

□   Indicate what action (if any) you would like the reader to take.

□   Give your first and last name, or at least two initials and a last name, your address, and daytime phone number. Sign your name.

What Not to Say

□   Don't bother ending your letter with "Think about it!" One editor says this line shows up routinely in letters and is just as routinely deleted. If your letter appears on the opinion-editorial (op-ed) page, the implication is that you want people to think about it; you don't need to say this.

□   Don't begin your letter with, "I know you won't dare print this letter." Editors say that they dare print a great deal, and they remove most of those beginning sentences. Newspapers willingly print letters critical of their reporting, editing, and editorials.

□   Avoid whining ("It's not fair," "It always happens to me").

□   Do not use pejorative adjectives ("stupid," "dumb," "ridiculous," "redneck," "bleeding heart liberal"). Certain readers will agree with your sentiments. Most, however, will see, quite properly, that such language indicates a weak and unreasoned argument.

□   Avoid name-calling and stereotypical categorizations ("You men are all the same," "Labor unions have always done this," "These crazy feminists," "The welfare rolls are full of . . .").

□   Never use threats—veiled or not. Resorting to coercion or mental or physical bullying betrays a weak position.

□   Publishers will not print anything that might be libelous, so there is no point in writing that sort of letter. This means you say nothing that can be proved to be malicious (even if it's true) and you say nothing that can't be proved (even if there is no intent to harm).

□   Although many regional publications will accept letters reflecting on a previously published letter, most national publications have policies against publishing letters about letters.

□   Avoid half-truths or inaccuracies. Letters are subject to editing for length, libel, good taste, newspaper style, and accuracy. Editors will check the facts in your letters.

Tips on Writing

□   Be brief; shorter letters are more likely to be used and less likely to be edited. A letter of one or two hundred words is just right, but a longer letter will get printed if it is narrowly focused and avoids side issues.

❑   Be sure your topic is important to more than one person (you). An op-ed page editor counsels against writing about something that is overly personal to one event in your life. For example, a newspaper cannot print all the thank you letters aimed at doctors or emergency room staff or ambulance drivers or good Samaritans; the letters to the editor department is not a thank you column.

❑   Be timely; editors rarely run letters that refer to issues weeks or months old. To comment on a specific article, write immediately after it is published.

❑   Stick to one narrow idea, omitting anything that doesn't touch directly on it. Letters that don't focus on one point or topic will be edited to do so.

❑   State your position clearly so that readers are in no doubt as to which side of the issue you are on.

❑   Be reasonable, moderate, rational, fact-oriented.

❑   To get a letter accepted in a competitive market, aim for pithiness, humor, a startling slant, unusual information, or a twist on conventional thinking.

❑   When you feel strongly about an issue, get others to write letters too so that the letters to the editor column reflects that many people feel the way you do.

❑   Have others read your letter; oftentimes you are too close to the problem to see how your letter may affect others.

❑   Most papers won't print letters from the same individual more frequently than every month or two, so if you've just had a letter published there's not much point in writing again soon.

❑   Most publications want letters that are original to them, not copies of letters sent to one or more other publications. There are exceptions to this, of course, but you may want to check your publication's editorial policy. If you are writing to several publications at once, advise them of this.

Special Situations

❑   Anonymous letters rarely get printed as most publishers believe their readers have a right to know whose views are being expressed. However, some circumstances justify anonymous letters, such as the prospect of physical harm to the writer or loss of a job. Editors consider requests for anonymity under those or similar circumstances and will print the letter over a "Name Withheld." You may feel better calling first to make sure this is possible. If you write, specify that the letter is to be published only if your name does not appear.

□   When asking for a correction or retraction of inaccuracies, misstatements, or incomplete information, begin by identifying the offending article by date, section, page, and column. Be polite, factual, and firm. Offer to supply correct data, proofs of your assertion, and phone numbers to call for verification.

□   Letters may be signed by many people, but rarely are more than two of the names published; most publications believe their readers are interested in reading opinions in the letters column, not lists of names.

□   Just before political elections, letters to the editor columns become particularly popular. Most newspapers will consider letters that support one candidate or criticize another as long as the focus remains on the issues rather than on personalities and the writers' attempts to support their judgments. However, editors easily recognize letters that are thinly disguised press releases or part of an organized effort to create a bandwagon effect, so avoid blatant politicking. Some papers will print no election-related letters during a period immediately preceding an election or on Election Day; this is to avoid being used to launch last-minute offensives.

Format

□   When possible, type rather than handwrite a letter to the editor. Any kind of stationery is acceptable.

---------------------------- **WORDS** ----------------------------

advice	contradict	infer
agree	controversy	inflammatory
annoying	convinced	insulting
approve	criticize	irritating
aspect	disagree	judgmental
assess	disapprove	misunderstanding
assume	dissatisfied	notion
attitude	dissent	offensive
believe	disturbing	omission
bias	doctrinaire	one-sided
commentary	dogmatic	partisan
conclude	embarrassing	perspective
conjecture	error	persuade
consensus	examine	position
consider	express	posture
contend	impression	prejudiced

premise   speculate   surmise
provocative   stand   unfortunate
rankled   suppose   view
slant

─────────────────────── PHRASES ───────────────────────

after reading your Sept. 29 article on

a May 3 *New York Post Dispatch* article
   spoke of

an affront to those of us who

cartoonist Humphry Clinker should be
   aware that

congratulations on your impressive
   November issue

did a slow burn when I read

difference of opinion

fail to agree

how can anyone state, as did Laetitia
   Snap (June 3), that

I agree wholeheartedly with

I am horrified by the Aug. 11 report

I am one of the many "misguided"
   people who was outraged by

I am puzzled by the reference to the
   long-term effects of

I am writing on behalf of

I disagree with the Reverend Septimus
   Crisparkle's premise (Nov. 13)

I found the short story in your
   September issue to be

I'm still fuming after reading

I must take issue with

in response to a July 3 letter writer who
   said

infuriating to see that

I read with great/considerable interest

I really enjoyed

I strongly object

I take exception to the opinions
   expressed by

it seems to me that

it was with great displeasure that I read

I was disturbed/incensed/pleased/
   angry/disappointed to learn that

letter writer Muriel McComber's
   suggestion (Aug. 9) was well-taken, but

made me see red

many thanks for your editorial/article on

on the one hand . . . on the other hand

point in dispute

presented a false picture

regarding Senator Sam Blundel's new
   bill for the hearing-impaired

several letters have commented upon

stirred up quite a controversy here at

take umbrage

the article on women in trades did
   much to

your editorial position on

your infuriating article on

your Sept. 17 editorial on

─────────────────────── SENTENCES ───────────────────────

A Dec. 9 writer is incorrect in claiming that the Regional Transit Board was abol-
   ished several years ago; we are, in fact, alive and well.

I am writing to express my appreciation for your excellent coverage of City Council
   meetings on the local ground water issue.

I commend you for your Nov. 13 editorial on magnet schools.

I disagree with Elizabeth Saunders' Apr. 5 column on city-supported recycling.

I expect to see a retraction in tomorrow's paper.

I look forward to seeing a published retraction of the incorrect information given in this article.

In Hennie Feinschreiber's Dec. 9 column on the living will, she uses statistics that have long since been discredited.

In his December 1 Counterpoint, "Tax Breaks for the Rich," Gerald Tetley suggests that out of fear of giving the rich a break, we are actually cutting off our noses to spite our face.

I think you were wrong to feature Lucy Gayheart on your cover last month.

I was disappointed that not one of the dozens who wrote to complain about the hike in municipal sewer rates noticed that the rates are actually lower than they were ten years ago.

Please consider the cumulative effect of such legislation on our children.

Please do not drop Flora Lewis/Cal Thomas/Ellen Goodman/George Will/Mike Royko from your editorial pages.

Several important factors were omitted from your Apr. 6 article on wide-area telephone service.

The writer of the Mar. 4 letter against triple trailers seemed to have little factual understanding of semi-truck traffic and professional truck drivers.

Your Aug. 3 editorial on workers' compensation overlooked a crucial factor.

Your June 3 editorial on child care failed to mention one of the largest and most effective groups working on this issue.

PARAGRAPHS

▷ The letters written recently on ethics in government seem to be missing the point. Candidates for high office need not only be innocent of criminal or unethical activities. They must also be perceived to be people of high ethics. It doesn't matter if they are legally and factually "clean" if they have appeared to act with impropriety, if they have associated with those whose ethics are questionable, or if they have seemed to be fuzzy about the standards required of government officials.

▷ Has anyone noticed that the city has become overrun with dogs in the last several years? Most of these dogs have no collars and run in packs of five to eight dogs. If I had small children, I would worry when they played outdoors. Where have these dogs come from? Whose problem is it? The city council's? The health department's? The police department's?

▷ Count at least six women (the undersigned) who were outraged at your "news story" on the recently appointed Episcopalian bishop for our area. You devoted several lines early on in the story (thus implying their relative importance) to Ms. Dinah Morris's clothes, hairstyle, and even the color of her fingernail polish. Do you do this for new male bishops?

▷ Your story on the newest technology in today's emergency rooms featured the views of hospital administrators, medical care-givers, and manufacturers' representatives. Nowhere was a patient mentioned. Is overlooking the patient also a feature of today's emergency rooms? (If it is, it's not new.)

▷ Henri Philipot has got to go! Day after day his column is trivial, superficial, and inane. Does anybody read the guy? Seriously, why do you keep him? What's the attraction? Anybody else agree with me?

▷   I would like to commend Meg Bishop for the use of "people first" language in her Jan. 2 column. By using expressions such as "people with severe disabilities" rather than "the severely disabled" and "people with quadriplegia" rather than "quadriplegics," Bishop helps change the way society views people with disabilities.

▷   Letter writer Charles Shandon neglected to mention in his long, rather hysterical diatribe against mayoral candidate Hugh Desprez that he is running Mary Shandon's bid for the mayor's office. He is also her husband.

▷   I notice that your magazine persists in using "man" and "mankind" to refer to both men and women. I'm enclosing a reading list of books and articles that make a very strong argument for the dropping of this inaccurate, unacceptable, and illogical convention. As one of the most respected monthlies in the country, you owe it to your readers to use language that includes everyone.

▷   A flurry of letter writers urges us to rally against the proposed congressional pay raise. I wonder if they understand the protection that such a raise would give us against special interest groups. Let's give this one a closer look. It may actually be a sheep in wolf's clothing.

▷   There was an error in your otherwise excellent article about the Lamprey Brothers Moving and Storage. In addition to brothers Henry, Colin, and Stephen (whom you mentioned), there is also brother Michael, a full partner.

SAMPLE LETTERS

Dear Mr. Scott,
    What happened to the ecclesiastical crossword puzzle you used to have every month in *The Abbot*?

. . . .

To the editor:
    Several months ago, you announced a "bold new look" for the paper. Could we maybe have the timid old look back?
    Sometimes I find the financial pages behind the sports pages, sometimes in a section of their own, and occasionally with the classified ads. Usually the advice columnists and funnies are run together in their own section, but more often they are separated and positioned variously with the sports pages, the community news, the feature section, or the food pages.
    I have tried to discern a method to your madness—perhaps on Mondays the sports have their own section, on Tuesdays they appear with the financial papers, etc. No such luck. Somebody down there must just roll dice and say, "Ha! Let them try to find the foreign exchange rates today!"
    Is there any hope for a more organized future?

. . . .

Dear Mr. Burlap:
    The excerpt from *Point Counter Point* in your June issue was excellent. I hope you will continue to offer us selections from lesser-known but high-quality literature.

. . . .

Dear Business Editor:

An article in the Aug. 3 morning edition reported sales for our company in the billions. Naturally that would be nice, but it should have read millions. We would very much appreciate your printing a correction in the next edition of the paper.

. . . .

Dear Editor:

I read with interest the proposal to add four stories to the downtown public library building at a cost of $5.3 million.

I am extremely concerned, however, that no provision has been made for user access. As it now stands, hundreds of thousands of books are all but useless since no one can get to them. There are a handful of metered street parking spaces, but you must be lucky to find one. And then you must not forget to run out every hour and insert four more quarters (the meter readers are particularly active in this area).

How many of you have driven around and around and around hoping for a parking place? How many of you have walked five or six blocks carrying a back-breaking load of books? How many of you have gotten $10 tickets because you forgot to feed the meter on time? It is utterly pointless to spend $5.3 million on a facility that no one can use.

. . . .

To the Editor:

The front page of your Nov. 3 issue carried a full-color picture of a car accident victim who later died.

We, the undersigned, worked with Hilda Derriford—some of us for only two years, some of us for as long as sixteen years. To see our good friend and co-worker displayed in her last moments for an unknowing and uncaring public was one of the most painful things we can describe. How her husband and children felt about the picture is another story, but we can't think they liked it any better than we did.

What is the point of using a photo like that? Can you defend such a practice in any logical, compassionate way?

See also: COMPLAINTS, DISAGREEMENTS.

18

Letters Dealing with Employment

"Most people like hard work, particularly when they're paying for it." (Franklin P. Jones)

Employment-related letters are important to employees because one's livelihood can be affected, directly or indirectly, by letters that run the spectrum from asking about job openings to requesting a raise to asking for clarification of retirement benefits. Employers also depend heavily on well-written letters to maintain good employee relations and to resolve personnel problems that obstruct the goals of the business or organization.

This chapter deals solely with letters involving employer-employee relations. For useful related material, check the index and the following list.

Employment Letters Deal With

- acknowledgments: applications/proposals/suggestions (see also AC-KNOWLEDGMENTS)
- advice/complaints/reprimands (see ADVICE, COMPLAINTS)
- announcements: layoffs/changes/company policies (see also AN-NOUNCEMENTS, INSTRUCTIONS)
- approvals: raise/promotion/projects/requests/changes (see also AC-CEPTANCES)
- congratulations/commendations (see also CONGRATULATIONS)
- interviews (see APPOINTMENTS, FOLLOW-UP, RÉSUMÉS)
- invitations: retirement parties/service anniversaries/awards ceremonies/speaking engagements (see also INVITATIONS)
- meetings: announcing/canceling/changing/postponing (see also AP-POINTMENTS)
- networking (see INTRODUCTIONS)

- references and recommendations (see REFERENCES)
- refusals: raises/promotions/proposals/requests (see REFUSALS)
- requests: raise/promotion/project approval/interview/meeting (see REQUESTS)
- resignations
- résumés and letters of application (see RÉSUMÉS)
- retirement (see also ACKNOWLEDGMENTS, ANNOUNCEMENTS, CONGRATULATIONS, INVITATIONS)
- terminations

How to Say It

□   When writing a cover letter to accompany your résumé, be brief, descriptive, and dynamic. Include: expression of your interest in the company or job; list of what you are enclosing; why you think you are suited for the job and what you can do for the company; expression of appreciation of the company (this is most effective if you specify what you like).

□   When you cannot make an immediate decision among applicants, write to each person acknowledging the receipt of their application or résumé or thanking them for their interview. Tell them you will need some time to make a decision but will let them know as soon as you do. (If you have some idea of how long this will take, say so.) Thank them for their interest in your organization.

□   When turning down an applicant for a position, include: your thanks for the person's application; a simple statement saying that you are unable to offer the person the position; if necessary or helpful, an explanation of the decision; positive comments on the person's credentials, abilities, interview, résumé; if applicable, an invitation to reapply at some later time; your good wishes for success in the person's search for a suitable position. Some companies do not bother notifying a job-seeker when their application has not been successful. However, it is courteous as well as good public relations to write a brief, tactful letter.

□   When writing to tell a job applicant that they are being offered the job, include: a congratulatory remark about being chosen and something complimentary about their credentials, experience, or interview; information about the job—duties, salary, supervisor's name, starting date; the name and telephone number of someone who can answer further questions; an expression of goodwill about the person's employment with the company. You may want to insert some positive remarks about the company to influence the person's decision to accept the offer.

□   When announcing changes in company policies, procedures, or regulations, include: a description of the new policy; a reference to the old policy,
if necessary for clarification; a brief reason for the change; expected outcomes of the change (benefits); the deadline for the change implementation;
instructions or enclosures that amplify on the change; the name of a person,
along with the telephone extension number, who can answer questions or
help with problems; an expression of your enthusiasm about the change.

□   In most organizations, raises are given in certain regulated ways, and
each company has its own evaluation process. However, if you should have to
write a letter asking for a raise, be brief and factual, supplying as much
supporting material (letters of commendation, patents, research papers,
sales records, evaluations, awards) as you can. Although in some companies
raises are more or less expected at certain intervals, nobody ever has a
"right" to a raise; do not let this attitude color your letter. Avoid threatening
to leave unless you really mean it. Do not compare your salary to others';
management does not appreciate employees who compare salaries, and they
may become defensive. Instead, show how your work has become more valuable to the company or speak of an "adjustment" to reflect additional hours,
duties, or productivity.

□   Notifying employees of layoffs or terminations has become fairly codified, partly because of labor unions, partly because of legal ramifications,
and partly because it is most efficient for large organizations to follow a
uniform manner of dealing with them. The standard government form commonly known as "the pink slip" is used in many cases. When a letter is
written, it is usually brief. In some situations a letter could include: a statement about the layoff or termination; an expression of regret at the necessity
of taking this measure; the date at which the layoff or termination becomes
effective; in the case of a layoff, the possible length of the time, if known;
details on company layoff and termination policies, career counseling, letters of recommendation, available public assistance, and any other information that will help the employee cope with the layoff or termination; the
name and telephone number of someone who can answer further questions.

□   When you resign from a company or organization, a verbal resignation
may be all that is necessary. Generally, however, it is useful for both employer and employee to have a written record of the resignation. The common practice is to resign in person, and then to follow up with a letter.
Begin by writing something positive or complimentary about the position,
company, or organization you are leaving. State that you will be resigning,
effective as of a specific date. In most cases, give a reason for resigning:
poor health or work-related health problems; age; greater opportunities for
advancement, higher salary or more desirable location with another company; someone in the family is being transferred; wish to change careers;
recent changes that have affected your position. If you are leaving because

of problems with management, co-workers, restrictive company policies, or other negative reasons, be vague: "For personal reasons, I am resigning effective March 1." You may want to offer to help find or train your replacement if this is a problem for the company and you are leaving in a friendly spirit. End on a pleasant note, expressing appreciation for what you have learned, for your co-workers, for being associated with such a dynamic company, for being part of a new development. In some situations, you can write a one-sentence letter of resignation, giving no explanation.

□   In accepting a letter of resignation, include a statement of acceptance "with regret," some positive comments on the person's association with your organization, and an expression of good wishes for the person's future.

What Not to Say

□   In our highly litigious society, you will want to avoid anything in your letter to employees or prospective employees that could be considered actionable. Common sense will provide a certain amount of guidance, but in any questionable instance, you should consult with your attorney on the phrasing of your most sensitive letters (reprimands and terminations, for example).

□   There is little excuse for allowing negative emotions to appear in letters between employees and employers. Avoid expressions of anger, revenge, disdain, hurt feelings, irritation, condemnation. Where you find yourself overly involved emotionally, it may be best to have another person write the letter.

□   Do not use a letter of resignation as a dumping ground for complaints and anger. It is best to take your leave in a polite, dignified manner—even if the truth lies elsewhere. For one thing, you may need a letter of reference. For another, despite confidentiality, angry letters have a way of following you about in your professional community. Then, too, you can't tell when you might have dealings with the company in the future. If you are leaving because of illegal or dishonest practices, you will be more effective taking your complaints (with as much documentation as you can provide) to outside bureaus or agencies.

□   If you have been asked to resign or have been discharged, your letter should not refer to this. State simply that you are resigning, so that it appears that way in the official records.

Tips on Writing

□   Clarity is extremely important in employee-employer letters; many problems can be avoided when informal agreements and decisions are spelled out clearly.

□   Brevity is one of the great virtues today. The proliferation of paper on the average desk (even in the computer age) may be depressing, frightening, or irritating, depending on your temperament. People will appreciate your letters (and will respond to them more quickly) if they are brief and to the point.

Special Situations

□   Many managers and executives find it rewarding to write occasional letters to employees to create goodwill, build morale, and show that they are aware of what goes on throughout the department or company. Include in such letters: expression of your appreciation for good work; compliments on specific projects, campaigns, or successes; comments on how their work relates to the good of the company as a whole; a mention of your availability for discussion; a reference to future plans, meetings, or hopes.

□   When reprimanding an employee, include: a positive or complimentary remark to begin with; a factual description of the unacceptable employee behavior; if appropriate, how this came to the writer's attention; why it is considered unacceptable (if necessary to explain); how the employee can improve or change; if appropriate, the penalties for continuing this behavior; an expression of hope that the person will deal with the situation. A reprimand should be tactful, brief, and positive (instead of saying, "Do not make personal phone calls while patients are in the waiting room," say, "Please confine personal phone calls to times when the waiting room is empty." Your goal in writing a letter of reprimand is not to get revenge or blow off steam—it is to effect a change in employee behavior. The best way to do this is to be encouraging and respectful. Avoid condemning, belittling, haranguing, preaching, scolding, or patronizing the recipient of your letter.

Format

□   The bulk of in-house correspondence consists of memos. Only the more official communications (promotions and resignations, for example) or letters that will eventually go in people's files, are typed on letterhead stationery.

―――――――――――――――――――――― WORDS ――――――――――――――――――――――

achievement	cost-effective	industry
application	cutback	morale
capable	dependable	objectives
competent	effective	operation
conduct	goals	oversee

policies	regulations	training
position	seniority	transactions
procedure	skilled	vacancy
process	supervise	well-trained

---------------------------------- PHRASES ----------------------------------

accepted another position

after much deliberation

an opportunity has recently arisen

appreciate the opportunity of having worked

appreciate your wanting to join our

ask you to accept my resignation

cannot presently offer you any encouragement

cease operation

closing the plant

company cutbacks/merger

considered for the position of

due to economic conditions

effective immediately

eliminate certain positions

entry-level position

expect to fill the vacancy

financial problems/difficulties have forced/obliged us

have no other option but to

highly motivated

I regret having to tell you this, but

it is my sad duty to/with regret that I inform you that

must advise/inform you

not adding to/expanding our staffs at the moment

proposed termination date of

recent energy crunch

see no alternative

submit/tender my resignation

trainee position

under consideration

with great personal regret/great reluctance/mixed feelings

---------------------------------- SENTENCES ----------------------------------

A heartfelt "thank you" to all of you who put in so many hours of overtime to make sure the Derwent job got finished on time.

Although your credentials are impressive, we are offering the position to someone who also has the grain futures experience we were looking for.

At the suggestion of Don Rebura, I'm writing to ask for an interview to discuss employment in your marine research division.

Before you leave, please be sure that Personnel has your current address and phone number on file.

I am deeply concerned by this flouting of safety regulations.

I am seeking a responsible, challenging position with a major brokerage firm offering new opportunities for professional growth and success.

I am proud to be part of such a creative and enthusiastic team—I hope you are too.

I appreciate all the encouragement, support, and technical assistance I have received here.

If you hear of any openings in the company, I would certainly appreciate knowing about them.

I have received a complaint from Lucia Davidge about Sherman Pew.

I have seen your wonderfully creative and appealing display windows.

I'm looking forward to a long and challenging association with Willard Electronics.

I must insist that this dangerous situation be cleared up immediately.

I will be most happy to recommend you highly to potential employers.

I would like to offer my services to your organization.

On behalf of the management of Steenson Engineering, I am happy to inform you that you have been promoted to Senior Research Engineer, effective March 1.

Our decision in no way reflects on your considerable qualifications/many skills.

Please accept my resignation, effective today.

Thank you for applying for the position of commercial plant specialist with Calvert Tropical Plants.

Thank you for your letter/résumé/application, which we received today.

The award belongs to the whole department.

The position for which you have applied has already been filled.

This is to advise you that you are being laid off in compliance with Article XXXI, Section 6 of our current labor agreement.

This is to tender my resignation from Toddhunter Associates as Media Specialist effective April 1.

Unfortunately we are not able to offer you a position with Roehampton, Ltd. at this time.

We accept your resignation with regret, and wish you well in future endeavors.

We appreciate your interest in our company.

We are pleased to offer you the position as warehouse attendant for Landor Textiles.

We are sorry to see you leave.

We have been favorably impressed with your credentials.

We have received a number of responses to our advertisement, and we ask your patience while we evaluate them.

We hope to be able to consider you for another position very soon.

We hope you will be available for recall.

We'll be glad to provide a good reference.

We will keep your application on file in case we should have any openings in the near future.

We will let you know/contact you/notify you/be in touch with you/write or call you about the status of your application sometime before June 1.

Your resignation has been received, and will be effective immediately.

You've all worked very hard on this project, and it shows!

PARAGRAPHS

▷   We have received complaints that employee attempts to guard against receiving bad checks have become overly intrusive, hostile, and humiliating. Several customers have said they will not return to the store. While we encourage every effort to prevent the writing of bad checks, your actions must be tactful, courteous, and respectful. Please reread your employee handbook for specific acceptable measures and for suggested phrases and actions for handling this situation.

▷   As I explained yesterday, I am obliged to resign my position with the Van Eyck Company because of ill health. I appreciate the good employer-employee relationship we have enjoyed over the years and will be watching the company's growth with much interest. If I can be of any assistance to my successor, I will be glad to help out.

▷   This is just a note to tell you that I met someone who thinks just like you do and who may be helpful with your present work. Why don't you give Jock Larne a call at 555-1988?

▷   It is with much regret that we advise you that we are unable to continue your employment after September 1. As you are no doubt aware, the company is experiencing severe—but temporary, we hope—difficulties. We believe that this layoff will also be temporary, although for the moment it is not possible to promise anything. In the meantime, please check with Personnel for information on letters of reference, company layoff policies, public assistance available to you until you find other employment, and career counseling.

▷   We have carefully considered your letter of application, résumé, and portfolio, and have been most favorably impressed. Please call the Human Resources Office at 555-6790 to arrange an interview with Enoch Emery, the Art Director.

▷   We are sorry to announce that Jeanne Beroldy has resigned from the firm effective July 1. She has accepted the position of Managing Director with Christie Packaging Corp. Although we will miss her, we wish her every success in her exciting new position.

▷   We are seeing more and more travel expenses turned in after the fact, whereas company policy states that all travel expenses should be preapproved. If you have any questions about how to handle travel expenses, talk to Michael Lambourne in Personnel, extension 310.

▷   Because of several complaints we have received lately, I thought it might be worthwhile to remind all employees that their job is to solve problems causing customer complaints, not aggravate them. I ask that you do not debate with customers, do not blame them (even when they may be at fault), and do not make excuses for us if we don't really deserve them. Let the customer know that you take their problems very much to heart and that you are prepared to do whatever you can to solve them. In the rare case when a customer remains unhappy and belligerent, refer them to me. Tactfully suggesting that they take their business elsewhere is one option I might have. But this is my option—not anyone else's.

▷   Veronica Roderick has left Wain International to pursue other business interests. Associate Director for the past three years, she will be replaced by Itzik Landsman, currently Assistant Director, effective October 16.

▷   Last month, we lost $3,780 worth of clothing to shoplifters. There is an informational seminar on shoplifting scheduled for June 16 at 3:00 p.m. In the meantime, we ask all employees to be especially vigilant.

▷   It is with regret that we accept your resignation, effective March 1. You have been one of the company's strongest assets for the past five years. Please accept our best wishes in your new position.

————————————————— SAMPLE LETTERS —————————————————

Dear Mr. Karkeek:

Thank you for submitting your recent letter and résumé concerning employment with our firm.

You have an interesting background. However, we feel your qualifications and experience do not match the needs of the account executive/trainee position presently available in our Chicago office.

We take this opportunity to thank you very much for your interest in Lessways International and to wish you much success in the attainment of your career objectives.

                                                    Sincerely yours,

. . . .

Dear Ms. Moncada:

As you know, I just celebrated five years with Tresham Paper Products. In that time, I have been challenged and stimulated by my work, supported by co-workers, and encouraged by management. I have very much enjoyed being a part of the Tresham team.

However, the recent reorganization has changed things considerably for me, and I question whether the next five years will be as fruitful for me as the last five, or whether I will continue to be as useful to the company in my new situation. Because of this, I am accepting a position with Walter & Co., Inc., where I am assured of opportunities for advancement as well as exceptional laboratory support.

Please accept my resignation, effective November 1, along with my appreciation for a satisfying and rewarding five years.

                                                    Sincerely,

. . . .

TO: All Employees
FROM: Lawrence Mont, Head Librarian
DATE: August 14, 1992
RE: Library usage

Some of you have expressed your frustration and irritation with the company library over the past six months. There are not enough carrels, there are usually long lines waiting for assistance from the librarian and for use of the computer card catalogs, and often the books you want are not available.

To resolve these problems, the library is adopting one rule change and is asking you to implement a usage change.

As of September 1, all library books will be due back in the library one month from the checkout date (the previous loan period was two months). For the first several months, we will be calling this change to your attention as you check out books.

To avoid crowded conditions, we suggest you use the library during off-peak hours. You should have no trouble getting help and using the card catalogs during the following periods: 8:00 a.m. to 10:00 a.m.; 3:00 p.m. to 5:30 p.m. The hours between 10:00 a.m. and 3:00 p.m. are our busiest times. We suggest that only those who absolutely cannot come earlier or later use these hours.

We always appreciate hearing your comments on the library—let us know how you think this is working out.

· · · · · · · · · · · ·

Dear Elizabeth Firminger,
Thank you for applying for the position of insurance adjustor with the Raybrook Adjusting Service. Your work history is outstanding, and you made a very good impression at your interview. As you know, however, we were looking for someone with experience in the inland marine area, and we did find a candidate with that qualification.

We very much appreciate your interest in our company, and would like to suggest that you reapply to us in six months when we expect to have several other positions open. We will keep your application on file until then.

It is clear that you will be an asset to the company that eventually hires you—good luck in finding the right place.
Sincerely,

· · · · · · · · · · · ·

TO: Dr. Betti Lancoch
FROM: Caradoc Evans
DATE: February 3, 1992
RE: Biodegradable plastics technology

As you are aware, we continue to be highly interested in your biodegradable plastics technology. It appears to be the cornerstone for several new products. I understand that you are pursuing patents for this technology. We would like to see your patent applications filed by May 1, 1992, so that we could initiate customer contact to clarify performance criteria for several of the products.

This note should serve to restate our need for your technology along with appropriate patent protection. Should you require additional support, please don't hesitate to call.

· · · · · · · · · · · ·

Dear Marguerite Lambert,
Thank you for your application for the position of litho stripper, your résumé, and your work samples. They are currently being carefully considered by our Human Resources Department.

We received a number of other applications, so it may be three or four weeks before we are able to make a decision. You will be notified either way as soon as we do.

Thank you for your interest in Greatheart Printing Company, Inc.
Sincerely yours,

· · · · · · · · · · · ·

Dear Marcus,
As you are no doubt aware, I recently received a raise, and I am of course grateful not only to have a job that I enjoy so much but to be appreciated in this very practical way.

However, I am not sure how the raise was determined. As I look back over my five years here, I see a fairly quick rise from the position I originally accepted (word processor) to my current position as department manager. All performance reviews have been particularly favorable, including the last one. Despite these outstanding reviews, and three successive promotions within the last two years, my recent raise was just 1.5% above the company average.

As my immediate supervisor, you are perhaps in the best position to tell me (1) if this is consistent with policy throughout the company—that is, if I perhaps really didn't "deserve" a larger raise; (2) if there is something I should be doing to let others know my achievements, qualifications, and general worth.

If you have time to discuss this in the next couple of days, I'd be grateful for your time.

Sincerely,

See also: ANNOUNCEMENTS, APPOINTMENTS, CONGRATULATIONS, REFERENCES, RÉSUMÉS, WELCOME.

19

Letters to Family and Friends

"Why it should be such an effort to write to the people
one loves I can't imagine. It's none at all to write to those
who don't really count." (Katherine Mansfield)

Letters to family and friends are informal, conversational, cheerful, newsy—and rare. Personal mail—letters plus holiday and greeting cards—makes up only about 6% of the total mail moved today. Steve Sikora, founder of LEX, The Letter Exchange, says that the decline of the personal letter has meant the near elimination of nonprofessional writers. He divides literature into three categories: writing not meant to be shown to anyone, such as a diary or journal; writing meant for publication, or "public literature"; and personal letters, which he says constitute the people's literature.

Electronic mail and phone calls (more than 40 billion long-distance phone calls per year) appear to have largely replaced letterwriting.

Jeanne O'Neill, media relations officer for the U.S. Postal Service points out, however, that "the beauty of the letter is that it can be read and re-read. It's a very personal communication. People seem to have more freedom expressing themselves in a letter. Also, they are improving their writing ability and creating a lasting record. Our history has been brilliantly illuminated by letters."

Letters to Family and Friends Include

- annual form letters (see SEASONAL GREETINGS)
- correspondence with out-of-town friends and relatives
- family "business": letters to camps/schools
- letters to young people: birthdays/congratulations on an achievement/away from home
- love letters
- notes and short letters to in-town friends and relatives
- pen pals

- special-event letters (see CONGRATULATIONS, SEASONAL GREETINGS, SYMPATHY, WEDDINGS)
- welcoming prospective or new in-laws

How to Say It

□ Talk about everyday happenings—whatever you've been doing lately.

□ Describe movies, books, plays you've seen or read recently.

□ Relate news of other family members or friends you have in common.

□ Tell future plans, events, travel.

□ Include anecdotes, jokes, and quotations that have caught your eye.

□ Give your opinion on current events that are particularly interesting or frustrating to you.

□ Discuss hobbies, collections, or interests you have in common with your correspondent.

□ Tell about sports events that you have either participated in or attended.

□ Give news of pets.

□ Offer some ideas—whatever you've been thinking about lately.

□ Talk about the seasons, the weather—what nature is doing in your backyard.

What Not to Say

□ Do not begin with "I don't know why I'm writing, because I really don't have anything to say," or "You know how I hate writing letters." Also avoid starting off with an apology for not having written sooner. Begin instead with something cheerful, positive, and interesting.

□ Do not end with "I've bored you long enough" or "I'd better quit before you fall asleep." Instead, say how much you'd enjoy hearing from them when time allows or how much you miss them or, again, how happy you are about their news.

□ Mark Van Doren said, "The letter which merely answers another letter is no letter at all." And Sigmund Freud said, "I consider it a good rule for letter writing to leave unmentioned what the recipient already knows, and instead tell . . . something new." Don't spend too much time responding to news from your correspondent ("The new car sounds great." "Your party sounded like a lot of fun." "I'll bet you were proud of him."). Instead, write about happenings from your own life, news of family or friends, discussions of ideas.

□   In general, avoid complaining (unless you can do it entertainingly) and detailing personal problems.

□   In writing to children avoid the use of the word "kid(s)." ("I'm so proud of you kids!" "Do kids still live on pizza? Here's a certificate good for a free one.") Many young people dislike such labels as: children, teens, teenagers, minors, adolescents, juveniles, youngsters, tykes, youths, and kids. If possible, avoid any label at all; if you must use one, try young person (up to perhaps age 17) or young adult (ages 18+).

□   Avoid writing down to young people. It is one thing to use simple sentences and vocabulary, but quite another to be condescending. Reread your letter as though someone were sending it to you or to some adult you know. Except for the reading level, does it sound okay?

□   When a child is away from home for a week or more for the first time, it is best to avoid telling them how much they are missed. You may say this lightly (perhaps a "We miss you!" at the end), but do not go into detail about how empty the house seems. Some children take these things very seriously and even feel responsible for their parents' feelings. It is also better to avoid detailing what everybody at home is doing; that too can make them sad. Instead, ask questions that will give them something to write back about: What time do you get up? What do you usually eat for breakfast? Do you have a swimming class? Who else lives in your cabin? Are there any animals there? Have you been in a canoe yet? What is your favorite activity? Who is your counselor? Have you made new friends? Who?

□   When writing to young people, avoid lecturing or trying to teach a lesson. It's not certain why preaching so often creeps into these letters, but it's not usually a pretty thing.

Tips on Writing

□   Adopt a cheerful, positive tone—unless, of course, you or your reader have been going through sad times. Check your letter for words like *don't, haven't, can't, won't* or words like *awful, terrible, bad, hard, difficult.* Are they all necessary?

□   Most people enjoy receiving cartoons, interesting clippings from the newspaper, snapshots, or other enclosures that reflect their interests.

□   Everyone likes a "newsy" letter—a potpourri of topics, from responses to your reader's last letter to happenings in your life to reflections on current events, books, movies, ideas. Choose items that your reader is interested in and make references to feelings and activities you have in common.

□   Remember your creative writing teacher's advice to "Elaborate! Elaborate!" Instead of merely reporting that you went camping, elaborate on the theme. Almost any sentence lends itself to some kind of elaboration, and that's usually the kind of detailed writing that's enjoyable to read.

□ Write about ideas that are important to you, opinions you hold, your reaction to current events. D. H. Lawrence said, "I love people who can write reams and reams about themselves: it seems generous."

□ When dealing with strong feelings, letters can be very effective because they distance people from each other and from the problem while obliging them to think through their thoughts enough to get them down in some reasonable order on paper. However, letters can also worsen the problem. Written words are not as easily forgotten as words spoken in the heat of anger; they can also be reread many times by a grudge-holder. Words without accompanying gestures, smiles, and apologetic looks are colder and more inflexible. Three cautions will help: think very carefully about the temperament of the person you are writing and determine an approach that the person will be able to "hear"; do not write in the heat of your strongest feelings—that is, it is good to write then, but do not *mail* it; reread and rewrite your letter several times over a period of days.

□ When writing to children include a stimulating, challenging, or curious statement. If you've just heard a bit of trivia, or if you have a thought problem, word puzzle, anecdote, or interesting story, tell it. Share your thoughts, discuss ideas, ask questions. Too often adults underestimate children, who enjoy being let into the adult world. Tell them about something that is important to you—an issue, a job problem, your garden.

□ Young people would rather be doing lots of things than writing letters. It is helpful to enclose with your letter several postcards or a self-addressed envelope with an unattached stamp (so that the stamp isn't wasted in case they don't write back). Construct a humorous letter for the child to return to you that consists of boxes to check off with various made-up statements and "news." This technique will probably net you a letter at least once.

□ Very young children appreciate mail even if they are unable to read. When you write remember that a parent will be reading it aloud; things sound different that way. You can include a colorful drawing or cut-out picture along with their name (which many youngsters recognize early on) and a small picture of you. Tuck in a balloon or fancy pencil or small toy, depending on what is appropriate for the child's age.

Special Situations

□ If you would like to exchange letters with people who share your interests, contact Steve Sikora, The Letter Exchange, P.O. Box 6218, Albany, CA 94706, for a description of how his popular and effective system works. International Pen Friends, based in Dublin, Ireland, has members of all ages; for information, send a self-addressed stamped envelope to: International

Pen Friends, Box 290065, Brooklyn, NY 11229-0001. Young people (ages 12 through 20) who want to write a foreign pen pal can contact: World Pen Pals, International Institute of Minnesota, 1690 Como Avenue, St. Paul, MN 55108. Also for young letterwriters are: The Student Letter Exchange, Box 2465, Grand Central Station, New York, NY 10163, and The International Friendship League, 55 Mount Vernon Street, Boston, MA 02108. Some organizations charge fees; ask for information.

□   When the families of an engaged couple do not know each other, there is often an exchange of letters expressing pleasure in the engagement of their son and daughter and perhaps arranging a visit. Although today many families meet each other for the first time at the wedding, it used to be that the man's mother was expected to write the woman's mother first, say how pleased she was, and suggest a visit. Today, either family may write first, and visits between the families of origin are often not even considered. Instead, many engaged couples will go together to visit first one family, then the other, arrangements being made by the son or daughter of the house with their parents. A courteous and graceful gesture is a note written before the visit by the prospective son- or daughter-in-law expressing appreciation for the invitation and pleasure in the forthcoming visit.

□   There are no general rules for writing love letters. Keeping the other person in mind as you write will help you imagine what they are thinking, feeling, and doing. In theory at least there should be more "you"s than "I"s in a love letter, but given the high interest of the reader in everything the writer says or does, there are few complaints of excessive self-revelation. Sincerity, simplicity, and directness are to be prized; the reader should be left in no doubt about their place in the writer's affections. If you're sending a series of love letters, you might include a new "why I love you" reason in each one. Recalling time spent together and planning for the future are time-honored ways of filling the page.

□   With so many people traveling today, it's likely that you will write "Bon voyage" notes to friends and relatives or send postcards and letters back home from your own trips. To prepare to write memorable cards and letters yourself, read Rudyard Kipling's *Letters of Travel*, Pierre Teilhard de Chardin's *Letters from a Traveller*, John Steinbeck's *A Russian Journal*, Michael Crichton's *Travels*. From Phillip Brooks' 1893 *Letters of Travel* to Joanne Sandstrom's 1983 *There and Back Again*, you'll find letters to inspire and entertain.

Format

□   Letters to family and friends can use any format you like. Acquaintances are a little different. The less well you know a person, the more formal the letter or note will be.

▫   Postcards are wonderful for keeping in touch with people you love when you haven't time for a letter. Keep a stack of colorful, funny, or oldtime postcards near your letterwriting area. Getting in the habit of sending off a couple a week will make you very popular and will relieve you of much of the guilt that a stack of unanswered mail produces in most people.

▫   Printed or typed letters to children are especially welcome as they are easier to read.

WORDS

activities	funny	pleased
affectionately	goings-on	proud
busy	happy	satisfying
events	healthy	vacation
friendship	news	weather

PHRASES

a warm hello	missing you
did I tell you that	remember the time
did you hear the one about	sorry to hear
did you know	such a good neighbor
did you see the movie/TV show	sympathize with
have you ever thought about	thinking of you
have you heard	we were so happy to hear that
how did you manage to	we wondered if
I enjoyed hearing about	what did you think of
I meant to tell you	whatever happened to
in your last letter you didn't mention	what would you say to
I sure hope that by now	when are you going to
I thought you might like to know	your mother/father says that you

SENTENCES

Are you planning to travel this summer?
Do write when you get a chance.
Friends like you are so special.
Have I told you lately that I love you?
Have you read any good books lately?
How are you?
How was Mexico?

I can't tell you how much I appreciated your letter.

If only I wrote as often as I thought about you!

I'll be counting the minutes till I see you.

I look forward to hearing from you.

I'm wondering how your open house turned out.

I think of you every day/so often.

I treasure the times we share.

It's been too long since I've written.

I was so glad to see your handwriting again.

Please write and tell me all the news.

So much has happened since the last time I wrote you.

Time seems to creep by when you're away.

We'd love to see pictures of the new house.

We thoroughly enjoy your letters—you can't write often enough for us.

What a dear letter!

What do you think of the new mayor?

What's new?

When will Martin graduate?

You're in my thoughts every minute of the day.

Your friendship is a special treasure.

Your last letter was priceless/delightful/a pleasure to receive.

Your letters always brighten my day.

Your letter was such fun to read—thanks!

———————————— PARAGRAPHS ————————————

▷   My daughter is very interested in attending Camp Goodwin. Enclosed please find a completed application form, a signed health certificate, and the registration fee of $75. Also enclosed is a postage-paid postcard addressed to Becky, as she would appreciate hearing from you as soon as her application is approved. Thank you.

▷   Just imagine me here in sunny Southern California, where it's been hovering in the 80s with beautiful pink sunsets and snow-covered mountains floating on the horizon. People here are already pulling out their beachwear and heading seaward for some ultraviolet rays and premature wrinkles. Those who aren't beach-bound have turned to the east and north where huge, crowded, snow-covered slopes await them. I went skiing a couple of weekends ago with some friends and had an absolutely giddy time.

▷   I can hardly wait for summer to get here. What's that you say? Summer has come and gone? The kids are back in school? But . . . but . . . Get my drift? I really don't know where the time goes.

▷   Sydney is the most beautiful city I've ever seen—and perhaps the most polyglot. We hear everything from Japanese to Italian to who knows what. The physical setting is breathtaking: the bay is surrounded by many small coves and inlets, complete with sandy beaches and cliffs. Backing these are white and brick buildings with red tile roofs. We stop often at a little place right on Sydney Cover, near Circular Quay where all the ferries dock and just a short distance from the Opera House. We order a couple of middies of Cooper's ale, a dozen Sydney rock oysters, and some smoked trout pâté. Sound good?

▷   Please say hello to everyone and tell Audrey thanks again for taking us out. We had a great time! Your family is so warm and fun to be around—so much energy and self-assurance! I miss you all!

▷   Will wonders never cease? Hannah is finally sprouting some teeth—believe it or not. I mean she's only seventeen months old! I was beginning to wonder if kids need teeth to get into first grade. Well, those teeth may have been slow in coming but at least they brought out the monster in her for four months. Actually she's been pretty good considering how sore her mouth must be.

▷   Bon voyage! No one could be happier or more excited for you than we are. We know how long you've planned for this trip. Say hello for us to the Eiffel Tower, the Coliseum, and anything else you think we'd be interested in. And don't forget to send us a postcard, even if you get home before it does! We'll look forward to hearing all about it when you return.

▷   This evening I'm having my first interview with a private adoption agency—at home, in my natural habitat. Next week I start paying them money and attend a two-day workshop. Then the following week there's another two-day workshop, then more interviews—all this to complete a home study. After that the search begins and could take anywhere from one day to eighteen months. It makes me nervous in the service because it's such a big step, but I think I'm ready for it.

▷   I'm sorry about this one-size-fits-all letter, but my negligence in corresponding with all of you finally got so oppressive that I had to take immediate steps. These immediate steps have taken me almost three weeks. Meanwhile, my brand-new personal computer was crying out, "Use me! Use me!" Then . . . Poof! Voilà Eureka! Hoover! . . . this letter was conceived and executed.

▷   I can't believe how long it's been since I've written you. I know I put that in every letter I send you. I should just order some stationery with "I can't believe how long it's been" printed on top. David, your letter was, among other things, an inspiration to me that a person *can* pull out of even the deepest letterwriting slump. I thought, "By golly, if he can do it, so can I!"

▷   Last weekend, Marv and I, our friend Bill, and his son Todd went to western Upper Peninsula to a remote place called Sylvania where everybody uses canoes, and there are restrictions on camping and fishing. You have to release all but one fish a day, and it has to be bigger than what the regular State conservation rules call for. How I loved that trip! We talked to the horned owls at night, and I almost stepped on a nesting loon. Later we watched it dance. We saw eagles nesting and tame baby ducks doing their thing while the mama waited. I walked along the shore with a flock of them, and they didn't seem in the least disturbed by me. A merganser almost hit my line while I was casting.

▷   Greetings! I usually can get as far as "Greetings!" but then I stall out. You'll never know how many intended letters never get past that stage. This one is unusual because I actually found it again, and didn't have to start totally from scratch.

▷   We spent the night camped at a remote campground in Badlands National Park. The stars were stunning, and there were buffalo everywhere—we had to drive through a herd to get to our campsite. Right now we're in Wall Drug eating breakfast. I really wish you were here with us.

_____ SAMPLE LETTERS _____

Dear Angela and Tom,

Parlez-vous français? That means "Sorry I haven't written lately." It all started when I ran out of lined paper at my office. I hate trying to write on this blank stuff, it's like trying to drive on a snow-covered road, only a little safer.

So how's the world treating you these days? We are winding down from another busy summer and hoping for a beautiful and serene fall. Whoever coined the phrase "lazy days of summer" ought to have their vital signs checked. I mean, who are we kidding here?

Both Kalli and Lauren are taking a gymnastics class, so we spend a lot of after-dinner time in the yard practicing what they are learning, with me as their "equipment." But it's fun, at least until the mosquitoes begin setting up their derricks.

I had a busy summer at the office, but September is slow as usual. The kids are back in school, the farmers are busy, and bow hunting season is here. It's actually a nice pace although hard on the budget. I think I would enjoy dentistry a lot more if I didn't have to make money at it.

I'm manager of our softball team this season. It's one of those things that doesn't sound like much, and shouldn't be, but *is*. I'd rate it about a 9.8 on the headache scale (of 10). We are winning at 11-3 and tied for first in our twelve-team league, but, honestly, the manager has nothing to do with that. Now if we were losing, *then* it would be my fault. The hardest part is collecting money from people for various things and making a lot of phone calls.

Well, that's all for now. Say hello to the kids for me.

With love,

. . . .

Dear Alice,

And how is my favorite aunt? Your letter came the other day and it was one of the nicest I've gotten in a long time. It was great seeing you over Christmas break.

Baseball is now in full swing (get it?), and we're running sprints every morning by 6:00 a.m. By 10:00 we're hitting off the machine. I can't wait for the weather to clear up so we can go outside to do all this.

Tell everybody "Hi" for me, and if Liz has any questions about college, she can write me. I can't answer them all but tell her the first quarter of the first year is the toughest, and it's all downhill after that!

Love,

. . . .

Dear Mrs. K.,

It was so nice to hear from you. I wish we could have had a longer visit at Easter. This semester has gone by so quickly—there are only three weeks left. Maybe we can get together when I come home for the summer.

I know you don't watch TV, so I'll tell you what Oprah Winfrey said. The average cost of a wedding is $13,000. Can you believe that? Mom tried to break the news to Daddy. He guessed the average wedding cost was $700 to $1,000. Poor Daddy.

Because there *is* going to be a wedding! We think next year. Can you believe I've written a whole page and haven't mentioned the love of my life? Jeff is fine, and sends his love too.

With a hug,

. . . .

Dear Lettie,

We recently became the proud and confused owners of a personal computer, and you are about to sample our first efforts.

We all enjoyed your last letter, and have taped the cartoons up on the refrigerator. Congratulations to Maria on her latest horseback riding award!

Somewhere I read that life, to a five-year-old, is full of alternatives. Tommy is forever asking, "Mommy, would you rather have me get eaten by an alligator, bonked on the head, or fall out of a skyscraper window?"

As usual we are crowding twelve months of living into the five months of decent weather we have evidently been allotted for our area.

I went bargain hunting at some rummage sales last weekend. I guess you could say I got my limit. The Lamberts were here for two days along with their little poodle, Muffy (French for "lint ball," isn't it?).

I bought a generic fruit punch that says one of its ingredients is "natural punch flavoring." What is a punch? I assume it grows on trees, and I'm guessing it needs a warm climate.

We're having a party Friday night—twenty-two people. It's been the best way I've discovered to get the spring cleaning done.

I wonder what Terry and Paul are going to name their baby. I'm guessing it's a boy—or maybe a girl.

This letter is more disjointed than most. I guess I don't try often enough to harness a thought, and now that I'm trying, my fingers are too weak to hold the reins. You like my metaphor? I ought to be a writer.

Give my love to everyone!

. . . .

Dear Alice,

Patrick has just told us that you two plan to marry, and I wanted to let you know right away how delighted we are. We've hoped for this for a long time, and I think you know how much we love you. We couldn't be happier!

We're still expecting you and Patrick over the Fourth—and we're saving a big hug for you until then.

With much love,

. . . .

Dear Christopher,

Congratulations on doing such a good job on your term paper. I read it through twice and learned so much. I'm not surprised you got an A + on it. I especially liked the way you paced yourself on this long drawn-out project. I remember you starting your note cards back in February, and then worked on it steadily all spring. I'm impressed!

Love,
Mom

See also: ADVICE, APOLOGIES, CONGRATULATIONS, "GET WELL," SEASONAL GREETINGS, SYMPATHY, THANK YOU.

20

Follow-Up Letters

A follow-up letter refers to an earlier letter, conversation, or meeting and is a graceful way of tying up a loose end, reminding someone to carry through on a promised action, building on something that went before, or spreading goodwill.

Letitia Baldridge, the New York writer of etiquette books and former White House social secretary, encourages following up meetings and lunches with letters. "This little personal touch, which takes three minutes, makes an enormous impression," she says. "The ones who do it regularly in business are such standouts. They're the ones who jump ahead."

Write a Follow-Up Letter When

- You have not had a response to a letter of yours and you need to remind someone that you are waiting for answers, information, confirmation, or merchandise.
- Your telephone messages have not been returned.
- You wish to sum up what was accomplished in a meeting or interview so that there is a record and so that your estimate of what went on can be verified by others.
- You need to confirm a meeting date, a telephone or other oral agreement, a message left with a third party.
- You wish to remind someone of an appointment, meeting, favor, request, inquiry, invitation, payment, or work deadline.
- A sales letter or product literature has not produced a response.
- A gift you sent has not been acknowledged and you want to know whether it arrived.

- You have visited a school, university, or college as a prospective student, or have attended a meeting as a guest and potential member, and wish to express your appreciation and impressions.

- Someone has visited your school, university, college, or organization as an applicant and you wish to express appreciation and the hopes that they are interested.

- You want to send omitted or supplemental material or to revise an earlier correspondence.

- Your initial sales letter brings a response (order, expression of interest, request for more information) and you want to amplify the material in your first letter, encourage the customer to order or to buy again, and to keep in touch with the customer for goodwill reasons.

- You want to follow up on a sales call or demonstration.

- You want to verify with a customer that a shipping problem or missing order has been settled to their satisfaction.

- After business lunches, dinners, meetings, or other hospitality you want to express appreciation and acknowledge what was accomplished.

How to Say It

☐   In a general follow-up letter, refer to the key idea (the meeting, your last letter, the unacknowledged gift) and mention the reason for writing the present letter ("as I hadn't heard from you" or "I wanted to remind you"). If you are asking your reader to do something, say so clearly ("Please telephone me," "Let me know if it arrived," or "Send your payment now").

☐   When following up a telephone call or face-to-face conversation, begin by referring to your meeting or telephone visit. Recap the conversation, repeating accurately the details of your talk: what decision was made, dates, times, quantities, plans, costs, people involved, and so forth. Ask the person to verify that this was the substance of your discussion. State what you expect next of the other person. Express appreciation for their interest or pleasure in the forthcoming meeting.

☐   When you must write a follow-up letter to an unanswered request, query, or letter, repeat your original message (or include a copy of it). You may want to go into a little more detail this time on the need or importance of the person's response and what consequences for you or for the other person might arise from a failure to respond.

☐   When following up a sales presentation, your letter is primarily a good sales letter, but you also thank the person for the time and opportunity to explain your product or service and you emphasize the one or two features that the person seemed most taken with during your presentation. Express your appreciation of their business, office, plant as well as your pleasure in the possibility of doing business with them.

☐   When a meeting or event has been scheduled many months in advance, it's sometimes necessary to send follow-up notes reminding people. Repeat all the information along with a pleasant remark about hoping to see the person.

☐   When sending a follow-up letter to an unacknowledged statement or invoice, include the necessary information (amount, account number, date due, days past due) with a simple "a brief reminder" notice. This is often all it takes since some late payments are simple oversights. (If this letter brings no response, see COLLECTION.)

☐   After interviewing for a job, you will probably want to write a follow-up letter. It is important to send this before a decision has been reached; sometimes a good follow-up letter makes the difference in getting the job. State how much you enjoyed the interview, how much you would like the job (mention something specific about the job requirements or your experience), and that you would be glad to provide any additional information or references. If there were any misunderstandings or any points you failed to make clearly during the interview, you might redress the situation in this letter.

What Not to Say

☐   Avoid implying that your reader is thoughtless, negligent, forgetful, or impolite when writing about an unanswered letter or unacknowledged gift. There is always the possibility of mail going astray. Even if they have been lax in responding, they won't like you any better for pointing it out to them. Try to keep your irritation or frustration from showing.

☐   A follow-up letter should not be a simple repeat of an earlier communication (except in the case of confirming an oral agreement or discussion). It should have some specific (even if thin) excuse for being written—to confirm receipt of something, for example.

Tips on Writing

☐   Many offices maintain a tickler file. When a letter is sent (inviting someone to speak at the awards banquet, for example), a notation is made on the calendar to verify several weeks later that a response has been received. It is a good idea to indicate in this way when to write a follow-up letter for the letter you are mailing today. All letters that may need follow-ups can be kept together, arranged by the date when the follow-up should be sent.

□   When you receive no response to a sales letter and send a follow-up, you begin by referring to your previous letter ("I wrote you several weeks ago to tell you about . . ." or "Did you receive the certificate we sent you, good for . . . ?"). The rest of the letter is primarily a good sales letter but should emphasize a different benefit or aspect of your product or service than your first letter did. This letter should also be shorter or longer than the first and perhaps different in tone.

□   When a customer requests product information or literature, you fill the request and write a good sales cover letter to accompany the material. It is customary to write a follow-up letter several weeks later. Refer to the earlier letter, thank them for their interest, offer further information, and then either mention a representative who will call on them, give them an order blank with a first-order discount offer, urge them to call a toll-free number to order, or make some other action-oriented proposal.

□   Too often communication ceases once the customer has paid for the product or service. However, aggressive businesses will keep in touch with such customers, sending follow-up letters to see how things are working out, to inform customers of new product lines, to remind them that you appreciated their business in the past and hope to serve them again.

Special Situations

□   If you give a gift that is not acknowledged, a follow-up letter can be written eight weeks later. Because business gifts are often opened by staff rather than by the intended recipient and because wedding gifts can be misidentified, describe the item so that it can be traced. Avoid sounding accusatory or blaming.

□   Follow-up sales letters are written after a customer shows some interest (requests a brochure, stops by your booth at a trade fair, calls with a question, responds to an ad). You won't want to wait too long before writing the follow-up, or customers may lose interest. Although these can be called follow-up letters, they are primarily sales letters.

Format

□   Most business follow-up letters are typed on letterhead or memo stationery. Social letters or brief reminder-type notes can be handwritten.

□   Although not widely used, "to remind" cards can be sent to follow up a telephone invitation. Handwrite the information in regular invitation format on printed cards, foldovers, or personal stationery: "This is to remind you that Mr. and Mrs. Louis Rony expect you on . . ."

WORDS

acknowledge
confirm
feedback
inform
mention

message
notify
prompt
remember
reminder

reply
response
review
suggest

PHRASES

about a month ago, we sent you/wrote
  you about
according to your letter
a little reminder
am writing to remind/inform you that
appreciate your concern/business/
  thoughts of us/your interest in/your
  calling our attention to
as I have not heard from you
as I mentioned on the phone this
  morning
as mentioned in your letter
as we agreed yesterday
beginning to wonder if you received
call to mind
did you receive the
I am still interested in
if you wish further documentation on
I know how busy you are, so/and/but
in reference/reply/response to

I wrote you three weeks ago asking for
jog your memory
just a note to remind you
just a reminder of
just to remind you
make sure you're aware of
now that you've had the opportunity to
  consider/an opportunity to familiarize
  yourself with
prompt you to
put a string around your finger
refresh my/your memory
since then I've heard nothing and
since we have not heard from you
thank you for your letter telling us about
this brief reminder
thought you might like to be reminded
to let you know
we haven't heard from you, and

SENTENCES

Did you receive the Blake River catalog and discounted price list that you requested?
Have you had an opportunity of reviewing the materials we sent last month?
I am wondering if you received my telephone message last week.
I am writing to follow up on our conversation about the three-party agreement
  among Clara Hittaway, Amelia Fawn, and Georgiana Fawn.
I appreciate the time you gave me last week to demonstrate our unique Lammeter
  Integrated Phone Service System.
I enjoyed meeting you very much.
If you did not receive my materials, I would be happy to send you another set.
I haven't heard from you, which makes me wonder if my invitation ever reached you.

I look forward to hearing from you.

I'm grateful for the time you took to meet with me today to explain the laboratory technician job.

I'm wondering if you received my letter.

I wanted to follow up on our phone conversation of yesterday.

Just a note to remind you of the staff meeting (3:30 p.m. Thursday in the teachers' lounge).

Just a note to see if you received the message I left for you Friday.

Now that you have had a chance to tour the proposed site, I'd like to set a date to discuss our options.

Thank you for your inquiry/expression of interest.

PARAGRAPHS

▷   I was delighted to meet with you at your home and hear your thoughts about our community. The best part of running for the Bonville City Council is the opportunity to talk with neighbors like you about our future. Please call my office with your concerns, and remember to vote on November 7!

▷   I'm looking forward to having dinner with you Friday evening. I'll be waiting in the lobby of the Rosalba Hotel at 7:00 p.m. See you then!

▷   You may have mislaid our earlier letter notifying you that your subscription to *Evening* expires with the current issue. To avoid interrupting your subscription (and missing one of the fine series of articles on bat behavior), please send in the enclosed postage-paid reply card today.

▷   Several weeks ago we sent you a packet of informational materials on Topaz Island Resort. Now that you've had a chance to look over the color photographs of our unique vacation paradise, would you like to reserve vacation time in one of the ultra-modern cabins? Our spaces fill up quickly after the first of the year, so make your choice soon!

▷   Thank you for the courtesy and interest you showed me yesterday when I stopped in to inquire about the opening for a child care advocate. I didn't expect to do more than pick up an application form, so it was a pleasure being able to discuss the job with you. As you could probably tell from our conversation, I am very interested in the position and think I am qualified for it. I'll have my references and résumé in the mail to you by the end of the week.

SAMPLE LETTERS

TO: Johannes Rohn
FROM: Oren Cornell
DATE: February 10, 1993

We have not yet received your year-end report. I'm enclosing a copy of my original letter and another copy of the form. Please turn in the completed form as soon as possible. We now have all the evaluations but yours, and need to process them before the winter recess.

· · · · · · · · · · · ·

Dear Ms. Edelman:

On September 16, I wrote you in response to your classified ad for a career services specialist. I included a résumé, several references, and a cover letter.

As I have had no response, I am wondering if you received my materials. Enclosed is a self-addressed stamped postcard. Would you please indicate to me whether my materials were received by you and, if not, if you are still interested in seeing them?

Thank you.

Sincerely,

· · · · · · · · · · · ·

Dear Ms. Collen:

We hope you are as pleased with your Safe-Home Security System as we were pleased to install it for you. Do let us know if you experience any problems in these first few months. Very few of our customers do, but we're available if anything should come up.

You did not choose to purchase our Monthly Inspection Service at this time. However, if you change your mind, we can easily arrange it for you.

It was a pleasure doing business with you!

Sincerely yours,

· · · · · · · · · · · ·

Dear Mr. Ayrton,

Just a note to remind you that I still haven't received my copy of the Brodie contract. It's probably in the mail, but with December being such a busy month, I thought I'd mention it.

Sincerely,

· · · · · · · · · · · ·

Dear Julia Avery:

I'm wondering if you received my letter of January 14 asking you to speak at the Society of Professional Engineers meeting to be held May 3. We are still very interested in having you present your recent work to the group.

If you did not receive my letter or if you would like additional information, please call me collect at 612/555-6613. We expect to send the program to the printers by the end of the month.

Sincerely yours,

· · · · · · · · · · · ·

Dear Professor Fansler,

As one of the contributors to the *Handbook of English Studies*, you will want to know that there have been two changes: (1) the handbook is scheduled to appear in early December of this year, not in May, as previously planned; (2) it will be published in four volumes rather than two.

Many authors exceeded their space allocations, making a two-volume set unmanageable (it would have run nearly 1,300 pages per volume). Also, a smaller size per volume and thus a lower volume price will result in a larger sales potential (each volume is available individually).

All authors who contributed to the original volume will still receive complimentary copies of volumes I and II, and those who contributed to original volume II will receive both volumes III and IV as complimentary copies.

Sincerely,

See also: ACKNOWLEDGMENTS, APPRECIATION, RESPONSES, SALES, THANK YOU.

21

Fundraising Letters

> "What's a thousand dollars? Mere chicken feed.
> A poultry matter." (Groucho Marx)

Intense and growing competition for the charitable dollar means that your fundraising letter has to pack the maximum of persuasion and appeal in the minimum of words. In the average home mail delivery, fundraising appeals will outnumber every kind of letter except sales letters. How do you convince readers to set *your* letter aside for a contribution?

It helps if you are writing on behalf of a long-established, genuinely worthy organization with a history of compassion and effectiveness and a good reputation. All appeals are stronger when they can establish the organization's credibility. After that, however, your rate of return will depend on vigorous writing: dynamic verbs, intriguing anecdotes, striking metaphors, graphic statistics, irresistible appeals to heart and purse. One way of learning to write good fundraising letters is to study effective sales letters.

Fundraising Letters Include

- asking for volunteers to help fundraise
- follow-up letters after initial appeal (see FOLLOW-UP)
- invitations: benefits/balls/banquets/fundraising events
- requests for contributions
- responses to fundraising letters (see also ACCEPTANCES, REFUSALS, RESPONSES)
- thanks for contributing (see THANK YOU)

How to Say It

☐ Arouse the reader's interest with an attention-getting opening.

☐ Clearly identify the organization and its purpose: what it does and for whom.

▫   Establish the need and convince the reader it is real and urgent.

▫   Tell how the person's contribution will be used.

▫   Appeal to the heart by the use of anecdotes, quotations, descriptions.

▫   Appeal to the head by use of statistics and information.

▫   Explain what contributing will do for the reader (give personal satisfaction, offer a tax deduction, provide entry to a select group of givers).

▫   Establish the credibility of the organization and assure the reader that their contribution will be used effectively.

▫   Make it easy to give by including a postage-paid reply envelope or a toll-free number where contributions can be made by credit card.

What Not to Say

▫   Avoid asking questions or making statements such as "Please pause now and reflect on the impact of the United Community Fund in your household. If you feel the United Community Fund activities have a positive impact, consider writing a tax-deductible check." Build from one strong message to another, and do not interrupt your sequence to give the reader a chance to reflect, "argue back," or rationalize.

▫   Do not allow a subtly harassing or moralizing tone to creep into your letter. People who feel strongly about a cause often think others "should" contribute, and this attitude colors their letters. Givers do not respond well to being told they ought to give; they prefer to feel it is a free-will offering springing from their own best impulses.

Tips on Writing

▫   Use positive language and images instead of negative ones. For example, instead of describing how poorly off someone will be if your reader doesn't contribute, describe how the person's situation will be improved if the reader does contribute.

▫   Be specific—specific in your examples of need, specific in the request you are making, specific in stating how you intend to use the donation.

▫   Convey a sense of urgency. The reader must not only give, but give *now*. The letter that gets set aside to be dealt with later often doesn't get dealt with at all. Ask for an immediate response and include at least one good reason for doing so.

▫   Your message can be effectively presented in two parts. Your vision statement gives the reader a strong picture of what can be: a healthy, well-nourished child, a bustling community center, people with disabilities working at a variety of jobs. Your mission statement tells concretely what you plan to do, how you expect to arrive at the previously painted picture: statistics, numbers, budget, steps, plans. The first appeal is largely emotional and subjective, the second is factual and objective.

☐   Give people a reason for wanting to give: alleviate suffering, improve the community, better someone's prospects. In subtle ways you can let them know they will feel better if they give and that it will please you (and important people associated with the organization). Other appeals can be based on popular approval of your cause, the usefulness of a tax donation (particularly at the end of the year), or a tug at the heartstrings.

☐   To establish your organization's credibility, you may want to enclose an annual report or fact sheet telling what percentage of funds go for administrative costs, naming the public figures who support it, and excerpting commendations from civic groups. You should also have available for those who request it an audited financial report showing how much of the budget was devoted to each of the organization's principal expenditures, to overhead expenses, and to fundraising activities. A descriptive list of the board of directors, trustees, or other officials is also helpful.

☐   Some fundraising letters begin by asking for one thing from the reader (to sign a petition, call a legislator, vote on an issue, participate in a letter-writing campaign), and then later in the letter ask for a contribution as well.

☐   Adding a postscript (P.S.) to your letter is an effective attention-getting device because it is visually set off and in a position of emphasis. The postscript can urge the person to take action immediately, express appreciation for the person's help and interest, or add one more telling bit of information.

☐   Avoid using your charm, influence, or power to pressure friends and co-workers into giving to your favorite organization or supplying you with lists of possible contributors. Manipulation and high-pressure tactics may occasionally bring you a grudging one-time contribution, but they are hardly likely to do you any good in the long run. These efforts are often, in fact, counterproductive because they engender feelings of resentment, guilt, and discomfort. Most of us have a little of the rebel in us, and react poorly to coercion. We like to think it's our generosity and not your pressure that leads us to contribute.

☐   Your letter should be signed by the president or other high-ranking member of your organization or by a celebrity or public figure.

☐   You may want to design a series of letters, each with a different emphasis. In appealing to the same person, sometimes one approach will be more effective than others.

□   Personal letters of appeal on business letterhead are effective but questionable. They should be written only with the express approval of your employer.

□   When writing to ask someone to be part of a fundraising committee, spell out exactly what you expect of the person as well as a description of the fundraising efforts and the overall campaign goals (financial and publicity).

□   Establish a bond between you and your reader or between your organization and the reader ("As a parent/teacher/physician/American, you understand what it means to . . .").

Special Situations

□   Although not considered fundraising in the strict sense, organizations can often better their circumstances by writing letters to the editor to raise people's awareness of their concerns or by writing politicians, legislators, and public figures about issues that affect them (see EDITOR).

□   Responding to fundraising appeals does not often involve a letter, or even a comment from you; most organizations simply want your check, which you tuck into the provided envelope.

□   If you want to inquire about organizations that are asking you for a contribution, you can obtain up to three reports on individual agencies free on request by writing to: National Charities Information Bureau, 19 Union Square West, NY 10003-3395. (It is a nonprofit organization so please enclose a #10 self-addressed stamped envelope.)

□   When inviting people to benefits and fundraising events, use the appropriate invitation form (see INVITATIONS), but be clear about what is expected of those who accept ("$100 donation suggested" or "Tax-deductible contribution of $500 per couple suggested"). Your wording may be limited by the allowable meanings of "tax deductible" and "donation."

Format

□   The vast majority of fundraising letters today are form letters. Although one might not expect people to respond to a generic request, these letters do in fact bring in large sums for their organizations, and well written form letters are not only acceptable but effective. The audience you target with this form letter is important to your success, however. Direct mail solicitation will be much less effective than letters directed to members of specific groups.

───────────────────────────── WORDS ─────────────────────────────

advocate
aid
appeal
ask
assistance
auspices
backing
befriend
benefactor
benefit
bequest
charity
compassionate
contribution
cooperation
donate
donor
encourage

endow
essential
favor
foster
furnish
generous
gift
give
grant
grateful
help
humane
necessity
need
offer
participate
partnership

patronage
petition
philanthropic
promote
public-spirited
relief
request
rescue
share
solicit
sponsorship
subsidy
supply
support
tribute
unsparing
urgent

───────────────────────────── PHRASES ─────────────────────────────

a campaign to stop/protect/
    encourage/support
acquaint you with
act in concert
adopt the cause of
all pull together
all you have to do is
as generous as possible
as soon as you can
a two-pronged campaign
be good enough to
broad program of services
call upon you for
can bring comfort to those in need of
champion of
come to the aid of
consider carefully
continue our efforts
counting on your contribution
deserves your thoughtful consideration

direct your attention to
do a service for
financial backing
for the sake of
give assistance
good/guardian angel
have the goodness to
helping hand
help to shape the future
humanitarian interests
I am confident that we can
in order to provide the necessary
    funds
it can make all the difference for
join forces
make room in your heart for
make this possible
matter of necessity
on account/behalf of
our immediate needs are

please join your friends and neighbors
  in supporting
pressing need
rising costs
there are no funds presently available for
the time has never been better to/for
this program really works because
those less fortunate than you
very special cause/program/need
we are struggling to cope with a
  world-wide shortage of

welfare of others
we urgently need you to
with open hands
without your contribution
working together, we can
your contribution will enable
your donation will make it possible
  for
your past/unselfish generosity
your tax-deductible gift

_____ SENTENCES _____

Almost all the money we need to help preserve the Bradgate River Valley comes from
  people like you.

Any amount/contribution is most welcome/appreciated.

But without your help, it cannot be done.

Can I count on you to be part of this effort?

Do it now, please!

Funds are scarce.

Help us work for a solution to this most tragic human problem.

Here are just a few of our goals.

Here's how you can help.

If each family gave only $7.50 we could meet our goal of $5,000.

I know you receive appeals from many worthy groups—why is this one different?

I'll call you next week to see if you can help.

I'm writing to ask you to join our campaign.

I need your immediate help to make sure our legislation continues to progress despite a fierce lobbying campaign against it.

In order to take advantage of bulk prices, we need to raise $10,000 before May 1.

I promise not a dime of your contribution will be wasted.

It *can* be done!

I thank you from the bottom of my heart.

It is people like you who truly make the world a better place to live.

I want to thank you for your generous help so far and tell you about some of the
  developments you have supported.

I will truly appreciate whatever you can give, and I know these young scholars will
  too.

Join us today.

Last year, your contribution helped more than 3,000 students come closer to their
  dream of a liberal arts education.

Now, more than ever, your continued support is needed to help keep the doors open.

Of course, your donation is tax deductible.

Only by working together can we make a difference.

Our deadline for raising $50,000 is April 1—could you please send your gift by then?

Please be as generous as you can.

Please consider our request seriously.

Please encourage as many of your friends and neighbors as you can to call legislators, sign a petition, contribute funds.

Please mail your tax-deductible check in the enclosed postage-paid envelope.

Please respond quickly and generously.

Please take some time to read the enclosed brochure.

P.S. Please write your check and make your phone call today.

Thanks for whatever you can do.

The Cypros Food Shelf presently faces a crisis.

The people of Port Breedy are counting on you.

The Raybrook Foundation is at a financial crossroads this year and we critically need your generous giving to sustain the important work we've begun.

We are looking to people like you to help us provide the dollars we need to continue our hospice program.

We are most grateful for any support you can give us.

We depend on you to fund much of what we do.

We invite you to become part of the Annual Giving Campaign.

We look forward to hearing from you.

We need your help to get us through this special period of need following the fire.

We're determined to win this battle.

We try our very best to be efficient and cost-saving, but we still find ourselves losing the battle to inflation.

Whatever you decide to send, please send it today—the situation is urgent.

When you contribute to the Belknap Foundation, you invest in the future.

Won't you support the Outdoor Youth group in your town today?

You don't have to give until it hurts—just give until it feels good.

Your contribution now really does make a difference.

Your contribution will help us expand our resources and do a far more extensive job of protecting our vulnerable waters.

Your generosity to the Boyle County Library Fund will ensure not only that we can preserve existing books, manuscripts, and archives, but that we can continue to supplement the rising acquisitions budget for new books and periodicals.

Your generosity will be recognized in *The Anchor*, the monthly organization newsletter.

Your gift of $20 or more now will help the Animal Rights Fund.

Your telephone calls, letters, and checks have helped.

 PARAGRAPHS

▷   All quality nonprofit organizations need financial resources to help achieve their goals. The Argante Human Services Agency has three basic means of financial support: foundations and corporations; fee services (based on ability to pay); and individuals. Your contribution is, and always has been, critical to our success.

▷   Many alumni and friends have "shared the wealth" of their Jarrett education by contributing to the tuition aid fund. Some of these tax-deductible gifts have been given directly to the development office, while others have been donated in memory of a loved one. This funding is available for students who are unable to pay all the necessary tuition fees and is a very satisfying way of feeling that you have passed on some of what you have received.

▷   We've accomplished a great deal. But so much more must be done. To continue our work, we need help—urgently—from the people who care about the quality of life—people, I hope, like you who are willing to support us in this struggle. Think about it. Then think about taking out your checkbook and writing us the largest check you can.

▷   The purpose of this letter is to ask you to contribute to a fund that will be used to provide additional learning opportunities for our children. District budgets are limited and cannot cover many items we want our students to have. It is our goal to raise $3,000 to provide the items on the attached budget.

▷   You are cordially invited to the Holiday Open House, to be held Saturday evening December 12, from 7:00 p.m. to midnight, at the Bildad Mansion on Meville Avenue. This annual parish fundraiser is open to the public and will feature Victorian Christmas carols and refreshments, old-time vaudeville entertainment at 10:30 p.m., and "Christmas Carol" characters circulating all evening long. Join us for a delightful and unforgettable evening of holiday magic. The suggested donation of $20/person is tax-deductible.

▷   I'm asking you to do two things. First, write your congressional representatives and senators and tell them you want a change. Second, help us meet the rising costs of lobbying and publicizing this issue with a gift of $10, $25, $50, or more.

▷   Would you like to be able to support the Merton Children's Council for future generations with a single stroke of the pen? All you have to do is name the Merton Children's Council as beneficiary of a certain percentage of your new or existing life insurance policy. For example, if you have a $100,000 policy, you could give 99% ($99,000) to your spouse and children and 1% ($1,000) to the Merton Children's Council. Just arrange with your insurance agent or a member of your local chapter of underwriters to sign a beneficiary change form. In just minutes you can ensure support for Merton Children's Council beyond your lifetime.

▷   Please indicate if your gift will be matched by your employer. (Your personnel office will provide you with the necessary information and forms.)

▷   Will you be breathing cleaner air next year or not? It's up to you. A bill currently before the state legislature (SF1011) will set new, lower levels of tolerable pollution for rural and urban areas. To convince lawmakers of the importance of this bill, I need you to sign the enclosed petition and return it to me at once. Time is running out—the bill comes out of committee later this month. A successful petition drive requires your signed petition . . . and your dollars. Along with your signed petition, I'm asking you to return a contribution of $15 or $25 to support lobbying efforts for this important measure. But please hurry!

▷   Your services as a volunteer fundraiser would be very much appreciated. We are meeting Thursday evening, August 25, at 7:30 in the school auditorium. Enclosed is a self-addressed postcard so that you can indicate whether you will be able to join us in this important effort. We sincerely hope you can!

▷   One person *can* make a difference and influence the course of human events. Please choose to support our efforts—if not with a check, then with your calls and letters to your legislators, and with your activist support in your community and among your friends. Please don't leave this important work up to "the other person." We need YOU!

▷   Because the School Enrichment Council is organized for the purpose of lobbying and influencing legislation, your gift or donation is not deductible under current IRA guidelines as a charitable contribution. It may, however, be deductible as a business expense. If you have questions, please contact the SEC or your tax accountant.

▷   This year the challenges we face are substantially greater than those of the past. We need you to join us and be part of this important movement. We need your support, and you need the benefits of our important work.

▷   Please try to send at least $15. Our only source of support is the voluntary dollars of those like yourself who are concerned about our vanishing wild flowers.

▷   A sizable percentage of Clara Hibbert's campaign funding consists of small individual contributions from people like you who live in the Fifth Ward. She is not the candidate of special interests. She is the candidate of the people who live and do business in your ward.

───────────────────── SAMPLE LETTERS ─────────────────────

Dear Mrs. Farrinder:

The Board of Directors of the James Area Community Councils recognizes your invaluable help to the J.A.C.C. in various capacities over the years. We also note with great interest your very successful fundraising efforts last year on behalf of the public library system.

We are asking for your support for the J.A.C.C. in a special way this year: Would you consider chairing the 1993 fundraising campaign?

This is of course a major commitment and you may have questions about it. Last year's chair, several members of the committee, and the Board of Directors would be happy to meet with you at your convenience to discuss what this position might involve.

We think you would be an effective and inspiring campaign chair, and we hope very much that you will be able to say "yes."

Sincerely,

. . . .

Dear Fred and Aline,

I deeply appreciate your contribution. Thanks to the outstanding people who have worked on the campaign, we have accomplished a great deal. My commitment to public education is stronger than ever. I am pleased to have your confidence and support.

The campaign has grown in scope and intensity. In the remaining days, we are reaching out to large numbers of voters in a variety of ways. There is still much to be done. Please remember to tell your friends and neighbors to vote on November 7.

After the election, I will have eight weeks before the important School Board work begins. I will continue to prepare myself for the issues and problems facing our schools. I look forward to your continued input now and in the future.

Thank you again, Fred and Aline, for your help.

Sincerely yours,

. . . .

Hello!

You might call this letter a "Newgate Update"—we wanted to get in touch with you who have donated vehicles to us within the past few years to let you know what's new at Newgate.

You may already know that we moved. We're located three blocks west of Highway 280 at 2900 E. Hennepin Avenue. This move brought Newgate to a bigger and better facility in which to provide more disadvantaged people with auto body repair training. We're training twenty students now and want to increase that to forty over the next two years, so we currently have openings for many new trainees in the program.

We're trying some new methods (newspaper articles and radio ads) to let people in the community know about Newgate's training program and our need for donated vehicles.

But what's been most important to Newgate in the past has been "word of mouth" referrals: people like you telling others about us. And so we'd like to remind you that we still need donated cars *and* they're still tax deductible. I've enclosed a brochure that you may want to pass along to a friend. We'd be glad to give an estimate of fair market value over the phone—just call us at 555-0177.

We thank you for your donation in the past, and hope you'll keep us in mind in the future.

Sincerely,

. . . .

Dear Monty Brewster:

On behalf of the Board of Directors of the McCutcheon Foundation and all those who benefit directly and indirectly from its work, I thank you for your most generous contribution. I think I can safely say we have not seen its like in all the years we have been asking individuals to help us with this important work.

Hundreds of people's lives will be materially and positively affected by the kindness and charity we have witnessed today.

Thank you, and may you reap one hundredfold the goodness that you sow.

Sincerely,

. . . .

Dear Adelaide Culver and Henry Lambert:

I would like to invite you both to become members and supporters of Citizens for the Arts, the only statewide advocacy group working to enhance all the arts at all levels.

As a political action group, Citizens for the Arts has been highly successful during the last sixteen years in its efforts to build support for the arts throughout the state.

Through our efforts, state appropriations to the arts increased from $500,000 in 1975 to over $8 million last year. We also successfully lobbied for increased funding to individual artists through the regional arts councils and for the establishment of public art as a component in newly constructed state buildings. On the national level, we lobbied to exempt artists from the tax capitalization requirements of the 1986 Tax Reform Act.

Citizens for the Arts can continue to work for a healthy arts environment only with your support. Many of our successes are currently being challenged, and most of our state arts programs are insufficiently funded.

As a member and supporter of Citizens for the Arts, you will receive monthly newsletters on arts-related legislation and various arts events throughout the state as well as a pass entitling you to discounts at over seventy-five state arts organizations and events.

Please join us today. Your support is needed by Citizens for the Arts and the arts community.

Sincerely,

. . . .

Dear Mr. and Mrs. Claggart:

You may wonder if people with severe disabilities really can live independently. Isn't it easier for a disabled person to be taken care of rather than hassle with the day-to-day decisions about how and where to live? Isn't institutional living cheaper for the taxpayer? The answer is a resounding NO to both questions!

Consider Eva, a thirty-three-year-old woman with developmental disabilities who has lived with her parents all her life. She came to the Denver Center for Independent Living last March and asked for assistance so she could live in an apartment in the community. She *wanted* to be independent. And her parents were concerned about what would happen to Eva when they could no longer care for her.

DCIL staff went to Eva's home, evaluated her situation, and helped her decide exactly what special help she needed to live independently. One-on-one training in laundry, cooking, cleaning, money management, and job interviewing skills were provided. Additionally, Eva participated in our recreation program and found a great buddy to do things with.

Today Eva has a job washing dishes, her own checking account, a best friend, and a roommate with whom she will be sharing an apartment as soon as she has saved up her share of the rent deposit. Her family is delighted with the self-confidence and independence Eva has developed through her work with DCIL.

DCIL provides training and support services to any person with a physical, emotional, or developmental disability who wants to live in the community or who is in danger of being placed in an institution. A recent study by the Colorado Department of Social Services shows a 40% savings to the taxpayer when severely disabled people live independently in the community. DCIL services help make that independence possible.

With your help, many more people like Eva can live productive lives. Please consider a tax-deductible end-of-year gift to DCIL to continue this important work. Your contribution directly enables persons with disabilities to become independent, contributing members of our community.

Thank you for your generosity, and happy holidays!

Sincerely,

See also: ACCEPTANCES, COVER, FOLLOW-UP, REFUSALS, REQUESTS, RESPONSES, THANK YOU.

22

"Get Well" Letters

"I enjoy convalescence. It is the part that makes the illness worthwhile." (George Bernard Shaw)

Some "get well" messages are easy to send—the illness is not serious or we know the person only casually and thus aren't too involved emotionally. However, at other times our feelings of helplessness, anxiety, and even pity either keep us from writing altogether or produce letters we're not particularly proud of.

It is helpful to focus more on the other person's anxieties, hurts, and experiences than on your own feelings of inadequacy. It also helps to say what you feel—if you are upset, say so. If you don't know what to say, perhaps you should say so.

The main purpose of "get well" letters is to remind people that they are not alone in their trouble, to offer them the undoubted power of love and friendship as a force for healing. Your "encouraging word" does not have to be lengthy, literary, or memorable; a few sincere sentences will do.

Occasions That Call for "Get Well" Letters

- Send "get well" messages when family members, friends, co-workers, neighbors, or acquaintances are ill, hospitalized, recovering from an accident, undergoing tests, or having surgery.
- Business customers, clients, and colleagues will appreciate (and remember) your thoughtfulness in sending low-key "get well" cards with a simple handwritten message. You may also want to write when there is an accident or illness in the family of a close associate, employee, or longtime customer.
- Friends or relatives in chemical dependency treatment or in treatment for depression, eating disorders, and other such conditions may also be glad to receive words of support and encouragement.

How to Say It

☐   State simply that you are sorry about (or sorry to hear about) the illness, accident, or surgery.

☐   Offer to help in some specific way, if appropriate: make the person's most critical sales calls the next week, finish a project, sit in on a meeting, bring in library books the person might enjoy, take children for the weekend or chauffeur them to school events, make the calls canceling a social event, provide meals for the family, bring mail to the hospital and help answer it, read aloud to the person, run errands.

☐   Although it is generally better not to visit people who are hospitalized or who are seriously ill at home, you might offer to stop by if the person will be laid up for a long time or if you think they would welcome a visitor. Suggest that someone give you a call with a time and date, but make it easy for the person to refuse your visit in case they aren't feeling up to it.

☐   Assure the recipient of your concern, thoughts, best wishes, love, or prayers.

☐   End with your hopes for a speedy recovery, rapid improvement, better health.

What Not to Say

☐   In general, avoid being unnecessarily and tactlessly specific about the illness or accident. Say "your car accident" instead of "that horrible accident that took two lives" or "your surgery" instead of "your ileostomy."

☐   Avoid the word "victim" with its negative overtones of tragedy, helplessness, and self-pity.

☐   Avoid empty phrases, clichés, and false cheeriness. While an upbeat, positive tone is very helpful, false cheeriness is not. Common offenders include: "It's probably for the best" (it doesn't feel "best" to them); "I know how you feel" (no, you don't); "God only gives burdens to those who can carry them" (this is arguable); "Every cloud has a silver lining" (not when the cloud is hovering over *your* bed); "Think on the bright side—at least you don't have to go to work" (the person might greatly prefer work to the sickbed); "I'm sure you'll be up and around again in no time" (the patient is sure of no such thing, and the time passed in bed does not feel like "no time"). Reread your letter to see how you, in the same situation, would feel about its tone.

☐   Do not criticize the care the patient is receiving or the medical choices being made unless there is a very good reason for doing so. Most people already have doubts about whether they are being cared for as effectively as possible; it is upsetting when friends add to these doubts. While the person closest to the sick person might act as the patient's advocate, asking questions, examining test results, and conferring with doctors, there's no need for more than one, or possibly two, supporters of this nature. Other people's speculations are not helpful.

□　Do not use dramatic words such as "tragic," "devastating," "affliction," "torture," "nightmare," or "agony" unless the situation truly calls for them. Characterizing the situation as catastrophic is not always helpful or cheering, and many people are very sensitive to what they perceive as pity. If a sick friend speaks in such terms, you may respond in kind, but take your cue from the patient and do not jump to conclusions as to how they might be labeling the situation. You can be sympathetic and emotional without overstating the facts or dramatizing your own reaction to them.

Tips on Writing

□　Write as soon as you hear the news. Putting off a difficult letter does nothing to make it easier. And although "get well" letters are welcome at any time, prompt ones carry a warmer, stronger message.

□　Edgar Watson Howe said that when a friend is in trouble, we shouldn't annoy the person by asking if there is anything we can do. Instead, he said, "Think up something appropriate and do it." Sometimes it is too much effort for the sick person to respond to a general "anything I can do to help" offer. But if you mention something specific in your letter, the person has only to say, "Yes, thank you," or "No, thank you."

□　Instead of a lengthy letter, which may be fatiguing or uninteresting to many ill people, enclose with your card and note a few amusing or intriguing clippings from the paper ("What do you think about THIS?!"), photographs, a pressed flower, a cartoon, a sachet of potpourri, a quotation, a child's drawing, or colorful postcards or pictures. Enclosures are also a good idea when the usual words don't come easily—in the case of the terminally ill, for example.

□　The recipient of your letter is a person, not just an illness, with all the usual human hopes, interests, relationships, and emotions. However, those with more serious conditions are often feeling a loss of competence, an uncertainty about the future, and an interruption of the plans and activities by which they defined themselves. Hospital patients often feel depersonalized, vulnerable, afraid, and even angry. It helps if your letter keeps the illness in perspective and treats the person much as you did before. To avoid the false note that can creep into a "get well" letter, watch out for advice-giving, a patronizing or pitying tone, or the subtle message that the person isn't quite what they used to be.

Special Situations

◻   Employees or business colleagues will appreciate a short, sincere note acknowledging their illness or hospitalization, especially if you reassure them about the situation at work—who is taking care of their responsibilities, what provisions are being made for temporarily replacing them—and about their medical benefits and sick leave policy. People often don't look carefully at such things until they are too sick to do much but worry about them. The person's immediate supervisor or someone from the human resources office can send information about insurance, sick leave, and other relevant company policies. Or, if you know the person well, your simple assurance that there is nothing to worry about may be sufficient. "Get well" messages from managers or executives—even when the employee is not personally known to them—inspire feelings of belonging and company loyalty, and thus are a good idea on both the personal and business levels.

◻   If someone you know is seriously or terminally ill, do not initiate the subject of imminent death or the danger of death; let them bring it up first. Also, avoid cards and messages that say "get well," since the person may know this is not possible. Reread your letter to make sure you have not subconsciously written a "sympathy" card to the person about their anticipated death. An appropriate letter says you are thinking about your friend and (if this is true) that you are praying for them. Include a shared memory, but avoid telling it as an epitaph ("I will never forget . . ." "I will always remember you as the one who . . ."). You might say instead, "I'm still thinking about your giant pumpkin. I'll bet it would have won first prize at the State Fair." Focus on those pleasures that are still possible for the terminally ill patient, for example, letterwriting, visits with family and friends, reading, old movies, card games, dictating memoirs.

◻   When writing those suffering from chemical dependency, eating disorders, and other such diseases, choose commercial cards that say "thinking of you" rather than "get well." In most cases, the less said the better, as others rarely realize all that is involved in such treatment and all that the patient experiences and struggles with. A simple note to let the person know you're thinking of them is often very well received.

◻   If a friend or relative becomes severely disabled, bedridden, or in need of constant care and supervision, you might want to write not only to the patient but to the person responsible for their care—spouse, parent, child, relative—and offer your sympathy as well as some help (running errands, chauffeuring, bringing meals, spending time with the patient so that the caregiver can have some free time).

◻   When writing to a sick child, say simply that you're sorry to hear they're sick, and then enclose something colorful, entertaining, and age-appropriate:

a word puzzle, riddles, a balloon, a cartoon or clipping from the paper, a story you made up or photocopied from a magazine, a sticker book. You could also hand-letter a "coupon" good for a stack of library books that you will bring over and pick up several weeks later, a carry-in meal from their favorite fast food place (if parents first okay the idea), thirty minutes of being read to, chauffeuring of friends to and from the patient's house or the hospital. If you think the child will be writing back, help them along by asking a few questions: What's the hospital room like? Who is the doctor? What is the best thing about being sick? The worst thing? What is their day like, from morning to night? What is the first thing they're going to do when they get well?

Format

□   Commercial cards are so available and appropriate for many different "get well" situations that their use is almost standard today. Some recipients will skip the printed verse to read your handwritten message, but others will carefully read every word of the commercial message as though you had written it expressly for them; for this reason, select your card with care. And always write something personal on the card—either a brief message at the bottom of the inside right-hand page or a longer message on the (usually blank) inside left-hand page.

□   Use personal stationery, notepaper, or engraved note cards for hand-written notes.

□   In the case of business contacts or very close friends, a typed message on business letterhead, personal-business stationery, or memo paper is as welcome as a handwritten note.

────────────────────── WORDS ──────────────────────

accident	heal	saddened
affection	health	sickness
cheer	hope	sorry
comfort	illness	suffering
concerned	indisposed	support
convalescence	mishap	sympathy
diagnosis	optimistic	treatment
discomfort	ordeal	trouble
disheartening	painful	uncomfortable
disorder	reassure	undergo
distress	recovery	unfortunate
experience	relapse	unwelcome

———————————————— PHRASES ————————————————

be up and about

bright prospects

clean bill of health

devoutly hope

early recovery

encouraging news

feeling a lot better soon

felt so bad to hear

fervent/fond hope

get better

good health

good omen

good prospects

greatly affected by the news that

have every/great confidence that

heavy news

hopeful that

keep your spirits up

quick return to health

rapid recovery

regain your health

restore/return to health

sorry/very sorry/mighty sorry to hear

so sorry to hear that

thinking of you

unhappy to hear about

wishing you happier, healthier days
   ahead

———————————————— SENTENCES ————————————————

Although we'll miss you, don't worry about your work—we're parceling it out
   among us for the time being.

Best wishes for a speedy recovery.

Do hurry up and get well/get better.

Don't worry about the office—we'll manage somehow.

Everyone at work feels so bad about your accident.

From what I understand, this treatment will make all the difference/will give you a
   new lease on life.

I am very concerned about you.

I am hoping that you are feeling better every day.

I am inspired by the way you are handling all this.

I certainly hope you are not too uncomfortable/miserable/in a great deal of pain.

I hope that you will soon be well/be back to your old self/be up and around/be up and
   about/be back in the swing of things/be back on your feet.

I hope you are getting some relief from the pain.

I hope your convalescence progresses quickly and pleasantly.

I hope you're not feeling too dejected by this latest setback/too miserable/weak/
   uncomfortable.

I'm glad to hear you're getting some relief from the pain.

I'm sorry that you've had such a scare, but so relieved to know you caught it in time.

It's no fun being laid up.

It was with heavy hearts that we heard you are battling your old Nemesis.

I've just heard about your accident/surgery/illness.

I was so sorry to hear about your illness/that you were in the hospital.

Knowing your unusual determination and energy, we are anticipating your speedy recovery.

The news of your emergency surgery came as quite a shock.

The office/this place is not the same without you!

We all miss you.

We all felt so bad when we heard about your accident.

We are both looking forward to/hoping and praying for your speedy and full recovery.

We expect to see you as good as new in a few weeks.

We just heard that you've been on the sick list this past week.

We just wanted to let you know how concerned we are.

We're all rooting for you to get better very quickly.

We're hoping for the best of everything for you.

We're hoping you'll be back on your feet in no time.

We're thinking of you and hoping you'll feel better soon.

What a bitter pill to come through the heart surgery with flying colors and then to break your hip!

You have all my best wishes for a speedy recovery.

You're very much on my mind and in my heart these days.

Your family said you were in a great deal of pain, but bearing up well.

Your many friends are hoping for your quick return to health/early recovery/rapid recovery.

Your job will be waiting for you when you are ready to come back.

PARAGRAPHS

▷   I'd love to hear from you when you feel up to writing. Until then, be patient with yourself and don't try to do too much too soon. I'm thinking about you every day.

▷   We're all relieved you came out of the accident so lightly—although from your point of view, it may not feel all that good at the moment. I hope you're not too uncomfortable.

▷   I was so sorry to hear about your arthritis. I hope you don't mind, but I made a contribution in your name to the Arthritis Foundation and asked them to send you a packet of informational brochures.

▷   Can I help with anything while you're out of commission? Because of my work schedule and the family's activities, I'm not as free as I'd like to be. However, some things I could do (and would be delighted to do) are: pick up any groceries you need on my way home from work (about 5:30), run the children to evening school events, have them over on Saturday or Sunday afternoons, make phone calls for you, run errands on Saturday mornings, bring over a hot dish once a week. I'd really like to help. You know very well you'd do the same for me if our positions were reversed! I'll be waiting for your call.

▷   I was so sorry to hear about your broken arm. Do you think you'll ever ride a horse again? I hope it mends quickly. Let me know when you're ready for a cup of a tea and a visit.

▷ I'm sending you some old *Highlights for Children* magazines and one new scrapbook. I thought you could cut out your favorite pictures and stories and paste them in the scrapbook. It might help pass the time while you have to stay in bed.

———————————————— SAMPLE LETTERS ————————————————

Dear Harry,

What a shock to get to work this morning and have Louie tell me that the only reason I punched in earlier than you for once was that you'd been in an accident. It was pretty gloomy around here until we got some information from the hospital. Your doctor evidently thinks the general picture looks good and you shouldn't be laid up too long.

Louie has divided up your work between Max and Charlie so don't worry about anything at this end.

Best wishes,

· · · · · · · · · · ·

Dear Mrs. Gummidge,

We were so sorry to learn that you have been hospitalized. I took the liberty of stopping your newspaper and mail delivery for the time being (the mail is being held at the post office). Since I had a copy of your house key, I went in to make sure all the faucets were off and the windows shut (except for leaving one upstairs and one downstairs open an inch for air). I've been going in at night and turning on a few lights so it doesn't look empty.

I wasn't sure you were up to a phone call, but I thought you'd want to know that the house is being looked after.

We are all hoping and praying for your speedy recovery. In the meantime, if there is anything you'd like us to do, please don't hesitate to call.

With best wishes,

· · · · · · · · · · ·

Dear Ms. Melbury,

The staff and management at The Woodlanders join me in wishing you a speedy recovery from your emergency surgery. We are all relieved to hear that the surgery went well and that you'll be back among us before very long. For one thing, you are the only one who can ever find the Damson files.

As far as work is concerned, please do not give it a thought; concentrate instead on getting well. Giles Winterborne has offered to take over any outstanding projects on your desk, and Felice Charmond will be answering your phone and taking care of things as they come up. I'm having Marty South send you a copy of company policy on hospitalization costs and sick leave (they are both, I think, very generous) so that you don't have to worry about the business side of things.

With all best wishes, I am

Sincerely yours,

· · · · · · · · · · ·

Dear Jay,

Word has it that you've been under the weather lately. As soon as you feel up to it, let me know and I'll call Daisy and Tom and Nick—there's nothing like a party for lifting the old spirits.

Best,

· · · · · · · · · · ·

Dear Eliza,

Grandma and I were so sorry to hear that you've got the chicken socks. We didn't know chickens wore socks, so we were very surprised. What's that? You say you have the chicken fox. What kind of an animal is a chicken fox anyway? What's that? You say you have a chicken box. Are you going to raise chickens in it? Oh, excuse me, you have the chicken rocks. We've never heard of them. Are they the latest fad, like pet rocks? Oho! We've got it now. You've got the CHICKEN POX. Maybe by the time you've read this long letter, you will be feeling a little better.

Grandma said to tell you to be sure not to scratch, but I'm sure you won't.

In a few days when you feel better we'll give you a call and you can tell us yourself how you're feeling.

Love,

· · · · · · · · · · ·

Dear Uncle Mordecai,

We all felt so bad to hear that your tricky hip has landed you in the hospital. Here's hoping that surgery is effective in clearing up the problem and that you aren't uncomfortable for too long.

I went over yesterday and cleared the leaves out of your gutters. I was afraid you'd be worrying about that.

We'd like to stop by the hospital some evening to see you, but I'm wondering if it isn't more important for you to get all the rest you can. If you feel up to company some evening, give us a call. Otherwise, we'll see you when you get home. Take care of yourself. You're pretty important to a few people around here.

With love,

· · · · · · · · · · ·

Dear Goldie,

I was very sorry to hear about Abraham's automobile accident yesterday. When I spoke to your daughter, she seemed to think that although he was facing some surgery and was fairly uncomfortable, the outlook was good. I hope all goes well and that he can look forward to coming home very soon.

According to your files, you have taken no compassionate leave in the eight years you have been with us, so there is certainly no problem with your taking as long as you like to be with Abraham. Patsy Tate has assumed responsibility for your station; she may call you from time to time with a question, but otherwise the situation is well in hand.

Although our hospitalization insurance is based on a preadmit system, this does not apply in the case of an emergency, such as Abraham's hospitalization. However, there are a few steps you should take in the next several days to regularize the situation. I've asked someone from Human Resources to call you about this.

If there is anything we can do to make things easier for you, let us know. In the meantime, you are very much in our thoughts.

Sincerely,

· · · · · · · · · · ·

Dear Olivia,

You realize, of course, that there will be no further bridge games until you are well! None of us is willing to invite a substitute—"Replace Olivia?" As Sam Goldwyn put it in two words: "Im Possible."

Don't worry about the homefront. George has things under control, and we are all taking turns entertaining your house guest, that nice Mr. Pim.

Give us the high sign when you are ready for phone calls or visits—or a game of bridge!

Love,

· · · · · · · · · · ·

Dear Horace,

We were all distressed to hear of your heart attack. Leo says you're doing well and all of us here at Giddens are looking forward to your full and speedy recovery.

You'll be happy to know that even in your absence, it's very much business as usual; your nephew Leo has been a quick study, and things are going very smoothly. We loaded the last shipment of the big Hellman order yesterday, and so far all schedules have been maintained.

It must be difficult to be away from a business you raised from a baby, but you need have no fears about it. I hope you can instead spend your energy regaining your health and strength.

Very best wishes to you and Regina.

Sincerely,

See also: ACKNOWLEDGMENTS, FAMILY, SYMPATHY, THANK YOU.

23

Goodwill Letters

"It is not enough to collect today's profits, for your competitor is collecting tomorrow's good will."
(*How to Write Letters That Win*, 1906)

Goodwill letters are a type of sales letter, but you are not selling a product or service directly. Instead, you are "selling" the recipient on your company's worth, reputation, friendliness, integrity, and competence. You want the recipient to think well of the company and to keep it in mind for future purchases, visits, service contracts.

Although many sales are based on price, color, dimensions, length of service contract, and other measurable properties, many more sales are based on feelings or attitudes about a company, product, or service. Goodwill letters are directed to the nonmaterial aspects of customer choice.

One type of goodwill letter has a specific ostensible purpose: to congratulate a customer on twenty-five years of business, to thank someone for a large order, to apologize for a delayed shipment, to express appreciation for a favor. Almost any occasion is reason enough to show interest in your customers. Writing such a letter is not necessary; nothing unfortunate will happen if you don't write it. However, when you do send such a letter, you reap extra interest, consideration, and appreciation from your customer. (For guidelines on these letters, see APPRECIATION, CONGRATULATIONS, THANK YOU, or another specific topic.)

The second type of customer goodwill letter is a simple "how are you doing/just keeping in touch" message that reminds customers of you and lets them know you are thinking of them.

Goodwill letters are also helpful within companies. It is not necessary to send a congratulatory message to an employee on celebrating an important personal anniversary or for publishing a paper, but doing so creates good morale and company loyalty.

Goodwill letters are too easily overlooked amidst the paper blizzard of urgent and necessary correspondence, but they pay off handsomely for those who will take a few minutes a day to write one or two "unnecessary" but always well-received goodwill letters.

Kinds of Goodwill Letters

- anniversaries: service/wedding
- announcements: change in prices/personnel/policies/address (see also ANNOUNCEMENTS)
- appreciation: good payment record/past business/customer referral (see also APPRECIATION)
- congratulations (see CONGRATULATIONS)
- customers' and employees' life events (see appropriate topic)
- holiday greetings (see SEASONAL GREETINGS)
- special events and offers: open houses/sales/discounts/gifts/samples/ certificates/coupons
- surveys/questionnaires
- thank you: previous business/current purchase/suggestions/assistance/ good work (see also THANK YOU)
- welcome/welcome back (see also WELCOME)

How to Say It

❑   State your main message (congratulations, thank you, happy holidays, "just want to see how you're doing," "so happy to hear that . . .").

❑   Expand on the message ("I'm particularly grateful because . . ." or "You've been a delight to work with because . . ." or "I hope the New Year is a happy and healthy one for you and your family").

❑   Close with pleasant wishes for success and a mention of future or continued contact.

What Not to Say

❑   Do not include a strong sales message in a goodwill letter. Often your products or services are only lightly mentioned or not mentioned at all.

❑   Save business news, requests, or comments for another letter. When you send a goodwill letter, don't dilute the impact by asking for business or for a favor or for higher work outputs.

Tips on Writing

❑   One type of "how are you doing?" goodwill letter is a survey or questionnaire about the customer's use of your product or service. If well constructed, the survey will be useful to you in a number of ways. The customer will appreciate being asked for an opinion and for your interest in their reaction. You can explain what use you plan to make of the survey. Express appreciation for their help.

◻   The biggest category of customer goodwill letters is probably the holiday or year-end greeting. If your message is a general calling-to-mind letter or card (insurance agent, publisher, bank), send it anytime. But if December is one of your important sales or donation months, and you want to jog people's memories about your particular charity or your place of business, mail your greeting early in the month before people have already shopped or written out their checks.

◻   Holidays are also an excellent occasion for goodwill letters written on behalf of company management, firm officers, or board of directors and sent to employees.

Special Situations

◻   Goodwill gifts—samples, trial sizes, the first in a series, something the customer can keep whether they purchase anything else or not—are accompanied by a cover letter. The sales message is not too strong as the free product is theoretically the sales "message." However, follow up this mailing with a letter a few weeks later. At that time you can intensify the sales message. (See also COVER, SALES.)

Format

◻   All goodwill letters should be typed on letterhead stationery, except for brief congratulatory notes to employees and colleagues that may be typed, or possibly handwritten, on memo paper.

◻   When sending holiday greetings to employees or customers or other general-message letters, a well-written form letter is customary and acceptable.

WORDS

admire	kindness	special
appreciate	memorable	superb
delighted	one-of-a-kind	terrific
enjoyed	pleased	thoughtful
grateful	remarkable	unique
happy	respect	valuable
impressed	satisfying	welcome
inspired	sensational	

───────────────────────── PHRASES ─────────────────────────

happy/pleased to hear
how are you getting along with
just thinking about you
just to let you know
keep us in mind
let us know if

like to keep in touch with
pleased to be able to
show our gratitude for
wanted you to know
wishing you all the best
would be glad to have you stop in again when

───────────────────────── SENTENCES ─────────────────────────

All of us here at Larolle International send you warmest holiday greetings and our
   best wishes for a happy, healthy new year!
As one of our longtime customers, you may be interested in our new, faster ordering
   procedures.
Congratulations on your ten years with us.
I heard something pretty special is going on over there!
To show how much we appreciate the responsible handling of your account, we are
   raising your credit limit to $10,000.
We never forget a customer!
We now have a special customer hotline—at no charge to the calling party—for all
   your questions and concerns.
We're having a one-day customer appreciation day, and you're one of the special few
   who are invited!

───────────────────────── PARAGRAPHS ─────────────────────────

▷   You used to order regularly from us, but we haven't heard from you in some
time now. To help you remember how easy it was to order and how much you
enjoyed our high-quality camping merchandise, we're enclosing a "welcome back"
certificate good for 15% off your next order. We sure hope you use it—we've
missed you!

▷   I noticed the handsome photograph of you and your husband in Sunday's paper—congratulations on twenty-five years of marriage! Do stop by the office the
next time you're in the store so I can congratulate you personally.

▷   Thank you so much for referring Stanley Purves to us. It is because of generous
and appreciative customers like you that Dorset Homes has been growing by leaps
and bounds. We will give Mr. Purves our very best service—and we are always ready
to help you in any way we can. Thanks again for passing on the word!

▷   You are cordially invited to an Open House on January 29 from 5:00 to 8:00
p.m. to celebrate our fiftieth anniversary. We are taking this opportunity to show
our appreciation to our many fine and loyal customers. Do come—we will have a
small gift waiting for you!

_____ SAMPLE LETTERS _____

Dear Jules,

I see that the bank is celebrating an important birthday—congratulations! You must be proud to see what a success Mignaud et Fils has become 100 years after its founding by your great-grandfather.

All of us here at Philips Deluxe Checks wish you continued success and prosperity.

Sincerely,

. . . .

Dear Mr. and Mrs. Charles:

It has been three months since your new floor tiles were installed. I hope you have been enjoying them. We have customers who still rave about floor tile they bought from us thirty years ago.

If we can be of any service to you in the future, do keep us in mind. We plan to have a storewide three-day sale on all floor coverings in late January in case you are interested in doing any other rooms.

Thanks again for choosing a fine floor product from Geiger Tiles.

Yours truly,

. . . .

Dear Hilda Cherrington:

Over the years, you have ordered a number of our fine products. You're one of the reasons that Lee Gifts is the premier mail order house that it is.

To thank you for your business and to introduce you to a completely new line of Christmas ornaments, we are enclosing the "Christmas Star" for your enjoyment. We think we you will admire the fine craftwork that went into this delicate ornament. It makes a wonderful keepsake gift for friends and relatives. Also enclosed is a copy of our current catalog, which shows all twenty-five of the new "Memories" series of ornaments.

We hope you enjoy your ornament!

Sincerely,

See also: CONGRATULATIONS, "GET WELL," SEASONAL GREETINGS, SYMPATHY, THANK YOU, WELCOME.

24

Letters of Instruction

"I wish he would explain his explanation." (Lord Byron)

Instructions are found in brochures, pamphlets, owners' manuals, packing slips, on the back of credit card statements, and at the bottom of invoices. However, occasionally it is necessary to write a special letter of instruction, most often in response to a customer query. Well-written letters of instruction serve as both goodwill and sales letters, so they should be looked on as a special opportunity to increase customer loyalty rather than as a routine and unimportant part of your correspondence.

Write Letters of Instructions For

- agreements/contracts/leases
- babysitters/daycare providers
- forms/applications/surveys
- house/plant/garden/pet care while away
- new policies/procedures/regulations
- operating instructions: appliances/tools/equipment
- payments
- product registrations/use/care
- requests for instructions (see REQUESTS)
- return, repair, or replacement of merchandise
- samples
- shipping instructions

How to Say It

□   If your letter is a response to an earlier contact, mention this ("Thank you for your letter asking . . ."). Otherwise, give the reader an immediate reference point ("To help you get the most out of your new software, we offer the following suggestions for use.").

☐   Number or otherwise set off the steps in your instructions.

☐   Tell the reader where they can go for further help.

☐   End with a pleasant statement of appreciation or with a mention of future business or enjoyment of the new product.

What Not to Say

☐   "Don't give instructions in the negative" is a negative statement. "Word your instructions positively" is a positive one. Use the positive form. Whenever you find "don't" and "never" and "should not" in your instructions, rephrase the sentence to read positively.

☐   In giving instructions, avoid words like "simple" and "obvious." Invariably, these words preface something that is neither simple nor obvious to the other person, and they carry the subtle sting of a put-down by implying that the instructions are clear to everyone but the puzzled reader.

☐   It seems superfluous to counsel against patronizing, insulting, or condescending language, yet these attitudes sometimes creep into letters of instruction. For example, many times a "broken" appliance is simply not plugged in. When compiling a list of troubleshooting instructions for appliance repair, the first step usually counsels users to check the outlet to see if the appliance is plugged in. Instead of poking a little sly fun at this kind of slip-up, phrase your instruction matter of factly.

Tips on Writing

☐   Instructions must be clear and intelligible. Especially when preparing a form letter that will be used thousands of times, have at least half a dozen people unfamiliar with its content read your letter for clarity. Some of the worst instructions in the world have been written by experts; because they know their field so well they cannot understand the mind of the uninitiated well enough to adequately explain anything. (Computer documentation used to be a good example of brilliant minds producing instructions that were often all but useless.)

☐   Be specific. If you say "soak contacts overnight," give the desired number of hours in parentheses. "Overnight" means different things to different people. If you instruct people to clean an appliance regularly, describe products and procedures that work best and tell what "regularly" means.

☐   Be diplomatic and polite. Some requests for instructions may appear inane to you and the answers so obvious you hardly know how to phrase your response. But people's brains work in wonderfully odd and divergent ways, and the person may actually be looking at the situation in a way very different from the way you ordinarily see it. Then, too, even if it is a "stupid" question, good public relations demand that you treat it as politely and helpfully as any other question.

□   Although it may mean a little more work for you, it is often helpful to the reader if you explain *why* as well as *how*. For example, "Do not use this compound when there is danger of rain followed by temperatures below 32 degrees." Many people will accept this instruction without question. But others will wonder what rain and cold have to do with anything, and still others will ignore it, thinking it unimportant. If you add, "because the compound will absorb the moisture, freeze, expand, and probably crack," users are far more likely to follow the instruction—and you will receive fewer complaints.

Special Situations

□   Cover letters often contain instructions. When sending someone a sample, a contract, or a product, for example, you may want to explain how to interpret or use the item.

Format

□   Instructions to customers are always typed on letterhead stationery.

□   Memos are used for in-house instructions and should be typed except for the briefest and most casual instructions.

□   Form letters are especially useful for letters of instructions.

_____ WORDS _____

advice	explanation	policy
approach	guidelines	procedure
avoid	how-to	process
carefully	illustrate	regulations
clarification	indicate	steps
demonstrate	information	system
description	method	technique
details	operation	warning

_____ PHRASES _____

alert you to

always check to see

as the illustration shows

before you use your appliance

be sure to

commonly used to

it requires that you

much more effective to

note that

once you are familiar with

recommend/suggest that you

standard operating procedure

you will find that

_____ SENTENCES _____

Certain precautions are necessary.

If you have more questions, please give me a call.

Please note the following guidelines.

We are happy to be able to clarify this matter for you.

You may be aware of most of this, but since I'm not sure just what you need to know, I'm including everything.

Your Aldridge electric knife will provide you with a lifetime of use if you follow these care instructions.

_____ PARAGRAPHS _____

▷   Enclosed is the final version of the contract, which constitutes the complete and entire agreement between us. Please read it carefully and consult with your attorney before signing all three copies on the bottom of page 5. Please also initial clauses C1 and D3 to indicate your awareness of the changes we have agreed upon. Return all three copies to me along with a check covering the agreed-upon amount. One copy of the contract will be countersigned and returned to you.

▷   Thanks for taking care of the hamsters while we're away. If you can stop by once a day, that'd be great. Give everybody one-quarter cup of hamster food. Fill their water bottles. Give Furball an apple slice and Marigold a banana slice from the fruit in the plastic box (they don't care if it's old and brown). The others don't need any special treats. We'll be back before the cages need cleaning, so don't worry about that.

▷   To obtain a credit card for another member of your immediate family, please complete the enclosed form, making sure that both your signature and the new cardholder's signature appear on the indicated lines.

▷   We would very much appreciate your filling out the enclosed survey. It will take only a few minutes. Use a number 2 pencil and carefully fill in the circles corresponding to your answer. Do not write in the white box in the upper right-hand corner. Fold the form along the dotted lines and seal by moistening the flap. Do not use staples or transparent tape. Your name and address are optional. Thank you!

▷   Please give Caddy a bottle around 8:30 (or earlier if she seems hungry). If she falls asleep with the bottle in her mouth, take it out. Leave her bedroom door open so you can hear her if she wakes up.

———————————————— SAMPLE LETTERS ————————————————

Dear Mr. and Mrs. Gauss:

Enclosed for your review is a Contract to Buy and Sell Real Estate for your property located at 1946 Storm Road, Jameson, IN 47438.

The contract requires your acceptance on or before July 1, and both of you must sign the contract and have your signatures notarized.

If you have any questions regarding this contract, please call me at 555-3369.

. . . .

Dear Mrs. Dollery:

We were sorry to hear that your AutoAnswer phone system is not satisfactory. All our equipment is carefully checked before leaving our Chicago factory. However, in rare cases, an intermittent problem may have been overlooked or something may have happened to the equipment during shipping.

Please return your system to us, following these steps:

1. Use the original carton and packing materials to ship the system back to us.

2. Address the box to: Customer Service, P.O. Box 1887, Woodlanders, IL 60031. (Do not use the California ordering and customer service address.)

3. Enclose a letter describing the problem (a copy of the letter you originally sent us would be fine) and mention whether the trouble occurred immediately or after use. The more information you can give us, the more quickly we can locate the problem.

4. Fasten the enclosed RUSH label to the top right-hand corner of your letter. This will ensure that you receive a fully functioning machine (your present system or a new one) within ten working days.

Thousands of satisfied customers are experiencing the delight and time-saving features of the AutoAnswer phone system every day; I want you to be one of them very soon.

. . . .

TO: Estabrook County Residents
FROM: Estabrook County Board of Commissioners
DATE: October 2
RE: Yard Waste

The amount of garbage each of us produces is enormous, and so are the problems and costs of disposing of it. During the summer months grass clippings make up 24% of residential garbage.

As you perhaps know, legislation passed earlier this year requires us to separate grass clippings and leaves—yard waste—from our regular trash after January 1.

How do we do this?

It's easy! We have four good options:

1. Leave grass clippings on the lawn. This is the most cost-effective and environmentally sound way to deal with grass clippings. They decompose, returning nutrients to the soil, and never enter the waste stream.

2. Bag grass clippings and take them to one of the six County compost sites—free of charge (list of compost sites is enclosed). Empty your bags of grass clippings and fill them with free compost for your garden.

3. Use grass clippings as mulch around trees and shrubs (if your grass has not been chemically treated).

4. Bag your grass clippings and pay a trash hauler to collect them separately.

For additional information call 555-2117, Estabrook County's Compost Center.

P.S. We've had a number of calls asking if grass clippings won't ruin the lawn if left on it. You can leave grass clippings on the lawn and still keep it healthy by: (1) not letting the grass get too long before mowing (clippings should be no more than one inch long in order to filter down into the soil); (2) using a sharp mower blade (the sharper the blade the finer the clippings and the faster they decompose); (3) avoiding overfertilization (very dense grass doesn't allow clippings to reach the soil to decompose); (4) removing excessive thatch (1/2 inch is ideal); (5) mowing the lawn when it's dry.

. . . .

Dear William D. Carmichael,

Beginning January 1, we will be adopting an exciting new program of flexible benefits. To become part of this program, we ask that you:

1. Read the enclosed brochure, which explains the program.

2. Sign up for the informational meeting that is most convenient for you (list enclosed).

3. Schedule an appointment with one of the Human Resources staff to discuss the program and to ask any questions you might have. At that time you will be given a confidential record of your personal benefit program and an enrollment form to fill out specifying the way you want to "spend" your benefits.

4. Return the form by October 1. This date is very important. If you fail to send in your enrollment form by October 1, you will automatically be enrolled in the "no choice" plan (see brochure for description).

If you have any questions about this process, call Human Resources at ext. 43.

. . . .

Dear Customer:

Thank you for your inquiry about home maintenance of your recently purchased VCR. We do not recommend that owners repair their own VCRs. Although it may be more costly, a professional repair job is a better choice in the long run.

However, if you are willing to accept the risks, there are some maintenance and small repair jobs you can attempt at home. You can clean the record and playback heads with a commercially manufactured cleaning cassette (read instructions before using). Note, however, that most of these special cassettes, particularly the dry kind, work by abrasion and can wear down your video heads. After unplugging your VCR, clean the interior with a soft painter's brush and—for hard-to-reach places—a can of compressed air. You can also replace belts, rollers, switches, and springs, and can lubricate gears, shafts, and other moving parts every few years. Using a light machine oil, *oil* parts that spin. *Grease* parts that slide or mesh (but don't use too much grease).

For further information, consult the manual that came with your VCR, check with a local repair shop, or write us with your specific question.

See also: ADVICE, RESPONSES.

25

Letters of Introduction

"I look upon every day to be lost, in which I do not make a new acquaintance." (Samuel Johnson)

Letters of introduction are not as common as they once were. First, the telephone has largely replaced the written word as a means of putting two people with common interests in touch with each other. Second, most people have enough social and business contacts for several lifetimes, and they are reluctant to suggest additional ones to friends unless they are sure the proposed introduction will be uniquely and genuinely beneficial to both parties. Putting two people in touch with each other is risky; it is not impossible that they will both end up resenting you if it was your idea and you pushed it too hard.

Although some letters introducing people to each other are still seen, today's letter of introduction is more commonly used to introduce a new sales representative, new product, or new service to customers.

The letter of recommendation often serves as a letter of introduction (see REFERENCES).

Write Letters of Introduction For

- business associates/employees
- friends moving/traveling to a city where you know people
- introducing business/product/services to newcomers in the area (see WELCOME)
- job seekers (see also RECOMMENDATIONS)
- membership in clubs/groups/organizations
- new address/office/division/outlet/company (see also ANNOUNCE-MENTS, WELCOME)
- new billing procedure/statement/payment schedule
- new employees/associates/partners/programs/policies/prices (see also ANNOUNCEMENTS)

207

- new products/services (see also SALES)
- requesting an introduction to someone from a third party
- researcher working in the other person's field

How to Say It

□   In the first paragraph state your reason for writing: to introduce your-self, to ask for an introduction to someone, to introduce someone to your reader, to suggest that your reader meet with someone.

□   Provide the person's full name, title, position, or some other "tag" to situate the person for your reader.

□   Tell something about the person to be introduced—whether it is your-self or a third party—that will make your correspondent want to pursue the introduction.

□   Explain why contact with this person is desirable.

□   State how the meeting can take place: the reader can contact the other person (include address and phone number); the person will call your reader; you are inviting them both to lunch.

□   Express your appreciation.

What Not to Say

□   Avoid dogmatic assurances that the two people will like each other very much. No one can predict who will take to whom. Phrase any such sugges-tion tentatively, and emphasize instead what they have in common so that your reader can decide what, if any, interest there might be in meeting the other person.

Tips on Writing

□   There are two ways of providing a letter of introduction. One is to give the letter to the person requesting the introduction; the person will then call upon the third party and present the letter. The envelope is usually left unsealed, which means your letter will be tactful. The second way is to write directly to the third party, asking if they would be able to meet with, enter-tain, or help the person requesting the introduction.

□   Provide several points of contacts between the two people who are to meet: interests they share, people they both know, work or school connec-tions. The object is to provide both people with a way of beginning a conver-sation or a relationship.

❑   When you are asking someone to offer hospitality to a friend or business colleague, write the person directly and ask that they respond to you. This spares the third party the embarrassment of presenting a personal letter of introduction only to be rebuffed because of lack of time or interest. It also spares your friend or acquaintance the awkwardness of being caught off guard and perhaps pressured into doing something they may not really want to do.

❑   When you are asking someone to introduce you to a third party, word your request so that the person can easily refuse.

❑   Letters of introduction used to present a very serious obligation to entertain or meet with the person presenting one. Illness, a recent death in the family, or some other serious obstacle were the only acceptable excuses for failing in this social responsibility. This is no longer true. You are being asked to do a favor and unless you feel greatly indebted to the person requesting it, you can send a brief refusal to both parties (see REFUSALS).

Special Situations

❑   Several letters should be written following a meeting of two people introduced by a third: Cyril will thank Liza for her letter of introduction to Rebecca and will thank Rebecca for the meeting; Liza will thank Rebecca for following through on her request to meet with Cyril; Rebecca may thank Liza for putting her in touch with Cyril, but at the very least she will assure Liza that it was no trouble and that she enjoyed meeting Cyril.

❑   It is always a good idea to introduce (by letter) a new sales representative to customers before the first visit. This not only smoothes the representative's way, it serves as a goodwill letter, letting customers know that headquarters is aware and interested in what goes on in the field. The letter should give enough information about the new sales representative to allow the customer to feel comfortable with the change and to see that you have every confidence in the person's ability to serve the customer well.

❑   Letters introducing new products and services have strong sales messages. Only a phrase like "we are pleased to introduce" qualifies it as a letter of introduction; from there on, it's pure sales.

❑   When introducing a change in billing procedures (new due date, automatic deposit, windowed reply envelopes) or a new format for your statements, explain why you instituted the change and, if possible, enclose a sample statement or envelope. Your explanation should focus on the value of the change to the customer, not its value to you. By expressing your appreciation for the customer's business and stating that the changes will improve service, your letter of introduction becomes a goodwill letter or even a sales letter.

Format

☐   Longtime convention dictates that social introductions be handwritten on personal stationery or foldover notes. However, typewriters and computers are at work even here, and handwritten letters seem to be reserved for only the most formal and most particular of your correspondents.

☐   Introductions to clubs, organizations, and other groups where the line between business and personal matters is not obvious may be handwritten or typed, usually on personal letterhead or plain bond paper.

☐   Business introductions (requests for them, the letters themselves, and thank yous) are typed on business or personal-business letterhead. A personal touch is commonly added by a handwritten note on your business card to be included with the letter or given to the person requesting the introduction.

☐   Form letters are useful when the same message of introduction must be conveyed to a number of people, and the message is not particularly personal. For example, introducing a new slate of officers to a far-flung membership, or introducing a new product line or new payment schedules to thousands of customers.

WORDS

acquaint	greet	propose
announce	hospitality	receive
associate	introduce	sponsor
colleague	meet	suggest
connections	notify	visit
contact	pleasure	welcome
co-worker	present	

PHRASES

acquaint you with	please don't feel obliged to
bring together two such	present to you
bring to your attention/notice	shares your interest in
get together with	similar background
give a nice reception to	the bearer of this letter
if you have time	this letter/note will introduce
I'm happy to introduce you to	we're pleased to introduce
I think you'll like	we would like to tell you about
I would like to introduce to you	you've heard me mention
known to me for many years	

_____ SENTENCES _____

Any courtesies you are able to show her will be appreciated.

Dr. Roselli plans to be in Rome for the next two years, so if you feel able to offer him any hospitality during that time, I would be most grateful—and I think you'd enjoy meeting him.

I'd appreciate very much any consideration you can extend to Mr. Chevenix.

I feel sure you would not regret meeting the Oakroyds.

I'll appreciate any kindness/courtesy you can show Harriet.

I think you and Nathan would find you have a great deal in common.

I've always wanted to bring you two together, but of course it will depend on whether you are free just now.

I've asked Adela to give you a call.

I've often thought you two should meet.

I will be most grateful for any help/time/courtesy you can give Claude.

Thank you for whatever you may be able to do for Ms. Ingoldsby.

There is little that Ms. Trindle does not know about the field; I suspect that you would very much enjoy talking to her.

This letter will introduce Nicholas Broune, president of our local professional editors network, who will be spending several weeks in New Orleans.

This will introduce a whole new concept in parent-teacher conferences.

We are pleased to introduce the Reverend Duncan McMillan, who will be serving as weekend presider as of June 1.

_____ PARAGRAPHS _____

▷   Hello! May I introduce myself? I'm Flora Mackenzie, and I'm running for city council from Ward 4. I'd like to give you a few reasons to vote for me on November 7.

▷   Sarah Purfoy of Clark Machinery will be in San Francisco February 3, and I've given her my card to present to you. I wasn't sure if you knew that Clark is working on something that may solve your assembly problem. If you haven't time to see her, Ms. Purfoy will understand.

▷   Dear friends of ours, Ellen and Thomas Sutpen, are moving to Jefferson later this month, and I immediately thought of you. They've just bought one hundred acres not far from you, and their two children, Henry and Judith, are almost the same ages as your two. I know you're very busy just now, so I'm not asking you to entertain them or to do anything in particular—I just wanted you to know that the Sutpens are delightful people, and I think you'll enjoy them. Remember us to them when you do meet them.

▷   I would like very much for you to meet Rachel Cameron, as I think she would be a wonderful person to run the Good Samaritan program. I'm having a small cocktail party Friday night, and I thought I could introduce you to her then. What do you think?

▷   A friend of mine whom I admire very much, Dodge Pleydon, will be visiting various galleries in Atlanta this next week, and I suggested he stop by to see you. I think you would be interested in his work. He is rather shy, so if you do not like what he is doing, he will take the hint very quickly. He is not at all like the artist you described who camped outside your office for days at a time trying to get you to change your mind!

▷   I've just learned that our favorite babysitter has moved next door to you. Not only is it a small world but are you lucky! Bob Vincy is dependable, resourceful, and full of fun. I wish I could introduce you to him personally, but I hope this note will inspire you to go over and sign him up immediately.

▷   I would like to arrange a meeting with Rosamund Redding to discuss setting up small investors' groups in rural areas. I know the two of you are good friends, and I thought it might mean something to her if I were to mention that you and I have been in the same investors' group and on the New Beginnings Center board of directors for several years. May I use your name when I write her for an appointment?

▷   I don't often do this, but I'm going to stick my neck out and say that I think you ought to see an engineer named Alec Harvey. The man can do anything, and I think he may be just the person to unsnarl your transportation department. I've asked him to give you a call, but do feel free to tell him you're busy if you don't want to see him. In fact, it was I who urged him to call because I'm so convinced it might be worthwhile for you to meet him.

———————————————— SAMPLE LETTERS ————————————————

Dear Ms. Cardross:
    The account you have established with us has been reassigned within our Telemarketing Department. I would like to introduce myself as your new representative here at Chambers Office Supply and take this opportunity of asking if we can be of any service to you at this time.
    You are currently set up with account AB 40021, and you receive a 15% discount off our list prices.
    I notice that the printer ribbons that you normally buy are on sale this month (25% off).
    If you have any questions regarding your account, or need assistance in any way, please contact me. I will be happy to help you out.
    Thank you for your continued business. I look forward to dealing with you in the near future.

                                        Sincerely,

                            . . . .

Dear Edwin,
    I'm going to be in New York for three weeks in June, trying to find a publisher for my book. I know that you have extensive publishing contacts there, and I wonder if you might know anyone in particular I ought to see and, if so, if you would ever be so kind as to provide me with a letter of introduction.
    I hope this is not an imposition, and I wouldn't want you to do anything you're not comfortable with, so I'll understand perfectly if you don't feel you have any information that would be useful to me.

                                        In grateful appreciation,

. . . .

Dear Henry,

Congratulations on finishing the book! I'm so pleased for you. And, as a matter of fact, I do know someone I think you ought to see while you're in New York. Maud Dolomore has her own literary agency that deals almost exclusively with biographies.

I'm enclosing a brief letter that will introduce you to her. In this case I feel that I am doing both you and Maud a favor by putting you in contact with each other—I suspect your book is something she would be pleased to handle.

Let me know how things turn out.

With best wishes,

. . . .

Dear Henry,

I'm so pleased to hear that you've finished the book! Unfortunately, I've looked through my files but don't see anyone who would be particularly useful to you or to whom I'd feel comfortable writing a letter of introduction.

Most of my contacts are now older and retired, spending their limited time and energy on their own projects. I hope you understand.

Sincerely,

. . . .

Dear Edwin,

I just wanted to let you know that I am so grateful for the letter of introduction you wrote to Maud Dolomore on my behalf.

I had lunch with her, and she decided to represent my book. From finding an agent to finding a book contract is a long way, but I am very pleased to know the manuscript is in good hands.

The next time you are in town for a conference, would you let me know ahead of time so I can take you to lunch?

I will of course let you know immediately if Maud manages to find me a book contract. Thanks again.

Yours truly,

. . . .

Dear Monica,

I've just received your letter asking for a letter of introduction to Herbert Pelham. As a matter of fact, I'm leaving tomorrow for San Francisco and will visit Herb while I'm out there. I'll sound him out about him seeing you. He is, however, something of a recluse and may not agree to it. I hope that when I explain your idea, he will be persuaded.

I'll be in touch sometime after the fifteenth.

Sincerely,

. . . .

Dear Mr. De Fontelles,

Thank you for your letter of August 16 asking me to write you a letter of introduction to my grandfather. Although I am very sympathetic to your project, I must say no to your request. My grandfather is not in good health, and even a letter from me wouldn't get you past the door.

I wish you luck interviewing some of the other former members of the Resistance.

Sincerely yours,

. . . .

Dear Robert,

This letter will introduce Ethel Ormiston to you. Since you are younger than I, you won't remember her. She's Grandma Nell's cousin, and the two of them were raised like sisters. She approached me about our family genealogical records, but I told her that Mother had given everything to you.

I hope you won't mind letting her look at what you have, and possibly photocopy them. Thanks.

. . . .

Dear Gordon and Madeline,

Some very good friends of ours, Nina and Charles Marsden, are going to be in Seattle August 18 to September 1. I usually hesitate to put strangers in touch with each other because too often it doesn't seem to work out. But in this case, I have a feeling you would very much enjoy meeting them. They are both officers of the Midwest Apaloosa Conference and are interested in arranging reciprocal shows with groups from outside the Midwest.

I've mentioned that I'd be writing you, but added that you are very busy and may not even be in town during the last part of August, so there is certainly no obligation to call them. If, however, you have time and think you'd like to meet them, they'll be staying at the Horseshoe Inn on Murray Road.

All our best,

. . . .

Dear Homeowner,

Let me take this opportunity to introduce you to Irmiter Contractors and Builders. Founded in 1921 by my great-grandfather, our sixty-eight years of experience have firmly established us in the home renovation, restoration, and remodeling industry.

We base our professionalism on the principles of old world artisanry and customer service. We are members of, actively participate in, and meet the requirements of the National Association of the Remodeling Industry (NARI) and the National Kitchen and Bath Association (NKBA). Our six decades and four generations of experience in the building trades assure you, the homeowner, of the best return for your home improvement dollar. We are dedicated to creating the perfect living space for you and your family. Irmiter Contractors does this by combining state-of-the-art products and up-to-date management techniques with time-honored traditions of quality workmanship and attention to your needs. We recently received a Regional National Kitchen Design Award from NARI and offer complete design and drafting services for any type of project. In short, we are the problem solvers for the modern family living in an older home environment.

We invite you to compare, to talk to our customers, visit our jobs in progress! You'll see what we've done, what we're doing, and what we can do for you!

Please send the enclosed card or give us a call today, and let's get started on our most important project this year—YOUR HOME!

Sincerely,

Tom Irmiter
President

P.S. We will accept invitations to bid on blueprints.

See also: REFERENCES, REFUSALS, REQUESTS, THANK YOU.

26

Invitations

All major and many minor life events are marked by social occasions to which we invite family and friends. Being social animals, we also celebrate non-events for the pure fun of it. Social gatherings offer friendship, entertainment, relaxation, and a certain necessary ritualization. Invitations can range from the casual "Come visit!" scrawled on a postcard to engraved, highly codified invitations to dinner-dances.

In the world of business, occasions such as banquets, dinners, lunches, cocktail parties, receptions, and open houses offer opportunities to conduct business, to improve employee morale, and to encourage or solidify relationships with clients, customers, suppliers, and others.

The blurring of lines between people's business lives and personal lives is a development with a positive side as well as a negative side. What it means for your correspondence is that there is no longer a sharp line between personal correspondence and business correspondence.

Write Invitations To

- exhibitions/fashion shows/new equipment or product shows/trade shows/book fairs
- fundraising events
- hospitality: lunches/dinners/teas/receptions/open houses/cocktail parties/buffets/brunches/parties
- meetings/workshops/conferences
- open a store account/credit card account or to accept trial membership/subscription/merchandise
- overnight/weekend hospitality
- recitals/performances
- religious ceremonies

- sales (see SALES)
- school events
- showers: baby/engagement/wedding (see also WEDDINGS)
- speaking engagements: conference/banquet/workshop
- tours: factory/office/plant
- weddings (see WEDDINGS)

How to Say It

□   State the occasion (open house, dinner dance, retirement party).

□   Give the date (month, day, year, and sometimes day of week) and time (include a.m. or p.m.).

□   Include the address (with instructions on how to get there, or perhaps even a map if it is difficult to find).

□   Mention refreshments, if appropriate

□   Include the charge, if any (for fundraisers, and certain other nonsocial events).

□   Enclose an engraved/printed reply card and envelope or include an R.S.V.P., R.s.v.p., Please respond, or Regrets only in the lower left corner of the invitation, along with an address or phone number where the response can be sent.

□   A telephone number is required with an R.S.V.P. (unless all the invitees are well acquainted with the host). When there is no R.S.V.P., a telephone number is optional.

□   The preferred dress (black tie, white tie, formal, informal, casual, costume) is indicated in the lower right corner (optional).

□   Inform overnight guests of when you expect them to arrive and leave, what special clothes they may need (for tennis, swimming, hiking), whether they will be sharing a room with a child, sleeping on the floor, or will need a sleeping bag, and whether there will be other guests. Ask whether they can tolerate animals, cigarette smoke, or other potential nuisances.

□   Additional information might include parking facilities, alternate arrangements in case of rain, and an offer of transportation.

□   Express your anticipated pleasure in seeing the person.

What Not to Say

□   Do not use abbreviations in formal invitations except for "Mr.," "Mrs.," "Ms.," "Dr.," "Jr.," and sometimes military rank. Avoid initials in names. In

very formal invitations, write out "Second" and "Third" after a name, although you may use roman numerals: Jason Prescott Allen III. (There is no
comma between the name and the numeral. There is, however, a comma
between the name and "Jr.") States should be spelled out (Alabama, not Ala.
or AL) and the time is spelled out ("half past eight o'clock").

Tips on Writing

☐   When you need to know who is coming, include a reply card. This card,
of the same paper, style, and format as your invitation, is enclosed with a
small envelope (at least 3 1/2 inches by 5 inches to meet postal requirements) that is stamped and printed or engraved with your address.

☐   When inviting a single person or, for example, a work acquaintance
whose spouse you do not know, be sure to indicate if the invitation (1) is
intended only for that person; (2) includes a friend; (3) can be taken either
way as long as you are notified ahead of time how many are coming.

☐   When inviting people to an in-house business event, you can simply
send a memo that includes: type of occasion (retirement, going-away, service anniversary); time, date, place; whether refreshments will be provided; if
a collection is being taken up; an extension number to call for confirmation
or information.

☐   There is a general and unfortunate laxity about responding to invitations today. Wedding couples report sending beautifully engraved invitations, complete with self-addressed, stamped response cards, which very
few of their invitees bother to return. The couple is then surprised (and
socially and financially embarrassed) when nearly everyone shows up at the
reception. To obtain an accurate account of the number of guests you can
expect at your reception, you may have to telephone all those who failed to
respond and ask if they're planning to attend. It might also help to replace
the "R.S.V.P." with something in plain English ("Please reply" or "Please
respond") although it appears that fewer and fewer people understand that it
is *always* necessary to respond to an invitation that carries an "R.S.V.P." or
"Please reply" on it.

☐   Formal invitations are generally engraved or printed on fine-quality
notepaper, use a line-by-line style, and are phrased in the third person
("Terence Mulvaney requests the pleasure of your company at a dinner-
dance in honor of his daughter . . ."). They may also be handwritten, using
the same format and phrasing.

☐   Informal invitations use either commercial fill-in cards or are handwritten on informal stationery or foldovers in usual letter style (first person,
run-in format). The invitation is usually written on the first page of a foldover

or, if this page has your name on it, you can add the details of the invitation below your name. You can answer informal invitations with the same type of stationery. If you have cards with your name or personalized stationery you can simply write under your name "accepts with pleasure/declines with regret the kind invitation of . . ." and complete the information.

▫ When issuing invitations to families with young children, if you want to invite the children, list them by their first names on the envelope on the line underneath their parents' names. (Never add "and family.") Older children (somewhere between thirteen and eighteen) should receive their own invitations. Be particularly sensitive to adults living in the family home; their names should not be tacked onto their parents' invitation.

▫ When you must cancel or postpone an invitation, much will depend on how much time you have. If you are able to have formal announcements engraved or printed, follow the original invitation closely in format, style, and quality of paper. Generally, you will handwrite the note, adopting a formal or informal style depending on the original invitation: "Mr. and Mrs. Hans Oosthuizen regret that it is necessary/that they are obliged to postpone/cancel/recall their invitation to dinner on . . ." or "We must unfortunately cancel the dinner party we had planned for . . ."

▫ When you must cancel an engagement that you have already accepted, call at once to let your host know and then follow up with a brief note apologizing for the change of plans. Stress your regret and offer a believable excuse. If you have to cancel at the last minute or if you know your cancellation is a serious inconvenience, you may want to send flowers along with your note.

▫ For many years, it has been considered improper to make any mention of gifts in an invitation. It is still highly inappropriate to suggest the kind of gift (by mentioning where one is registered for wedding gifts or specifying that money is the gift of choice, for example). However, the problem remains of how to tell invitees that gifts are not wanted (for example, by the person celebrating an eightieth birthday who has no need of gifts and no room for them). This little rule can be broken if done gracefully. People celebrating a twenty-fifth wedding anniversary who have all the appliances, china, and knick-knacks they can comfortably live with might write, "Your friendship is very special to us. We ask that you bring no other gift." Or, by requesting that guests bring a particular "gift," you let them know that nothing else is expected. Such "gifts" might include a favorite recipe; a potluck dish to share; old pictures, clippings, or written-out anecdotes for a scrapbook; something that is primarily symbolic of the gathering's theme (each person to bring a candle, favorite cartoon, sheet music, etc.).

▫ When sending invitations to a fundraising event, enclose a postage-paid reply envelope to make it easy for people to buy their tickets. You may want to note whether their ticket is tax-deductible. If you do not include a reply envelope, make it clear where to send the check and how to obtain tickets. Some fundraisers fail because potential donors are busy people who can't take the time to read the small print or guess how they should handle the request.

☐   If you are planning a sit-down dinner, you may want to specify two times on the invitation: the time you hope to see your guests and the time you expect to dine. People are often casual about arriving late, and dinner can be spoiled by having to be put back. This will allow you to begin dinner on time.

☐   Timing is important. Invitations to an important event involving out-of-town guests may need to be mailed as early as six months ahead of time. Invitations should be sent up to four or five weeks before a dinner or any formal event involving local people, two to four weeks before a reception or cocktail party, and two weeks for more casual dinners and get-togethers. If you are using engraved or printed invitations or are hand-addressing a large number of invitations, you will need to allow even more lead time.

☐   Invitations to religious ceremonies should include: date, time, place, type of ceremony, information about reception or gathering afterwards, an expression of pleasure at the thought of seeing them and hopes that they can attend. Invitations to a bar mitzvah or bat mitzvah can be engraved, printed, or handwritten, should be sent at least a month in advance, and should include: the young person's full name; time, date, place; details about recep-tion or celebration afterwards.

☐   An invitation is issued in the name(s) of the host(s). It is no longer true that all but the most formal social invitations are issued and replied to over the wife's signature even when both husband and wife are hosts or guests. The matter of names for women that appear on invitations ("Which is proper—married name, business name, birth name?") is fairly simple: the woman uses whatever name pleases her, and the prospective guest responds using that name. When you are issuing invitations and you are unsure of how to address the woman, call her office or her home and ask. This is a perfectly acceptable question today. For business invitations, hosts often have their titles and company names after their own names. Friends may issue invitations together. Even groups ("The Castorley Foundation invites you . . ." or "The Central High School senior class invites you . . .") may issue invitations.

☐   Response cards and self-addressed, stamped envelopes encourage prompt replies and are invaluable when you need to know the exact number of guests. The cards are printed with a simple formula: "M_____ [guest's name to be filled in] _____ regrets _____ accepts [one or the other checked off] for Thursday, May 14, 1991." In some case the words "accepts" and "regrets" stand alone, and the guest is to cross out the word that does not apply or circle the one that does. Printers generally have samples and can advise you how these should be done.

□   When you want to know in advance how many will be accepting your invitation, place R.S.V.P or R.s.v.p. at the bottom left corner of the invitation to indicate that a reply is expected. French for "Respond if you please" ("Répondez s'il vous plaît"), the phrase may be replaced by "Please reply." You may also use "Regrets only." In this case, people call or write only if they are unable to attend, the assumption being that all others will attend. Indicate where your invitees are to respond. When an invitation is issued by several people in honor of someone else to be held at an unfamiliar address, it may not be immediately clear where the reply should be sent. An address or phone number should be included directly beneath the R.S.V.P. When inviting a large number of people to an exhibition, reception, open house, cocktail party, or other less intimate gathering, omit the R.S.V.P. When you do not hear from people, even after enclosing reply cards or inserting an R.S.V.P., you may have to call them or send follow-up notes to determine whether they are coming.

□   The types of dress you might indicate for your guests include: "black tie" or "formal," which generally mean the same thing, that is, a tuxedo for the men and an evening dress for the women. ("Black tie" applies only to the men; the women can wear a gown of any color or length.) "White tie," which is a rarity nowadays, means white tie and tails for the men and long, formal gowns with over-the-elbow gloves in cooler weather for the women. "Semiformal," an all-encompassing term generally used for early-evening gatherings or cocktail parties, can mean just about anything except a long gown.

□   When inviting someone to speak at your conference or organization's meeting, your invitation should include: the name of the conference and sponsoring organization; the date, time, and place; the type of audience (size, level of interest, previous exposure to subject); the kind of speech wanted; the length of time allotted; equipment available for use; accommodation and transportation information or directions to the meeting site; whether there will be a question and answer session; a description of the program; meals available; name of the contact person; details of the honorarium; an offer of further assistance; an expression of your pleasure at having the person speak to your group. You might also include a request for biographical information on the speaker to use in the program.

Special Situations

□   Invitations to social events related to a début are issued by the parents, whether married, widowed, divorced, or separated: "Sir Arthur and Lady Dorcas Clare request the pleasure of your company at a dinner dance in honor of their daughter Millicent on Saturday . . ." When simply receiving, the invitation can read: "Mrs. Sybil Fairford and Miss Elizabeth Fairford will be at home Sunday the second of June from five until half past seven o'clock, One Cooper Row."

□   Many sales letters use an "invitation" approach—some are brief and worded like a formal invitation. They invite the customer to come to a special showing, sale, or demonstration or to become a member, account holder, or subscriber. Others use the phrase "you are invited to . . ." in the first paragraph, and then go on to develop the message like a regular sales letter.

□   If your local newspaper is one of the few that still report special social events, you can write a letter to the society editor that includes: time, date, and place; type of event; reason for it; description of flowers, decorations, food; guest list; background information on the guest of honor or any high-profile guests; anything that makes the event special; a promise to call just before or after the event with any corrections; an expression of your appreciation and an offer to provide additional information if necessary. Timing may be important, so telephone for guidelines before submitting your material.

□   Annual meetings are usually announced with the formal notice required by corporation by-laws, but invitations may also be sent, especially if there is a banquet or dinner following. No reply is necessary in order to attend the meeting, but a reply is usually requested for the dinner.

Format

□   Formal invitations are engraved or printed on good-quality foldovers or notecards. Printers, stationery stores, and large department stores can offer you a number of styles, types of paper, inks, and designs.

□   Business invitations range from elite engraved invitations to lower-quality printed (but still formal-appearing) invitations to invitations typed on letterhead stationery, memo paper, personal-business stationery, and even postcards.

□   Personal invitations may be handwritten on foldovers or personal stationery.

□   Invitations that are actually sales letters may be constructed as form letters and mass distributed.

□   There are a number of commercial fill-in-the-blank invitations on the market; there is nothing wrong with using these for casual gatherings. Some of them are even quite cheerful and clever.

□   If you entertain regularly you may want to order engraved or printed invitations with blank spaces to be filled in as needed. In either formal or informal format, the invitations might read: "Mr. and Mrs. Desmond Mulligan request the pleasure of [name's] company at [event] on [date] at [time] o'clock, 1843 Thackeray Street."

_____ WORDS _____

attend	event	rejoice
cancel	honor	salute
celebration	installation	solemnize
commemorate	postpone	welcome
début		

_____ PHRASES _____

accept with pleasure
be our guest
give a warm reception to
have the honor of inviting
in commemoration/celebration of
in honor of
invite you to
kindly respond on or before
looking forward to seeing you

obliged to recall/cancel/postpone
owing to the illness/death of
Piper's Village Inn cordially invites you to
request the company of/the pleasure of the
   company of
we are celebrating
we would like to invite you to
you are cordially invited

_____ SENTENCES _____

A revolutionary new service is now available to valued customers—and you're among
   the first invited to enroll.
Can you and Aunt Amelie join us this year for Thanksgiving dinner?
Come hear noted Reformation scholar and professor of history Dr. Margaret Heath
   speak on September 12 at the 8:30 and 11:00 services at Gloria Dei Lutheran
   Church, 1924 Forster Avenue.
Do drop in—if only for a few minutes.
I have asked a few friends to stop by after work on Friday the 20th—can you join us?
I'm looking forward to seeing all of you again.
I'm pleased to invite you to acquire the Golden American Bank Card.
It will be so good to see you again.
I urge you to look over the enclosed materials and consider this special invitation now.
Mr. and Mrs. Alex Polk-Faraday regret that it is necessary to cancel their invitation to
   brunch on Sunday, the sixteenth of August, because of the illness of their daughter.
Owing to the illness of Mr. Barclay, Lettice Watson and Thomas Barclay are obliged
   to recall their invitation for Thursday, the sixth of July.
Please confirm by June 6 that you can attend.
We are looking forward to seeing you again.
We hope to see you there.
We hope you can join us.
We invite you to apply for an account with us.

You are invited to a special evening showing of our new line of furniture from European designers.

─────────────────────── PARAGRAPHS ───────────────────────

▷   The family of Mr. and Mrs. Frank Jervis invite you to help Laura and Frank celebrate their Golden Wedding Anniversary! An Open House will be held at the Russell Eagles Hall, from 1:00 to 4:00 p.m. on Sunday, March 10, 1992.

▷   You are invited to attend the Fall Family Festival this Tuesday evening from 6:00 to 9:00 p.m. at Temple Beth Shalom, 14 Burnsville Parkway. There will be puppet shows, activity booths, games, and refreshments!

. . . .

Kindly respond on or before
September 18, 1993

*M*_____

accepts/declines
Number of Persons _____

. . . .

▷   You are invited to hear the National Liturgical Choir under the direction of Maugrabin Hayraddin at 4:00 p.m. Sunday, September 28, at Quentin Methodist Church, 1823 Scott Avenue. The sixty-voice chorus will sing Russian liturgical music by Gretchaninof and Kalinikof and selections by Bach, Shaw, and Schutz. The cost is $5 ($3 for seniors and students).

▷   You are invited to join the Henderson Video Club for one month—at absolutely no cost to you. Tell us which four selections to send you, and they will be sent out the same day we receive your order.

▷   The tenth annual Public Works Open House will be held on Tuesday, October 3, from 4:00 to 7:00 p.m. at the Evans Street yards, a block south of Owen Avenue. There are things to do and things to see for the whole family. Get your picture taken up on a Public Works "cherry picker." Car buffs can tour the biggest maintenance and repair shop in the city, and you will have a chance to win your own traffic signal. There will be giveaways, drawings for prizes, music, food, and entertainment. Some lucky winner will take home an actual traffic signal used for fifty years on the corner of Blodwen and Marquand Streets.

▷   Please plan to attend the Hargate open house this Thursday, September 26, at 7 p.m. You will have the opportunity to meet the school staff, sit in on each of your student's classes during a simulated (but greatly shortened) school day, and talk to other parents during the social hour that follows. (A contribution for the refreshment table will be greatly appreciated.)

_____ SAMPLE LETTERS _____

Lucas-Dockery Importers, Inc.
cordially invites you to a
cocktail hour and reception
in honor of their merger with
Sheridan International Associates
Friday, the tenth of November
from five to half past eight o'clock
Mansfield Gardens
One Mansfield Commons

. . . .

Dear James Ayrton,

You are invited to become a member of the Brodie Community Anti-Crack Coalition. Formed eight months ago, this coalition of three community councils and six community organizations was formed to oppose the activity and effects of illegal drug use and trafficking in Easdaile and especially in the Brodie neighborhood.

Block clubs have been formed, and an information meeting was held last week at the Easdaile High School.

The Brodie Community Council already has two delegates to the coalition, but we believe it would be helpful to have at least one other delegate. Your name has been mentioned several times as someone with the necessary experience and enthusiasm.

I will call you later this week to discuss the possibility of your participation.

Sincerely,

. . . .

Agnes Leslie Graham and Robert Graham
request the pleasure of your company
at a dinner-dance
on Saturday, the twenty-first of May
at seven-thirty o'clock
Harcourt Inn

R.S.V.P.

Dear Dr. Denny:

It is with great pleasure that I invite you to the 43rd Annual Engineering Society Conference. This year's Conference will be held at The Citadel Hotel in downtown Dallas from September 23 through September 27.

We are offering a valuable program with industry-wide applications, speakers who are recognized experts in their field, and topics with many implications for the future (see enclosed brochure). Ample time is scheduled for discussion periods. In addition, tours to two outstanding instructional materials centers have been arranged.

With your budget in mind, we have obtained special meeting rates from the management of The Citadel. Information on accommodations, transportation, and registration is enclosed.

If you have any questions, please call the session coordinator, A.J. Cronin at 610/555-1889.

Sincerely,

. . . .

Houghton-Maguire Marine

cordially invites you to its

First Annual Marine Electronic Equipment Exhibit

1:30 p.m. to 6:30 p.m.

Saturday, May 2, 1992

Highway 32 and County Road C

Refreshments

Drawings

. . . .

Dear Mrs. Lucas,

We are having a reception on Sunday, May 5, from 1:00 p.m. to 4:00 p.m. to celebrate our joy in the adoption of our new son, Philip. It would mean a great deal to us to have you join us.

Sincerely,

. . . .

Haidée Czelovar Power and Raoul Czelovar

cordially invite you to a reception

celebrating the

Golden Wedding Anniversary of

Simone Rakonitz Czelovar and Karl Czelovar

Sunday, the second of April

at eight o'clock

Wyatt's Village Inn

Indianapolis

R.S.V.P.   *Formal Dress*

555-1980

. . . .

Special Savings Invitation!

Dear Martin Lynch Gibbon:

As one of our Preferred Customers, you are invited to save 10% on every purchase you make at Murdoch Jewelers on July 14 and 15. This discount applies to both sale-priced and regular-priced merchandise, and includes our line of dazzling Iris diamonds, the ever-popular Headliner watches for men and women, and our complete selection of wedding gifts.

You deserve the best, and for two days this month, "the best" comes with a discount just for you!

Note: The discount does not include labor or service charges.

. . . .

The liberated hen party, 3rd edition

Come join some of the great women
you never have enough time to chat with
to discuss your life, your loves, your stress level,
the projects that are turning you on,
the things that are making you old, and
howtheheckcanwesurvivethismadpacewithgrace&dignity?

When: Friday, March 10, 1989, 7:30 p.m.
Where: 107 Virginia Street 55102
How nice of you to offer: You really don't
mind bringing a quick/easy hors d'oeuvre/snack? Thanks!

*Joanna * Mary Kaye * Anna*
. . . .

Dear Major and Mrs. Caswell,
    We are planning to celebrate Mother and Dad's fortieth wedding anniversary with a dinner-dance at The Azalea Gardens on September 16, at 7:00 p.m. We would love to have you celebrate with us.
    Please let me know if you can join us.

                                            Fondly,
. . . .

The Board of Directors
of the Finsbury United Aid Society
requests the pleasure of your company
at a dinner-dance
on Saturday, the fourteenth of May
at half past seven o'clock
Finsbury Community Ballroom
for the benefit of
The Finsbury Children's Home

Suggested Contribution $50   Black Tie

See also: ACCEPTANCES, ACKNOWLEDGMENTS, REFUSALS, RESPONSES, SALES, THANK YOU, WEDDINGS.

27

Letters Dealing with Orders

"The propensity to truck, barter and exchange one thing
for another . . . is common to all [people], and to be
found in no other race of animals." (Adam Smith)

Most ordering today is done on standardized order forms, purchase forms, and requisition forms, and is handled by means of standardized procedures. Together with telephone ordering, which has surged to new highs in recent years, forms have eliminated most individual letters about orders. As long as there are human beings ordering and filling orders, there will be errors, exceptions, special requests, and problems to write about.

Write Letters About Orders When

- acknowledging/confirming receipt of order/telephone order/delivery date (see also ACKNOWLEDGMENTS, CONFIRMATIONS)
- asking for additional information (see also REQUESTS)
- canceling/changing an order
- complaining about an order (see COMPLAINTS)
- explaining procedures/policy changes/overpayments
- inquiring about order/delivery date/how to return merchandise
- instructing how to order/return goods (see INSTRUCTIONS)
- late payments (see COLLECTION, CREDIT)
- placing an order
- refusing/returning an unsatisfactory order

How to Say It

□   If you are ordering without a form (the form is missing from the catalog, you are responding to a magazine ad), include: the description of the desired item, the quantity, the size, color, personalization/monogram, and the price. Include your own name, address, and zip code, and state your method of payment. If you are paying by bank card, include its number, expiration date, and your signature. If you are buying from a company in your home state, add sales tax to the total. Also include any stated handling charges. Specify shipping directions or any special considerations.

□　When responding to orders received, it is helpful to have an all-purpose form for problem orders. After saying something like, "Thank you for your order. We are unable to ship your merchandise at once because . . ." list a series of possible problems so that one or more can be circled, underlined, or checked off. Some suggestions: Payment has not been received. We no longer fill C.O.D. orders—please send a check or money order. We do not have a complete shipping address. We are currently out of stock—may we ship later? We no longer carry that item—may we send a substitution of equal value and similar style? We need to know the size (quantity, style, color, etc.). You neglected to include shipping and handling charges in your payment.

□　When you must return an order that is unsatisfactory, include in your cover letter: your name and address; a description of the enclosed merchandise; a copy of the sales slip, invoice, or shipping label; an explanation of why you're returning it; your request for a refund, credit to your account, or replacement merchandise; an expression of appreciation. If returning the merchandise is difficult (in the case of a large appliance, for example), write first and ask how it should be returned. Always ask for (although you may not always get) reimbursement for your shipping costs.

□　When you are canceling a prepaid order or when asking for a refund, give all possible information: order/invoice/reference number, date of order, description of merchandise. Specify whether your payment should be returned to you as cash or check (if you paid by check), as a credit to your account or your bank card (if you charged it), or as a credit to your company's account.

What Not to Say

□　Avoid including other business (request for a new catalog, complaint about a substitution in a previous order, request for preferred-customer status) when placing an order. It may delay the order.

Tips on Writing

□　Arrange your order on the page so that it can be deciphered at a glance. Instead of phrasing an order as a long sentence ("I would like to order six pairs of size 11 men's white ankle socks and four pairs of size 11 men's black ankle sox, at $7.95 per pair . . .''), arrange the information in columns. Set off data so as to be quickly read—there will be a smaller chance of error in your order.

□   If you need merchandise or supplies by a certain date, state it clearly. By making explicit in your letter the importance of the delivery date, you will in most instances be able to cancel the order without forfeiture if you fail to receive it in time; the letter can serve as an informal contract.

Special Situations

□   If your first order should go astray and you send in a second, emphasize that it is a duplicate order. Too often, the first order eventually turns up and is also filled.

Format

□   Orders were made for forms, and vice versa. Although no two order forms are precisely alike, a few items are standard: customer's name, business name or title, address, zip code, and telephone number with area code; customer's account number; description of merchandise, page where it appears in catalog (optional), quantity wanted, size, color, type; monogram or personalization; price per unit; total price for each item; shipping and handling chart; sales tax information; amount enclosed; shipping information (options available plus approximate length of shipping time); space for bank card number, expiration date, and signature; spaces for signatures from purchasing department or other authorization.

□   Individualized letters dealing with orders are generally typed on letterhead or memo stationery.

□   If writing about a personal order from your home, a handwritten note is acceptable if clearly written.

_____ WORDS _____

articles	expedite	merchandise
billed	freight	overpayment
cancel	goods	receipt
change	handling	rush
charge	immediately	stock
confirm	invoice	urgent
depot	items	warehouse

_____ PHRASES _____

as soon as possible/at once
being shipped to you
confirm your order
delivery date of
enclosed is my check for
if you have any further problems
I would like to order
must cancel my order of

please advise us/let us know
please bill to
prompt attention
retail/wholesale price
return receipt requested
ship C.O.D.
shipping and handling charges

_____ SENTENCES _____

Along with your order I'm enclosing our spring catalog as I think you'll want to
know about our new lower prices (many are lower than last year's!) and our completely new line of Strato work clothes.

If you cannot have the storage cabinets here by October 3, please cancel the order and
advise us at once.

Please bill this order to my account # JO4889.

Please cancel my order for the Heatherstone china (copy of order enclosed)—the
three-month delay you mentioned is unacceptable.

Please charge this order to my Carlyle First Bank Credit Card # 333-08-4891, expiration date 11/95 (signature below).

Please check on the status of my order #90-4657 dated March 1.

Please confirm receipt of this order.

Please include your account number/invoice number/order number on all correspondence.

Thank you for your order.

We hope you enjoy your personalized stationery, and will think of us for your other
stationery needs.

We look forward to serving you.

You should receive your order by August 1.

_____ PARAGRAPHS _____

▷   This is to confirm receipt of your order #104-1297 dated June 17, 1992. It will
be shipped on or about June 26. Please allow two to three weeks for arrival. If you
need to contact us again about this order, use our reference number, 442-48895.

▷   I'm sorry, but we no longer ship C.O.D. Please send a check or money order for
$782.11 so that we can expedite your order.

▷   Please note that you received a special price on the sheet protectors. Your refund
check for the overpayment is enclosed.

▷   We are trying to match exactly the interior folders we use for our hanging files.
The ones shown in your current catalog, page 217, look very much like ours. Could
you please send us samples in several colors so that we can be sure before ordering?

▷   With one exception, your order is being shipped to you from our Gregsbury warehouse this week. The six portable desktop calculators, however, are coming from our Chicago warehouse, and we have been experiencing some delays from that warehouse recently. You may not receive the calculators until approximately March 8. Please let us know if this is acceptable.

———————————— SAMPLE LETTERS ————————————

Dear Dr. Sturmthal:

   Thank you for your purchase order # H459991, which we received on June 3, for the TEM-500 Transmission Electron Microscope. Your order has been sent to our Administration Department and your Purchasing Department will be advised directly as to the confirmation of terms and shipping dates.

   Teresa Desterro, Manager of the Sales Department, located in our Gillespie Office, will advise you of confirmed delivery dates and can provide you with answers to questions on order processing or shipment expediting. Alec Loding, National Service Manager, also located in our Gillespie Office, will send you complete information on the installation requirements of your new TEM-500. Both Ms. Desterro and Mr. Loding can be reached directly by calling 212/555-1212.

   We appreciate your order and the confidence you have shown in our company and in our instruments. We look forward to hearing from you either now or in the future if there is any way in which we may be of assistance to you.

                                                              Sincerely yours,

. . . .

Dear Ritson Projectors:

   We have just received the audio cassette front- and rear-screen slide projector we ordered from you on November 3 (copies of order and invoice enclosed). One of the lenses appears to have been broken in transit.

   Please let us know whether we should return the entire projector to you, take it to a service center if you have one in the vicinity, or have it repaired and bill you.

                                                              Yours truly,

. . . .

TO: Conford Confections
FROM: Alexander Trott
DATE: June 3, 1992

   I have been buying your Conford Confections for family, friends, and business acquaintances twice a year (Easter and Christmas) for many years. I will be traveling in Europe this summer and would like to take along Confections to offer friends and business acquaintances there.

   My questions:

   1. Do Confections need to be refrigerated, either to maintain good quality and appearance or to ensure that there is no product spoilage?

   2. Do you have outlets for your product in Europe? (I would not like to cart them along as a "special treat" and then find them being sold everywhere over there.)

3. Is there any other reason that would prevent me from taking Confections with me? (Do they melt easily, for example?)

If you can reassure me on the above points, please place my order for:

6 boxes	8 oz. Gift Box	$ 7.95
10 boxes	14 oz. Supremes	$12.95

My check for $197.83 (including sales tax and shipping and handling) is enclosed. Please ship to the letterhead address.

If you think I'm liable to be unhappy traveling with the Confections, I will appreciate your saying so and returning my check.

See also: ACKNOWLEDGMENTS, ADJUSTMENTS, APOLOGIES, COLLECTION, COMPLAINTS, CONFIRMATIONS, CREDIT, INSTRUCTIONS, REFUSALS, RESPONSES.

28

Letters About
Organizations/Clubs

"Please accept my resignation. I don't want to belong
to any club that would accept me as a member."
(Groucho Marx)

There are over 20,000 national and international organizations listed in the *Encyclopedia of Associations* (Gale Research Company), and many other clubs, societies, and groups function in less formal ways to provide people with ways of sharing interests, goals, lifestyles, professional information, and recreational activities.

Most club or organization correspondence is brief, routine, and easily written. But every announcement, invitation, or letter also represents the organization to its members and to the public and thus should be carefully prepared and attractively presented.

Write Letters Dealing with Clubs/Organizations For

- announcements: meetings/changes/reminders (see ANNOUNCE-MENTS)
- invitations: organization events/speaking engagements (see also IN-VITATIONS)
- meetings: canceling/changing
- requests: membership/sponsorship/applications/volunteers/information/copies of agenda or minutes
- recommending new member (see also REFERENCES)
- resignations
- welcoming new members (see also WELCOME)

How to Say It

□   When announcing a meeting, include: the name of your organization; the date, time, and place of the meeting; a phone number for further information; at least one reason why a person would want to attend the meeting (celebrity guest speaker, special election, panel discussion, book signings).

□   When inviting someone to speak to your group, include: your organization's full title; a list of members, if possible, with an estimate of how big the audience might be; a description of the group's interests and backgrounds so that the speaker can target the audience better; directions or a map to the meeting place; the name and phone number of someone who can give the speaker additional information. You might also want to mention what equipment (overhead projector, microphone) is available.

What Not to Say

□   Avoid putting anything down on paper that could be construed as negative. Personality conflicts, disagreements and disputes over policies, and shifting allegiances all give groups their dynamism and distinct character, but they are best handled face to face. Committing delicate situations to letters that go in public files is unwise.

□   Most groups today have a collegial rather than hierarchical spirit, so beware of paternalistic, top-down letters to members.

Tips on Writing

□   Unless you write on behalf of a small, casual group, keep letters to members businesslike and somewhat formal. Spuriously intimate letters are offputting to some people, whereas a reserved letter may strike others as less warm but certainly not offensive.

□   Be obsessive about spelling members' names correctly. We have all gotten used to the mutilation of our names on generic mailing labels, but no one likes to see it from their professional or social group.

Special Situations

□   You may be asked to do a favor or write a recommendation for someone in your club or society whom you don't know well. By virtue of association and club kinship, there is a subtle pressure to respond positively. But you are no more obliged in this case than in any other (see REFUSALS).

Format

☐   Type all club or organization business correspondence. An exception might be a social club in which the members know each other very well and might handwrite memos to each other.

☐   Postcards are wonderfully useful in getting out meeting notices, announcements, invitations, and short messages.

☐   For an organization of any size, your mailing list should be computerized; combined with the merge function of most word processing systems, corresponding with members is simple and quick.

WORDS

affiliation	consortium	policies
allegiance	constitution	procedures
alliance	guild	qualifications
association	headquarters	regulations
bylaws	league	rules
coalition	lodge	society
committee	nominate	

PHRASES

a credit to the organization	have been elected a member of
affiliated/associated with	join forces
belong to	minutes of the meeting
board of directors	slate of officers
committee chair	would like to nominate you for

SENTENCES

Congratulations on your election to Pi Delta Phi, the honorary French academic society.

I am sorry to inform you that family illness obliges me to step down from the club vice-presidency, effective immediately.

It is with great pleasure/regret that I accept/decline your nomination to the Board of Directors of Montmorency House.

I would be happy to discuss any question you have about the Club over lunch some day next week.

I would consider it a privilege to put your name forward for membership.

I would like to recommend/wish to propose Brander Cheng for membership in the Burke Orchestra Society.

Join now and take advantage of this very limited offer to new members.

Please accept my resignation from the Rembrandt Society.

To join the Frobisher Society today, simply indicate your membership category on the enclosed form and return it with your check.

We offer our members extensive personal benefits unavailable from any other organization.

Would you please place the following three items on the agenda for the November meeting?

PARAGRAPHS

▷ The Belford Area Women in Trades Organization invites you to attend its next monthly meeting, Thursday, June 14, at 7:30 p.m. in the old Belford Union Hall. Get to know us. See what we're trying to do for women in trades in this area. And then, if you like what you see, join up! Introductory one-year membership is $45, and we think we can do as much for you as you can do for the Organization!

▷ This is to acknowledge receipt of your membership application. You will hear from us as soon as we have received all your references and evaluated your application. Thank you for your interest in the Society.

▷ I understand you and some other employees have formed several noon-hour foreign language clubs. I would be interested in joining your Italian-speaking group. Can you put me in touch with whoever is in charge of it? Thanks.

▷ Congratulations to our new officers, elected at the September 12 meeting: Truda Silber, president; Martin Lynch Gibbon, vice-president; Andrew Davies, secretary; Maria Eleonora Schoning, treasurer. They will be installed at the beginning of the October 15 meeting. Our most sincere gratitude is extended to last year's officers, who saw the Club through a remarkable expansion and a rewriting of the bylaws. Thanks, Fran, Leo, Rose, and Dennis!

▷ Notice: The Professional Educators Network will *not* hold its regularly scheduled monthly meeting on February 10 at 7:30 p.m. We regret any inconvenience this cancellation may cause you. The next meeting will be held March 8 at 7:30 p.m. in the Schley Library meeting room.

▷ We are all, of course, very sorry to see you resign, but we understand that you have many other obligations at this time. We will be happy to welcome you back whenever your circumstances change. It's been wonderful having you with us.

▷ Thanks so much for helping to clean up after the dance last Saturday. It's certainly not a popular job, which makes me appreciate all the more the good-hearted folks who did pitch in. The next time you're on the committee, you can put me down for clean-up!

————————————————— SAMPLE LETTERS —————————————————

Dear Hugh,

As a member and current secretary of the Merrivale Philatelic Society, I'm always on the lookout for other stamp collectors. Someone happened to mention yesterday that you have been collecting for years. Would you be interested in joining us?

Because some of the members have quite valuable collections, we are careful to accept newcomers only on the basis of three references in addition to the recommendation of a member.

I would like to propose you for membership, if you think it's something you would enjoy. I'm enclosing some information that will tell you a little more about the group and its activities.

Let me know if you're interested, because I'd be pleased to sponsor you.

Sincerely,

· · · · · · · · · · ·

Dear Friend,

There is something remarkable and unique about the Tropical Fish & Aquarists Club. For one thing, it really is a club, not an organization whose "membership benefits" amount to little more than having your name on a mailing list and receiving a monthly magazine.

When you join the Tropical Fish & Aquarists Club, you don't belong to it—it belongs to you. You have the option of meeting with other hobbyists in large, small, or special-interest groups as often as you and your co-enthusiasts want. You are entitled to four free five-line ads per year in a magazine that reaches thousands of other hobbyists. We'll extend your subscription to the magazine for one year if you contribute an article for publication. And . . . at the end of each year, we share any profits from membership fees and magazine revenues with members.

You don't belong to the Club; it belongs to you!

Yours truly,

· · · · · · · · · · ·

To: Board of Directors

It is with much regret that I resign my position as Secretary of the Macduff Drama Club. Family complications necessitate that I withdraw from any evening activities at least for the foreseeable future.

I have thoroughly enjoyed my association with the Macduff Club and am particularly sorry to give up my office. If I can be of any help to my successor, I am available by telephone.

Best wishes to all of you. I will look forward to joining again as soon as possible.

· · · · · · · · · · ·

TO: Admissions Committee
FROM: Paul Dombey
DATE: April 16, 1992
RE: Recommendation for membership

It is my pleasure to propose for membership in the Granger Social Club Louisa and John Chick. I know Louisa and John both personally and professionally; he is a fellow merchant, owner of Chick Book & Stationery, and she is Louisa Dombey, my sister. I recommend them to you very highly.

They are both graduates of Walter Gay University, members of Trinity Lutheran Church, and hosts of a weekly book club. In addition, Ms. Chick is currently president and part-owner of The Women's Collective and Mr. Chick has served as vice-president of the local merchants' group.

They are charming people, committed and accomplished tennis players, and assets to the community. I think the Club would benefit from their addition to its rolls.

Sincerely,

See also: ANNOUNCEMENTS, FUNDRAISING, INVITATIONS, REFERENCES, REFUSALS, REQUESTS, RESPONSES, WELCOME.

29

References and Recommendations

Letters of recommendation and letters of reference are so closely related that guidelines for writing them are nearly identical. A letter of reference vouches for a person's general character. It situates the person in time and space, verifying that they do indeed have a history and are known to people of substance. Most often, the writer of the reference letter doesn't even know where the letter will end up; it is aimed at "prospective employers" or at some unfamiliar name, title, and company.

The letter of recommendation is narrower and more specific. The writer of this letter knows both the subject of the letter *and* the person or company to which it is directed. In this way, the person essentially says: I know both of you, and I suspect you have enough in common to merit getting together.

A letter of reference will get a person into an interview by assuring a prospective employer that they are a decent, law-abiding sort. A letter of recommendation will add weight to an individual's application as it is being evaluated.

Letters of Reference and Recommendation Include

- asking someone to write a letter on your behalf
- club membership (see also ORGANIZATIONS)
- credit references (see CREDIT)
- recommendations: individuals/ideas/companies/projects/products/ services/programs/workshops/new procedures/managerial decisions/ plans of action

- references: former employees/students/friends/family members/customers/neighbors/babysitters
- refusing to write (see also REFUSALS)
- requesting information from a previous employer or from a reference cited by an applicant
- thanking someone for writing (see also THANK YOU)

How to Say It

□   When asking someone to write a letter of reference or recommendation for you, describe in detail the type of reference information that will be most helpful to you. When a prospective employer asks someone to provide a reference for an applicant, it is most effective to describe the type of employment the candidate is seeking. The person can then relate the applicant's background to the position.

□   When giving a reference for a former employee, include: the employee's full name, length of employment, and job title and duties; a description of the qualities that made the person a good employee; an expression of regret at their leaving (if this was the case); an offer to provide further information, either on the telephone or in writing; your name, address, and telephone number.

□   When writing a general reference for someone, include: length of time you've known the person; the kind of relationship you have with them (teacher, neighbor, former employer); comments on the person's trustworthiness, sense of responsibility, or other characteristics; your reasons for thinking the person would make a good employee, member, candidate, scholarship winner; an offer to provide further information if necessary. A general letter of reference focuses more on the person's character than on employment background, since often you aren't sure who will be receiving the letter and which particular job skills should be emphasized. Prospective employers assume that the better you know the person and the more enthusiastic you are about them, the more detailed your letter will be. Therefore, if you feel positively disposed toward the subject of your letter, give as much concrete detail to support your claims as you can. You will want to consider, too, that very often the person you are writing about will have access to the letter. In this case, the person needs a general letter that can be photocopied as many times as necessary and given to prospective employers, college admissions boards, scholarship committees, and so forth.

□   When recommending someone for a specific position or to a specific company, first find out as much as you can about the situation. In this way, you will know whether the person and the situation are really a good match.

If they are, you can write a very effective recommendation. Include: the person's full name; the length and type of your association with the person ("I have been Mr. Drake's immediate supervisor for the past six years"); the person's best qualities along with detailed examples supporting your statement; your reasons for thinking the person is of interest to the reader; a summary statement of your confidence in the person; an offer to provide additional information if necessary.

□   When recommending a service or product to someone, confine yourself to a description of your own experiences with that service or product. If a friend moves to your former town and asks you to recommend a physician, you can certainly name your former physician and describe the kind of care you received. But it is a little risky to unreservedly recommend things to other people whose perceptions, experiences, and criteria may be different from yours. It is best to pepper such a recommendation with "in my opinion" or "You may want to check with a few of your new neighbors for their recommendations too," or "I don't know if the Crossland Clinic is everyone's cup of tea, but we were very satisfied."

□   When thanking someone for writing you a recommendation or reference, include in addition to your thanks any news of your job search, membership application, college admission efforts—or at least a promise to let the person know what happens. Even if you don't get the position or choose not to take it, you will want to express your gratitude to the person for writing on your behalf.

□   When you are making a formal recommendation or proposal for a specific course of action, advocating a policy change, supporting a decision, or giving advice in an area of expertise, include: a subject line or first sentence stating clearly what the letter is about; a summary of your recommendation; statements, statistics, anecdotes, and other support for your recommendation; your offer to accept further negotiation, to engage in further research, or to submit additional information. If your recommendation is critical of previous actions, decisions, or policies, word it in the passive voice, do not point verbal fingers at anyone, and be constructive. Point out the benefits along with the disadvantages, stating perhaps that the latter outweigh the former. Do not apologize for your recommendation. The tone should be matter-of-fact and unemotional.

What Not to Say

□   Although its use is not a major gaffe, "To whom it may concern" has fallen out of favor as a salutation for letters of reference or recommendation destined for people you don't know. Instead, you can use "TO:/FROM:/

DATE:/RE:" or entitle your letter "Introducing Letitia Fillimore," "To Prospective Employees," "Recommendation of Helena Landless," "Letter of Reference for William Einhorn," or give it any other suitable heading.

❑   In writing recommendations or references avoid such statements as "I'd hire her in a minute if she were applying here," "If I were you, I'd snap this one up," or "I can't think of anyone more deserving of this scholarship." Most people resent being told their business. You supply the information; they make the decision.

❑   Avoid saying something you can't prove. This is often not so much outright dishonesty as misplaced enthusiasm, but it can work to the subject's eventual disadvantage.

Tips on Writing

❑   The single most important advice in writing effective recommendations and references is: be specific. It is a principle of good writing not to *tell* the reader but to *show* the reader. Instead of saying merely that someone is honest, you might explain that the person had access to the cash register, and even when experiencing personal financial hardship, the person's receipts were always accurate to the penny. Instead of saying someone is compassionate, tell about the time they missed a dinner party to help a troubled co-worker.

❑   Don't be too lavish or use too many superlatives—it undermines your credibility.

❑   When you can speak from your own knowledge of a person's honesty, loyalty, competence, or easygoing temperament, do so. These qualities are usually important to the prospective employer, especially whenever the position involves sensitive information, access to the employer's family, handling money, or representing the employer to the public.

❑   Even though the person you are recommending may have a dozen outstanding personal characteristics and abilities, try to focus on just two or three. When a letter appears too effusive and the subject too perfect, the reader tends to discount the entire recommendation. Emphasize the person's strongest qualities and give anecdotal evidence to support your opinion. List other positive character traits later, for example, "Mrs. Dudeny is also cooperative, cheerful, and always willing to stay late in an emergency."

❑   You can sometimes help a person write you a more effective letter of recommendation by spelling out in your request the kind of letter you need and offering as many guidelines as possible. Outline the type of job you are seeking and the qualities needed for it and mention that the more specific they can be the more helpful it will be for you. You can't tell a person what to write, but someone with your interests at heart will then focus on those qualities of yours that match the job description. To make it convenient, enclose a stamped business-sized envelope addressed to the prospective employer. In a few cases, if you know the person well, you might offer to draft a sample recommendation.

□   If handled carefully, acknowledging that a person has a weakness or two in the midst of an otherwise enthusiastic recommendation can be effective, but this tack is not for everyone. "If Ms. Rickards has a fault, it is her tendency toward perfectionism. She will not allow a slipshod letter to leave the office, even if this means several retypings."

□   When you write a letter of reference or recommendation and give it directly to the subject of the letter, you generally leave the envelope unsealed so that the person can read it if they wish. When your letter is mailed directly to a personnel office, scholarship committee, or other inquiring agency, it is sealed and perhaps also marked confidential.

Special Situations

□   When you believe that writing a positive letter of reference or recommendation for a former employee is unjustified or, in some cases, irresponsible, you can either decline to provide one or write a brief, carefully worded one. Most employee records are accessible to employees, who may be inspired to legal action if they do not care for what you have written. According to a study by Charles W. Langdon and William P. Galle, Jr. of the University of New Orleans, employers are so wary of lawsuits from disgruntled ex-employees that over half the firms surveyed said they would not give out any information at all on former employees without their written consent; 80% are reluctant to give bad references; 47% said they wouldn't write a bad reference even when they possessed proof of employee wrongdoing; and 10% are so cautious that they never under any circumstances provide references. A survey by the National Association of Corporate and Professional Recruiters showed that nearly half of all companies contacted have a policy against giving references on current or former employees. And with good cause: defending a defamation suit before a jury can cost as much as $250,000, even if the company wins the suit. Nearly a third of all libel cases are filed by workers who sue former employers about bad references. On the other hand, failing to write a letter for someone may deprive them of a job, although the responsibility for this lies ultimately with the unsatisfactory employee. If the faults did not involve dishonesty or dangerous practices, you may be able to write a restrained letter that tells the truth but suggests that the person might be able to cope better in another position. You can also write a letter in which you simply verify the dates the person worked for you.

Format

◻   Letters of reference and recommendation should be neatly typed (with a fresh ribbon) on letterhead paper.

◻   Thank you notes addressed to people who have written letters of reference or recommendation may be typed or handwritten on plain personal stationery or foldovers.

◻   In-house recommendations dealing with minor matters of policy may be typed on memo paper.

—————————————— WORDS ——————————————

accurate	ethical	praiseworthy
admirable	excellent	productive
appreciate	experienced	professional
approve	first-rate	promising
capable	forte	recommend
commendable	friendly	reliable
competent	hardworking	remarkable
congenial	helpful	reputation
conscientious	honest	resourceful
considerate	imaginative	respect
cooperative	indispensable	responsible
creative	ingenious	self-motivated
creditable	integrity	sensible
dependable	intelligent	substantial
deserving	invaluable	successful
diligent	inventive	suitable
discreet	loyal	superior
dynamic	meticulous	tactful
effective	originality	thoughtful
efficient	outstanding	trustworthy
endorse	performed	upright
energetic	personable	worthy
esteem		

_____ PHRASES _____

able to communicate her/his ideas to others
able to energize a group of people
a complete knowledge of
acquits herself/himself well
a creative problem-solver
an asset to any organization
an energetic and enthusiastic worker
a take-charge person
attentive to detail
broad experience/range of skills
can attest to
can heartily/wholeheartedly recommend
caution you about
considered an enthusiastic worker
conversant with
dependable/eager/hard worker
did a great deal to improve/increase/better/upgrade
discharged his/her duties satisfactorily
distinguished herself/himself by
every confidence in her/him
everyone here speaks of her/him in the highest terms
first-rate employee
full of initiative
give her/him every consideration
good critical thinking skills
grasps new ideas quickly
great aptitude for
greater respect for

has not been completely reliable
has three years' experience in
have no hesitation in recommending
held in high regard here
held positions of responsibility
highly developed technical skills
I can recommend with complete confidence
I have been impressed with
in response to your request for information about
I would not hesitate to recommend
many fine contributions
matchless record
not an altogether happy arrangement
nothing but praise for
one in a thousand
outstanding leadership abilities
put in a good word for
rare find
responsible for all aspects of security
satisfactory in every way
set great store by
skilled in all phases of light clerical duties
sterling qualities
takes pride in his/her work
this is to recommend
vouch for
well thought of
worth his/her salt

_____ SENTENCES _____

Although I am unable to write you the recommendation you requested, I certainly wish you good luck in finding a suitable position.

Although the flexible-benefits program is optional, we strongly recommend that employees read the enclosed booklet and consider enrolling as it is the most complete coverage we offer.

Ann Shankland has highly developed sales and marketing skills and has also proven herself invaluable in the recruiting, training, and supervising of an effective sales team.

Both co-workers and supervisors were very enthusiastic about Jeremy Melford.

Charles Herbert has strong verbal and written communications skills and an ability to work with almost anyone.

Dr. Mayer was without a doubt the best stage manager the Metropolitan Opera House ever had.

Elizabeth Endorfield is one of our most knowledgeable people when it comes to custodial chemicals, equipment, and techniques.

Hiram G. Travers worked for me/was in my employ for ten years.

I always found her work, character, and office manner most satisfactory.

I believe any organization would be fortunate to have Mr. Trent.

I believe Mr. Dilling would be an asset to any company.

I can't offer you a reference letter, but please accept my best wishes in finding more satisfying employment elsewhere.

I feel very comfortable recommending Ellen Huntly to you.

If I can provide additional information, please don't hesitate to ask.

I highly recommend Amelia Jordan.

I'm pleased to have the opportunity of providing a reference for Bridget Derricks.

I'm very grateful to you for writing such a wonderful letter of recommendation— I'm sure it helped me get the job.

In response to your inquiry about Chester Nimmo, it is only fair to say that he seemed to need constant supervision and our association with him was not an altogether happy one.

I've known Richard Musgrove as a neighbor and employee for six years.

I will be happy to answer any questions you might have about Dr. Lakington's employment with us.

I would prefer not to comment on Jean Emerson's employment with us.

James Rodman left our employ for personal reasons; we were completely satisfied with his work.

Mary Treadwell worked as an X-ray technician at Porter General Hospital from 1985 to 1990.

Mr. Tamson's record with our company was excellent.

She is also able to work under deadlines.

We are obliged to let Mr. Dunne go because of financial difficulties; this should in no way reflect on his considerable abilities.

We found his/her services more than satisfactory.

We were all very sorry to see her/him leave/go.

Your comments will be held in the strictest confidence.

PARAGRAPHS

▷   Emily Wardle has asked that I write a letter of recommendation based on our professional association over the past several years. I've found Ms. Wardle to be honest and straightforward in her approach to her work, business, and family. She has demonstrated a high degree of loyalty and trustworthiness to her work and to her associates and has carried out her obligations with vigor and resolve. She believes in giving an honest day's work for an honest day's pay. She will certainly be an asset to any group with which she associates and works. I would recommend her without reservations.

▷   In order to fully evaluate your suitability for the sales position you applied for, we need to speak to at least four former employers or supervisors. Please provide us with names, addresses, and daytime phone numbers of people we may contact. You will hear from us as soon as we have made a decision.

▷   The position turned out to be very different from what I'd expected and I ended up declining it. I'm grateful to you for the very positive recommendation you wrote (one of the reasons they wanted to hire me, I know!), and I'd like to use it again sometime. I'll let you know what happens.

▷   You asked what I thought of the Vanever-Hartletop contract. After looking into the matter, my best recommendation would be to return the contract unsigned with a request for renegotiation of the default clause.

▷   In response to your request for information about Tasker Lithography, I must say that we have had nothing but exceptionally fine dealings with them for the past eight years. Deadlines were always met, and the quality of their work has been superb. The few times we had to ask for changes, they were carried out quickly and cheerfully. It is possible that others have had different experiences with Tasker. I can only say that we are very pleased with their work.

▷   It is a pleasure to confirm Kenneth Eliot's employment with Meynell Associates from 1987 through 1992. During his tenure here, Kenneth performed his responsibilities with diligence and punctuality and was a definite employee asset. We have no reservations about recommending him highly.

▷   Lucas Cleeve comes to this job with a long history of community involvement. He has been a strong advocate for neighborhoods during his two terms on the city council. He has served as chair of the Rules and Policy committee and of the Energy, Environment, and Utilities committee; financial specialist with Sybil county; legislative aide; member of the Human Development Commission, the Board of Health, the Board of Water Commissioners, the Housing Redevelopment Authority, the Financing and Bonding Commission, and the Task Force on Neighborhood and Community Action. How can we afford NOT to return such an experienced, committed advocate to the City Council?

▷   Paul Arthur Presset has applied to us for a position as a third-grade teacher and has given us your name as a reference. Would you be so kind as to describe what you know of his character, classroom abilities, and interpersonal skills based on what you observed when he taught at Jennings Elementary? I will naturally hold this information in strict confidence. Enclosed is a self-addressed stamped envelope for your reply. Thank you.

SAMPLE LETTERS

Dear Ms. Tartan,

You once offered to write me a letter of reference if ever I needed one. I would like to take you up on your kind offer now.

I am applying for a part-time teaching position in the Glendinning-Melville School District and have been asked to supply several letters of reference. In the hopes that you have the time and are still willing to write a letter, I'm enclosing an instruction sheet from the school district outlining what they need in a letter of reference as well as a stamped envelope addressed to the district personnel offices.

If for any reason you cannot do this, I will understand. Know that I am, in any case, grateful for past kindnesses.

Sincerely,

. . . .

TO: Office of Admissions
FROM: Dr. Charles Kennedy
RE: Steve Monk
DATE: November 15, 1992

I have known Steve Monk for four years. During his first two years at Isherwood Central High, he was a student in my Earth Sciences class and in my C.P. Biology class. During his junior year, I was Steve's advisor for an independent study in biology, and this year he is carrying out an extracurricular research project for which I am providing some guidance.

This young man is one of the brightest, most research-oriented students I have encountered in eighteen years of teaching. His SAT and achievement test scores only begin to tell the story. I understand he is sending you copies of several of his research projects; this will provide you with more evidence of his understanding of the principles of scientific inquiry, of his passion for exactitude, and of his bottomless curiosity. However, it is only in talking and working with Steve that the full extent of his talents is revealed.

In writing you this letter, I hope to persuade you of one thing: to arrange a meeting between some of your science faculty and Steve. There is no doubt in my mind that you will be interested in this young man. I am much more concerned about his financial situation, and I believe that once you see what caliber of student and scientist Steve Monk is, you will find some way of dealing with his financial needs.

I am very much interested in Steve's situation and will be happy to provide any further information.

. . . .

Dear Ms. Burnell,

You requested employment information about Dan Burke.

Mr. Burke was employed with us from 1986 through 1990 as a structural engineer. His work was satisfactory, and I believe he left us to pursue a more challenging job opportunity.

If we can be of additional assistance, please call.

Sincerely,

See also: INTRODUCTIONS, REQUESTS, RÉSUMÉS, THANK YOUS.

30

Refusals

"To know how to refuse is as important as to know
how to consent." (Baltasar Gracían)

Refusals (also known as regrets and rejections) are never easy to write. It will help if you are clear in your own mind that you do indeed want to say "no"; any ambivalence will undermine your letter. One very good reason for saying "no" is simply "I don't want to." When you have a specific reason for saying no and want to name it, do so. However, the fact that someone else wants you to do something confers no obligation on you to defend your decision. People who become angry with you for saying no, who try to manipulate you, or who make you feel guilty are confusing requests with demands.

Write a Refusal When Giving a Negative Response To

- adjustment/claims requests
- applications: employment/franchise
- gifts
- invitations: personal/business
- proposals: contracts/bids/books
- requests: contributions/credit/introductions/time/volunteering/pro-motions/raises/loans of money or possessions/appointments/meet-ings/interviews
- sales: presentations/offers/invitations
- wedding invitations (see WEDDINGS)

How to Say It

☐   Thank the person for the offer, request, invitation (which you describe or mention specifically).

□   State your "no," expressing your regret at having to do so.

□   If appropriate, explain your position.

□   Suggest any other resources the person might try.

□   Close with a pleasant wish to be of more help next time, to see the person again, or for good luck with their project.

What Not to Say

□   Avoid lengthy, involved excuses and apologies; they are far from convincing, even if true.

□   "Yes but no but yes but no." Let your "no" be a firm "no"; no waffling.

□   Avoid phrases like "you appear to think," "according to you," "you claim," "if you are to be believed." Restate the person's request, complaint, or angry letter in an unemotional, factual way.

□   Do not attribute your refusal to someone else's actions ("my wife/husband doesn't care for . . ."), except in the incidental way that, for example, an illness in the family prevents you from doing something.

□   Avoid outright lies. It is too easy to be caught out, and you will be a lot more comfortable with yourself and with the other person the next time you meet if you stick to some version of the truth.

Tips on Writing

□   Start out your refusal with a "thank you," if appropriate: "Thank you for your résumé/request/suggestion/manuscript/ proposal."

□   Be tactful. Avoid reflecting on the person you're writing to or on their program/project/invitation. State your refusal in terms of some inability on your part ("another meeting that day," "will be out of town," or simply "will be unable to attend").

□   Even when responding to outrageous or inappropriate requests and letters, keep your reply even-tempered and detached.

□   When possible, try to lessen the writer's disappointment in some way: offer to help at a later date; suggest someone else who might be able to provide the same assistance; agree with them on some point; apologize for your inability to approve the request; try to show some benefit to them from your refusal, if possible; thank them for their interest/request/concern.

□   Such a small thing as reversing the order of your phrases may help. Give the reason for your refusal before actually stating the refusal. For example, instead of saying, "I will not be able to attend your graduation because I'm going to be in California that week," say, "I am going to be in California the week of June 2, which means I won't, unfortunately, be able to attend your graduation."

Special Situations

□   If your invitation is issued in the name of more than one person, mention all of them in your refusal and mail it either to the person listed under the R.S.V.P. or to the first name given.

□   For a discussion of how to respond to an invitation from the White House, including a refusal, see ACCEPTANCES.

□   When you are obliged to cancel a previously accepted engagement, include the name of the event, its date and time, and give an explanation, if appropriate. If you are canceling your attendance at a large professional workshop, you need not explain. If you are canceling for a small dinner party, you should give an acceptable reason. Use the same format as a regular refusal.

□   Canceling an account, appointment, meeting, order, reservation, service, or social event is handled like a combination refusal and apology: mention the event, date and time; apologize for having to cancel; give a simple, reasonable excuse for your cancellation; for social events, close with your hopes that the event goes well, that you will see the person soon, that you will be able to attend the next event.

□   In declining to arrange a requested introduction, be tactful and, if possible, give a reason. However, this is a favor and you are under no obligation to explain your refusal. Close on a pleasant note—wishing you could have been of help, hoping the person finds some other way of achieving their goals.

□   When you must refuse an adjustment or claims request, do so in a way that maximizes the chances of keeping the customer. Be tactful and considerate. Offer an alternative or compromise solution whenever possible. Tell the customer that you understand their position, that their complaint has been given every consideration, and that you wish you could say yes. Then give a reasonable and credible explanation of your "no." You may want to appeal to their sense of fair play. Point out what would happen if all such requests were granted. Use any facts in the case to show that an approval is not really justified. Most customers will be satisfied with a brief, clearly written refusal. A few will write back and argue, point by point. When that happens, a firm "no" with no further explanations can be sent.

□   Sometimes it is necessary to refuse a gift. This happens most often in business when you are offered an unacceptably expensive gift or when the acceptance of gifts is prohibited by your organization. Be gracious and express your gratitude for the person's thoughtfulness and for the choice of gift. Explain why you must return it ("Employees are discouraged/prohibited from accepting gifts from suppliers," or "I hope you will understand, but I would feel very uncomfortable accepting such an expensive gift from a client").

□ Most fundraising appeals are mass-produced and the ones you choose not to respond to will go straight in the wastebasket. However, when you receive a personal letter with first-class postage, written over the signature of someone known to you, you will no doubt take the trouble to respond. Compliment the person on the work the organization is doing, give a plausible excuse for not contributing, and wish them well. You are not obliged to give any more detail than you choose; a vague statement that you are currently overcommitted elsewhere is fine. If you are refusing because you disagree with the organization's goals or policies, say so.

□ When you must refuse a request for credit or a loan, be sure of your facts, be tactful, and keep in mind that the person is still a potential customer. Thank the person for applying and express appreciation of their interest in your company. Emphasize positive factors in the credit history and tactfully suggest how the person might improve their chances of obtaining credit from you the next time. Indicate what resources you have relied upon to arrive at your decision (the application, employer's recommendation, background check, credit bureau file). You might suggest ways of improving their credit standing, alternative sources of credit, or reapplying to you after a certain period of time or after resolving certain financial problems.

□ Be tactful when denying an expected or hoped-for promotion. Your letter should (1) show appreciation for the employee's contributions, listing specific talents and strengths; (2) explain very honestly and concretely why the promotion was denied; (3) offer specific suggestions on how the promotion might be earned or, if the promotion depended on external factors (too many managers, budget shortfalls), what changes might affect a future promotion.

□ If you must turn down a formal invitation and wish to explain your reasons, you are not required to adhere to the mirror-image response format. You may send instead a handwritten informal letter.

□ Many companies and government agencies have specific and strict procedures for handling bids. When you have a choice, notify bidders of your requirements as soon as possible. In rejecting bids, be courteous and supportive, and, when possible, explain briefly why the bid was rejected (especially if it concerned failure to follow directives or to stay within certain guidelines) or why the winning bid was accepted. Information like this is useful to your contractors. Close with an expression of appreciation and a reference to the possibility of doing business with them at a later date. You do not need to name the winning bidder.

□   When writing to terminate a business relationship, friendship, or dating relationship, aim for a no-fault "divorce": do not blame the other person or bring up past grievances. Help the other person save face by implying that this is what they want too and by taking the responsibility for the separation on yourself. Be as honest as is consistent with tact and kindness. Above all, be brief and unequivocal; over-explaining or "keeping your options open" can be fatal if you truly want to end the relationship. Conclude with an encouraging, complimentary remark.

Format

□   Business letters of refusal are typed on letterhead stationery.

□   Personal letters of refusal are most often handwritten.

□   Form letters are used to reject manuscripts, to state that a company is not currently accepting any applications, or to make any other routine refusals.

□   In declining an invitation, use the same format as the invitation itself: If it is handwritten, handwrite your reply. If business letterhead stationery is used, reply using your own business letterhead. If the language of the invitation is informal, your reply should also be informal. In the case of formal invitations, use the same words, layout, and style as the invitation in your reply. For example:

Dr. and Mrs. Horace Willkerson

request the pleasure of

the Reverend and Mrs. Robert Porteous's company

at a dinner-dance

on Friday, the fourteenth of May

at eight o'clock

Winstonbury Inn

. . . .

The Reverend and Mrs. Robert Porteous

decline with regret

the kind invitation of

Dr. and Mrs. Horace Wilkerson

to a dinner-dance

on Friday, the fourteenth of May

at eight o'clock

Winstonbury Inn

—————————— WORDS ——————————

awkward	indisposed	sorry
contraindicated	obstacle	turndown
decline	opposition	unable
difficult	problem	unavailable
dilemma	refuse	unfavorable
doubtful	regret	unfeasible
impossible	reject	unfortunately
impractical	reluctantly	unlikely
improbable	respond	

—————————— PHRASES ——————————

after much discussion/careful
  evaluation
although I am interested in
although I am sympathetic to your
  problem/plight/situation
although the idea is very appealing
appreciate your asking me/us, but
at a considerable disadvantage
because of prior commitments
beyond the scope of the present study
can never be
cannot consider/supply/offer/provide/
  accept/comply/consent/extend any
  more time

company policy prohibits us from
current conditions do not warrant
difficult decision
disinclined at this time
dislike throwing cold water on
does not qualify/warrant
do not have enough information
do not presently have
don't want to discourage you, but
due to present budget problems
have a small chance/no chance whatever
have enough at this time
have no desire at this time

hope this will be of some help even
  though
I am sorry to disappoint you, but
I appreciate your asking me, but
if it were possible
I know how understanding you are, so
  I'm sure
I'm sorry to tell you
I must say no to
I regret that I cannot accept/that we must
is not possible/helpful/available
it is, unfortunately, out of the question
  that
it's a wonderful program, but
it's presently impossible
I wish I could say yes, but
I would like to help, but
I would normally be delighted, but
must decline/demur/pass up/withdraw
  from
negative response
no alternative but to
no significant advantage in
not a choice I can make right now
not an option at the moment
not currently seeking
no, thank you
nothing would please me more, but
not likely/possible
on no account

out of the question
previous commitments
prohibited from
puts me in something of a dilemma
regret to inform you
remain unconvinced of the value of
runs counter to
say no to
sincerely regret
sorry about this, but
sorry to say
stumbling block
the chances are against
there is a lack of interest here
the trouble with
this pointblank refusal
thumbs down
ticklish situation
unable to help/comply/grant/send/
  contribute
we appreciate your interest, but
we are unhappy to report
we find that we cannot
we have concluded with regret
we have now had a chance to review
without adopting an adversarial
  position
won't work out
would rather not
your idea has merits, but

SENTENCES

Although we appreciate your interest in Dempsey Toys, we do not feel that your
  product is one we could successfully market.
Although your entry did not win, we wish you good luck and many future successes.
At this time there does not appear to be a position with us that is suited to your
  admittedly fine qualifications.
Best of luck with selling your idea elsewhere.
Fundraising is not one of my talents—is there anything else I could do for the
  committee?
However, we will keep your résumé on file.
I am obliged to cancel my workshop reservation.

I am sorry not to be able to give you the reference you requested in your letter of November 3.

I appreciate very much your offer of assistance, but I want to try a few things before I go outside the firm for a solution.

I don't think this will work for us.

If you reread your contract, specifically clause C1, you will see that we have no legal obligations in this regard.

I have read your recent submission with interest, and regret that I must return it.

I have taken on more projects than I can comfortably handle.

I hope this will help you understand why we are unable to furnish the additional funding you are requesting.

I hope you can make other arrangements.

I know we'll be missing a wonderful time.

I'm not able to help with/attend/have you stay at that time, but I'm free the following week.

I'm overextended at the moment.

I'm really sorry, but I can't/I've got to say no.

I'm sorry, but I'm going to be out of town that evening.

I'm sorry I can't help.

I'm sorry that it is necessary to write this letter.

I'm sorry this one doesn't make the grade, but I hope your next proposal will be more successful.

I must part company with you on this issue.

I only wish I could!

I regret that I'm unable to accept your kind invitation.

I sympathize with your request and wish I could help.

It is particularly difficult for me to have to turn this down.

It is very difficult to say no to you, as you can imagine.

It's possible we would be interested sometime after the first of the year.

I wish I could be more helpful, but it's just not possible now.

I wish I didn't have to refuse you, Jerry, but I cannot see my way to making you a loan at this time.

I would prefer that you not use me as a reference.

May I take a raincheck?

Our present schedule is unfortunately very inflexible.

Perhaps you could check back with me sometime next year.

Please accept my sincere regrets at not being able to join you.

Regarding your request to use my name in your fundraising literature, I must say no.

Thank you, but we have had a regular purchasing arrangement with Burnside Office Supplies for many years.

Thank you for the opportunity of considering your application.

The Board has unfortunately turned down your request.

The position at Locksley International for which you applied has been filled.

The return of your manuscript implies no criticism of its merit, but means only that it does not presently meet our needs.

This is a difficult letter to write.

Under other circumstances, I would be happy to help you.

Unfortunately, I'm not in a position to make you the loan.

Unfortunately, it does not suit our needs at this time/it's just not possible now.

Unfortunately, this is not a priority for Pettifer Grains at this time.

Unfortunately, your request comes at a particularly difficult time for me.

We appreciated being able to review your credentials.

We appreciate your asking us, and hope that we will have the opportunity of saying "yes" some other time.

We are currently overstocked.

We are obliged to deny you the extension on your loan.

We are sorry, but the warranty on your watch has expired/we cannot comply with your request.

We are sorry that we cannot help you, and we hope most sincerely that you find another solution to your problem.

We are so sorry to have to miss your open house.

We are unable to approve your loan application at this time.

We are unable to issue a refund without a receipt.

We are unhappy to report that your work was not selected for inclusion in the symposium.

We have decided to accept another proposal.

We have reviewed your credit application and regret to inform you that we are unable to offer you a bank card at this time.

We must decline your request for an extension on your loan.

We must unfortunately decline to offer you a special low price; doing so would be most unfair to our other customers.

We regret to inform you that Spenlow Paint & Tile is no longer considering applications for its sales positions.

We regret to say that a careful examination of your résumé does not indicate your suitability for the position under consideration.

We've had a chance to look at your proposal carefully, and I'm sorry to say it's not right for us.

We very much regret that because of a previously scheduled engagement we will not be able to join you for dinner next week.

We wish you luck in placing your work elsewhere.

You've unfortunately caught me at just the wrong time—I'm over-scheduled for the next two months.

─────────────────────── PARAGRAPHS ───────────────────────

▷   Because we are financially committed to several charities similar to yours, we are unable to send you anything. However, please accept our best wishes for successful continuation and funding of your work—we certainly appreciate and admire what you are doing.

▷ Thanks for sending "Love in the Place Dauphine." Although this particular story isn't quite right for us, I'd like to see anything else you've done. I apologize for the long delay in getting back to you.

▷ Dr. Gerda Torp regrets that because of a previous engagement she is unable to accept the kind invitation of Mr. and Mrs. Esdras B. Longer for Sunday, the third of June at 8:00 p.m.

▷ I've checked our production schedule and see no way of moving up your deliveries by two weeks. We are dependent on materials shipped to us by suppliers in other states who are unable to alter their timetables.

▷ For a number of reasons, I am uneasy about writing you a letter of introduction to Sir Harrison Peters. I have discussed it with my superior, who would prefer that you find some other avenue of contact. I hope you will understand.

▷ Thank you for your second shipment of tea cozies. I'm sorry to say that these still do not seem to be what we are looking for in a high-quality Irish tea cozy. We are therefore returning to you the second shipment, complete. Thank you.

▷ Thank you for your résumé. We considered your application very carefully but have decided to offer the position to someone else. We will keep your application on file, however, and will contact you if we have a similar opening later. Please accept our best wishes as you seek a challenging and rewarding position.

▷ We've just received your kind letter inviting us to Howards End. You can imagine how we would enjoy seeing you and Margaret again. However, Julia is graduating from college that weekend, so we will have to say no this time. Thanks so much for thinking of us.

▷ I am sorry to report that we are unable to extend credit to you at the present time. Our decision is based primarily on your lack of a credit record and on the brevity of your current employment. We would be happy to discuss your request with you again in six months.

_____ SAMPLE LETTERS _____

Dear Dean Arabin:
   I very much regret that I am unable to represent Barchester College at the inauguration of Dr. Eleanor Bold as new president of Century College on September 16. I was unable to reschedule a previous commitment for that day.
   My wife is a graduate of Century, so I would have particularly enjoyed being part of the ceremony. Thank you for thinking of me. I was honored to be asked to represent the College and would be glad to be of service at some other time.
   I hope you are able to make other arrangements.
                                             Sincerely,

. . . .

TO: Friends of the Library Committee
   Thank you for your kind letter asking me to direct the annual fundraiser. I am flattered that you thought of me.

Because of several other time-consuming commitments, I am unable to accept your invitation. I would have enjoyed working with you and contributing in some way to our fine library system, but I feel sure that you will find the right person for this important project.

With best wishes, I am

Sincerely yours,

· · · · · · · · · · ·

Dear Tony Cryspyn:

Thank you for submitting your work to us. As editors of the *Windsor Castle Review*, we have given your material careful consideration; every manuscript submitted to this office is read by one or more of us.

We regret that "The Ninth Son" is not suited to the current needs of the magazine, but we wish to thank you for having given us the opportunity of reading it. Unfortunately, the volume of submissions and the press of other editorial responsibilities do not permit us to make individual comments or suggestions.

Sincerely,

· · · · · · · · · · ·

Dear Chris and David,

Thank you for sending us the information on your real estate trust investment opportunity.

Although it looks very appealing, this is not something we are prepared to get into at the moment. I sent the prospectus on to my brother in Denver. It is possible he would be interested.

I'm sure you will find all the capital you need, and I wish you every success.

Best wishes,

· · · · · · · · · · ·

Dear Ms. Murchison,

We were so sorry to hear about the problem with your Wimsey Electronic Typewriter.

Although your machine is still under warranty, we are unable to repair it for you free of charge. It appears that the terms of the warranty have been violated; misuse of the machine renders the warranty null and void. The machine was plugged into a European 220-volt outlet when it was intended for use only with 110-volt outlets or for 220-volt outlets *with a converter*. (This is explained in the owner's manual, and a small tag is affixed near the plug warning to use only 110-volt current.)

If you wish us to repair the machine at an approximate cost to you of $120, please let us know. Otherwise, we will return it to you.

We wish we could be more helpful, but the terms of the warranty are very carefully spelled out. We really cannot afford to make exceptions, no matter how sympathetic we might feel.

Sincerely,

See also: APPOINTMENTS, CREDIT, DISAGREEMENT, RESPONSES.

31

Reports and Proposals

> "Reports in matters of this world are many, and our resources of mind for the discrimination of them very insufficient." (John Henry Cardinal Newman)

Although long proposals and reports do not qualify as letters, shorter ones are sometimes written as letters or memos. They use plainer language, do not have heads, subheads, and clauses, and in general are less formal and less complicated than lengthier reports and proposals. Sometimes a proposal-letter is a proposal to write a proposal, and a report is a preliminary report to a longer report; in these cases, they can borrow from the other material—from an abstract or summary, for example.

Reports and proposals can be solicited or unsolicited. In a solicited proposal, someone asks you to submit a bid, estimate, or proposal for doing some specific work or for performing a certain service. Your proposal is thus a sort of sales letter in which you convince the person that you can do the job better than anyone else. With a solicited proposal you usually have a precise idea of what the buyer wants and are able to tailor your proposal to those needs. However, there is also usually keen competition when proposals or bids are solicited.

In an unsolicited proposal, you try to sell someone on something they have not expressed a specific need for. Your letter is not oriented toward outdoing your competition, but toward convincing your readers that they need your product or service in the first place.

Reports and Proposals Include

- acceptance of proposal/bid
- acknowledgment of receipt (see ACKNOWLEDGMENTS)
- bids and estimates
- credit reports (see CREDIT)
- proposals: books/products/grants/projects/programs/sales and services
- recommendations/suggestions (see also REFERENCES)

- rejection of proposal/bid/report (see REFUSALS)
- reports: annual/monthly/progress/management/staff/technical
- responses to inquiries/requests (see RESPONSES)

How to Say It

☐   When you write a letter-report, include: a key sentence identifying the topic of the report; a statement of why you are sending the report ("as requested," "for your information," "Charles O'Malley asked me to send you a copy"); the main body of the report; a one- or two-sentence summary; if appropriate, what you expect the person to do with the information; an offer of additional information if needed.

☐   When writing a letter-proposal, state the topic of the letter in the beginning (or use a subject line); describe the idea in detail; give costs, specifications, deadlines; tell the reader what the next step is ("call me," "sign the enclosed contract").

☐   Issue memos are reports that summarize important information so that policy decisions can be made. The memo is an ideal format for the fact-oriented report. It may include: background information or history of the issue; options available and their pros and cons; costs and fiscal impact; recommendations; suggested next step (meeting, negotiation, vote).

☐   When writing grant proposals, there are three admonitions that will cover all types: (1) follow directions scrupulously; (2) present your material faultlessly—neatly typed, clean, well spaced; (3) make sure the content is high quality. Certain organizations specialize in helping grant applicants, and sometimes people in your field will critique your material.

☐   If you cannot respond to a proposal or report right away, acknowledge its receipt to the sender and assure the person they will hear from you as soon as you have evaluated the report or proposal. People usually spend some time putting together reports and proposals and then are eager for results. They will wait more patiently if their letter has been acknowledged.

☐   When reporting in response to a request for information, refer to the person's request, give your report, and express appreciation of their interest.

☐   Many progress reports have some specified format, but others may be written in narrative letter form. Include: what has been done during the reporting period; what is currently being done; what outstanding projects are waiting for attention; good news and bad news during the reporting period; other comments that will give the reader an appreciation of the progress of the group, student, employee.

What Not to Say

◻   Do not bring in other topics or business. The report or proposal is necessarily a very focused document.

Tips on Writing

◻   In addition to its main body, a full, formal report may contain a foreword, preface, introduction, acknowledgments, table of contents, an abstract, conclusions or recommendations, summary, appendix, and bibliography. If you want to write about the report in a cover letter or without sending the entire report, consider excerpting parts of the report. The abstract and summary are particularly useful. Then, if your correspondent is interested, you can send the entire report.

◻   Give credit to those who worked on the report or proposal.

◻   Have someone who has nothing to do with the proposal or report read it over for clarity. One of the biggest failings of technical writers is understanding material so clearly and completely that they cannot describe their work intelligibly to outsiders.

◻   Aim for one page. It will not always be possible to reduce a proposal or report to one page, but in trying to do so, you will weed out unnecessary and wordy passages.

Special Situations

◻   If you think the proposal is going to be acceptable to the other party, you can turn the proposal letter into a contract letter or binding agreement by adding at the bottom something like, "Read and approved on [date] by [signature and title]." If the proposal is part of a larger contract insert, "pursuant to the Master Contract dated March 2, 1992, between Raikes Engineering and Phillips Contractors" (see also CONTRACTS).

Format

◻   Letters containing reports or proposals should be typewritten on letterhead or memo stationery.

◻   Forms with blanks to be filled in are very convenient for credit reports, school progress reports, weekly production reports, and other reports that depend on numbers or short descriptions.

—————————————————— WORDS ——————————————————

abstract	evaluate	preliminary
account	exhibit	presentation
acquaint	explanation	problem
agenda	exploration	procedure
analysis	exposition	program
applications	findings	project
appraise	forecast	projections
approach	gauge	proposal
arrangement	guesstimate	prospectus
assess	information	recommendation
calculate	inquiry	record
commentary	inspect	representation
compute	instruction	research
conclude	introduction	results
conditions	investigation	review
consider	issue	statement
contents	judge	strategy
critique	layout	study
decision	method	subject
description	monograph	suggest
design	notification	summary
determination	offer	system
diagram	opinion	technical
disclose	outcome	terms
discussion	outline	text
display	performance	thesis
draft	plan	undertaking
establish	policy	venture
estimate	preface	

—————————————————— PHRASES ——————————————————

a considerable/significant/important
  advantage
address the problem of
advise of
along these lines
as you can see from the above/
  foregoing/statistics
ballpark figure
close/exhaustive inquiry

copy of the proceedings
detailed statement
educated guess
estimated value
give our position on
gives me to understand
go on record
in-depth account of/look at
institute inquiries

make an estimate

make inquiry/known/public

map out

matter/question at hand/in dispute/ under discussion/at issue

planning stages

plan of action

position paper

rough computation/calculation

rough draft/guess

subject of inquiry

supplies/offers/provides some distinct advantages

take into consideration

take measures/steps

this report summarizes the progress of

under consideration/discussion

SENTENCES

Below is the information you requested.

Enclosed is a sample service contract that we believe would suit all your maintenance needs along with a fee schedule that is one of the most reasonable you will find anywhere.

I am happy to send you this report of our activities for the past six months.

I propose that we set up a subcommittee to study flex-hours for all salaried employees.

The following report was prepared by Robert Famish and Narcissa Topehall.

This is to acknowledge receipt of your report on current voter attitudes.

We are happy to accept your estimate for refinishing our Queen Anne dining room suite.

Your proposal was most impressive/well conceived/highly professional.

PARAGRAPHS

▷ Your book proposal has been read with great interest. We will want to have several other people read and evaluate it before submitting it for discussion at our weekly acquisition meeting. I will let you know as soon as we have made a decision.

▷ Since our letter of September 3, in which we compared electroplating and sputtering for production of thin alloy films for recording, we have done some additional research on this subject. We have found that as long as the proper microstructure is achieved, both electroplating and sputtering are effective. It appears too early to exclude either of the processes. It may be helpful, however, to do a rough cost analysis either as more data from research in these two areas become available or by making a number of assumptions.

▷ This report is a summary of your benefits and any optional coverage you have chosen as of January 1. Your benefits booklet provides further details. If you have any questions, please see your supervisor or the Benefit Information Coordinator. Although this report has been prepared for you as accurately as possible, the Company reserves the right to correct any errors.

——————————————————— SAMPLE LETTERS ———————————————————

Dear Etta,
Re: Proposed Budget for Design of Streets DRS—821.01
We have estimated the design cost to produce final plans for the relocation of Concannon Street from the bypass to the railroad tracks, and for Concannon Bypass from Blake Avenue to Nicholas. The design of Concannon Street is for a length of approximately 2,000 feet and consists of five traffic lanes, curb and gutter, and a raised median over 25% of its length. The Concannon Bypass design covers approximately 2,500 feet and includes curb and gutter along the outside lanes and median, pavement widening, intersection improvements, acceleration and deceleration lanes, and signals at three locations. The cost works out to $55,000, and we therefore propose that a budget for this amount be approved.
Please call me if you have any questions concerning our estimate. Thanks.
Sincerely,

· · · · · · · · · · ·

Dear Arnold,
I talked to John Culver last week about the sample of shielding film I'd sent him earlier, and he said it was just what they'd had in mind. He had a few questions about the electrical connection and the wiring pattern. He explained what they are currently doing and said they will send me a sketch of the preferred pattern.
I promised to send him some mesh samples as soon as Hildegarde has prepared them, and we agreed to set up a date to further discuss their needs.
Yours truly,

· · · · · · · · · · ·

TO: Residents in the Larkin Road neighborhood
FROM: Larkin Road Task Force
DATE: April 12, 1991
A citizen task force composed of interested persons was formed last May and met almost the entire year to make recommendations to the Planning Commission which, in turn, made its report to the City Council.
Residents living near the south end of Larkin Road wanted the road connected to the freeway immediately to ease traffic problems during rush hour. Our representatives asked that the problem of where to funnel the traffic at the north end be resolved before such a connection is considered.
There were, however, several areas of complete agreement, among them resolutions to have a direct westbound connection to relieve some of the traffic on neighborhood streets and to reduce the Larkin Road speed limit to 35 mph as soon as possible. An Environmental Impact Statement was also suggested by the task force.
Unfortunately, the Planning Commission reversed the two major points of neighborhood agreement and did not recommend them to the City Council. The City Council said that the direct westbound connection was a future possibility that they could not now consider. It did, however, vote in favor of the Environmental Impact Statement and supported the enforcement of the current 45 mph speed limit.

See also: ACCEPTANCES, ACKNOWLEDGMENTS, CREDIT, INSTRUCTIONS, REFERENCES, REFUSALS, RESPONSES, SALES.

32

Letters of Request and Inquiry

"Knowledge is of two kinds. We know a subject ourselves,
or we know where we can find information upon it."
(Samuel Johnson)

Letters of request and letters of inquiry are sometimes treated as two separate categories. In fact, however, these letters are similar. When you want to *know about something*, your letter is, strictly speaking, a letter of inquiry. When you want to *ask for something*, it is a letter of request. However, oftentimes what you are asking for is information, which turns your request into an inquiry. Query letters, in which you write to ask what someone thinks of an idea for a book, article, or proposal, are also a type of request letter.

These letters are critical in maintaining the flow of ideas and resources between people and organizations and must be good ambassadors for their writers. Often they are the first point of contact between businesses and potential customers, between those seeking something and the employers, publishers, and vendors they are seeking it from.

Letters and memos of inquiry and request, along with query letters, are among the most common communications in business life today. Many of them are simple letters of one to three sentences.

Write Letters of Request/Inquiry When You Want

- adjustments (see ADJUSTMENTS, COMPLAINTS)
- advice (see ADVICE)
- appointments/meetings/interviews (see APPOINTMENTS, EMPLOYMENT, RÉSUMÉS)
- assistance: business/personal
- bids and estimates
- contributions/donations (see FUNDRAISING)
- documents or copies of business/personal records
- favors: business/personal

269

- goods/services: prices/samples/information/brochures/product literature
- information/explanations/instructions
- information on a credit rating (see CREDIT)
- introductions (see INTRODUCTIONS)
- payment (see COLLECTION, CREDIT)
- permission to reprint/use copyrighted material
- raise in salary (see EMPLOYMENT)
- speakers for your conference/banquet/workshop
- to borrow money (see CREDIT)
- to check on an unacknowledged gift
- to learn if a company has any job openings
- to query an editor about a book or article idea
- zoning changes

How to Say It

☐   Open with a clear, polite statement of what you want to know or what you are requesting.

☐   If appropriate, explain the use you intend to make of the material or why you need it.

☐   State the specific action or response you want from your reader.

☐   Explain why your reader might be willing to respond to your request.

☐   Let the recipient know where to send the information or where to telephone with a response (if your stationery does not show this information).

☐   Specify the date by which you expect/need a response.

☐   Express your thanks or appreciation for any help that may be forthcoming.

☐   Enclose a self-addressed stamped envelope, if appropriate.

What Not to Say

☐   Don't ask for "any information you have." At least begin with a specific request and then, if you aren't sure what else they have that you might want, you could add "and anything else along these lines" or "and any additional information." If you don't give specific examples of the kind of information you want, you are likely to be less than satisfied with what you receive. Many companies have dozens and sometimes hundreds of brochures dealing with their products and services. A vague request for "any information you have" may oblige the recipient to pick and choose randomly from among these informational offerings.

❑ Avoid implying that you have a right to the information, service, or favor, or assuming that it will automatically be given to you—you are making a request, not a demand. Because you never take a positive reply for granted, you are always grateful when receiving one.

❑ Avoid apologetic phrases such as "I hope you don't mind," "I hope this is not too much trouble," "I'm sorry to bother you," "Please do not hesitate to call me if this is not clear," or "If this is inconvenient . . ." There is no need to feel apologetic about making requests—everybody asks for things. You yourself have probably received hundreds of requests to which you said either yes or no and thought very little of it. Be matter of fact and unapologetic.

❑ Several letterwriting authorities object to ending a request letter with "thank you" on the theory that it seems to signal an end to the exchange. They suggest an expression of appreciation instead. And there is always "I am looking forward to hearing from you," which is pleasant and forward-looking. However, "thank you," or more commonly "thank you in advance," is seen everywhere; it is part of the landscape by now and if you use it, few people will notice or care. Some people like the brisk wrap-up sound of it and use it automatically.

❑ When writing lawmakers about an issue, avoid oversimplification—a one-sentence solution to a problem that has been plaguing the country for decades, for example. If you do not wish to write several pages showing your grasp of the complexities of the issue, at least acknowledge that you understand how many factors are involved. Also avoid hostile, accusatory remarks. They will not endear you to the recipient, who may be in a position to help you. It is rare that one individual is completely responsible for the passage or nonpassage of a bill or for the problem you are writing about, and you may be railing at the wrong person.

Tips on Writing

❑ Be direct, simple, brief, and specific. Your first sentence should fix your reader's attention on the precise nature of your request.

❑ Long explanations of why you need something aren't necessary. Exceptions exist, of course; if you are writing the county pathologist for information on procedures in a murder case, it helps to explain that you are a mystery writer looking for background rather than a prosecutor building a case. Asking someone for general advice on mid-life career changes will be less helpful than detailing your situation and asking for specific advice on it. Especially when writing people who receive large volumes of mail—legislators, for example—you need to keep your letter as short as possible if you want a speedy reply.

☐   Use a subject line to quickly orient your reader. For example: Subject: WATS line service. Re: Guidelines for grant proposals. Subject: Eurail Saverpasses. Re: Speakers bureau. With a simple request, you do not need a salutation; the subject line can stand alone.

☐   If your request is anything but brief and straightforward, phrase it in the form of several numbered questions (from most to least important), so that the recipient can tick off each item as it is responded to.

☐   Be sure your reader is clear about what you want; in a longer letter, restate your request in the last paragraph.

☐   Give all numbers, dates, and other information that will help your respondent give you the most complete answer.

☐   Make it easy for someone to respond to you: enclose a survey or questionnaire; provide a postage-paid postcard printed with a message and fill-in blanks; leave space under each question on your letter so the person can jot down replies and return it in the accompanying self-addressed stamped envelope.

Special Situations

☐   When requesting a change of address, be sure to give both new and old addresses—and the old address should be given exactly as it appears on the mailing label.

☐   The query letter can be considered a combination request letter and sales letter. Although you are actually inquiring to see if an editor would be willing to consider your book manuscript or story idea, you also need to make the project appear attractive. The first paragraph includes all pertinent information: the type of book (biography, reference, children's), its title, length, and intended audience. The second paragraph describes the book in terms that make the editor itch to read it. This paragraph must be some of your finest writing. A third paragraph might include information showing that there is a market for your manuscript and that you are the best person to write it because of your background and experience. In the last paragraph you say that you are enclosing a self-addressed stamped envelope for the editor's reply, and you thank the person for their time and attention.

☐   When requesting estimates or bids, be very detailed: give precise specifications, quantities, special needs, deadlines (for bid and for completion of work/delivery of materials); types, model numbers, colors; a list of everything you expect to be included in the total. To ensure that no important consideration is omitted, use the eventual contract that will be offered as a model for your bid request letter.

▫ When asking someone to speak at your meeting or conference, be sure to indicate the expected length of the talk, the probable size and makeup of the audience, and any available equipment (overhead/slide projector). A professor of astronomy, for example, needs to know whether the audience consists of members of a social organization interested in a wide variety of topics, hobbyists who are grinding their own lenses, or professional astronomers from a nearby lab.

▫ When writing to an elected official to request or recommend a course of action, mention the issue or legislation you're writing about in the first sentence or in a subject line ("Re: property taxes" or "Subject: HR4116"). State your opinion clearly ("I strongly disapprove of . . . /I urge you to . . ."). Give reasons for your position. If there are several, list them separately, set off by numbers, asterisks, or bullets. Indicate the course of action you would like the person to take or the response that you expect. Offer to serve as a resource if the issue is something you are particularly knowledgeable about. End with an expression of appreciation for their interest and time.

▫ When writing to ask whether an unacknowledged gift was received, describe the item, tell when you sent it, and offer a face-saving "out" for the person ("I know how busy you are"). You could also mention that you are inquiring because you insured the package and if it did not arrive, you want to follow up on it, or that you are wondering if you should put a "stop" order on the check. You don't have to give a reason for your inquiry, but doing so is more tactful. Although failing to acknowledge or send thanks for a gift is a serious breach of etiquette, it is also very common. It is hardly worth the high blood pressure to be irritated by those cavalier friends and relatives who were never taught how to respond appropriately to gifts.

▫ When requesting permission to use copyrighted material, make it easy and attractive for the person to say "yes." Include either a special form or a copy of your letter that the person can sign and date. Also include a self-addressed stamped envelope. Making the acceptance a one-minute job increases your chances of getting permission. In the letter (or on the permission form), state precisely what you want to use (title of book or article, page numbers, line or paragraph numbers, first and last phrases of the excerpted material). Tell how you are using the material (the name of your book or article, approximate publication date, publisher, price, expected number of copies, and anything else that might reflect the anticipated audience and distribution). Include the exact credit or permission line you plan to use so that the author can approve it. Offer to send a complimentary copy of the book, if you wish. Express your appreciation and, if you wish, your admiration for the person's work.

▫ When making requests for hotel or motel reservations, include such information as the number of persons in your group, how many rooms you need and whether you want single or double beds, your times of arrival and departure, and any extras you'll need (crib, poolside room, connecting rooms, additional bed). Ask for confirmation of your reservation, and indicate how the rooms are to be billed—to you, to a credit card, to your company account—and if you are entitled to a discount of any kind.

□   Requests for zoning changes must be factual, unemotional, and businesslike. Your letter will become part of the public record, so be sure all facts, property descriptions, and mentioned zoning regulations have been checked for accuracy. State your reasons for requesting the change, modification, or variance. Include as much information as you can showing that, first, a zoning change will not harm the environs and, second, that there are potential benefits. Attach statements from neighbors, petitions, assessments, and any other documents that can conceivably bear on the issue.

Format

□   Business requests that go outside the company are typed, usually on letterhead stationery. Memo paper is used for brief, casual, or routine requests.

□   Personal requests may be typed or handwritten on business or personal stationery. The more personal the request (advice, favors), the more suitable it is to handwrite the note on a foldover or personal stationery.

□   Postcards are very useful for one-line requests.

□   If you need to make the same type of request repeatedly, use a form letter or memo paper with blank space to fill in the title of the article or sample you're requesting.

––––––––––––––––––––––––––– WORDS –––––––––––––––––––––––––––

accommodate	grateful	query
appeal	help	question
ask	hope	questionnaire
assistance	immediately	quickly
brochures	information	reconsider
consider	inquiry	refer
cooperation	instructions	reply
donation	need	request
expedite	obtain	require
favor	permission	rush
furnish	permit	seek
generous	problem	solicit
give	products	urgent
grant	prompt	want

_____ PHRASES _____

acquire information
additional information/time
all available information
anticipate a favorable response
apply/ask for
appreciate any information/your
  cooperation
as soon as possible
at once
be good enough to
be so good as to
by return mail
can you help me with
count on/upon
direct me to the appropriate agency
expect to hear from you
give me some assistance
have the goodness to
help us out with
hope you are able to
hope you can turn a willing ear to
  this request
hoping for a favorable reply
I'd appreciate having/receiving/
  obtaining
if you can do this
if you can find time in your busy
  schedule to
if you could answer the following
  questions
if you think this might be possible
I'm writing to ask you
institute inquiries
interested in receiving information/
  learning more about

it would be most helpful
I will return the favor when
I would appreciate your assessment of
I would be grateful/most grateful if/for
I would like to ask you
I would very much appreciate
let me/us know
look forward to hearing from you
look for your response
make inquiries
matter of necessity
of great help to us
on account of/behalf of
please call me to discuss
please let me have your estimate for
  this job by
please provide us with/send details
  about
please send me
pressing need
sincere appreciation
subject of inquiry
take into consideration
thank you for your efforts in/to
thank you/thank you so much for
trouble you to/for
truly/greatly/very much appreciate
we would appreciate your taking a few
  minutes to
will be greatly appreciated/received
would appreciate it if
would it be possible to
would you be willing to

_____ SENTENCES _____

A prompt reply will be most appreciated.

Because of increases in base compensation and the overhead burden for the fiscal
  year just ending, we respectfully request the Standard Hourly Billing Rates be
  escalated by the 8% maximum stated in Section 1.B. of the contract.

Can you tell me which government agency might be able to give me background information on Minamata disease in Japan?

Enclosed is a self-addressed stamped envelope/an International Reply Coupon for your reply.

How can a private citizen be named to the task force on the Resolution Trust Corporation?

How do you plan to vote on this issue, and why?

I am counting on you.

I appreciate your help.

I ask that you not only support this bill, but that you use your considerable influence to convince other legislators of its value.

If I can in any way return the favor, it will give me great pleasure to do so.

If possible, I would like to have the room on the second floor overlooking the park that we've had the last two times we stayed with at the Hôtel Henri IV.

If you would like to discuss this, I could meet with you at just about any time that is convenient for you.

I have a favor to ask of you/would like to ask a favor of you.

I'm in a rather difficult situation at the moment.

I'm wondering if you can find the time to give us a little guidance.

I respectfully request a zoning change for 1954 North Eliot from the current retail business designation to industrial.

It occurred to me that you might be able to give me some assistance with my research project.

I will appreciate any information you can give me and will of course keep it in the strictest confidence.

I will be most grateful for your help/your considered opinion on this.

I would appreciate a phone call as soon as possible/a reply by return mail.

I would appreciate receiving this information in the next two weeks.

I would be interested in seeing some of the material that went into the preparation of your most recent occupational titles handbook.

I would like to know your position on handgun control.

I would like to meet with you to discuss Jackie's progress so far this year—can you give us twenty minutes sometime next week?

Many thanks for any information you can send me.

May I ask a favor of you?

May I count on you?

May I use your name as a reference when applying for a cashier position with Mawson's Country Inn?

Please let me know if you have enough information to proceed with this request.

Please send me an application for your Golden Bank Card with variable interest rate and no annual fee.

Please send me any literature you have on postal regulations for bulk mailing/home maintenance contracts/industrial abrasives/small business loans.

Please send me copies of any free booklets or leaflets you have on vitamins.

Please send me information on your company—its services, staff, and descriptions of previous work.

Please send product literature along with prices for the following items/materials/workbooks.

Please send the materials C.O.D./third class/first class and bill us for any extra postage.

Thank you for your consideration and understanding/for your prompt attention to this request/for your time and attention/for any cooperation you can give us.

We do not understand footnote (b) of Exhibit H—could you please explain it?

We need to have this information by July 1.

We request that the Board take action on this resolution at its next regular meeting.

We would like the bid in writing.

Will you please follow up on this with the appropriate City staff to make the necessary dedication?

Will you please provide the as-built drawings as soon as possible?

Will you please send me a copy of your current catalog and price list?

Will you please send me a list of those trash haulers in Willard County that contract by volume rather than by flat fee?

Would you please forward this letter to the appropriate person?

Would you please send me an application form?

You've been so good to me in the past that I feel comfortable asking this.

———————————— PARAGRAPHS ————————————

▷   I am interested in flying from Denver to Hong Kong sometime after June 7 and returning to Denver from Hong Kong approximately three weeks later. I will need two round-trip tickets Denver-Hong Kong, and I am hoping you can find the most inexpensive seats available. I understand that if I purchase tickets by March 1, there will be a price break. My plans are fairly flexible as to departure and return dates if that helps obtain lower-priced tickets. Please call me as soon as you have some information.

▷   My Maundrell watch, which is still under warranty, has stopped running for no apparent reason. I'm told there is nothing wrong with the battery. Please tell me where to bring or send it for repair under the warranty.

▷   Please send a copy of your guide to the best American colleges. Enclosed is my check for $7.95.

▷   The flyer that came with this month's telephone bill describes a telephone answering system that is available for $8.95 per month. It is not clear to me whether this is an outright purchase (if so, how many months of payment are involved?) or a lease arrangement. Please send me complete information.

▷   Would you be interested in seeing a 20,000-word juvenile biography of Marie Marvingt, the Frenchwoman who was known as "the Fiancée of Danger," "the most incredible woman since Joan of Arc," and "the most complete sportswoman the world has ever known?"

▷   The Pallant County Arts Board is attempting to determine whether it is meeting the needs of county artists, writers, playwrights, and musicians. Would you be so kind as to take a few minutes to fill out the enclosed questionnaire and return it to us in the self-addressed, stamped envelope? Please do not fold the questionnaire as results will be tabulated by computer.

▷   I was unable to attend your talk on "Texture Performance of Metals" but would greatly appreciate reprints or preprints of anything you have written in this area. Thanks.

▷   Will you please place my name on your mailing list to receive all announcements, newsletters, and information regarding business mailing regulations and tips? If you have booklets or materials of general interest, I would appreciate copies. Let me know if there is a charge. Thank you.

▷   I'm wondering if you could give me about five minutes of your time on the phone some time next week. I am writing a research paper on global economics, and think that you may have answers to some of my questions. I found when I interviewed other people that it takes from three to five minutes—no more. If you are unable to do this, I will understand. Enclosed is a self-addressed postcard—please indicate on it a time when I could call you.

▷   I understand that the basement meeting room of the Oakdale Community Church is available for use by various small groups. Would it be possible for our study group to meet there one evening a month? Our own church does not have any such facilities, and we have found it difficult to move around to a different home each month. We could meet on nearly any Tuesday, Wednesday, or Thursday evening that is convenient for you.

▷   Will you please send me the necessary forms for copyrighting a literary property? I would also appreciate any instructions on filling out the forms properly and background material on copyright law. Thank you.

▷   We have just moved to the area and are interested in changing from our out-of-state insurance agent to someone local. Please send complete information for the following types of insurance: auto, home, whole life. We prefer that you do not follow up with a call or visit; as soon as we have studied the material, we will call you if we have questions or if we would like to schedule a meeting. Thank you.

▷   We are interested in replacing the decorative stone brick on our home and would like you to give us an estimate on your lightweight "cultured stone." Please call either of us at work during the day or at home during the evening (see enclosed business cards) to set up an appointment. Thank you.

▷   Several bowling teams in the tri-county area are establishing a league that will sponsor a series of competitions. We will be needing trophies, plaques, and ribbons. We are also interested in seeing your line of name tags, medals, incentives, T-shirts, caps, and jackets. Please send your catalog and price lists. Thank you.

▷   I will be calling on barbers in your area the week of June 4-June 11 to show a line of completely new Swedish barbering tools. Made of tempered steel, guaranteed for twenty years, and sold with a service contract at no extra cost, these implements have already won three first-place Mentions of Merit from the American Academy of Barbers. I would like to stop by The Hair Bear sometime during that week. Enclosed is a self-addressed, stamped postcard—please indicate a time that would be convenient for you. To thank you for your time, I will be bringing you a gift.

▷   The Somers County Extension office is revising its brochure on spot removal. We understand that you have been doing some interesting research in this area. Could we have copies of any relevant papers? We will of course credit you in the brochure. Also, if you know of any other especially good resources on this topic, we would appreciate knowing about them.

▷   I am interested in learning more about Metro University. Would you please send me: (1) a catalog, (2) any brochures you might have, (3) financial aid information, (4) application forms for the 1993-94 school year, and (5) information on setting up an interview with the Admissions Office and a tour around the campus.

▷   I know you've been especially busy these last few weeks trying to settle into your new home, but I'd like to make sure that you received a package I mailed you a month ago. It was a housewarming gift, of course. I did insure it, so if it's lost I can have a tracer put on it. Do let me know, won't you, if it hasn't shown up?

SAMPLE LETTERS

Dear Axel,
    I plan to be on Sanburan Island in the near future, and am wondering if you could schedule a tour for me of the Tropical Belt Coal Company. Coal is one of my hobbies.
    Enclosed is a self-addressed envelope and an International Reply Coupon for your response.
    Thanks so much for your time and attention.
                                                                Sincerely,

. . . .

Dear Mr. Babington:
    I would like your permission to reprint the following material from your book, *Diplomacy Today*:
    page iv: paragraph 2: "Since 1701 . . . and nothing was said."
    page 294: final sentence: "If it appears that . . . only Henry VIII knows the truth."
    This material would be used in my book, *The New Diplomacy*, to be published by Baines-Gandish in 1994. The book will retail for $16.95 and is expected to have a somewhat limited market. I will send you a complimentary copy, and you would of course be given credit as follows:
    Reprinted with permission from Spencer Babington, *Diplomacy Today* (New York: Goddard Publishing, 1982), pp. iv, 294.
    I'm enclosing two copies of this letter. If you agree to grant me permission, please write "permission granted," sign and date one of the copies, and return it to me in the enclosed self-addressed stamped envelope.
    I will very much appreciate being able to use those two excerpts. Your book was an eye-opener when it appeared, and it has remained a standard for me of fine writing, clear thinking, and inspired research.
                                                                Sincerely,

. . . .

Dear Representative Ewbank,
    I was appalled to learn that only 1% of the total plastic materials produced in this country are recycled. Are you aware of this? I have three questions.

1. What is your position on recycling and what are you currently doing in this respect?

2. Can you give the names and addresses of any effective groups currently working on this problem?

3. Where can I most effectively address letters urging action—which government agencies or lawmakers?

I appreciate any information you can give me.

. . . .

Dear Mrs. Hawkins,

I would like to reserve a single room at the Admiral Benbow Inn for July 7-17. I will be arriving late on the evening of July 7 so please hold the room for my arrival. Enclosed is a check for the first night.

Thank you.

Sincerely,

. . . .

TO: Emmerick Demolition and Salvage

In September 1991 you submitted a bid to Brooker Real Estate to remove two structures, one at 1898 Stratfield and one at 1921 Cabell. Since that bid, two additional properties have been purchased by Brooker Real Estate and will require demolition this summer.

I invite you to submit a rebid to include the two additional sites plus tank removal at another site (please see attachment for description and addresses of sites).

Contact me if you will be submitting a bid as I would like to schedule a meeting to discuss this project further and to answer your questions.

. . . .

Dear Morris,

I'm thinking of leaving Langdon Glass Works (I'll tell you why next time I see you) and am currently on the lookout for a good sales management position.

You seem to know everyone in the industry (and everybody knows you)—would you mind letting me know if you hear of any openings?

I appreciate being able to ask you this. Let's get together soon.

Sincerely,

. . . .

TO: LeRoy Investment Services

Please send me information on investment opportunities for the small, independent investor. I would specifically like to know:

1. Requirements, interest rates, and other information on certificates of deposit, treasury bills, municipal bonds, mutual funds, and other investment programs.

2. The commission your company charges for handling such investments.

3. The performance records on your investment programs over the past two years.

4. The names of several people who have used your services recently.

. . . .

Dear Mr. Ruggles,

Thank you for your inquiry about Red Gap. We are enclosing some Chamber of Commerce brochures, a map of the area, and a list of events and activities through the end of the year.

If we can be of any further assistance, please let us know. We very much hope that you enjoy your stay in Red Gap.

Sincerely,

. . . .

TO: Orme Woolen Products
FROM: Shamrock Gifts
DATE: June 4, 1992

As we plan our Fall inventory, we are again in the market to buy woolens. We are principally interested in the traditional Aran sweater (men's and women's cardigans and pullovers), and would like to request a sample.

Please also send information on any other knitwear that your company produces and a current price list.

If you plan to have a representative at the Chicago Trade Fair at the end of July, please advise us of your stand number so that we can contact you at that time. (Note our new address and telephone number.)

Thank you in advance for your attention.

. . . .

Dear Laura Payton:

Our longtime supplier of plastic tubing has recently informed us that they are discontinuing their plastic tubing division. Our vice-president of purchasing will be visiting several plastic tubing manufacturers in your area next week.

Would it be possible for you to schedule a meeting and plant tour for him on Tuesday or Wednesday of next week? Enclosed are data on our projected needs for plastic tubing, our production schedules, and delivery requirements that may be helpful to you in preparing for his visit.

Thank you.

Sincerely,

. . . .

TO: Representative Meg Kissock

It is my understanding that the national debt is now around $3 trillion. This amount of debt is so staggering and has grown so quickly that I'm afraid few Americans understand its implications and consequences. I would like to know:

1. Your views on this situation and what concrete plans, if any, you have to help lower the national debt. With elections coming up in the fall, I think it is important to know what candidates think about this issue.

2. What an individual person can do to alert others to this serious situation. Are there groups working on this? Do you hear from other concerned citizens? Who are they and how can I get in touch with them?

I will appreciate your time and effort in responding to my very serious concerns about the national debt.

. . . .

Dear Mr. Eldrige:

Would you be willing to speak to the Challis University English Department about your recent book *Grammar and the Grammarian* sometime this next spring? Several department members have heard you speak; all of us have read your book. We meet the third Wednesday of every month and hope that one of those Wednesdays will fit into your schedule.

If you think this is possible, please call me to discuss the honorarium.

Hoping for a favorable reply, I am

Sincerely yours,

. . . .

TO: Zoning Commission
FROM: Barbara Topham
DATE: March 10, 1992
RE: Zoning File 9117, Children's Playschool

I am writing to urge you to approve the Special Condition Use Permit sought by Children's Playschool. As we live directly across the street, we would be one of those most affected, and I believe it is important for you to know that the change would not appear to adversely affect the neighborhood.

. . . .

Dear Archie,

At the last meeting of the Open Door organizing committee, we discussed the need for new members. Your name came up several times as someone who has spent a good deal of time, money, and energy at the Food Shelf. We all felt you could add creativity, excitement, and inspiration to our efforts.

Would you consider a one-year commitment to the committee? This would involve one general monthly meeting, one weekly subcommittee meeting, some telephone work, and your regular weekly volunteer hours. I think you are currently spending about ten hours a week at the center. If you need to cut down on those hours to devote time to the committee, that would be fine.

Although this is something you'll need to think about, we are hoping to have your answer within the next two weeks so that we can publish the new roster in our year-end appeals. We are all hoping very much that you'll say "yes" but will understand if you cannot. In any case, we are grateful for the time and talent you have already given the center.

With best wishes,

. . . .

TO: Metropolitan Council

I understand that you are funding a special multi-family recycling program for those who live in apartments or condominiums with twenty or more units.

I am writing on behalf of our neighborhood association, as we have a number of such buildings, and residents are interested in such a program. Please send information. We would also be interested in having someone from the Council speak at one of our meetings to explain the program.

Sincerely,

. . . .

Dear Mr. and Mrs. Hall,

Please cancel all reservations that we have made at the Coach and Horses. This includes the following dates: August 18-25, November 9-11, and December 1-4.

Thank you very much.

Yours truly,

See also: APPOINTMENTS, COLLECTION, CREDIT, EMPLOYMENT, FUND-RAISING, INVITATIONS, ORDERS, RESPONSES, SALES, THANK YOU.

33

Responses

"I was gratified to be able to answer promptly.
I said I didn't know." (Mark Twain)

In business, prompt and thoughtful responses to incoming mail may be as important as the carefully drafted sales letters you send out. For responses that are clearly "yes" or "no," see ACCEPTANCES and REFUSALS.

Write Responses To

- apologies
- complaints
- congratulations
- expressions of sympathy
- inquiries
- invitations (see also ACCEPTANCES, REFUSALS)
- letters addressed to someone temporarily absent
- requests: information/instructions/samples/introductions/contributions/payments/letters of reference

How to Say It

□   In the first sentence, mention the letter, memo, or invitation you are responding to and its central point so that your reader knows immediately what you're referring to.

□   Respond briefly and completely, giving all requested information.

□   When responding to a number of questions or to a complicated letter, organize your letter elements by using numbers, bullets, or asterisks and leave plenty of white space.

□   When responding to an invitation, repeat the date, time, and, possibly, the place and kind of event.

□   If appropriate, offer further assistance.

□   If you are unable to respond completely to an inquiry, include names, addresses, and phone numbers where more information can be obtained.

What Not to Say

□   In most cases, avoid giving more information than your reader has requested. It is costly and unproductive.

□   Respond respectfully to every letter, even those that you consider offensive, uninformed, inane, or a waste of time. On such small things is a company's reputation based over time.

□   The birth of a child with defects or a handicap is often the occasion of some unfortunate remarks. In responding to this news, avoid the following: "You're not going to keep it, are you?" "I think you should sue the hospital." "Is one of you a carrier for this?" "Maybe the baby won't live; that would be best all around." "Whose fault was it?" "Did you drink while you were pregnant?" "I guess it could have been worse." "God only sends burdens to those who can bear them." Beware of being inappropriately and overly sympathetic. Although this situation can entail countless difficulties and heartbreak, it does not call for a sympathy letter. Until you know how the parents are feeling (devastated, concerned but basically optimistic, happy to have the child at any price), do not reveal your own feelings—they may be wide of the mark. Instead, say that you've heard that they have a new little one, that there seem to be some problems, that you are thinking of them, and that you are willing to help out in any way you can. Avoid commercial "new baby" cards. Later, when you know how the parents are feeling, you can respond on a more emotional level.

Tips on Writing

□   It is imperative to respond when an invitation carries an R.S.V.P. There is currently an epidemic of failures in this respect, resulting in horror stories of empty places at wedding feasts, huge overpayments for no-show guests, or guests showing up with uninvited children or friends in tow. It is the number-one complaint of people who send invitations. If you are an extremely important, powerful, rich celebrity, people may cravenly forgive your failure to respond. If you are anyone else, you will lose credibility and respect with your acquaintances, and you may receive embarrassing phone calls questioning you about your plans. Please respond.

□   Instead of R.S.V.P., you may see "Regrets only" followed by a telephone number. Call only if you are unable to attend; the assumption is that otherwise you will be there. If your invitation includes no R.S.V.P., no "Regrets only," and no reply card, you are not obliged to respond. This type of invitation is used for large affairs—political gatherings, fundraising events, business cocktail parties, large conventions.

☐   Customer inquiries should be handled with the utmost respect, speed, efficiency, and good cheer—inquiries are generally forerunners of sales. Answer questions as completely as possible and enclose supplementary lists, articles, reports, brochures, flyers, or catalogs. Always make it possible for the inquirer to follow up (place an order, find a local distributor, call a toll-free number for more information). If for any reason you cannot respond at once, at least acknowledge receipt of the letter.

Special Situations

☐   Letters of complaint should receive a speedy response. If you are not ready with a solution, acknowledge the person's letter, stating that you are working on the problem and will contact them as soon as possible. If the complainant is correct, do everything possible to right the situation; be gracious and apologetic when replying (see APOLOGIES and ADJUST-MENTS). If the complainant is wrong, thank them for writing, explain tactfully your position, and end with a pleasant wish for continued custom (see REFUSALS). Try to leave the customer feeling good about the company and about your efforts on their behalf.

☐   When responding to a request for a charitable contribution, mention the sum you are donating, ask for a receipt (for tax purposes) if you wish, and enclose a filled-out matching gift form if your organization participates in this program.

☐   If you are invited to a Bar or Bat Mitzvah but cannot attend, you will want to send a congratulatory note or commercial greeting card with personal message added; only those who attend the ceremony are expected to send a gift.

☐   In responding to congratulatory messages that are very flattering and enthusiastic about your talents and achievement, say "thank you" first of all. Then be gracious. Eleanor Hamilton says, "A compliment is a gift, not to be thrown away carelessly unless you want to hurt the giver." It is easier to handle a compliment if you reflect it back to the giver ("how nice of you to write," "your letter touched me," "how thoughtful of you").

☐   When asked what you or someone close to you would like for a graduation, anniversary, birthday, or seasonal gift, mention a broad gift category (books, for example) that will provide a range of prices for the giver. It is unacceptable to name a specific item.

◻   You must respond to invitations (acceptance or refusal) and you really ought to respond to announcements (congratulatory card or note), but must a response include a gift in the case of graduations, showers, and birth/adoption or engagement announcements? Not necessarily. If you do not attend a celebration and are not particularly close to the host or guest(s) of honor, you are not obliged to send a gift along with your response.

◻   Expressions of condolence require a response, which can take a number of forms, from handwritten formal notes of thanks (see THANK YOU) to printed newspaper announcements of appreciation (see ANNOUNCE-MENTS). In the case of a public figure, acknowledgments can be sent to large numbers of people who were not personally known to the family (see ACKNOWLEDGMENTS). Responses may be very brief, may be sent up to six weeks following the funeral, and may be written by someone on behalf of the person closest to the deceased.

◻   A truly negative letter—bitter, hostile, accusatory, unfairly critical—requires careful handling. At one end of the spectrum, where you feel the writer could be actively dangerous, you will consult with the police or an attorney. At the other end, where the person just seems to need to express feelings, you can reply with "I am sorry to hear you feel that way" and suggest any action on their part or yours that might alleviate the situation. In between, reply to the letter as you would to a "normal" letter, overlooking the angry tone. You are not obliged to respond to an abusive letter.

Format

◻   Choosing a format for a letter or note of response is very simple: do as you were done unto. If the original letter was typed, type yours; if it was handwritten, handwrite yours. If the invitation was formal, your response should be written in the third-person formal manner. If it was informal, first-person style on personal stationery, you respond in a similar manner. If nontraditional language is used ("invite you to share in our love"), use the general format and approximate words, but you may alter them slightly if you feel uncomfortable using them.

◻   If you use formal notes engraved or printed with your name, you may respond to invitations by penning in "accepts with pleasure" or "declines with regret" under your name. Add the date so that your recipient knows which invitation you're responding to.

◻   Forms are particularly useful in responding to inquiries, as many of them are narrow in scope and routine in nature. Design a brief, general form letter that thanks the person for the inquiry and indicates what information is being forwarded. You might include a checklist of available publications so that you can indicate those that are of interest to the customer and that you are either enclosing or mailing under separate cover. You can also leave blanks: "Thank you for your inquiry about _____." Or design a form with every conceivable response and then check off the appropriate one ("Your order has been sent." "We are temporarily out of stock." "Please reorder in _____ days." "This is a prepaid item, and your payment has not yet been received." "Please indicate a second color choice.").

--- **WORDS** ---

acknowledge	inform	respond
answer	notify	response
confirm	regarding	return
feedback	reply	

--- **PHRASES** ---

according to/as mentioned in your letter

appreciated your thoughts of us/your interest in

appreciate your calling our attention to

appreciate your concern/your business

greatly regret your dissatisfaction

how much I appreciated your kindness and help

if you want further documentation on this issue

kind/warm expression of sympathy

meant a great deal to me

pleased to receive

sincerely sorry to hear that you were not satisfied with

sorry for the inconvenience/confusion/ mix-up/misunderstanding

thank you for your letter telling us about

to let you know

until you are completely satisfied

we have carefully/thoughtfully considered your letter, and

will receive immediate credit

your sympathetic/delightful/helpful/ comforting/encouraging letter/note

you were entirely right about

--- **SENTENCES** ---

As requested, we are submitting a budget figure for construction surveillance for the water and sewer line project.

Enclosed are the materials/brochures/reprints you requested.

If I can be of further service, please contact me again.

If we can answer any other questions, please call or write.

I have received your apology, and hope you will not give the matter another thought.

I hope that this information will be useful to you in resolving any remaining title issues, but if I can be of further assistance, please give me a call.

I hope this letter provides you with the information you need about the tank closure.

In response to your request for sealed bids, a bid from Dale Heating and Plumbing is enclosed.

Letters like yours have been a great comfort to us all.

Mary Postgate has asked me to respond to your letter about the settlement agreement dated January 30.

Our greatest concern is to please you.

Please accept my sincere apologies for the error in your May bill.

Please find enclosed three copies of the requested articles.

Thank you for writing/for calling this to our attention.

Thank you for sharing the lovely memories you have of Father with me.

Thank you for taking the time to write, and please excuse my delay in responding to your letter.

Thank you for your thoughtfulness/for being so thoughtful.

Thank you so much for your kind words/for your letter.

The information you requested is enclosed.

We always feel bad when a customer is not satisfied with our services.

We appreciate the time and effort you spent letting us know about this.

We are pleased to send you the enclosed product literature.

We are sorry that the lounger arrived in damaged condition.

We regret the circumstances that obliged you to write us.

We thank you for your inquiry, and are pleased to enclose a sample snack bar.

You have asked me to estimate the fees that would be required for our services.

You have every right to be upset/angry/offended.

Your annoyance is understandable.

Your apology was very welcome, and I thank you.

Your letter of October 3 has received our complete attention.

Your letter was a great comfort.

PARAGRAPHS

▷   Thank you for your inquiry about Gabbadeo Wines. Enclosed are several brochures describing our vineyards and products and a list of vendors in your area.

▷   Thank you for taking the time to let us know of your recent experience with Fennel Bread. We are always interested in hearing from our customers but regret that it was this type of occurrence that prompted your letter.

▷   We received your very impressive résumé today and look forward to meeting with you. Because of the large number of responses we received to our advertisement, however, it may be two or three weeks before you hear from us.

▷   Thank you for your generous and sincere apology. I am entirely willing to put the incident behind me, and I look forward to continuing our old association.

▷   Thank you for your letter of May 24 describing the employee rudeness you encountered on three different visits to our Lowton Street store. We are investigating the situation and will let you know the results. In the meantime, please accept our most sincere apologies for the embarrassment and unpleasantness you experienced.

▷   In response to your letter of September 16, we have made a number of inquiries and are pleased to tell you that most of the staff here is agreeable to helping you with your research project. Please telephone the department secretary Arthur Eden to let him know what day or days you would like to spend with us.

———————————————— SAMPLE LETTERS ————————————————

Dear Ms. Stedman:

Thank you for your interest in our Quick Mail program. Due to an overwhelming demand, requests for our brochure and video cassette have far outpaced our supplies. However, a new shipment has been ordered, and we'll send you your materials as soon as we receive them.

Once you receive our kit, you'll learn all about the money-saving ideas that our program has to offer—reducing your mail float time, accelerating your cash flow, escalating your postage discounts, and still other techniques.

Thank you for your patience. Your materials should be arriving shortly.

Sincerely,

. . . .

Dear Mrs. Painter,

Thank you for telling us about the infestation in our Wheatley cereal. We are sorry you had this experience and want you to know we share your concern.

Consumer satisfaction is most important to us, and we sincerely regret your recent experience with our product. Our company has very strict standards of quality control. We carefully examine each lot of raw materials when it arrives. Sanitarians inspect our manufacturing plant continually and, in addition, make periodic checks of our suppliers' facilities. Food samples are collected all through the manufacturing process and are analyzed in our laboratories. We enforce these stringent procedures to ensure the production of high-quality, insect-free products.

The information you gave us about our product is being brought to the attention of the appropriate company officials.

Again, thank you for writing.

Yours truly,

. . . .

Dear Mr. Einhorn:

In response to your inquiry of December 3, I am sorry to tell you that Mr. Belton was with us for only a very short time and our records do not indicate a forwarding address. I believe he used to also work for Lorraine Linens. You might try them.

Sincerely,

. . . .

Dear Barbara and Garnet,

Your love and support these past few weeks have been a great comfort to all of us. I am especially grateful for the way you took over with the children when I couldn't. And, Garnet, thank you for being a pallbearer. I know Edward would have wanted you there. I hope you have not exhausted your reserves of friendship, because I feel I am going to need your kindness and understanding for a while yet.

With love and gratitude,

. . . .

Dear Mr. Willard:

Thank you for your letter of July 18. We are always happy to hear from our customers and pleased to be of service to them.

We are embarrassed to learn of your unfortunate experience with one of our products. We are always alert to constructive criticism, for we appreciate the enviable reputation our brand names enjoy in the marketplace with consumers the world over.

We would like you to know that as soon as we received your letter we held a special meeting with the resident managers of our Juvenile Puzzle Division, as well as our Quality Control Division. They are now looking into the problem.

In the meantime we are forwarding to you, with our compliments, several of our newest products, which we are certain will bring many hours of pleasant entertainment to your household. We appreciate your taking the time to write us and hope that you will continue to look for our brand names whenever you purchase "things to do" that are fun for everyone.

Sincerely,

See also: ACCEPTANCES, ACKNOWLEDGMENTS, ADJUSTMENTS, APOLOGIES, CONFIRMATION, COVER, FOLLOW-UP, REFUSALS, THANK YOU.

34

Résumés

"We judge ourselves by what we feel capable of doing,
while others judge us by what we have already done."
(Henry Wadsworth Longfellow)

Although a résumé is not, strictly speaking, a letter, it is included in this book, first, because it is sometimes written in letter form and, second, because many of its elements are used in employment-related letters.

A résumé provides prospective employers with a written summary of your qualifications. Its main purpose is to convince the reader that you are a good candidate for the job and should be called for an interview.

A good résumé is a kind of sales tool: you want to sell a prospective employer on the idea of hiring you. Although it lacks most of the features of a sales letter (few employers want to be dazzled with extravagant claims and catchy language), it is good to keep the "selling" aspect firmly in mind. Does your résumé present you in a good light while still being strictly accurate? Does it make it easy for the employer to pick out the salient points, the aspects of your background that match the company's needs?

Before you begin writing a résumé, you will need to assemble two kinds of information: facts about yourself and facts about the job you want.

The employer is particularly interested in learning how you performed at other jobs. Does your résumé give a prospective employer a fair idea of you as an employee?

When applying for a job, you might use one or two of the following: a *résumé* is a businesslike summary of your work history and career goals; a *cover letter* is a brief letter written to accompany a résumé; a *letter of application* is a combination cover letter and résumé, although less formal and shorter than a résumé.

The information in this chapter can also be used to write a letter of application, although this type of letter has a fairly narrow use today. Most applications are made either on a form provided by the applied-to organization or by means of a résumé accompanied by a cover letter. However, in some instances, a powerful, selling one-page application letter that includes résumé material can be more effective than a conventional résumé and cover letter. And some organizations continue to rely on letters of application to gauge the applicant's overall self-presentation and command of the written language.

Whether you are offered or refused a job depends not so much on your education, experience, and skills as it does on how closely you match the prospective employer's needs. To emphasize this match, you need to learn about the company and to target your résumé directly to them. It is not difficult to spot a generic résumé, and when prospective employers come across one that has obviously been written especially for them, they will give it more than the sixty seconds that most résumés get. By presenting as clear a picture of yourself as you can in terms of the employer's needs, you make it easy for them to determine quickly whether there is a possible match.

When to Send a Résumé

- each time you apply for a job
- when responding to an employment ad
- when inquiring about openings at a company
- when applying to universities/degree programs
- when applying for membership in certain organizations

How to Say It

☐   Include your name, address, and a daytime telephone number.

☐   State the specific job or kind of job you are applying for.

☐   The heart of the résumé is the detailing of work experience (paid and volunteer) and job skills. There are two basic approaches:

1.   The traditional reverse chronological employment format starts by listing your most recent position and going back through time. This is the easiest format to use, but it has its weaknesses if there are gaps in your job history, if you're new to the job market, or if your previous jobs don't seem to relate well to the one you are seeking. The emphasis here is on external facts: how long you worked somewhere, job titles, list of duties. For this type of résumé, include: dates of employment, name and full address of employer, job title, job duties, and reason for leaving (readily accepted reasons include moving, returning to school, seeking a better position). You do not need to mention the reason for leaving; if the employer wants to know, this will be brought up in the interview.

2.   The nonchronological résumé (sometimes called a skills-oriented or functional résumé) stresses your skills, accomplishments, and relevant qualifications in a way that allows a prospective employer to determine whether you are what they need. In this résumé you group job experiences according to a specific skill. For example, under "Leadership Skills" you might write, "Supervised night shift at Hooper & Co. for two years." Under "Interpersonal Skills" write, "As the mayor's troubleshooter, I was often called upon to intervene in disputes, negotiate contracts, and otherwise deal with constituents, politicians, and city personnel under difficult circumstances." "Organizational Skills" might include: "I was hired at Arnold-Browne to reorganize the accounting department, which was barely functioning at the time due to staff turnover, low morale, lack of department guidelines, and poor use of office space. At the end of two years, I was commended by the company president for 'unparalleled organizing skills.'"

Another option is to combine the chronological listing and the job skills listing. Under each job listed in reverse chronological order, group skills used in that job. Or you can slant your résumé directly toward the job under consideration by listing the general qualifications and specific qualifications you have for it.

☐   Education: name of school, city and state where it is located, years you attended, the diploma or certificate you earned, the course of studies you pursued.

☐   Special skills: familiarity with office machines, tools, equipment.

☐   Publications.

☐   Honors, awards, scholarships you have received, organizations to which you belong, leadership positions you have held including class offices, hobbies, volunteer work not mentioned elsewhere, and other relevant qualifications.

☐   List of references, or a mention that they will be supplied upon request.

☐   You will also want to include a cover letter with your résumé. Address the letter to the person you would be working for (call the company to find out the correct spelling of their name and their exact title). Open with a pleasant remark about the company—something they have done recently, one of their successes, a project under development, an article in the business section of the paper about them. Or you could mention a name—someone who referred you to the company, someone who has spoken well of their employment there, someone who deals with the company as supplier or buyer. The use of names is slightly risky, but in general it provides a good way to begin your letter. Then briefly highlight your qualifications in reference to the advertised position and refer the person to the résumé for a complete description. Close with a request for an interview, and your appreciation for the person's time and interest. You may want to type your phone number under your name; although it will also appear on your résumé and on your letterhead, it can't hurt to make it very visible.

☐   In some situations you may want to attach work samples, publications, or other supplementary materials.

☐   If you are writing a letter of application (that is, a combined résumé and cover letter), open with an attention-getting sentence or paragraph, describe the skills you have that are appropriate to the job, summarize your experience and education (your employment history can be greatly shortened in a letter of application), tell why you think you are qualified for the position, and request an interview. Provide a complete address and daytime phone number and either supply references or state that they will be furnished on request. Close with a pleasant forward-looking statement: you hope to have the opportunity of discussing the position further; you will be glad to provide additional information; you appreciate the person's time and consideration and look forward to meeting them.

What Not to Say

☐   Robert Half, founder of Robert Half International, a large white-collar recruiting firm, says that in a résumé, "flippancy, careless errors, tactless remarks, irrelevant or extraneous material and attempts at humor should be avoided at all costs."

☐   Do not emphasize what you expect the company to do for you. ("I see this position as a wonderful opportunity to learn about the marketing side of the automotive industry.") Emphasize instead what you think you can bring to the company.

☐   Don't present your accomplishments so that they say, "Here is what I've done." Instead, phrase them to say, "Here is what I can do for you." For example, "I have the experience and ability to help you increase production efficiency. While I was supervisor at Fortis & Co., department overruns decreased 32%."

☐   Do not include such personal information as age, weight, height, marital or financial status, and religious or political affiliation unless it is relevant to the situation you are seeking. For example, if you are applying for a position as chief staffer to a state senator, you will want to note your political party affiliation. Or if you are applying for a position as church organist, it may be helpful—although not always necessary—to mention your religious background. It is often illegal for prospective employers to ask questions about age, sex, race, and religion.

☐   Avoid adjectives and adverbs. Take out every "very" you find and such lukewarm words as "good," "wonderful," "exciting." Use instead strong, perhaps even unusual, nouns and verbs.

□   Omit any mention of salary; this is better discussed in an interview. When you state a salary requirement first (or list previous salaries, thus tipping the prospective employer off to the range that you might accept), you lose a small advantage. Try to get your interviewer to mention a figure before you give your salary expectations.

□   Avoid embellishments, exaggerations, half-truths, and of course outright lies. These are not always discovered, although many companies have résumé fact-checkers. If you are found out, you will be immediately dismissed, will suffer at the least a great deal of embarrassment and humiliation, and may be liable to civil charges. Trying to make yourself sound better than you are for a position is often a tip-off that you may not be well qualified for it; would you be happy in such a job?

□   Just as you would avoid exaggerations and embellishments, avoid also being modest. This is not the time to play down anything you have done. It is often helpful to have someone who knows you look over your final draft.

□   Don't tell every single thing you've ever done. Sometimes filler material detracts from a strong résumé. People who throw in all the little extras and asides on the theory that it "can't hurt" may be wrong.

□   Omit information about work you've done in the past that you don't care to do again (unless, of course, this would leave large unexplained holes in your résumé). If you have always disliked dictaphone work and have a number of other tasks you can list under your last secretarial position, omit any mention of the dictaphone duties.

Tips on Writing

□   Present your information using simple, short sentences. Avoid jargon and long, involved phrases.

□   Use strong, active verbs. Instead of the weaker "I did this" or "I was responsible for that," write "I managed," "I developed," "I directed."

□   Read *What Color Is Your Parachute* for some excellent insights into effective résumés.

□   Do not use a standard, boilerplate résumé. Each job résumé should be typed or printed freshly (no photocopies) and should be tailored to the individual situation.

□   For a heading, use "Résumé," "Summary of Work History," "Professional History," "Skills, Education, and Experience," "Experience," or no title at all.

□   If this is true, let a prospective employer know that you are interested in more than a salary. The job may afford you a learning opportunity, a chance for advancement, the chance to use skills you haven't before found marketable. However, reasons such as proximity to your home will probably not carry any weight.

☐   It is essential that you have a clear idea of the job you are applying for. If you are not sure exactly what is involved, call the company to ask questions. Do research on the company in the library. Speak to people who work there or who know the company. When you tell a prospective employer what you can do for their company, the implication is that you have studied the company enough to know where you might fit in; this is very appealing. Although you cannot change the facts of your employment history, you can emphasize certain skills and qualifications if you know that this is what the employer is looking for. The employer may want creativity, for example, and none of your previous jobs emphasized it. You can then check other areas of your life to see where you have shown creativity—taking art classes, hobby photography, teaching night classes in pottery. If you haven't studied the job description and fail to note the call for creativity, you will miss an excellent opportunity to present yourself as an appropriate candidate.

☐   When writing a letter of application, tailor it to a specific company, and address it to a specific person in the company (call to find out the name and ask for the spelling, even if it's a simple name—"Barbara" could be Barbra, "Neil" could be Neal). Employers will spot a canned letter, and it is a little unlikely that you could send exactly the same letter to several different companies and appeal to all of them. Personalize your letter.

☐   The letter of application (and to a lesser extent, the résumé) is not meant to be an exhaustive list of everything you know and have done. Select the most important items (and those most relevant to the open position) and leave the rest for the interview. The two objectives are to tell enough so that the person can see you are well qualified for the job and to present this in such a way that the person wants to interview you. Do not try to cram in too much; you will force the reader to search for the important points. Use white space, bullets, or even capital letters (for job titles and skills) to help the reader quickly find your most telling points.

☐   In most cases, a résumé should be concise and compact—not more than two pages and one if you can manage it. There will always be instances in which a longer résumé will serve you better, but consider the situation carefully before sending ten pages. A short résumé might mention publications "in such professional journals as *AJA, Astro,* and *AR Monthly,*" while a longer résumé might list all the articles you've published. The best time for elaborating on a résumé is during an interview. The purpose of a résumé is to show that you are qualified for the job opening; at the interview you can fill in more detail to justify this opinion. Keep paragraphs short, and leave enough white space to make it easy reading.

□   It is impossible to overemphasize the importance of a neat, correctly written résumé. After you proofread your final draft, have at least two other people proofread it for you. The error that two of you miss will jump out at your prospective employer.

□   If you choose to list your work background chronologically, start with the most recent job you held. Put the dates of employment on the left side of the page. Beside each date, list the name of company where you worked during that period. Underneath give the title of your job there and a brief job description.

□   Describe your work experience in terms of successful outcomes. Even if you only helped increase sales, decrease expenditures, or come in under budget for the first time in ten years, it is valuable to say so. And be specific. Report those successful outcomes in numbers, percentages, dollars—how many people you supervised, how many copies of your books have been sold, how many projects you oversaw, how much time or money you saved the company, the size of the budget you were responsible for, percentage reduction in absenteeism in your department, percentage increase in productivity at your station.

□   When possible, emphasize your flexibility and ability to learn new tasks and adapt to new situations. In a world where information and technology are developing at breakneck speeds, this is an important qualification for most jobs. One way to do this is to make your past jobs sound different from each other. For example, if you have held several positions as a secretary, you might want to list under one position that you reorganized the filing system, under another that you trained employees in the use of the new telephone system, under yet another that you managed the office for three months while your supervisor was taking a leave of absence.

□   You may choose one of three styles for your résumé: (1) the first person ("I managed the Midway Pro Bowl for three years, and saw it double in profits in that time"); (2) the third person ("She has worked in a number of areas of radio broadcasting, including . . ." or "Dr. Patikar organized a new patient outcare service"); (3) without any pronoun ("Developed a new method of twinning steel"). Each style has advantages and disadvantages. The first can be wearying with all its "I"s (try to omit as many as possible), the second can appear remote and pretentious, and the third may strike a reader as abrupt. You are best off using the style you feel most comfortable with, regardless of what you perceive as its benefits or disadvantages.

□   You may not be used to looking at your work history in terms of job skills, so it may take some time to analyze what you have been doing in terms of broad skill categories. (Examples: effective communication skills, organization and management skills, interpersonal skills, promotional skills, negotiating skills, new product development skills, training program development skills, design and implementation of employee programs, workshop planning skills, leadership skills, office management skills, supervisory skills, copywriting skills.) Under each category, support your claim with examples from your work experience.

□   The purpose of a résumé or a letter of application is to get you an interview. Reread your material with this in mind: would you want to talk to the person who wrote this?

Special Situations

□   In certain lines of work, you may be asked to furnish a brief biographical sketch for such things as the program notes of a conference, a newspaper article on a recent achievement, or a company newsletter that features different employees each month. Although based on your résumé, such a sketch is always written in narrative fashion, is far briefer and less specific than a résumé, and aims rather to capture the essence of who you are professionally.

□   Young people seeking their first full-time job may encounter the classic frustration: They won't take me because I don't have experience, and I don't have experience because I can't get a job. Nonetheless, it is possible to put together an appealing résumé even without a significant work history. Look for school-related data that could interest an employer: name of educational institutions, dates, courses taken, degrees granted, major fields of study, GPA, awards, honors, scholarships. List groups you have belonged to (French club, chess club, sorority or fraternity), offices you have held, volunteer work you have done, and extracurricular activities and athletics for junior high, high school, and college unless they are too trivial or irrelevant. This type of résumé benefits from a "job skills" treatment rather than a precise listing of work experience. You might want to list such qualifications as "Dependability: received perfect attendance award for 9th and 11th grades; missed no days of work at summer job; earned award for dependability as a paper carrier." Or: "Learns quickly: took over for cashier at work with no notice and quickly learned cashier duties; as laboratory assistant at the University, learned new duties quickly and efficiently."

□   If you are given an application form to fill out for a job, you may always attach a résumé to it.

□   If you don't want your present employer to know you are job-hunting, request that inquiries be directed to your home address and that references from your present employer be delayed until both you and the prospective employer feel surer of the match.

□   Letters of application are also written to camps; clubs and organizations; colleges, universities, and trade schools; franchise organizations;

private elementary and secondary schools; and for volunteer positions. Although the content will be different from that of job application letters, many of the general guidelines in this chapter can be used.

□   It is still possible for the average person to apply to colleges or universities or to community colleges or trade schools without too much difficulty. If, however, you are a student at the very high or very low end of your graduating class or you have any special needs (particularly if you need financial assistance), you are advised to look for special help in this area beginning with the high school counseling office, private counseling services, and some of the numerous publications available. For some students, the process of applying for admission to college education can take many months and require much specialized information.

□   If you are on the other side of the desk and are asked to design a job application form, be certain it doesn't violate state and federal antidiscrimination laws. (Job applicants should be aware of their right not to answer certain questions.) You may not ask applicants to fill in such information as: age, race, sex, height and weight, color of eyes, hair, or complexion; birthplace; dates of public school attendance; arrest record, type of military discharge, past workers' compensation claims; whether they own their own home, have ever been sued, or had a surety bond or government clearance denied; work transportation arrangements; non-job-related handicaps; activities, memberships, and hobbies not directly related to the job; how they heard about the job opening. Many of these questions are prohibited because they could allow an employer to deduce an applicant's age, sex, or minority status. It might be wise to have a lawyer check your rough draft for possible state or federal discrimination violations.

□   When applying for a franchise, you will want to pay close attention to FTC guidelines and may also want a lawyer to help you with some of the correspondence.

Format

□   All résumés should be typed, printed, or machine-produced on good bond paper (white or off-white) in sharp black elite or pica type (no script or other special type). They should look professional, conservative, and straightforward. In a few fields, you might get a job using a highly creative résumé with graphics, colored inks, and an offbeat design. To do this, however, you must be very familiar with your market—to the point perhaps of knowing someone at the company who obtained their job that way. This type of résumé gets many admiring glances but is often passed over for the more "stable"-looking résumé.

□   There is only one correct format for a résumé—a logical, readable one. Your name and address may go in the upper left, upper right, or center of the page. Your material may be typed block or indented style. You have great latitude in setting up the material, so choose the format that seems to arise out of the arrangement of your material. White space helps. It's hard for a reader to spot the highlights if a résumé is run together, with no space between job listings, for example.

☐   Letters of application are always typed, either on personal letterhead or on good bond business-size paper. You will pay heavily for typographical errors, a worn-out ribbon, and poor spacing, grammar, or spelling.

WORDS

ability
administered
background
capable
contributed
coordinated
created
credentials
developed
directed
effective
enthusiastic
experience
goals

guided
handled
honest
imaginative
industrious
initiative
loyal
managed
objectives
operated
opportunity
organized
originated

oversaw
participated
performed
planned
professional
prospective
qualified
redesigned
responsible
restructured
skills
supervised
trained

PHRASES

ability to get along with people
able to present facts clearly and
   succinctly
a good working knowledge of
analytical and critical thinking skills
believe I have a strong aptitude for
considered an enthusiastic worker
conversant with
design experience
excellent communications skills
extensive experience with
good candidate/match for the job
good judgment
good sense of

have specialized in
I believe I could contribute
in response to your advertisement
in this capacity
I was responsible for
leadership abilities
may I have fifteen minutes of your
   time to discuss
my five years as
of considerable value to you
qualities that would be very useful in
sales ability
satisfactory arrangement
serious interest in

sound understanding of
specialized in
supervisory abilities
take pride in my work
technical skills
the experience to qualify me for
to arrange a meeting at your
  convenience

very interested in pursuing a career
  with
well suited for
would enjoy attending/working/
  belonging
would be willing to travel
would like to gain warehouse
  experience

———————————————— SENTENCES ————————————————

As you will see from my résumé, I have a great deal of experience in program
  development, administration, contract development, and budget planning.

I achieved an 18% capture rate on grants proposals submitted to local funders.

I am a skilled operator of the bridgeport mill and radial drill.

I am interested in your part-time position for a truck unloader.

I am responding to your advertisement in Sunday's paper for a senior analyst pro-
  grammer.

I believe I am well qualified to apply for your opening for a water quality extension
  agent.

I can refer you to people with whom I've worked on various accounts.

I consider myself a high-energy person.

I feel I could contribute something to your organization.

I have experience with light clerical duties.

I have three years' experience in product development.

I met every deadline while working at Brooker Associates, some of them under fairly
  difficult circumstances.

In my last position I performed complex CNC turning operations on diversified
  parts with minimum supervision, and also had Mazatrol experience.

In my two years at Arrow Appliance, I helped increase productivity by approximately 25% and decrease absenteeism by almost 20%.

I successfully reduced stock levels while maintaining shipping and order schedules,
  resulting in lower overhead costs.

I understand you are looking for a form tool grinder.

I was responsible for all aspects of store management, including sales, personnel,
  inventory, profit and loss control, and overseeing the annual budget.

I will be glad to discuss the matter of salary with you at a personal interview.

I will telephone your secretary Monday morning to see if you might be able to
  schedule an interview next week.

I would appreciate the opportunity of discussing this position with you.

I would be willing/am able to travel.

I would like to apply for the advertised position of data intake coordinator.

May I call you next week to set up an interview for the loan officer position?

My work skills include data entry, alphabetical and numerical filing, photocopying,
  typing skills, good organizational skills, an affinity for detail, and previous experience in a legal office.

Previous employers have found me responsible and innovative.

Recommendations/references are available upon request.

This is in response to your advertisement for a visual merchandising coordinator.

PARAGRAPHS

▷   As you know, I have been managing the Albany branch of your Woodstock Bookstore for three years. I understand that you plan to franchise several of your bookstores, and I would like to apply for the franchise for this store if it is available.

▷   All my previous jobs have involved public contact. As a result I feel comfortable dealing with people on many different levels. As an academic advisor in the MBA program at McKeown College, I provided academic guidance and course selection assistance to adult graduate students and program applicants, recruited students, and promoted the program in talks and seminars. As the city personnel manager of Darby, I was responsible for all human resource functions including recruitment, labor relations and negotiations, and employee wellness programs.

▷   My responsibilities at Edwards International included invoicing, logging deposits, resolving billing problems related to data entry, managing four other accounts receivable employees, and filing a monthly report on the department.

▷   I am highly skilled in the use and interpretation of specifications drawings and measuring instruments, generally knowledgeable about mechanical and electrical principles, and have experience in the construction, maintenance, and machine repair industries. Specifically, I have analyzed malfunctioning machines and systems (electrical, hydraulic, pneumatic), recommended corrective action, and, upon approval, made repairs or modifications. I also have a working understanding of recovery equipment, instrumentation, systems, and facilities, know how to use complicated measuring and sampling equipment, and can repair machines and equipment, working from written or oral directions and specifications.

▷   Part of my duties as music director and liturgist involved instrument acquisition and maintenance, including revoicing seven ranks of the organ, constructing small percussion instruments, enlarging the handbell set from sixteen to thirty-seven, and acquiring a new studio piano for the choir. I also obtained estimates and made plans for a major overhaul of the forty-rank 1926 Casavant organ.

▷   I am currently employed in an engineering environment by a large independent transportation firm, but I am interested in making a career change into the investment/financial services field. I have recently obtained my CFP designation and hope to find a position as a broker trainee. I am enclosing my résumé for your review and consideration for such a position.

▷   Selected career accomplishments: broke a fifteen-year collection record during the first two months of employment as a collector of delinquent medical accounts. Promoted to unit manager as a result of high achievement levels, and later to office collection manager. Was consistently the leading collector at the Denver branch of the Montjoy Agencies.

———————————————— SAMPLE LETTERS ————————————————

Dear Ms. Lownie:

As an editor with eighteen years' experience, I think I may be well qualified for the position of Editor that was advertised in *Engineering Today*. You will see from the enclosed résumé that I have edited both technical and trade publications. In each case, I was able to raise the standards of the editorial content, increase ad sales (in one case by 120%), and attract new subscribers in significant numbers.

Having met and exceeded my goals in my present position and feeling that the assistant editor is more than capable of taking over, I want to challenge myself with a more demanding position. *Engineering Today* appeals to me very much as this type of challenge.

Thank you for considering my application.

Sincerely,

. . . .

Dear Margaret West,

Libraries have been a second home to me for years, and I have decided to major in library science. In the meantime, I would like to apply for the summer job opening in your children's room.

Although my work background is slight (see résumé), I think I can offer you a deep and genuine interest in library science, a strong desire to excel at this kind of work, and library skills that come from many hundreds of library visits. As the oldest of five children, I also have considerable experience and a high comfort level in dealing with young people.

Thank you for your time and attention.

Sincerely,

. . . .

Dear Mr. Baillie:

The requirements for the branch manager position you advertised describe almost perfectly my own background.

As assistant manager of Gulliver Travel, I have been responsible for overseeing eight full-time agents. I am a travel school graduate (Charlson International) with a great deal of experience and a good working knowledge of the travel industry in all its phases—from issuing tickets and seat assignments and assisting with ticket assembly to PARS computer experience. I have two years of experience in domestic reservations, one year of experience working with corporate international travel operations, and a thorough understanding of international tariffs.

I would like to discuss this position with you and will be happy to come in for an interview at your convenience.

Sincerely yours,

. . . .

Dear Ms. Chuffnell,

We have just moved to Seabury and have been told by friends what an asset the Seabury Country Club is to the community. My husband, three children, and I are interested in applying for membership.

I am enclosing the three required member recommendations as well as the one-time nonrefundable processing fee of $50. If you need any further information, please call me during the day at 555-2498 or in the evening at 555-9980.

We are all looking forward to enjoying the Seabury Country Club for years to come.

                              With best wishes,

                    . . . .

JOAN PENROSE

Present Address	Permanent Address
14 Grace Lane, #4	Route 9N
Chance, UT 84623	Fairfield, UT 84620
801/555-2241	801/555-2789

OBJECTIVE

An entry-level management position in transportation and logistics with the opportunity to contribute to the efficient operation of a firm and to earn advancement through on-the-job performance.

EDUCATION

Bachelor of Business Administration, May 1992, from Merriam University, with a major in Transportation and Logistics and a minor in Psychology. Major G.P.A.: 4.0; cumulative G.P.A.: 3.4.

Coursework: Logistics Law, International Transportation and Logistics, Strategic Logistics Management, Transportation and Public Policy, Transportation Carrier Management, Transportation Economics; Accounting I and II, Business Communications, Business Law, Community and Regional Planning, Computer Science, Economics, Operations Management.

Financed 100% of college expenses through work, work-study programs, and grants.

EXPERIENCE

Merriam University Computer Lab, 1989-1992; supervised three other students; oversaw hardware repairs and updating of software library;

assisted users with various software (15 hours/week, September to May only).

Swinney's Book Store, summers, 1988-1990: assembled and packed book, magazine, and giftware shipments; trained twelve employees (20 hours/week).

Creston Food Stores, Inc.: Deli Manager and Clerk, summers, 1988-1990; controlled all facets of delicatessen, including catering large and small events; worked at five different stores (20 hours/week).

Lorimer Industries, Salt Lake City, June and July 1991, Transportation/Distribution Intern: facilitated the relationship between Transportation and Customer Support Inventory Planning and Purchasing; assisted in the routing and controlling of inbound raw materials; gained experience in outbound logistics management, including warehousing and distribution.

Blaydon Logistics Case Study, August 1991: one of seven students selected to participate in logistics project at Blaydon Corporate Headquarters, San Diego; evaluated performance measures used in the areas of transportation, customs, and export administration; presented initial findings and suggested alternative measures.

STRENGTHS

Communication: communicate well when speaking and writing; able to act as liaison between different personality types; comfortable and effective communicating with both superiors and staff.

Leadership: able to motivate a project team; background in psychology provides wide range of interpersonal skills to encourage and instruct others.

Responsibility: accustomed to being in positions of responsibility; self-motivated and willing to set goals and work to achieve them; never assume "the other person" is responsible.

Organization: use time and resources effectively; consider efficiency, planning, and accountability very important.

Computer expertise: experienced in Lotus 1-2-3, WordPerfect, BASIC programming, Saturn-Calc spreadsheets, MicroSoft Excell, Aldus Pagemaker, Harvard Graphics, and BITNET, an international electronic mail service.

Other: willing to relocate anywhere; have traveled to Europe (three times) and to the Orient (once) and thus have a global awareness of business and politics; quick learner and trained in analytical problem-solving skills; solid work ethic that finds satisfaction and pleasure in achieving work goals; daily reader of *The Wall Street Journal*, *The Journal of Commerce*, *Christian Science Monitor*, and *The Utah Times*.

ACTIVITIES

Treasurer, Transportation/Logistics Club
Member, University Finance Club
Member, Intramural Volleyball Team, four years
Campus Chest (student-operated community service organization), business manager, 1990, public relations, 1991
Member, Professional Women in Transportation, Utah Chapter
Coordinator of the Business Council Peer Advisory to Transportation and Logistic Undergraduate Students

AWARDS

Creston's Employee to Employee Courtesy Award
Dean's List, eight semesters
Golden Key National Honor Society
Phi Eta Sigma National Honor Society
National Collegiate Business Merit Award

INTERESTS

Astronomy, computer strategy games, bicycling, reading.

REFERENCES

Available upon request.

See also: APPOINTMENTS, COVER, EMPLOYMENT, FOLLOW-UP.

35

Sales Letters

"The advertisement is one of the most interesting and
difficult of modern literary forms." (Aldous Huxley)

Almost every letter that's sent out by a company, business, or organization is essentially a sales letter. Even "nonbusiness" letters like sympathy notes, congratulations, thank you letters, or apologies carry a second-level message that asks the recipient to think well of the firm.

In 1988, nearly 62 billion pieces of direct mail advertising weighing 7.6 billion pounds were delivered by the Postal Service—that's 250 pieces and nearly 31 pounds for every woman, man, and child in the United States.

In 1988 revenues from direct mailing advertising amounted to $270 billion; they are expected to have nearly doubled by 1992 to $500 billion. This is big business, and sales letters may be the most financially important ones you write.

Although computerized mailing lists have considerably reduced direct mail marketing costs, only about five out of every one hundred mailings are even opened by the recipient. This has two implications: you may want to use the envelope itself in such a way as to entice the person to open it; you will want to make those five opened letters so appealing that you get more than the average three out of five responses.

Sales letters aren't appropriate for all products and services, but they can usually get the reader to make the call or visit the store where the real selling can be done. Because they are productive and economical (compared to print and video advertising, for example), they are an integral part of most firms' marketing strategies. For many small businesses, they are the only practical and affordable advertising tool available.

Whether you're selling a product, a service, an idea, space, credit, or good-will, the sales letter requires more work before you begin to write than it does to actually write it. Henry Ford said, "Before everything else, getting ready is the secret of success." You need to know everything about your product or service. You need to know your reader, assembling as much data as possible. Then you must pinpoint and develop a strong central selling point. A number of other factors may be considered as well (timing, developing a coupon or sample). Only when a great deal of preparatory work has been done can a successful letter be written. Do not begin to write too soon.

Because they are so essential to a company's success, sales letters have become sophisticated and professional to the point that many corporations and businesses no longer generate their own. The buzzword today is "integration," and many large companies use full-service agencies to handle every aspect of their advertising needs, including sales letters. You can locate such firms in the Yellow Pages under Direct Marketing, Advertising Agencies, or Public Relations Counselors.

Kinds of Sales Letters

- announcements: changes/new products
- congratulations: purchase/new account/payment
- direct mail advertising
- follow-up: inquiries/sales letters/sales
- form letters
- goodwill (see GOODWILL)
- introducing new products/services
- invitation: open house/sale/membership/new account
- questionnaires/surveys
- responding to inquiries
- special promotions/sales/free gifts and services
- thank you: sale/new account/revived account
- trial offers: products/programs/services/subscriptions

How to Say It

- ☐ Get the reader's attention.
- ☐ Establish contact.
- ☐ Create an interest in what you're selling with a strong central sales message.
- ☐ Arouse the reader's desire for your product by using specific, vivid words and images to describe it
- ☐ Convince the reader that responding to your offer is a smart move, offering "proofs" (samples, testimonials, statistics) of your assertions
- ☐ Tell the reader how to obtain your product or service
- ☐ Stimulate and encourage the reader to take immediate action.

What Not to Say

□   Do not say, "We never hold a sale! Our everyday prices are so low that we don't need to." Human nature likes a sale. Even customers who regularly use your products or services and think they are reasonably priced like a bargain. By offering occasional discounts, sales, clearances, and special purchase promotions, you'll create a sense of excitement and willingness to buy in both old and new customers.

□   Avoid the first-name, palsy-walsy approach. Business columnist Louis Rukeyser received an impressive amount of reader response after a column on form sales letters. According to him, "The artificially intimate stuff appears particularly irritating."

□   Avoid subtle (and unsubtle) threats such as "You'll be sorry if you don't order now," "Yours while they last," "Don't miss this opportunity," "Don't pass this up." While a few readers may allow themselves to be stampeded by the hurry-hurry line, many more will call your bluff. Weigh this sort of approach carefully. A similar approach tells prospective customers that since they have not ordered anything during a certain period, their names will have to be removed from the mailing list if they don't order soon. This is actually effective in many cases as people fear missing out on something later on. While it doesn't work all the time and is a type of sales threat, it can be effective with judicious use.

□   Do not scold customers, correct them, condescend to them ("you probably don't know this, but . . ."), tell them they're going about things the wrong way by not buying/using your product, laying down too many rules, regulations, requirements.

□   Avoid jargon or concepts that make it difficult for the reader to quickly grasp your message. In pitching an engineering book to engineers, you will use some technical language, but the letter should still be intelligible at some level to laypeople.

□   Although warnings could be issued against badmouthing competitors and making unwarranted claims for products, both these tactics have been used (although not often) and used successfully (again, not often). Your use of such approaches will depend on your perception of your firm and product as being "above" this or not.

□   Do not make too many points in one letter. Concentrate on your strongest one or two sales points, add one in the postscript if you like, and save the others for follow-up letters.

□   In general, don't ask questions. It is poor psychology to get your reader into a "dialogue" in which they might not answer your question "correctly." Questions also derail your reader from the one-way train of thought that leads to a sale. Once you start building toward a certain conclusion, don't interrupt your sequence with questions. In particular avoid negative questions like "How can you afford to turn down this offer?" or "Why would anyone not want to own one?" Questions like these bring the idea of refusal to full consciousness.

☐   In most cases, you are better off without such hyperbolic claims for your product as astounding, revolutionary, incredible, sensational, extraordinary, spectacular. Use instead concrete features, benefits, details, and product claims. Understatement is often very effective.

Tips on Writing

☐   There is complete agreement on how to begin a sales letter: with a bang! There is no agreement, however, on what sort of a "bang" will work for you. Possibilities include: a surprising fact or statistic; a touching or dramatic anecdote; the offer of a gift, coupon, or booklet; a thought-provoking question or quotation; a joke or riddle; a celebrity endorsement, quote, or tie-in; a who-what-when-where-why paragraph; your strongest selling factor; nostalgia; addressing the reader by name (although this is not always agreeable to the reader) or as "someone special" singled out for the letter; perhaps even a negative or unexpected statement.

☐   There are a few more concrete guidelines for ending the sales letter. Because your main goal is to incite the person to immediate action, you tell them what you want them to do (order, call, mail a card, come to the store) and tell them how easy it is to do this ("enclosed is a postage-paid reply envelope"); echo your letter opening in some way—if you started off quoting a celebrity, finish by saying something like, "And that's why So-and-So won't drive anything but a . . ."

☐   Keep your paragraphs short.

☐   Beginning, middle, and end, the focus must remain on the prospective customer. Describe the product in terms of benefits to the customer, how it relates to their needs, problems, and interests, how it can improve their lives, save them money, make them feel more confident. The customer has only one question: "What is this going to do for me?" It's up to you to develop a strong client-centered message and persuade potential buyers that they need your product not so much because it's a great product, but because it is great for *them*. You will be using the words "you" and "your" frequently in such letters.

☐   It is rare that a sales message does not include somewhere the cost of the item or service. There is good reason for it; customers tend to ignore the message otherwise on the assumption that they can't afford it. Cost is a determinant in most purchases; if the customer has to call to find out, the extra trouble is often not worth it when a competitor's cost is available in its sales message.

☐ Make it convenient and desirable for the reader to respond. Convenience means orders blanks accompanied by postage-paid reply envelopes, prepaid form postcards asking for a sales rep to call or for additional information, a toll-free number to call for local distributors or to place orders, order now-pay later, a listing of store hours and locations. To increase the desirability of responding, offer discounts, bargain prices, delayed no-interest payments, gifts, in-store certificates, coupons, brochures, samples, or a free trial period.

☐ Although both are necessary, emotional appeals tend to be more effective than intellectual appeals. Your letter should be underpinned with an appeal to some basic human emotion: love ("your child will have hours of fun!"); the need for love ("heads will turn when you wear this"); prestige ("your home will be a stand-out with this . . ."); ambition ("learn new management techniques overnight"); security ("smoke-alarm with built-in battery tester").

☐ Repetition is helpful in emphasizing a main point, in clarifying complicated material, and in lending an attractive rhythm to your letter.

☐ State very clearly what you want your reader to do: send for this, buy that, call this number, send in the coupon, order from this catalog.

☐ How long should a sales letter be? Most advice would probably come down in favor of the one-page letter. On the other hand, some well-written four-page letters have enjoyed a high response rate. And of course a poorly written letter is in no way redeemed by being short. It is perhaps more logical to concentrate on what absolutely needs to be said—whether that takes one page, two, or four.

☐ You can create and foster credibility by means of testimonials, case histories, research studies, statistics, company reputation, product usage test results, comparison with similar products, free samples or trial periods, guaranties/warranties, celebrity endorsements, photographs of actual use, user polls.

☐ Sales letters aimed at former customers emphasize your appreciation for past business, your desire to serve the customer again, products or services introduced since your last contact with them, your confidence that you can satisfy their needs. You could ask if there is a reason that they no longer bring their business to you. This may provide you with useful information. Or it may remind the customer that there *is* no particular reason.

☐ Give the person a good reason for acting right now: limited supplies, expiration date of sale offer, prices going up later, early-response discount, etc.

☐ When possible, quote satisfied customers (particularly well-known ones) who can testify to the product's or service's usefulness.

☐ Whenever possible, guarantee the buyer's satisfaction in some way.

☐ Some sales messages can make effective use of such attention-getting devices as colored ink or paper, graphics, boxed information, unusual type faces or paper finishes, or such design elements as heads, subheads, white space, indented material, and bulleted lists. Important parts of your message can be handwritten, underlined, capped, italicized, or set in some combination of these. This attention-getting approach is not for every sales letter. If you are selling bank cards, life insurance, healthcare services, or other "serious" products and services, you would do better to adopt a more traditional format.

☐   The postscript has become extremely popular in sales letters—probably because of its effectiveness. Repeat your most powerful selling point here, or feature a new and strong sales point such as a money-back guarantee, a time limit for the offer, an additional bonus for buying now.

☐   Keep your letter exciting, pithy, and active. Use colorful descriptive words (words that are too general leave no trace in the reader's mind), strong verbs, appealing images. Sometimes a sales letter writer is so intent on either educating the prospective customer or building up a case via statistics, background information, and reports, that they forget how boring and how un-client-centered such a message is.

☐   There is a fine line between the clever gimmick, hook, ploy, or attention-getter and the too-cute-for-its-own-good approach. When taking a risk with a novel overture, have a number of people from different backgrounds read and evaluate your letter. If it is clever, the rewards are great. If you stray on the side of coy or insensitive, the results can be fatal.

☐   Convey to your reader that responding positively to your offer is the only sensible course of action to take.

☐   Consumers love free gifts, samples, and coupons!

☐   Dale Carnegie once said, "I deal with the obvious. I present, reiterate and glorify the obvious—because the obvious is what people need to be told." Never assume anything on the reader's part, and do not be afraid to state the obvious.

☐   For a select audience, you may want to use good quality stationery, first class postage, and an individually typed address to ensure that your recipient opens it.

☐   Choose a specific tone for your letter and maintain it throughout. Is your product one that can be described well in a friendly, neighbor-to-neighbor tone? Or will readers respond better to a serious, intellectual tone? Other tones include: humorous, brisk and businesslike, urgent and hard-hitting, sophisticated, lively and fast-moving, technical, soothing and reassuring, mysterious, informational, emotional.

☐   Sometimes a series of letters is effective. When you have good reason to believe a segment of the market is susceptible to your product (because of previous purchases, for example), you may want to contact them several times—but not with the same letter each time. The letters can differ from each other either by focus (highlight a different benefit of your product or service in each letter), by intensity (time is growing short, our offer will expire soon), or by offer (two-for-one price in one letter, a discount in another).

Special Situations

☐   A sales message is often combined with another message. For example, a letter congratulating someone on their new business mentions how the sender's products might be useful. A cover letter accompanying the new spring catalog points out new products or an improved ordering system. Thank you letters, announcements, letters of welcome, and seasonal greetings have all been used to carry a sales message.

☐   When you send samples, product literature, or information in response to a customer's request, the cover letter must be a sales letter of the best type. Although the enclosure should sell itself (or the product it describes), the cover letter can carry a strong sales message and additional incentives to become a regular customer (describe other benefits, enclose a cents-off or discount coupon, include a catalog and order form).

☐   With a versatile product or service (or a number of different products in your line), you will want to match up certain features or certain products with a particular segment of the market and target them with a letter tailored to their needs. For the same product, you might send out six different letters to six different types of customers. A greenhouse manufacturer might write different sales letters to farmers, suburban homeowners, businesses, apartment dwellers, and even college students (the desktop miniature greenhouse).

☐   When you are already selling a certain group of customers one product or service, you may want to target them with a sales letter promoting another product or service that, out of long habit, they don't "see" anymore. For example, customers who regularly use a hair salon may forget that they can also buy an extensive line of hair-care products, use tanning booths, or schedule manicures.

Format

☐   Most sales letters are computer-generated form letters—either standard form letters or letters in which individual names, addresses, and salutations are filled in using a mass mailing merge feature. The latter gives form letters a more personal look (unless you are also inserting the person's name here and there throughout the letter, which actually gives the opposite impression).

□ Some form letters are printed on good-quality paper, signed individually, and mailed first class.

WORDS

absolute	electronic	nostalgic
acquaint	exclusive	optional
adaptable	expert	portable
advantages	exquisite	powerful
affordable	extensive	practical
all-new	feature-packed	precision
attractive	flair	privilege
authentic	flexible	productive
available	free	professional
bargain	genuine	profitable
benefit	guaranteed	rapid-action
brand-new	half-price	rebate
breakthrough	handy	revolutionary
brilliant	helpful	state-of-the-art
classic	high-quality	stunning
clever	indulge	successful
comfortable	inexpensive	super
compact	informative	thrifty
convenient	ingenious	tremendous
dazzling	innovative	unbreakable
delightful	invaluable	useful
dependable	low-cost	valuable
discount	low-priced	versatile
durable	luxurious	warranted
economical	money-making	waterproof
effective	natural	wholesale
efficient	new	worth

PHRASES

absolutely free
acquaint you with
add a new dimension to
advanced design
a great gift idea
all for one low price
all in one easy operation

all-in-one portable convenience
all of this at your fingertips
an impressive collection
an incredibly low introductory
   rate/price of
appreciate your business
a price you'll appreciate

a revolutionary approach

as an added bonus

at a discount

at a fraction of the cost of

at Culver, it's been our commitment since 1921 to

at great savings/no expense to you

at your discretion

benefits and privileges include

blends in beautifully with any

both practical and beautiful

budget-pleasing prices

build upon the excellence that

built-in features

can choose from over 20 styles/cards/ models/varieties

can make a dramatic difference to you

carefree upkeep

come in and try

compact design

complimentary copy

contemporary/gracious design

custom personalization

did you know that

direct-to-you low prices

direct your attention to

discover how you can

does three jobs at once

easier and more enjoyable

easier to use than ever before

easy and comfortable to wear and use

easy/carefree maintenance

easy-to-follow instructions

elegant styling

engineered for dependability

enjoy it year round

every item is offered at a discount

exciting details/offer

experience the pleasure of

extremely pleased to be able to offer you

fast, efficient way to

fast, safe, easy-to-use

finely crafted

fit-any-budget price

for just pennies each

friendly and helpful

full refund

fully automated/warranted

get full details

gives you your choice of/the opportunity to

greater safety, convenience, and pleasure

guaranteed for two full years

have the satisfaction of knowing

hundreds of daily uses

if not completely satisfied

if you accept this invitation, you will be joining the select company of those who

if you respond right away

if you send payment now, you'll receive

I'll think you'll discover that

I'm writing to tell you about

in these fast-moving times

invite you to

it can pay for itself in

join millions of others who

just a reminder that

lasting beauty

lets you enjoy more of your favorite

low, low prices

loyal customers like you

mail the enclosed card today

makes any day special

may I send you this

money-back guarantee/offer

money's worth

more advanced features

more powerful and sensitive

more than fifty years of service

no matter which set you choose

no more mess/lost sales/typing errors/fuss/worry

no-risk examination

no strings attached

not at all as costly as you might expect

now, for the first time,

now is the time to learn more about

of particular importance to you

one of the largest and most respected daycare centers

one size fits all

on the enclosed Charter Invitation

our top-seller

outstanding features

over 50,000 satisfied customers

please take this opportunity

practical and decorative

preferred customer/rates

previously sold for

professional quality

prompt, courteous service

proven reliability

provides the finest home hair care at the least cost

puncture-resistant

ready to spoil you with its powerful features

reasonably priced

reduced price

reward yourself with

risk nothing

rugged and dependable

satisfaction guaranteed

simple to operate

so unusual and striking that they will be enjoyed again and again

special introductory offer/value

step in the right direction

stop those costly losses with

surprise that special someone with

take advantage of this opportunity

take a giant step forward now, *today*, towards

take a moment right now to look over this

takes the gamble out of choosing between

the intelligent way to

the many advantages of

the most versatile, powerful, and exciting study aid available

the perfect gift for yourself or a loved one

there's a world of enjoyment waiting for you with

the whole family can enjoy

this is one reason among many to order

time is growing short, so do send today for your

timeless elegance

to fit all your gardening needs

to suit your individual taste

unconditional money-back guarantee

under no obligation to

under our simple plan

unequalled savings and convenience

unique and invaluable

unique limited edition creations

urge you to

use it anywhere, anytime

user friendly

we expect a tremendous response to this offer, so

we look forward to sending you

we're making this generous offer because

we urge you to send today for

what better way to

why not order today/take advantage

with all this, you might expect these casseroles to cost as much as $25 apiece, but

with no obligation on your part

with our compliments

won't cost you a thing to

won't find better quality anywhere

won't you take a few moments right now to

worldwide provider of quality

you have been selected to receive

you'll be amazed to discover

you're a winner with your favorite

your key to peace of mind

your money back

your name has been proposed as someone who might like to own

you will appreciate the outstanding quality of these

———————————————— SENTENCES ————————————————

And don't forget—your fee includes a free gift!

And there's more I haven't mentioned—its dependability, for example.

At this low price, every home should have one.

Be the first in your community to have one!

But act now—we expect a sizable response and we want to be certain that your order is processed.

But that's not all.

Call today to arrange a demonstration.

Compare the savings, protection, and service you are currently paying for with what you could be getting with American Auto Insurance.

Discover savings of up to 50%.

Discover the elegance of a genuine leather briefcase with discreet gold initials.

Don't miss out!

Do your holiday shopping the easy way.

Enjoy it for a 15-day home trial.

Final notice!

Give us a call at 1-800-555-2110.

If you are not completely satisfied, simply return it for a full credit.

In order to make this offer, we must have your check by September 1.

It's a first!

It's a no-strings offer.

It's simple to get your free, no-obligation information on rates, available discounts, special services, and easy claims filing.

It's time for a change/for a new approach!

Join us today.

Just bring this letter with you when you come in to sign up.

Just what makes the Blount Filing System so great?

Mail the coupon now.

May I make an appointment with you next week to explain/show/demonstrate our latest line of products?

No other car can offer you this degree of prestige and affordability.

Now there's a new magazine just for you.

Offers like these don't come along very often.

Order one for every family member.

Orders are subject to credit approval.

Please do it promptly.

Please do not send any money now!

Please don't delay your decision—we expect a heavy demand for the Ellesmere filet knife.

Please don't hesitate to call for a free demonstration.

Please look over this offer very carefully.

P.S. To lock in these great rates, we must receive your deposit by October 15.

Returning the postage-paid reply card does not obligate you in any way.

Send for your free copy of the Bemerton planning guide.

Send in the card now, before you forget.

Send no money now—we'll bill you later.

Take a look at the enclosed brochure for a sneak preview.

Telephone now for an appointment.

Telephone Sarah Lash, your personal representative, for an interview.

Thank you so much for reading my letter, and I look forward to hearing from you.

The Art Deco look fits almost any decorating scheme.

There is absolutely no risk on your part when you order.

There's no cost or obligation of course.

There's plenty more!

These low prices are effective only until June 1.

This is just one more reason why our products have won such overwhelming acceptance.

This is why I'm writing you today.

To get your full-color booklet, just complete and return the enclosed postage-paid reply card.

Try a sample . . . free!

Use the order form and postpaid reply envelope enclosed to receive your first Holiday Bell absolutely free.

We cannot extend this unusual offer beyond May 25, 1993.

We invite you to complete the enclosed reservation request form and return it now to confirm your choice of dates.

We'll bill you later, after you've made up your mind.

We'll start you off with your first issue/book/figurine free.

We note that you have not used your charge account recently.

We're determined to win you over to Dalgarno office furniture.

We're making this unprecedented offer to a select group of homeowners.

We take all the risks.

We've missed you.

We want to make it as easy as possible for you to order.

What could be simpler?

Why not do it now, while the form is handy?

Why not say "yes" today?

Won't you join us by being among the very first to become a Charter Subscriber?

Won't you please let us hear from you right away so we can include your order with the many others we expect?

You can choose from over 150 different programs.

You can now acquire a snowblower for far less than you ever thought possible.

You'll appreciate these fine features.

You'll like our convenient evening and weekend hours; you'll love our brand-new equipment and experienced teachers!

You'll see that Rockminster China isn't like other china.

You'll wonder how you ever did without it.

You may not have ever bought/invested/tried, which is why we are making you this no-risk trial offer.

You must see the complete series for yourself to appreciate fully how it can enrich your life.

---------- PARAGRAPHS ----------

▷   Are you still paying premiums for the same homeowner's policy you signed up for ten years ago? Have you thought about comparing what's available today with what you bought ten years ago?

▷   If for any reason, at any time, you are not satisfied with your Haverley Air Cleaner, you can return it to us for a complete and prompt refund. No questions asked.

▷   P.S. The cookbook of your choice and the lucite book stand are both yours free—without obligation. All you need to do is send in the enclosed form.

▷   Send no money now. You will be billed at the time of shipment for any items ordered, plus shipping and sales tax (if applicable). But you do not have to pay until you are totally convinced of the high quality and value of our lithographs and prints. If you are not delighted in every way, just return your purchases within 10 days, and you'll owe nothing!

▷   The enclosed Special Introductory Invitation can be guaranteed for a limited time only. We urge you to reply within the next 21 days.

▷   There's only one sure way to convince you that Bryerley Bath Beads are the last word in luxurious skin-softeners. We're enclosing sample packets of two of our most popular Bryerley scents, Gardenia and Lily of the Valley. Try them and see if you don't notice a big difference!

▷   Congratulations on your election to membership in the Society for Historic Preservation! If you accept this membership offer—and I certainly hope you will— you will become part of a unique and influential group. As a member you will enjoy such important benefits as voting privileges on matters of national importance, a subscription to the monthly magazine, *Preservation*, and many more. Please mail the enclosed Confirmation of Election by May 31.

▷   P.S. This is your last chance to buy the kits at these low prices. Rising material costs require a moderate price increase effective later this year.

▷   You want to give that special child in your life the finest reading—his or her very own books—but you don't have the time to look at thousands of children's books to find the best. That's where we come in.

▷   Is a housecleaning service for you? We think so because you want the best for yourself and your family . . . and that takes time. Time you don't always have after working all week and meeting important family needs after hours. We can offer you thorough, reasonably priced once-a-week housecleaning that will make all the difference in your life. Think about what you could do with the hours you now have to spend on housework. Think about walking into a clean house at night. And then think about giving us a call to schedule an estimate interview.

_____ SAMPLE LETTERS _____

Dear Executive:

According to several management studies, the single most important character-
istic of an effective executive is the ability to manage time.

Are you meeting all your deadlines? Can you list your current projects in order
of importance? Do you have a good idea of where you are headed over the next week,
month, year? Can you find things when you need them? Do you assign work in the
most time-effective ways?

If you answered no to any of these questions, you're sure to benefit from our
popular, effective Time Management Workshop.

In just two days you will learn how to set priorities, how to use special tools that
will help you organize your time, and how to develop interpersonal skills that will
help you deal with unnecessary interruptions, inefficient staff, and group projects.

In fact, we don't want to be one of those interruptions, so we suggest that you save
time by making time for the next Time Management Workshop in your area. You
can do this in under a minute by checking off a convenient date and signing the
enclosed postage-paid reply card or by calling 1-800-555-1707 to register.

This is one workshop that won't be a waste of time!

                            Sincerely,

                   . . . .

Dear Marietta Lyddon,

You were a member of the Atlas Fitness Club from March 15, 1990, to November
18, 1990, and according to our records you worked out regularly.

Whatever your reasons for not being with us the past several years, you may want
to know about some changes that have taken place since you were last here:

New this year: Olympic-size pool with extended hours, 5:30 a.m. to midnight. A
lifeguard is on duty at all times.

New this year: Membership packages designed to fit your use patterns. You may
now choose between an all-use pass or a pass that specifies morning hours, early
morning hours, after-five hours, evening hours, late evening hours.

New this year: Peripheral services that our members—most of whom are busy
working people like yourself—have requested: a personal check-cashing service; yo-
gurt, soup, and mineral water machines in the lobby; a telephone for the use of
members making local calls; all-new padlocks for the lockers.

New last year: We now have 50% more equipment in the weight lifting room, and
three new Nautilus units.

If you liked us before, you'll love us now. I think it's worth a look, and I'm so
convinced of this that I'm going to offer you a two-week membership for FREE.

All you have to do is bring this letter with you when you come to give us another
look!

                            Sincerely yours,

                   . . . .

Dear MasterGold Cardmember,

A revolutionary new service is now available to valued MasterGold cardmembers—and you're among the first invited to enroll.

CreditReport service is a valuable new credit tool that will allow you to guard your privileged credit status. Membership in CreditReport entitles you to:

□ Unlimited access to copies of your CreditReport record. This is the one many credit managers and loan officers see. Now you can know what's in your credit report before you apply for credit or financing and avoid potentially embarrassing situations.

□ Automatic notification when anyone receives a copy of your CreditReport files. This way you know exactly who is receiving your credit report, and when.

□ Your financial profile—this valuable tool lets you organize your personal finances in one convenient document. Once completed, you may place your all-purpose credit/loan application on our computers—ready to be electronically transmitted to any participating credit grantor—in an instant.

□ Convenient application for loans or financing at participating credit grantors. A membership card is recognized at thousands of credit grantor locations—where shopping for the best credit terms can mean big savings on interest payments.

□ Credit card protection: At no extra charge we'll register all your credit, charge, and ATM cards in case of loss or theft. And we'll also provide for change of address for all your cards should you move.

Best of all, your membership includes an unconditional money-back guarantee, so you can enjoy all the privileges of membership without risk.

This is a valuable service for MasterGold cardmembers. I urge you to look over the enclosed materials and consider this special offer now.

Sincerely,

See also: ANNOUNCEMENTS, CONGRATULATIONS, CREDIT, INVITATIONS, ORDERS, SEASONAL GREETINGS, THANK YOU.

36

Seasonal Greetings

"Here's to your good health, and your family's good
health, and may you all live long and prosper.
(Washington Irving)

Holidays, particularly those at the end of the year, generate a great deal of heart-warming and supportive mail. They provide friends with the opportunity of renewing their relationships and exchanging news, and they provide businesses with the opportunity of sending goodwill letters to customers, colleagues, and employees. Fundraisers also know that people are more willing to give during the holidays and therefore schedule some of their most important appeals in late fall. It is not surprising that first-class canceled mail peaks substantially in December.

The United States Postal Service encourages us to "mail early" in an attempt to equalize the flow of the huge volume of holiday mail and reduce the expense of overtime hours for carriers. A typical metropolitan post office that ordinarily cancels eight or nine hundred thousand first-class letters per day will handle nearly three million per day right before Christmas (most of it scheduled for local next-day service) unless people mail early, distributing the postal burden more evenly over a longer period of time.

Of all personal mail, 43% is accounted for by holiday cards. Other greeting cards make up 21% and letters the remaining 36%.

Seasonal Greetings Include

- Christmas
- Columbus Day
- Easter
- election day
- Father's Day
- form/annual letters
- goodwill letters

- Hanukkah
- Halloween
- Independence Day
- Labor Day
- Martin Luther King, Jr.'s Birthday
- Memorial Day
- Mother's Day

- New Year's
- Pesach
- Purim
- Rosh Hashana
- St. Patrick's Day

- Thanksgiving
- Valentine's Day
- Veterans Day
- Yom Kippur

How to Say It

▢   Express appropriate seasonal greetings.

▢   Inquire about the other person, if a personal letter; express appreciation for the other person, if business.

▢   Wish the person happiness, success, health.

What Not to Say

▢   The seasonal greetings that many businesses send their customers may be sincere expressions of the joy of the season. But they are also written to nurture customer goodwill and to send a subtle sales message—if nothing more than "Remember us." Sales messages need not be subtle for some holiday greetings. Valentine's Day, for example, is made for strong sales messages from florists, candymakers, greeting card manufacturers, and gift shops. However, if you send an overly aggressive sales message with Christmas greetings, they are often perceived as self-serving and materialistic. Although no other period of the year is more commercial than the Christmas season, people don't like to be reminded of it.

Tips on Writing

▢   Although it is certainly not "wrong" to send a well-chosen card with nothing but your signature, it is strongly recommended that you add a few words of your own. If you truly have nothing to say to the person beyond the sentiments of a mass-produced greeting card, it is possible you should omit the gesture entirely. Most people find it disappointing to open a card and find no personal message.

▢   When one member of the household writes the messages and signs the greeting cards, it doesn't matter if they put their name first or last.

▢   The foregoing list of holidays may seem excessively long, but you may want to remember friends and customers even on the less celebrated holidays if the day means something special to them. Also, businesses can send goodwill letters to specific markets for whom these holidays are meaning-ful. Many sales letters are linked with a seasonal message.

☐   Not every household is a happy one. Among your customers and friends are people who have lost loved ones, who have financial worries, illnesses, and other burdens. When you are not sure of the other person's situation, choose seasonal greetings that are low-key and can convey your good wishes without an insistent and perhaps offensive cheerfulness.

Special Situations

☐   Those who send greeting cards to everyone they know for Hanukkah or Christmas can piggyback other news on their season's greetings: the an-nouncement of a new address, an engagement, or a new job. In the case of a divorce, for example, where informing one's acquaintances is still somewhat problematic, it is convenient and tactful to append the news to year's-end letters. Be sure to mail your greeting extra early to save friends the minor embarrassment of sending their greetings to you as a couple.

☐   Businesses that send seasonal greetings to their employees find that do-ing so generates a great deal of goodwill and company identification. After wishing the employees every personal and professional happiness, the letter might convey congratulations for a good year just past and appreciation for the employees' productive and cooperative work ethic. Avoid using this letter to "get a point across" or to chide the group or to transmit office news.

☐   Some people find form letters completely unacceptable while others enjoy writing and receiving them. Some letterwriting authorities advise against them but others believe they serve a useful purpose. Whatever one thinks of them, they are a fact of life and unlikely to be outlawed by eti-quette mavens in the foreseeable future. They provide a practical solution for many people who must choose between sending a form letter and not writing at all. People used to live and die in the same town; their pool of friends and acquaintances was small and did not require written communi-cations. Today's family might have hundreds of names in their address file: friends from elementary school in one town, high school in another, from college, from a junior year abroad, from the first three cities in which they worked, neighbors who have moved away, friends of their children, as well as aunts, uncles, and cousins on both sides. Form letters don't have to be boring, and many aren't. In the polycopied part of your letter, tell your general news: the year's highlights, changes in your lives, travels, work and school happenings. You can organize your letter chronologically or by giving each family member a paragraph or by topic. Your letter will be more inter-esting if you discuss ideas as well as activities: your concerns about the environment, a good book you recommend, a lecture you attended, the state

of television today, even your political views. You can also include anecdotes, quotations, photocopied clippings of interest, or snapshots. In the
handwritten part of your letter (which is really a "must," even if it's only a
line or two), speak to the concerns of your readers, commenting on their last
letter, asking about their lives. If you receive a fair number of photocopied
letters in your year's-end mail, you are probably safe sending one yourself. If
none of your correspondents use this form, it's possible that you are marching to a different drummer—which may be why they like you.

□   Because some holidays have a strong religious base, businesses need to
be careful about offending customers' belief systems. This means avoiding
religious cards and sentiments unless your audience is carefully selected
and well known to you. Do not casually bring religious elements into your
goodwill letters; it will be perceived as hypocritical and self-serving. Take
your cue from what other businesses in your area have attempted successfully in the past. You may also want to consult with adherents of different
faiths to see how your message appears to them.

Format

□   Greeting cards have grown tremendously in popularity and variety over
the past decade and are always acceptable, but they should be accompanied
by a handwritten message. If your name is printed or engraved on the card,
add a handwritten message when writing to close friends. Some people still
send printed greeting cards to numerous acquaintances with whom they are
not intimately connected. In some areas, this exchange of impersonal greeting cards is acceptable and even viewed very favorably. Do not use social
titles when having your name printed. For example, "Eddie Swanson,"
"Goldie Rindskopf," "Bill and Sarah Ridden" (not "Mr. and Mrs. William
Ridden") or simply "Bill and Sarah." Children's first names are usually listed
on the second line. In the case of a single parent with a different name
("Grace Larkins"), the children's last name is given ("Annie, Miriam, and
Minnie Wells").

□   Business letters carrying seasonal greetings are generally typed, although some companies send greeting cards, postcards, or specially printed
letters with colored graphics. A letter can be made more personal than a
greeting card and can carry more information. Investigate the cost differences between greeting cards and letters. The latter are generally less expensive even if you use special effects, decorations, and a colored envelope. You
might want to keep an idea file of some of the clever seasonal creations other
businesses have used over the years. Eye-catching letters are not, of course,
appropriate for all purposes; banks, legal firms, insurance companies, and
others are more harmed than helped by overly "creative" letters.

WORDS

blessings
celebration
happiness
health
holidays

peace
prosperity
rejoice
remembrances

season
success
well-being
wishes

PHRASES

all the best of the season
at this time of year
be prosperous
compliments of the season
during this holiday season
during this season and always
good luck/wishes
grateful for your patronage over the
    past year
great/happy/festive time of year
happy memories
holiday greetings
in commemoration/celebration of
magic of the holiday season

much to look forward to
our own personal joys seems to center on
quiet pleasures and happy memories
season filled with gentle joys
season's greetings
sincere wishes for
smiles of fortune
this festive season
warmest regards/wishes to you
wishes for a joyous season
wishing you love
with warm personal regards
wonderful holiday season

SENTENCES

As we at the Bennett Company look back over 1992, we remember with appreciation
    our friendly, faithful customers.
Best wishes for a bright and beautiful season/for a New Year of happiness.
Everyone here at Taunton-Dawbeney sends you their best wishes for happiness,
    health, and prosperity throughout the coming New Year.
Happy Hannukah/Easter/Thanksgiving/Passover/Holidays!
Holiday greetings and best wishes for the New Year.
I hope that 1992 was a good year for you and that 1993 will be even better.
I hope that the beauty of this season will be with you throughout the year.
I send my warmest wishes for a joy-filled and bountiful season.
I wish you a world of peace during this season and always.
May this be the best year yet!
May all the blessings of this happy season shine upon you.
May all your days be filled with prosperity, peace, and good health.
May peace, love, and laughter fill your holiday season.

May the beauty of this season bring you many special joys.

May this season's simple joys be with you always.

May you and your family have a joyous holiday season.

May you be inscribed and sealed for a happy, healthy, and prosperous year.

May you receive an abundance of love and joy this holiday season.

May your holiday season be filled with wonder.

May your shadow never be less!

Merry Christmas!

On Rosh Hashanah it is written . . . On Yom Kippur it is sealed.

Skip this part if you are allergic to form letters, if you don't care *what* we've been doing, or if you can't remember who we are.

The best part of this beautiful season is keeping in touch with special friends like you.

This comes with our blessings and love.

This is just a note to say we're thinking of you at Thanksgiving/Christmas/Easter.

This time of year inspires us to count our blessings—and good customers like you are chief among them!

Warm wishes to you and your dear ones this holiday season.

We hope you all have a very Merry Christmas and a Happy New Year!

We wish for you the gifts of love, friendship, and good health.

We wish you all the best in the coming year.

We wish you and your beautiful family much peace, health, and happiness.

PARAGRAPHS

▷   This Thanksgiving, as you reflect on your blessings—and perhaps even on some of the challenges that have helped you to grow—take a minute to consider those who have few blessings to count, those whose "challenges" have overwhelmed them. Help us provide traditional home-cooked Thanksgiving dinners with all the trimmings for the hungry and homeless during this Thanksgiving season. You can feed ten hungry people for $13.90, twenty for $27.80, or one hundred for $139. Won't you help?

▷   To start the New Year off right and to show our appreciation for your patronage last year, I'm enclosing a certificate good for one free meal with the purchase of another of equal or greater price.

▷   Ever mindful of cautions against "good news only" Christmas letters, I can tell you that we struggle with some of the same things you probably struggle with: the rather frantic pace and perpetual busyness, responding simultaneously to conflicting but equally important demands, the frustrations of a world that becomes more complicated and impersonal while systems and people and computers break down with distressing regularity, the hard-work side of parenting, trying to answer for ourselves as we hit our mid-life years the question that six-year-old Matt asked me a few weeks ago: "What's the point of being alive? I mean, what is the point of it all?"

▷   They don't call them Easter "bonnets" anymore, but the idea is the same! Come in and see our fantastic selection of spring hats: delicate straws from Italy, smart little toques from France, wacky and colorful sun-skimmers from Haiti, elegant felts from England, and much more! Buy a hat before Easter and receive a free stuffed bunny (wearing the latest in bunny bonnets) for the special child in your life.

▷   Eileen, who's now a sophomore, spent a month in Germany this summer, surviving a no-show on her luggage, a tick bite that required serum treatment, and a bomb threat on her return flight. As for me, I've been working with a local group to promote a recycling program here—we can talk trash, even in front of the children. Now you are thinking, "Great! I got out of hearing about their latest remodeling project." Sorry. This year we turned the pantry into a bathroom, and . . .

▷   Mother's Day is coming soon, and Rowley Floral Shops (with twenty-three metro-area locations) are offering a Mother's Day special you'll want to consider. Choose from one of six stunning floral arrangements (and six surprisingly low prices) to tell that very important person in your life how much she means to you. Included in your one low price is delivery anywhere in the metro area and a special Mother's Day card with Anne Taylor's charming verse:

> Who ran to help me when I fell
> And would some pretty story tell,
> Or kiss the place to make it well?
> My Mother.

Come in today and see which of the six arrangements will bring a smile to YOUR Mother's face!

▷   One tacky thing seems to lead to another, you know? One day you're wearing your trenchcoat over your nightgown to go out for the mail and the next thing you know you're sending form Christmas letters. Where will it all end?

▷   Although we feel rooted in joy, our mood this year is shadowed by family illnesses, the deaths of several dear people, and by unacceptable conditions that continue to exist in the world today. But being believing people, we want to join you in working for and hoping in a more just, more peaceful tomorrow.

―――――――――――――― SAMPLE LETTERS ――――――――――――――

TO: All Norton employees
FROM: Marda Norton, President
RE: Martin Luther King, Jr. Day

Beginning this year, Martin Luther King, Jr. Day will be a paid holiday for all employees. This day has particular significance for us as I believe Norton represents in many ways the lived-out reality of the dream for which Martin Luther King, Jr. lived and died.

There is no obligation, but we urge employees to devote at least a part of the day to some community service. Bob Gates in Personnel has a list of suggestions if you are interested.

Also, for this, our first holiday, you are invited to a potluck dinner in the upper cafeteria at 6:00 p.m. on January 16. Please call Bob Gates, ext. 42, with your reservation, and bring a covered dish. Depending on the interest shown in this year's potluck, we may continue the tradition.

. . . .

Dear Friends,

We think of you, celebrating Thanksgiving, the High Holidays, Hannukah, Christmas, New Year's, and hope that you are enjoying an abundance of health and happiness.

We are very grateful for blessings of the past year—a potpourri of events and challenges that included tubing down the Apple River . . . *Twelfth Night* at the Guthrie . . . Lisa's creampuffs, Kathy's pumpkin pies, Matt's banana bread . . . spending their 50th anniversary with Dave's parents . . . my brother Kevin adopted eight-year-old David . . . looking for rocks in Montana . . . Lisa and I marching for peace in Central America . . . visiting and being visited by friends and relatives . . . drinking Perrier and lime with brother Mark before he left for a job in Cairo . . . a Laurel and Hardy retrospective at the Walker Art Institute . . . Kathy with braces . . . Lisa hearing that she doesn't have to worry about scoliosis anymore . . . Matt concluding a year of vision therapy . . . Kathy and friends horseback riding in the bitter cold and wind on her birthday . . . me learning to live happily with a computer . . . having drinks with Dad at the airport on his way through town . . . Dave and I discovering new things about each other while working with engaged couples.

We send you our warmest wishes for a bright and beautiful New Year.

Margaret and Dave Herries
Lisa, Kathy, and Matt

P.S. Hello, Bob and Eliza! It has not been the same neighborhood since you left. You must be in the throes of college decisions with Angus just now—where is he thinking of going? If he wants to come look at Compton-Burnett, he can stay with us. Give Roberta, Hermia, and Madeline hugs from us. I'll call for a telephone visit after the first of the year.

. . . .

Dear Parent,

What perfect timing! Just as you're worrying about getting the children outfitted for the winter months, along comes Columbus Day! The children have a free day, and WE'RE having our lowest-prices-ever children's outerwear sale!

During our big Columbus Day sale (special hours 9 a.m. to 9 p.m.) we'll have free balloons and cookies for the children . . . and great prices and selections on over twenty name-brand children's coats and jackets.

Did we say it already? What perfect timing!

See also: CONGRATULATIONS, FAMILY, GOODWILL.

37

Letters of Sympathy

> "No one really understands the grief or joy of another."
> (Franz Schubert)

The condolence letter is one of the most difficult to write. People who feel sad, helpless, and tongue-tied are writing to people who are grief-stricken and vulnerable. Two common shortcomings are saying too little (glossing over what has happened or using euphemisms to describe it) or too much (offering inappropriate "comfort" and advice). However painful they are to write, letters of sympathy are strictly necessary if you have a personal or business relationship with the deceased's family or friends. It will not be easy for them to overlook your lack of response to something as all-important as the death of a loved one.

Send Letters of Sympathy

- To friends/neighbors/relatives who have suffered the death of a spouse/child/parent/family member/friend.
- To customers/clients/employees/colleagues who have experienced a loss.
- To the immediate family of an employee who has died.
- To those who have sustained misfortunes: loss of job/bankruptcy/ burglary/violent crime/hospitalization or long illness of a child.
- To those who have been involved in natural disasters: flood/hurricane/ drought/storms.
- To the recently divorced.
- To those who have had a miscarriage or stillbirth.
- To those hospitalized because of a serious or terminal illness or an accident (see also "GET WELL").
- To someone whose longtime pet has died.

- To accompany funeral wreaths, flowers, Mass offerings, contributions to charity.

- In the absence of one's superior. A secretary or assistant might acknowledge a death or serious illness if an absent supervisor would normally send a sympathy letter.

- To a grieving spouse or parent on the anniversary of a death, on birthdays or wedding anniversaries of those who have died, or on other occasions when you know the person might be thinking of their loss. Those who plan class reunions might send cards or flowers to parents of classmates who have died to reassure them that their children are remembered.

How to Say It

☐   "I'm sorry." In some simple, direct way, express your sorrow about the other person's loss or trouble.

☐   Mention by name the person who died or the specific sad event that occurred.

☐   In the case of a death, relate an anecdote about the person, a happy memory, some advice they gave you, the virtues, achievements, or successes for which they'll be remembered, something they said or did that touched you. The more specific your story, the more meaningful your letter will be. Instead of referring to a neighbor's "generosity," for example, recall how he always had a pocket full of peanuts in the shell for neighborhood youngsters.

☐   Offer condolences in the form of sympathy, thoughts, prayers, good wishes.

☐   If you are writing to one particular member of the family, mention the others in your closing.

☐   Offer to help in some concrete way. If you say you will call later to check on them, note this on your calendar.

☐   You might add that you know how burdened the person is at this time and that although you would love to hear from them, they should not feel that your letter requires a reply. By the time the bereaved person has written thank you notes for flowers, condolences, memorials, honorary pallbearers, and special assistance, there is little energy left to acknowledge sympathy letters.

☐   Depending on your relationship with the deceased, local or religious custom, and family preference, you may want to send along with your sympathy note flowers, donations to a charity, a Mass offering, or other type of appropriate memorial. (You would not, for example, send flowers for certain Jewish funerals.)

□   Close with an expression of sympathy or affection or with a wish for consolation.

What Not to Say

□   Avoid excessively dramatic and hyperbolic language ("the worst tragedy I ever heard of," "the dreadful, horrible, appalling news"). This measure of feeling properly belongs to the grieving friends and family. Do express what you feel—if you were appalled at the news, say so—but avoid becoming overly sentimental, flowery, effusive, or macabre. A simple "I'm sorry" is effective and comforting.

□   Avoid pious clichés, simplistic "explanations" of the tragedy, or undue readings of God's activities, intents, or involvement in this sorrow. If you share a similar faith life with the recipient, it may be helpful to enclose prayers or readings, but sometimes even the most spiritually involved are not ready for abstract comfort. Then again, a letter of sympathy based on spiritual truths may be the very best kind. To talk about a serious loss in a faith context means knowing your recipient very well indeed.

□   Do not give advice, and especially do not encourage big changes (leaving town, moving into an apartment, selling the spouse's model ship collection). It is usually many months before survivors can make well-thought-out decisions.

□   Avoid generic offers of help such as "Let me know if I can help out," or "Feel free to call on us." This requires a response from people who already have much to deal with, and most people will not take you up on such vague invitations.

□   As someone once said, "Most of our misfortunes are more supportable than the comments of our friends upon them." (C.C. Colton) Anyone who has received the condolences of others has encountered some of the well-meaning but hurtful clichés, false cheerfulness, and optimistic platitudes that pass for expressions of sympathy. Avoid phrases like the following:

> Chin up. Be brave. Don't cry. You'll get over it. She is better off now. Time heals all wounds. He was too young to die. Life is for the living. Keep busy, you'll forget. I know just how you feel. God never makes a mistake. Be happy for what you had. He's in a better place now. It's a blessing in disguise. At least she isn't suffering. He was old and had a good life. Every cloud has a silver lining. She is out of her misery at least. At least you had him for eighteen years. I feel almost worse than you do about this. God had a purpose in sending you this burden. You're young yet; you can always marry again. I have a friend who's going through the same thing. God only sends burdens to those who can handle them. Life must go on—you'll feel better before you know it.

Tips on Writing

□   The most important thing is to write in the first place. What you say is less important than the fact that you write. And it's never too late to write— even if you hear the news long after the event. Because so many people feel powerless in the face of tragedy or unhappiness, they end up doing nothing, saying nothing. Feelings of guilt usually ensure that they avoid the bereaved person thereafter.

□   Write customers, clients, employees, or colleagues just as you would friends or relatives, although your note will be shorter and a little more formal. Avoid philosophizing, religious messages, or overly personal re- marks. It is enough to tell the person you are thinking about them at this time, extend sympathy on behalf of the company, and convey condolences to other members of the person's family. (And there is, of course, no sales message or other business information included.)

□   Keep descriptions of your own feelings to a minimum (a bereaved per- son is not much interested or impressed by dramatic expressions of how you felt when you heard the news or how you haven't been able to eat or sleep since). Many sympathy letters seem to focus more on the writer's distress than on the bereaved person's. A simple statement that you are sorry or that you feel bad is sufficient; the recipient generally assumes a certain sorrow on your part—you do not have to document it.

□   Short is always better than long when writing a sympathy letter—at least initially. In the weeks and months and even years following a person's death, the surviving family and friends may greatly appreciate long, newsy, loving letters. In the time immediately following the death, however, letters should deal simply with the loss, expressions of sympathy, and offers of help. Writing people you don't know very well shouldn't take more than the in- side of a foldover note. For friends and relatives, you could extend your letter to the back side of the note—but no more.

□   Some people are uncomfortable with such blunt words as *death, dead, died, killed,* and even such milder and questionable euphemisms as *passed on, passed away, departed, left this life, gone to their reward, gone to a better life.* If you know the person you are writing feels that way, you can say instead, "sad to hear about Katherine," "sorry about your loss." Murder, suicide, or particularly tragic or gruesome deaths need not be mentioned as such, but for most people the word *death* seems to be used comfortably, and the older, roundabout terms like *the deceased, the dear departed,* and *her passing away* are no longer much seen.

□   Observe the fine line between sympathy and pity. Sympathy respects the person's ability to survive the unfortunate event; pity suspects it has beaten them. Read your letter aloud to see if it sounds patronizing or makes the recipient appear a helpless victim.

□   The greatest insurance against saying something untoward is to imagine yourself in the other person's place.

Special Situations

□   Losing a child through miscarriage or stillbirth is a devastating experience. Express your sympathy in the same way you would for the death of any child. Be careful not to minimize or discount the experience. Avoid such "consoling" (and, unfortunately, often used) remarks as: "You already have two lovely children. Be grateful for what you have." "This may have been the best thing. There might have been something wrong with the baby, and this was nature's way of taking care of the problem." "You're young yet. You can try again." "It was God's will." And the worst yet: "Don't feel so bad. After all, it isn't as though you lost a *child.*" The person *has* lost a child.

□   Responding to news of a divorce is difficult, unless you know the person you are writing very well. Neither expressions of sympathy nor congratulations are entirely appropriate in most cases. However, whether the person is "better off" or not, the divorce process is never without its sad aspects and mourned losses, and some expression of sympathy may be indicated.

□   In the case of a death by suicide, offer your sympathy as you would to any other bereaved family. However, although it is generally appropriate to say you were "shocked to hear about" someone's death, it is better to avoid the phrase in this case. It is also a great temptation in this kind of death more than in any other kind to want to ask questions. If you are close enough to the bereaved to feel justified asking such questions, save them for a conversation; do not include them in a sympathy letter.

□   When someone close to you has lost a longtime spouse, you might want to remember the person with a special note on the anniversary of the person's death and also on the couple's wedding anniversary date. Don't worry about "bringing up sad memories." The person will hardly think of anything else on those days, and will be grateful for the supportive note that says somebody remembers.

□   A letter to a terminally or seriously ill person is more of a sympathy letter than a "get well" letter but be careful not to anticipate someone's death. Avoid any mention of imminent death unless the person has introduced the subject first and shows a willingness to talk about it. Instead, say how sorry you are to hear that the person is ill and that you are thinking of them. You might talk about the good memories you have of doing something with the person, and refer to those pleasures that are still possible— like visits with family and friends. Instead of a "Get Well" card, choose one of the "Thinking of You" or no-message cards. (See also "GET WELL.")

❑   Although AIDS is quite unlike anything else, those who have it are still first of all your friends, neighbors, and relatives, and only second someone with an invariably fatal illness. Write as you would to anyone with a serious illness, and don't assume that the person's time is short. Some AIDS patients have good years ahead of them in spite of recurrent crises. It's more important to be supportive and to send a card than to say exactly the right thing. However, it will help if you focus on letting the person know they're in your thoughts rather than dwell on their illness, their prognosis, the sadness of it all. You might also want to ask if the person would like company. Because of the perceived nature of AIDS, some people are unwilling to visit, so your friend may appreciate a visit from you all the more.

❑   When you send flowers to a funeral home, address the accompanying small card's envelope to "The funeral of Emily Webb Gibbs." Inside should be a plain white card from the florist or your own visiting or business card with a brief message ("Please accept my sincerest sympathy," or "My thoughts and prayers are with you and the children"). If you send a donation to a charity in the deceased person's name, always give their name and address as well as your own. The charity will want to send a notice of the contribution to the family and acknowledge to you that the donation was received.

Format

❑   Sympathy letters are almost always handwritten on a foldover note. Although you can substitute a commercial greeting card, it is rarely acceptable to simply sign your name under the printed message. Add at least a line or two of your own. The notepaper should be plain—no bright colors or fussy design. You could also use personal stationery.

❑   It is sometimes appropriate to type a sympathy letter, for example, if you are writing to the spouse of a customer, client, employee, or colleague whom you didn't know well but with whom you had business dealings. In this case, use business-personal rather than full-size letterhead stationery.

_____ WORDS _____

affection	comforting	difficult
anguish	commiserate	disaster
appalling	compassion	distressed
bereavement	concerned	dreadful
bitter	condolences	endure
bleak	consolation	faith
blow	devastating	grief
burden	devoutly	grief-stricken

hardship
healing
heartache
heartbroken
heartsick
heavyhearted
help
hope
hurt
loss
misfortune
mishap

mourn
nightmare
ordeal
overcome
pain
regret
saddened
severe
shaken
shocked
sorrow

sorry
suffering
sympathy
tragic
trouble
trying
unacceptable
unfortunate
unhappy
unwelcome
upset

———————————————— PHRASES ————————————————

a grand person
a great sorrow to all of us
a heavy blow
at a loss for words
very special loss for you
broken heart
deepest sympathy
deeply saddened
deprived of
during this difficult time
extend our condolences
extremely/terribly/so sorry to hear of
  the death of
family sorrow
feel fortunate to have known
feel the loss of
greatly/sadly missed
greatly saddened
great shock
grieved to hear/learn of your loss
grieve/mourn with you about
have my heartfelt sympathy
heart goes out to
heavy blow/news
how deeply I feel for you
how much we sympathize/regret/feel
  for you in your sorrow
in your time of great sorrow
I remember so well

I was saddened to learn/so sorry to
  hear that
just heard/learned
long be remembered for
many friends share your grief
no words to express my great/
  overwhelming/sincere/deep sorrow
offer most sincere/heartfelt/deepest
  sympathy
our heartfelt sympathy
profound sorrow
sad change in your circumstances
sad event/news
send my condolences/our deepest
  sympathy
sharing in your grief/sorrow/misery
  during this difficult time
shocked and profoundly grieved
shocked and saddened
sick at heart
so sorry to learn about your accident
stunned by the news
terrible blow
there is little comfort in words
touched to the quick by the news
tragic news
trying time
upsetting news
want to extend our condolences/send
  you our deepest sympathy

warmest sympathy
we all share
will be greatly missed
wish to extend our
  condolences/sympathy
with feeling/great personal sorrow

with sincere sympathy/sorrow and
  concern
your great loss/sad bereavement
your sorrow is shared by everyone who
  knew and loved

———————————————— SENTENCES ————————————————

All of us are the poorer for Patrick's death.

All of us here/at the office are feeling Ted's loss very much/will miss Polly more
  than we can say.

All of us send our deepest sympathy; we only wish we could be with you in your time
  of sorrow.

Anthony will be sorely missed.

Dora was a wonderful person, talented and loving, and I know that you and your
  family have suffered a great loss.

How sad I was to hear of Hsuang Tsang's sudden death.

I admired Beatrice very much, both personally and professionally.

I am thinking of you in this time of sorrow.

I feel for you in your loss/sorrow.

I feel privileged to have counted Fanny as a friend.

I have just heard the sad news/learned of Eugene's death.

I hope that you can find some comfort in your many special memories and in the
  thought of the happy years you shared.

I hope you don't mind, but Marion Halcombe told us about your recent bad luck and
  I wanted to tell you how very sorry we were to hear it.

I know Phillip had many admiring friends, and I am proud to have been one of them.

I'm thinking of you.

I never knew anyone who had as many friends or who deserved them more.

I remember the way your mother made all your friends feel so welcome with her
  questions, her fudge, and her big smiles.

It seems impossible to speak of any consolation in the face of such a bitter loss.

It was with great sadness/sense of loss that I learned of Ramona's death.

I want to express to you my most heartfelt sympathy.

I want you to know how sorry I was to hear what happened.

I was devastated/shocked/saddened/grieved to hear of your great loss.

I was so sorry to hear about the divorce—it must have been a very upsetting and
  painful time for you.

I was so sorry to hear that Mr. Golovin's long and courageous battle with cancer has
  ended.

I was so very sorry to hear of your bad news/the change in your circumstances/your
  loss/Mrs. Danvers's death.

I will always remember Ishmael and feel very fortunate to have known him.

I wish I could be with you at this time.

I wish there was something I could say or do to comfort you.

I write this with a heavy heart.

Like so many others who were drawn to Yancy by his charm, courage, and warmth, I am deeply grieved and bewildered by his unexpected death.

May the love of family and friends comfort and strengthen you in the days ahead.

May the thoughts and prayers of all those who love you help sustain you at this difficult time.

My deepest sympathy to you on Antonia's death.

My hearts/prayers/thoughts/sympathies are with you and your family.

Our thoughts/love/heartfelt sympathy are with you both at this sad time.

Please accept my/our sincere condolences/sympathy.

Please extend our condolences to the members of your family.

Please know that you are very much in my thoughts and heart/prayers at this time of sorrow.

Professor Bhaer will always remain very much alive in the memories of those who loved, respected, and treasured him.

The loss of your warm and charming home saddened us all.

There is not much one can say at a time like this.

The world has lost someone very special.

This must be a very difficult time for you.

We all held him in the greatest affection and respect.

We always enjoyed Dr. Stanton's company and respected him so much as a competent, caring physician and surgeon.

We are thinking of you.

We extend our most profound sympathy to you and the children.

We were all/both grieved/saddened/so very sorry/devastated to hear of your great loss/of Evangeline's death.

We were stunned to hear that you lost your job, but are very hopeful that someone with your experience and qualifications will find something suitable—maybe even better.

We who knew and loved Varena have some idea of how great your loss truly is.

We would like to stop in Thursday evening to see you, if that's convenient.

While no words of mine can ease your loss, I just wanted you to know that I am grieving with you and thinking about you constantly.

You and the family are much in our thoughts these days.

You have all our love/heartfelt sympathy/warmest thoughts.

Your grief is shared by many.

PARAGRAPHS

▷   We felt so bad when we heard about the burglary. Something similar happened to us, and it affected me much more deeply and took longer to get over than I would ever have expected. I hope you are not too undone. May we lend you anything? Help put things back in order? Type up an inventory of what's missing? Give us a call, will you? I know you'd do the same for us.

▷   There is no good time for a tragedy, of course, but I know that you were in the midst of finalizing plans for the national conference. Would it help if I tied up the loose ends for you on that project? You are so organized I am sure I will have no trouble following your notes. Just say the word if this is something I could do for you. And, again, please accept my most sincere sympathies on your sister's death.

▷   Helen's death is a sad loss for you and for many others at Zizzbaum & Son. We too will sorely miss her, both from a personal and from a professional standpoint. As you know, we could not have been more pleased with her work for us over the past five years. She made many good friends here, and we all send you our heartfelt sympathy.

▷   It's been a year today since Clinton died, and I wanted to tell you that we think of him often and with great affection. You must still miss him very much. I hope you are keeping busy and managing to find small happinesses in everyday things. We plan to be in California in March and hope to see you then.

▷   The staff and student body join me in extending our sympathy to you on the death of your father. I have heard the stories you tell about this delightful and determined man, and I am sure this is a great loss for you. A special donation has been made to the scholarship fund; next year, one of the scholarships will carry his name.

▷   I was so sorry to hear about your wife's death. She was one of those truly gracious individuals who make life so much more pleasant for everyone around her. You will miss her very much, I know.

────────────────── SAMPLE LETTERS ──────────────────

Dear Mary and Jessie,
    We were all so sorry to hear about your father's death. He was a fine man, and all of Cranford is in mourning for him. I remember seeing him take the two of you for a walk each evening after dinner when you were just little girls. I hope your memories of him will be some comfort to you.
    Please accept our sympathy and good wishes.
                                            Sincerely,

· · · · · · · · · · ·

Dear Jeremy,
    I was so sorry to hear of Percy's death. I'm sure you'll miss him very much. Brett & Coleman have been such a pair for so long and many people will be grieving with you. Please accept my condolences on the loss of your longtime friend and partner.
                                            Sincerely,

· · · · · · · · · · ·

Dear Lydia,
    I was shocked to hear of Noel's death; you must be devastated. You and Noel were always closer than any married couple I know. I can only hope that your years of happiness and your many good memories will enable you to live with this sad loss.
                                            Affectionately yours,

· · · · · · · · · · ·

Dear Miss de Cintré,

This will acknowledge your letter of the 16th. Mr. Newman is unfortunately vacationing in a wilderness area this week, but I know he will be most distressed to learn of your brother's death when he returns. Please accept my sympathy on your loss—Mr. de Bellegarde visited here only once, but he left behind the memory of a charming, generous man.

Mr. Newman will be back in the office on the 25th, and I would expect you to hear from him soon after that.

Sincerely yours,

· · · · · · · · · · ·

Dear Dr. and Mrs. Primrose,

Please accept my sympathy on the fire that leveled your home. I understand you and your family are staying temporarily with the Thornhills. As soon as you begin rebuilding, please let me know—I would like to help. In the meantime, if there is anything I can do, give us a call.

My husband joins me in hoping that you and the children will soon be back in your own home.

With best wishes,

· · · · · · · · · · ·

Dear Jody,

We were all very sorry to hear the sad news. Flag was much more than a pet, I know, and you must be wondering if you'll ever feel happy again. I'm enclosing a picture that I took of you and Flag about a month ago. I hope it doesn't make you sad, but brings back good memories instead.

Love,

· · · · · · · · · · ·

Dear Mrs. Latch,

I was so sorry to hear of Mr. Latch's death. Although I haven't seen you since I left Barfield, I have often thought with great affection and pleasure of those wonderful days we spent together at the races. Please accept my sympathy on your sad loss.

Yours truly,

· · · · · · · · · · ·

Dear Eden,

Harriet tells me that your divorce from Alayne is now final. Please accept my sympathies for the difficult experience this must have been. I also send my very best wishes for a bright and happy future. I'll call you next week to see if you have time to get together.

Your friend,

· · · · · · · · · · ·

Dear Ms. Abinger:

I was sorry to hear of the recent flooding you've had at the Corner Stores. It is one of those horror stories that haunt the dreams of self-employed business people everywhere. I wish you all good luck in getting things back to normal as quickly as possible.

I wanted to assure you that although I will temporarily order my supplies elsewhere, I will be bringing my business back to you as soon as you are ready. I appreciate our long association and am looking forward to doing business with you again.

Sincerely,

. . . .

Dear Mrs. Miller,

Saturday is the first anniversary of Daisy's death, and I couldn't let the day go by without writing to see how you are getting along and to tell you that all of Daisy's friends here in Switzerland miss her as much as ever. Her beauty, innocence, and enthusiasm will always live in our hearts.

With warmest regards and renewed sympathy, I am

Sincerely yours,

. . . .

Dear Leora and Martin,

Please accept our most heartfelt condolences on your miscarriage. I know how much you were both looking forward to welcoming this child into your lives.

Will you let us know the moment you feel up to a quiet visit? We would like to stop by with a couple of our warmest hugs.

With love and sympathy,

. . . .

Dear Kitty and Chris,

We were stunned to hear the tragic news about Oliver. Everyone who knows you must be appalled and heartbroken at the loss of your bright, charming, lovable son. There are no words to adequately express our sympathy for the devastation and profound loss you must be feeling. Please know we are thinking of you and praying for you every minute.

In talking with Chris's mother, we learned that you are without a car because of the accident. We're leaving one of the demo cars for your use as long as you need it. Please let us do this; there is no need to call or to discuss it.

We'll be seeing you in the next couple of days. Until then, we send all our love and deepest sympathy.

Sincerely,

See also: ACKNOWLEDGMENTS, ANNOUNCEMENTS, "GET WELL," RESPONSES, THANK YOU.

38

Thank You Letters

> "Gratitude is something of which none of us can give too much. For on the smiles, the thanks we give, our little gestures of appreciation, our neighbors build up their philosophy of life." (A.J. Cronin)

Thank you letters are one of the pillars of good relationships; you cannot write too many of them. Yet next to letters of condolence, thank-you letters are possibly the most difficult to write, which is why so many of them arrive late or not at all.

What tends to paralyze most letterwriters is either feeling unworthy in the face of another person's generosity or needing to thank someone out of a mechanical sense of obligation or for a gift, dinner party, favor, or advice that wasn't at all to our taste.

In the first case, it helps to remember that people do what they want to do. If someone has overspent on a gift for you, entertained you far more lavishly than the situation called for, or given you a gift when you did not reciprocate, you must assume it was the person's free and willing choice. It also helps to forget about saying thanks for the gift as a whole, and concentrate on those smaller aspects of the gift or hospitality that pleased you.

In the second situation, focus on the giver rather than on the gift. Express your appreciation for thoughtfulness and generosity rather than for the gift or favor itself. It is generally possible to find something to say that is both truthful and positive of either the gift or its giver.

If you are ever in doubt about whether a thank you is necessary, err on the side of "necessary." Even when you have graciously thanked someone in person, a written thank you is often expected or required. It is better to express your appreciation too often than not often enough.

Thank you notes need not be long. However, they should be written promptly and should show a little life. If you are not sure whether yours qualifies in the lively division, pretend that you are receiving it from someone you don't like very well. Would you be critical of it?

In the instances listed below, an oral thank you rarely replaces a written one.

Write Thank You Letters For

- appreciation/congratulations/recognition
- contributions: fundraising drives/memorials/charities
- employee suggestions/outstanding efforts/jobs well done
- expressions of sympathy
- favors/kindness/assistance/special help/advice
- gifts: business/personal
- hospitality: business/personal
- information/materials/requested documents
- job interviews
- money: gifts/bonuses/loans
- orders: new/unusual
- patronage: new account/first purchase/good customer
- referrals: customers/clients/patients
- wedding and wedding shower gifts (see WEDDINGS)

How to Say It

□ Mention in some detail what you are grateful for.

□ Express your gratitude in an enthusiastic, appreciative way.

□ Elaborate on your appreciation (why you like it; how you are going to use it; one thing you particularly enjoyed about your stay).

□ Close with one or two sentences unrelated to the object of your gratitude (expressing affection, promising to see the person soon, sending greetings to family members, saying something nice about the donor).

What Not to Say

□ Avoid sweeping, general remarks ("Thank you for your lovely gift/the nice present.").

□ If you should receive duplicate gifts, do not mention this to the givers.

□ Do not ask where the gift was purchased so that you can exchange it.

□ There are two schools of thought on mentioning the amount of a money gift. Some authorities recommend omitting any mention and speaking instead of the giver's kindness, generosity, or, perhaps, extravagance. However, if you feel that both you and the gift-giver will be comfortable with a

mention of the amount, know that it is an acceptable if not highly recommended choice.

❑   A few letterwriting experts dislike the "Thanks again" that concludes
so many thank you letters and notes. However, it is a popular and benign
way of bringing the reader back to the point of departure, reminding them
of the purpose of the letter. If you like it, use it.

❑   "Never express more than you feel" is a good rule of thumb, especially in
thank you letters, where we are tempted to make up in verbiage for what we
lack in enthusiasm. A simple "thank you very much" goes a long way.

Tips on Writing

❑   Although "promptly" is the best answer to the question, "When do you
write a thank you note?" there are other suggested guidelines: for a stay in
someone's home, write within one to three days, but certainly within a
week; for gifts, two weeks at the most; for dinners and other hospitality,
within a day or two; for expressions of sympathy, up to six weeks because of
the special hardships involved; for "get well" gifts, as long as you need until
you are well enough to write (you may want to ask a friend to acknowledge a
few gifts for you in the meantime). Writing promptly usually means a better
letter; you are more likely to be feeling grateful and able to write a genuine,
artless letter if you write in the first flush of gratitude.

❑   Mention specifically what pleased you about the gift, favor, kindness.

❑   A thank you letter should generally not do double duty; save your news,
information, questions, and comments for another letter. Concentrate solely
on thanking the person.

❑   You are not *obliged* to write a thank you (although of course it is always
in excellent taste and will be greatly appreciated if you do) for: a party at
which you were not the guest of honor; a casual dinner, lunch, or cocktail
party; birthday, anniversary, congratulations, and "get well" cards and
greetings; favors and hospitality extended by people with whom you are
very close (a sibling, a neighbor) and with whom you have reciprocal arrangements. In these cases, thank the person by telephone or the next time
you see them.

❑   Overnight hospitality always warrants a thank you note—and usually a
gift, which you may bring with you or send afterwards (popular items are
specialty foods, houseplants, flowers, something for the house, or toys for
the children). When you write a family, address the parents, but mention the
children by name (and if you say something complimentary about them, you
will have more than justified your invitation). If you write to only one
member of the family (the one who invited you or the one who was primarily

responsible for your comfort), ask that your thanks be extended to the other household members.

Special Situations

□   A late "thank you" is harder to defend than any other kind of delayed message, but it is still better to write late than not at all. Don't spend more than a phrase or a sentence apologizing for the delay. ("My thanks are no less sincere for being so unforgivably late." "I am sorry not to have told you sooner how very much we enjoyed the petit fours.")

□   Yes, you do send a thank you note for a thank you gift, if for no other reason than to let the person know it arrived.

□   When someone donates money to a charity in your honor or in memory of a deceased relative of yours, the charity will acknowledge the contribution to the donor, usually with a printed card or form letter, but you must also write a thank you note.

□   Although the guest or guests of honor at an anniversary party, birthday party, or shower always thank each friend warmly for gifts as they are opened, thank you notes are still required. The party host should receive a special thank you as well as a small gift.

□   A good job-seeking technique as well as a gesture of courtesy is to write a thank you note to the person who interviews you. But write the note immediately after the interview before a decision can be made. Mention what you liked about the interview, the company, the position.

□   Even though business entertaining is often taken for granted, a brief thank you is appreciated and builds good relations. There is a curious belief in the business world that sending notes of thanks, appreciation, or congratulations makes a person look "soft" and may lead to others taking advantage of them. However, writing a positive note to someone—colleague, client, employee, supplier—actually inspires loyalty, enthusiasm, and increased productivity. Write follow-up notes of appreciation and thanks after business lunches, to particularly good speakers. When you receive a gift from a business contact, write a thank you, even though you know hundreds of them were probably sent out. If a gift is too costly for you in all conscience to accept, avoid any subtle accusation of poor taste on the giver's part when you write your thank-you-but-I-must-refuse letter; explain simply that your firm does not allow you to accept gifts.

□   When gifts arrive early for a wedding, golden anniversary, or other special day, do not acknowledge them or write thank you notes until after the day.

□   Thank you notes are sent for every gift the baby receives. Even if you thank each person warmly at the baby shower as you unwrap the gift, you still need to send a note. The shower host should receive a special thank you as well as a small gift.

□   Many letters contain a "thank you" sentence although they are not truly "thank you" letters. In business, receipt of applications, résumés, information, orders, and other letters are acknowledged with a "thank you." Customers are often thanked for patronizing a business, for making a first sale, for reactivating an account; these are essentially sales letters. In the same way, invitations (to speak at a workshop, to attend a dinner) are accepted in letters beginning, "Thank you for your kind invitation." They are also refused in letters beginning that way.

□   When you receive a gift from more than one person, you must send a thank you note to each person individually, and the notes should not just be copies of each other—try to make each one personal. The two exceptions to this rule are when you receive a gift from a family (even when all six of them signed the card) or when you receive a gift from a group with a particular identity: your bridge club regulars, the other teachers at your school, the people with whom you work. You can write one letter to the group but be sure that it is circulated or posted so that everyone concerned sees it.

□   After a death in the family, thank you notes must be written to people who sent flowers, donations, charitable contributions, or who helped with hot meals, hosted dinners, put up out-of-town visitors, lent chairs, or were otherwise supportive. When the person closest to the bereaved is unable to manage all the correspondence, a member of the family or close friend may write thank you notes on their behalf. The notes need not be long, and need not even be sent as soon as other types of thank you notes; traditionally, you have up to six weeks after the funeral to send thank you notes. To keep track of who sent flowers, attached cards should be collected by a family member or funeral home official and a careful description of the flowers made on them.

□   When you fax a document to someone, the recipient pays for the fax paper, the time the letter occupies the machine, the depreciation on the machine, etc. In most cases, this is acceptable as you are also presumably receiving faxed material from the other person, and you both benefit. The one clear exception—for obvious reasons—is a business thank you: Do not fax it.

Format

□   Personal thank you notes are almost always handwritten on foldovers, note cards, or personal stationery.

□   Formal printed or engraved stationery can be used to write thank you notes for formal or very important events. (It is most often used for wedding gift thank yous.)

◻   Business thank yous are typed on letterhead stationery, personal-business stationery, or good bond paper.

◻   Commercial foldovers with "Thanks" or "Thank you" are convenient and acceptable; a handwritten note goes on the inside page. Contemporary thank you cards with sentimental or humorous messages are also appropriate as long as a handwritten message is added.

◻   When you have a large number of people to thank, it is appropriate in some situations to insert a thank you notice in the local newspaper. For example, recently elected public officials might want to thank all those who worked and voted for them. People sometimes want to publicly thank the nurses, doctors, and hospital staff who helped them through a long and demanding illness. The funeral of a public figure often generates an enormous response, which is best acknowledged in a newspaper announcement.

─────────────────── WORDS ───────────────────

admire	grateful	satisfying
affection	happy	sensational
appreciate	hospitable	special
benefactor	impressed	stunned
bountiful	indebted	superb
captivated	kindness	surprised
charming	large-hearted	tasteful
compliment	lovely	terrific
delighted	memorable	thoughtful
enchanted	one-of-a-kind	thrilled
enjoyed	overjoyed	touched
fascinated	overwhelmed	treasure
favorite	perfect	treat
flattered	pleased	unique
generous	remarkable	valuable
gracious		

─────────────────── PHRASES ───────────────────

absolutely perfect choice for me
am pleased/grateful
an excellent idea
appreciate this opportunity
appreciate your confidence/interest/
   kind words/referral
a rare treat
as a token of our gratitude

cannot tell you how delighted I was
consider me deeply in your debt for
convey my personal thanks to
   everyone who
deeply appreciate
deep sense of gratitude
delighted in
derived great pleasure from

did us good/our hearts good

enjoyable and informative tour

enjoyed it/ourselves enormously

excellent/splendid suggestion

felt right at home

made us feel so welcome

for the most agreeable/pleasing/
  delightful/enjoyable evening

from the bottom of my heart

generous gift

greatly affected by

heartfelt thanks

hearty thanks

how kind/dear/thoughtful/sweet of
  you to

I am indebted/very much obliged
  to you for

I appreciated

I cannot thank you enough for

I deeply/certainly appreciate

I felt honored that/by

I have seldom seen such

I'll long remember

I plan to use it for/to

I really treasure

it is difficult to adequately express
  our gratitude/thankfulness/
  appreciation to you for

it was a great pleasure

it was very hospitable of you to

it was very/so/extremely kind of you to

I want to thank you for

I was delighted with

I will never forget

I wish to express my sincere

kind of you to ask us

know how inconvenient that was for
  you

know that I am grateful for

look forward to seeing you again soon

many thanks

meant a great deal to me

more people have remarked on the

most sincerely grateful to you for ⚹

much appreciated

much obliged

my personal thanks

one of the most memorable days of my
  trip

one of your usual inspired ideas

perfect gift/present

please accept my gratitude/our sincere
  appreciation

pleased as Punch

quite out of the ordinary

really appreciate your help

return the favor

seventh heaven

show my appreciation

thank you so much for the delightful

thank you very/so much

this is to thank you for the super job
  you did on

thoroughly enjoyed myself

tickled our fancy

took a great fancy to

truly a marvel

useful/appropriate/attractive/delightful
  gift

vastly entertaining

very special occasion

very thoughtful of you

want you to know how much we
  appreciate

we are so grateful/thankful to you for

we sincerely/truly appreciate your

we want you to know how much we
  value

we were especially pleased because

we were simply thrilled/delighted/
  stunned with

what a joy it was to receive

with your usual inimitable flair/style

wonderful surprise

your kindness/generosity

your kind remarks/words

your thoughtful expression of
  sympathy was

your very generous gift

you shouldn't have, but

_____ SENTENCES _____

Again, thank you for a thoughtful and unique gift.

All of us were touched by your thoughtfulness.

As soon as we decide what to do with your wonderful gift [money] we will let you know.

Consider me deeply in your debt.

How dear of you—we are delighted!

How did you know we needed one?

How especially thoughtful of you to know just when we needed help with the moving in.

How sweet/dear/thoughtful/kind of you to remember us/think of me.

I am grateful for all your assistance/help, and only hope that I can reciprocate some day.

I appreciate your gift/advice/hospitality/help more than I can say.

I can't remember when I've had a better/more pleasant/more relaxing/more enjoyable time.

I can't thank you enough for chauffeuring me around while the car was in for repairs.

I couldn't have had a more charming/better/more delightful host/guide.

I don't know what I would have done without you/your assistance.

If I can in any way return the favor, please let me know.

I had a lovely time last night.

I hope I can reciprocate/do something as nice for you some day.

I'll cherish your gift always.

I love it!

I'm grateful to everyone who worked on the banquet.

I owe you one!

I plan to use your gift to buy a wok—we have always wanted one.

I really appreciated your help.

I really treasure the paperweight, and it will always remind me of you.

It was a great pleasure to spend some time with you.

It was a much-needed gift/a wonderful surprise.

It was extremely kind of you to let me know about the job opening—I'll keep you posted.

It was so thoughtful of you to remember me.

It was very hospitable of you.

It was very kind of you to ask/include us.

I very much appreciate your concern.

I want to thank you for watching the children while I was ill.

Many, many thanks to both of you for a lovely evening.

Many thanks for your usual good work/for all you have done for me.

More people have remarked on it!

My delay in acknowledging the surprising and wonderful packet of stamps is inexcusable.

On behalf of the family of Violet Effingham Chiltern, I would like to thank you for your kind expression of sympathy.

Please convey our thanks and admiration to the entire staff.

Seeing you all again was simply wonderful.

Special thanks to the doctors and the nurses at Trewsbury County Hospital.

Thanks a million/a bunch.

Thanks for your cooperation and perseverance in this matter.

Thanks for your order and for the interest in Leeds Sporting Goods that prompted it.

Thank you for arranging the interview; I will let you know what happens.

Thank you for being the kind of friend I can count on/for making us feel so welcome.

Thank you for opening a charge account with us recently.

Thank you so much for referring Elizabeth Trant to our company.

Thank you for shopping regularly at Farrell Power & Light.

Thank you for the absolutely perfect weekend/for the excellent service we enjoyed yesterday/for the time you spent with me. Thank you for thinking of/remembering me at this special time.

Thank you for your cheerful note—how did you remember it was my birthday?

Thank you for your generous donation to the Dunstone Foundation in memory of James Calpon Amswell; he would have been very pleased and I appreciate your comforting gesture very much.

Thank you for your kind hospitality last night; I have never felt less a stranger in a strange city.

Thank you for your workable and badly needed suggestion!

Thank you from the heart.

Thank you so much for making my visit to Miami a memorable one.

Thank you so much for the delightful/agreeable/pleasing/entertaining/enjoyable evening.

Thank you very much indeed.

The letter of reference you so kindly wrote for me must have been terrific—Goodman & Co. called yesterday with a job offer!

The tour was as enjoyable as it was informative.

To show our thanks and appreciation for your prompt payments this past year, we are raising your credit limit to $3,000.

Visions of Paradise is a stunning book, and we are all enjoying it very much.

We all thank you for the tickets to the science museum.

We appreciate your referral of Don Amador to this office.

We are grateful/thankful/appreciative.

We are particularly grateful because we know of the many demands on your time.

We are thrilled with the handsome brass bookends you sent!

We both send our love and thanks for your thoughtful gift.

We both wish to express our gratitude for the time and trouble you took caring for the house while we were gone; the yard has never looked better!

We enjoyed the evening/the theater tickets/the book enormously.

We feel blessed to have such loving, faithful friends.

We'll think of your hospitality with appreciation and pleasure for a long time to come.

We will never forget the autumn glories of the North Shore—thank you so much for inviting us to share your cabin with you last weekend.

We will think of you every time we use your clever gift.

What a terrific idea for a gift!

What a wonderful time I had!

What would we have done without you?

You can see what a place of honor we've given your gift the next time you stop by.

You couldn't have given me anything that I wanted/would enjoy more.

You must be a mind-reader!

Your gift was right on target.

You're much too generous!

You're so thoughtful.

Your expression of sympathy on the death of my father was greatly appreciated.

Your good advice was very much appreciated.

Your help went far beyond what I'd hoped for, and I am grateful.

Your interest and concern were appreciated by all of us.

Your kindness to a stranger was very much appreciated.

Your lovely/beautiful/thoughtful gift arrived just now.

Your presence meant a great deal to us.

Your suggestions were as helpful as they were welcome; thank you.

Your unexpected gift delighted us all.

Your words of comfort and your anecdotes and stories about Alex meant a great deal to us during this sad time.

You shouldn't have, but I can't help being glad you did/but since you did, may I say that your choice was absolutely inspired!

You were a big help to me, and I hope I can repay you some day.

—————————————————— PARAGRAPHS ——————————————————

▷   Thank you so much for agreeing to write a letter of recommendation for me, especially since I know how busy you are this time of year. I'm enclosing a stamped envelope addressed to the personnel officer at Strickland Construction so that you can just drop your letter in the mail. I will, of course, let you know at once if I get the job. In the meantime, thanks again for your kindness.

▷   We are still talking about the wonderful weekend we spent with you—thank you, thank you! You are the busiest people we know, yet you welcomed us into your home as if nothing in the world were more important. We particularly enjoyed the comedy at the Wharton Theater—sharing a laugh with dear friends is surely one of life's greatest pleasures.

▷   I want to thank you for all the time you put into coaching your Crossley-area baseball team this summer. It was a joy to watch you and your enthusiastic players model sporting behavior and team spirit to some of the younger teams. The assistance of our volunteer coaches is crucial to the survival of this program, and the Board of Directors joins me in sending you our gratitude and thanks.

▷   On behalf of the directors, staff, and employees of Mallinger Electronics, I want to thank you for the splendid job you did arranging the Awards Banquet Night. Decorations, food, program, and hospitality were all first-rate. Please convey our admiration and thanks to your committee chairs. If you can possibly face the thought, we would like you to head up next year's celebration. The evening was an outstanding success in every way, primarily due to your organizational abilities, creativity, and interpersonal skills.

▷   Thank you so much for the graduation check. As you know, I am saving everything I earn for college, so when I received your card and gift, I knew right away what I was going to do with it! I've been needing and wanting a decent watch for a long time, and I can hardly wait to pick one out. Every time I look at my new watch, I will think of you with affection and gratitude.

▷   It is my understanding that you wrote a letter supporting my nomination by the Department of Materials Science and Engineering as a Distinguished Professor. I am happy to inform you that I was indeed honored with this title on June 3, 1991. I am deeply appreciative of your kind support in this regard. Many thanks.

▷   The kindness and generosity you showed to all of us at the time of Edgar's death are much appreciated. What a good idea to send a plant instead of flowers; we've put the chrysanthemums in Edgar's perennial garden. Thanks too for the hot meals, the lovely letter that I know you put your whole self into, and for your constant support. We're very blessed to count you as a friend.

▷   What a wonderful engagement gift! We haven't even begun to think of planning our wedding as we've heard it's so much work and so complicated. With this marvelous book on wedding planning, I think we can quit worrying.

▷   Your dad said you picked out my tie all by yourself. Thank you very much! Aunt Belinda just took a picture of me wearing the tie and eating a piece of birthday cake. When we get the pictures developed I'll send you one so you can see how nice I look in my new tie.

▷   I would like to thank one of your salesclerks for being helpful, tactful, and speedy—all at the same time! I foolishly tried to buy a wedding gift on my lunch hour, and I am a poor shopper at the best of times. Within minutes, this young man helped me select the absolutely perfect gift at the price I wanted to pay. It was all done so smoothly that I was out of the store before I knew it—and before I thought to ask his name. The initials on my sales slip are R.J. Can you identify him and pass on my thanks?

▷   This is a belated thanks for the Mozartkugeln—they were wonderful. I told the family about them but didn't share any! One of my favorite annual rituals is watching the Wimbledon tennis finals in bed (they start at 7:00 a.m.). The women's final was great, and that's when I ate the Mozartkugeln—they were deliciously decadent. When I lived in Salzburg there was a place about a mile from where I lived that made them daily. They cost about a quarter each then, and every day after class I made my little journey there to get one.

▷   Thank you for all the assistance, information, and encouragement you offered us when Hannah was applying to the U.S. Air Force Academy. We are convinced that her acceptance was due in no small measure to your support and advocacy.

▷   Thank you for your most welcome letter of September 28. I am impressed with your generosity in sending complimentary subscriptions of the magazine to our doctors and nurses presently working in Tanzania. They will make good use of them—they estimate that each copy of the magazine is held by over fifty pairs of hands!

▷   The extravagantly flowering azalea plant absolutely transformed my hospital room and has given me a great deal of pleasure these past few weeks. I'm looking forward to thanking you in person once I get back on my feet.

▷   I very much enjoyed this morning's discussion of the research position you want to fill. I was pleased to know that my advanced degree is definitely an asset. I've been "overqualified" for several jobs, and was beginning to wonder if my extra years of study were of any value in the job market. Thanks so much for your time and for the congenial interview.

———————————————————— SAMPLE LETTERS ————————————————————

Dear Aunt Esther Koskenmaki Lilley,
    Thank you so much for sending us a copy of your book *Father Said, "Eat, Don't Giggle!"* You are quite right in thinking that our collection of folklore materials can benefit from your contribution, especially since Finnish folklore is of particular interest to our Folk Arts Division.
    Again, thank you for your book.

                                        Sincerely,

· · · · · · · · · · ·

Dear Mr. Hollingford,
    Thank you for remembering my five-year anniversary with the company. I really didn't think anyone would notice except me! I have enjoyed working here and plan to stay as long as you'll have me. Thank you, too, for the gift certificate to Sweeney Inn. I have another anniversary coming up (three years of marriage), and I know where we'll celebrate it.

                                        Sincerely,

· · · · · · · · · · ·

Dear Elsie and Joe,
    You made our day with your funny anniversary card and warm message. In one way or another, you've been a part of many of our "big" days, so it was good to have you with us again, in a manner of speaking, on our twenty-fifth wedding anniversary.
    We both send our thanks and love for your faithful friendship (with the promise of a letter to follow).

                                        Fondly,

· · · · · · · · · · ·

Dear Colonel Lambert:
    Thank you so much for agreeing to speak to our study club. We are very much looking forward to hearing your presentation.
    Our district includes ninety-seven veterans, although usually only twenty-five to thirty attend the study club meetings.
    The best way to reach the Flitestone Motel from Centralia is to take I-80W to I-35 N, then exit onto Highway 20, which you'll take North to the intersection

of Highways 169 and 7. The Flitestone is on the Northwest corner of that intersection.

Again, thank you.

Best regards,

. . . .

Dear Agnes and Walter,

Thank you for the lovely silver piggy bank you gave Anabel. It's such a classic, and I know she will treasure it all her life. In the meantime, it has a place of honor on her dresser, and we've gotten into the habit of putting our change in it at the end of the day.

Can you come by to see your new little grand-niece sometime next week? We're all feeling rested by now and would love to see you. Give me a call.

With much love,

. . . .

Dear Millicent,

The dinner party was lovely, and we were delighted to be included. I don't know anyone who has as much flair and style as you do when it comes to entertaining!

Fondly,

. . . .

Dear Vincent Crummles:

Thank you so much for your contribution of $200 to the Alumni Annual Giving Campaign. As stipulated on the donor card returned to this office, your gift will be designated for the Annual Giving Fund to be used where most needed.

We also appreciate your use of the Langdon Co. matching gifts program and look forward to receiving their one-for-one matching gift. This matching gift will also be directed to the Annual Giving Fund.

Thank you again for your generosity, which will make it possible for many worthy young women and young men to have the advantage of a quality education.

Very truly yours,

See also: ACCEPTANCES, ACKNOWLEDGMENTS, RESPONSES.

39

Wedding Correspondence

> "There is no more lovely, friendly and charming
> relationship, communion or company than
> a good marriage." (Martin Luther)

Because there is a great deal of correspondence that surrounds a wedding, all wedding correspondence will be found in this chapter. However, you may find it helpful to check under such related topics as ACKNOWLEDG- MENTS, ANNOUNCEMENTS, CONGRATULATIONS, INVITATIONS, REQUESTS, and THANK YOU.

The word "traditionally" appears often in this chapter. Past and present usage are given side by side, because some people will want weddings planned in the more formal, more traditional manner. The principal rule today in weddings is that there are virtually no unbreakable rules. But if you want to know what has been done, you will be alerted by the word "traditionally." Some old traditions respect a certain dignity and appealing formality, but others reinforce outdated (and invariably sexist) ways of thinking that can be offensive. If you are the wedding couple, you have a right to do things your way at least on this special day. Nevertheless, you may want to think about why some traditions have given way to other ways of doing things. For example, the old notion (which pervaded all wedding correspondence) that the woman was being given by one man to another is generally considered unacceptable today.

Wedding Correspondence Includes

- acknowledging gifts
- announcements: newspaper/printed or engraved
- cancellation
- congratulations on wedding
- families of wedding couple exchanging letters

- informing ex-spouse of remarriage
- invitations: showers/wedding/parties
- postponement
- responses: invitations/announcements
- selecting ceremony participants: attendants/presider/organist/musicians/reception helpers
- showers: invitations/thank yous
- thank you: gifts/favors/greetings/assistance

How to Say It

☐   Hosts of wedding showers are increasingly making use of commercial shower invitations, but you may also send handwritten invitations that include: the name of the honoree or honorees (showers now include gift parties for brides-to-be, grooms-to-be, and couples); the type of shower (kitchen, tool, bath, garden, recipe, household); the time, date, and place; an R.S.V.P. or Regrets only; the name, address, and telephone number of the host. Although each guest is thanked for their gift at the shower, thank you notes should still be sent to each person (even those who "went in together" on a gift) soon after the shower. The shower host should receive a small gift as well as an especially warm thank you.

☐   When you invite some people to the wedding and others to both wedding and reception, your wedding invitation mentions the ceremony only. Enclose a card (about 3 inches by 4 inches, and of the same style stationery as the invitation) with an invitation to the reception. It is a shortened form of the wedding invitation: "Nora Hopper and George Trimmins request the pleasure of your company at their wedding reception [or: a reception following their wedding], on Saturday, the twelfth of June, Walter Village Inn, 55 North Walter Street. R.S.V.P." If all guests are invited to both the wedding and reception, you add, after the place of the wedding on your invitation, "and afterward at . . ." or "Reception immediately following" or "followed by a reception at . . ."

☐   Enclosures in a wedding invitation might include: a reception card (if not everyone invited to the wedding is also invited to the reception); an at-home card; a name card announcing what name the couple or the bride will be using after the marriage; pew cards for a large wedding; maps indicating location of ceremony and reception; admission cards, if the ceremony or reception is being held in a public place.

☐   For a small, casual wedding, invitations may be handwritten (perhaps a friend with exceptional handwriting will make a gift of their calligraphic skills) on good-quality white or off-white notepaper or foldovers in blue or black ink. You may write in the first-person, in the same way that you would extend any informal invitation. Printed or engraved invitations are rarely sent for a very small wedding. However, if large numbers of people are to be informed of the wedding afterwards, printed or engraved announcements can be sent. Your invitation should include: names of bride and groom; date, time, place; mention of hospitality to follow, if any; expression of pleasure at having guests celebrate with you. The invitation may be issued by the couple, by both their parents, or by the woman's parents, and should be mailed at least four weeks in advance.

□   Newspapers publish two types of wedding notices. One is a brief announcement, much like the engagement announcement. The other, more rarely seen today, is a feature article describing the wedding and participants at some length. Depending on how your paper handles weddings, include as much of the following information as allowed: bride's and groom's full names; date, time, and place of wedding; name of officiator or presider; names of members of the wedding party (and relation to the wedding couple); names, hometowns, and occupations or accomplishments of the couple's parents (and occasionally grandparents); information on the couple's education and careers; description of the flowers, music, and wedding party's clothes; where the reception was held; the couple's address after marriage. (If the woman is keeping her birth name or if the couple is adopting a hyphenated name, this is a good place to let people know: "Marian Belthem and Augustus F.G. Richmond will be living at 1871 Meredith.") Avoid nicknames and abbreviations. Call your newspaper in advance to get their guidelines on submitting wedding announcements; they may have special requirements. Some newspapers will publish information about weddings only if they have some news value. Others charge a fee for announcements. Some will publish either an engagement notice or a wedding announcement, but not both. And others will not print an announcement if it is "old news"—arriving more than several weeks after the wedding. Or they want the information about three weeks before the wedding so that it can be run the day after the wedding. In the short announcement-type newspaper notices, marriages were traditionally announced by the woman's parents. This practice has been largely replaced by couples announcing their own wedding, or the parents of both bride and groom making the announcement. Wedding announcements can also be sent to employee newsletters, alumni magazines, or other affiliation publications.

□   Printed, engraved, or even handwritten announcements are sent to people who were not invited to the ceremony or reception and are modeled on the wedding invitation. The same type of stationery is used, and the wording is similar. If formal invitations were sent, the announcements will also be formal; if the wedding was small and informal and invitations were handwritten, the announcements will also be handwritten. They are mailed as near the wedding date as possible (address them in advance), and may include at-home cards. Traditionally the bride's family made the announcement ("Mr. and Mrs. Raymond Gray announce the marriage of their daughter Polly to . . ."), and there were rules to govern cases in which her parents were divorced or deceased (one or both). Today, wedding couples often make the announcement themselves ("Camilla Christy and Matthew Haslam announce their marriage on Saturday, the fifth of June . . .") or it is made by both sets of parents ("Evelyn and Peter Gresham and Bridget and Henry Derricks have the honour of announcing the marriage of their daughter and son, Audrey Gresham and George Derricks, on Friday, the third of April, One thousand nine hundred ninety-two, Emmanuel Lutheran Church, Golding, Nebraska").

□ When replying to a wedding invitation, you will most often use the enclosed formal reply card. If a reply card is not enclosed, use the same format and degree of formality as the invitation to either "accept with pleasure" or "decline with regret." It is not improper, however, to reply informally to a formal invitation. What is absolutely imperative is that you do respond to wedding invitations. Failure of people to reply is the number-one complaint of wedding hosts. (You do not need to respond if you are invited only to the wedding ceremony itself.)

□ When you must decline an invitation to a wedding, use the enclosed reply card or respond on personal stationery or plain, good-quality foldovers using the same style as the invitation. If the invitation is formal, imitate the word and format; if it is informal (first-person, run-in format), reply informally.

□ When you are unable to write immediate or at least timely thank you notes for wedding gifts (because of a large number of gifts, extended honeymoon), send a handwritten or printed/ engraved acknowledgment card after you receive each gift. This serves two purposes: to let the person know their gift arrived safely, and to assure them that you will take great pleasure in writing them a personal note as soon as you can. Acknowledgment cards in no way replace thank you notes and should be followed by them as soon as possible.

□ Etiquette on thank-you notes for wedding gifts is inflexible: a handwritten thank you must be sent for every gift, even if you thanked the individual orally or if you see the person at work every day. One exception that used to be mentioned in etiquette books is a gift from your new spouse or from your parents; neither required thank you notes. You may want to rethink this. Both the man and the woman may and should be responsible for thank you notes. Whoever writes should mention the spouse ("Mae and I appreciate . . ." or "Hugh joins me in . . ."). Traditionally you had one month after the honeymoon to complete thank yous, but guidelines today allow you up to three months. If you receive a number of gifts during the busy time preceding and following the wedding, send acknowledgment cards. Each thank you note should include: a specific mention of the gift ("the silver bread tray," not "your lovely gift"); an expression of your pleasure; some mention of how you plan to use it, why you like it, how much you needed it; a sentence or two unrelated to the gift ("so good to see you at the wedding" or "hope you will come see our new home"). Keep a careful list of gifts as they arrive—nothing is worse than finding several unidentified gifts after the wedding. Do not mention the amounts of money gifts in your thank yous, but do tell how you plan to spend the money. Write separate and different thank yous to friends who have sent joint gifts, unless such a gift is from a large group, such as co-workers. If you use commercial thank you foldovers or note cards, choose the plainest type. When a wedding gift is not to your taste, focus on the kindness of the giver rather than on the gift. For additional guidelines on writing thank you notes, see THANK YOU.

□ Although many arrangements are made by telephone, your general wedding correspondence might include letters to the temple, church, or other location for the ceremony; to the officiant /presider/rabbi/priest/minister; to the sexton, organist, soloist, musicians; to your attendants; to the photographer and videotaper; to the florist, jeweler, bakery; to hotels to make honeymoon arrangements; for all the reception arrangements; ordering gifts for attendants, the aisle carpet, candles, ribbons, decorations. Although these are all very different letters, three things are important: give all possible details; ask everything you need to know at the outset; keep copies of everything. When asking friends or relatives to serve as attendants, be very clear about what you are asking; spell out firmly who pays for what; offer them a graceful way of refusing so that they don't feel pressured; express your appreciation for their friendship.

What Not to Say

□ In formal wedding invitations and announcements, do not abbreviate anything except Mr., Mrs., Ms., and some military ranks.

□ When accepting an invitation to a wedding reception, you may accept only for those people named on the invitation. If your children are not listed, they are not invited. It is highly improper and awkward, as well as expensive for the wedding family, for you to bring them to the reception. In the same way, if your envelope doesn't have "and guest" written on it, you may not bring someone with you. Ignoring this simple rule causes much outrage and inconvenience to wedding reception hosts.

□ When writing thank you notes for wedding gifts, never ask where a gift was purchased so that you can exchange it, and do not mention duplication of gifts.

Tips on Writing

□ The wedding invitation may be issued by the couple ("Julie Hallam and Keith Lockhart request the honour of your presence at their marriage"); by the couple's parents ("Mr. and Mrs. Theobald Pontifex and Mr. and Mrs. Philip Pope request the honour of your presence at the marriage of Charlotte Pontifex and Sydney Pope"); by the bride's parents ("Mr. and Mrs. Sancho Philipe request the honour of your presence at the marriage of their daughter Lucia"); by the bride's widowed parent ("Laura Morland/Mrs. James Morland/Mr. James Morland requests the honour of your presence at the marriage of her/his daughter Mary Rose Morland"); by the bride's divorced parents ("Laura Edmonstone Yonge and Philip Morville request the honour of your presence at the marriage of their daughter Margaret"); by a family friend of the bride, grandparent, or other relative ("Arthur Martindale requests the honour of your presence at the marriage of Caroline Moss to Evan Rhiw"); by the groom's parents ("Mr. and Mrs. Adrien Levine request the honour of your presence at the marriage of their son Etienne Levine to Camille de Jong"); by the wedding couple and both their parents ("Eliza Pentland and Bert Holly join their parents Major and Mrs. Thomas Pentland and Mr. and Mrs. Barnabas Holly in requesting the honour of your presence at their marriage").

□ Addressing wedding invitations: on the outer envelope, list full names and addresses, with no abbreviations if possible. On the inner envelope, repeat last names only ("Mr. and Mrs. Hollingrake"). If you are inviting young children in a family, do not include them on the outer envelope; list their first names under the parents' names on the inner envelope. (Never add "and family.") Older children (somewhere between thirteen and eighteen) should receive their own invitations. You may address one invitation using both full names to an unmarried couple living together. Your return address goes in the upper left-hand corner, unless you are using embossed or engraved envelopes, in which case it is on the back flap. (Note that the U.S. Postal Service discourages placing return addresses on the back flap.) To address the envelopes, use a good-quality fountain pen, felt tip, or calligraphy pen (if its tip is not overly wide). Attach attractive commemorative stamps. Note that you can pick up the invitation and announcement envelopes in advance so that you can begin addressing them early on.

□ Traditionally, the phrase "the honour of your presence" indicates a religious ceremony and "the pleasure of your company" is used for civil weddings or for wedding receptions.

□ You may use either "one thousand nine hundred ninety-three" or "nineteen hundred ninety-three" for your invitation or announcement.

□ If you are using reply cards, invitees will know how to respond. If you are not, insert an address or telephone number below the R.S.V.P. so that they know where to address their responses.

□   Watch for nonparallel forms in referring to the woman and the man in your invitations, announcements, and other wedding correspondence—for example, "the marriage of Adela Polperro to Mr. Lucian Gildersleeve." Either use honorifics for both (Ms. and Mr., for example) or for neither (neither is preferred).

□   Good timing is an essential ingredient of the successful wedding. Wedding books give more details on the subject, but general guidelines include: asking friends to be your attendants as soon as you have a date; ordering printed or engraved invitations at least three months prior to the wedding; beginning to address invitations two months or more before the wedding; mailing all invitations at the same time—between three and six weeks before the wedding.

Special Situations

□   If you are invited to a wedding ceremony but not to a reception afterwards, you do not need to reply. If you receive a wedding announcement, there is no obligation to send a gift, but it is customary to write your congratulations.

□   If your wedding congratulations are belated, write anyway. Most people understand the multiple pressures under which we all live and will be pleased that you remembered at all. Apologize only briefly for the delay.

□   Wedding cancellation announcements should be similar in style and format to the invitations you sent. If formal, engraved wedding invitations were sent, formal cancellation announcements must be sent. They should not be as lavish or as decorative as the invitations, but they should not be in an entirely different class in terms of quality and price.

□   If you want to let people know when you'll be ready for visitors and to inform them of your new address after marriage, you can enclose an at-home card in your wedding invitation or announcement. It is usually of the same style as your other wedding stationery, about 2 3/4 inches by 4 inches: "Linda Condon and Arnaud Hallet will be at home after the sixth of June at 1918 Hergesheimer Road, Lowrie, Wisconsin."

□   Each person invited to a formal wedding should receive an invitation. If you want a friend to be able to bring a guest, the best approach is to call and ask for the person's name and address so you can send them their own invitation. If this is not possible, write "and Guest" on your friend's invitation.

□   If you receive wedding reception acceptances on which people indicate that they are bringing their children (whom you have not invited), write a brief note saying you are pleased they can come to the wedding but that the reception is for adults only. You may have to write a similar note to people who indicate they are bringing an uninvited friend or visiting relative. If you have unattached friends who may not know anyone at the reception, it is a good idea to plan for them to bring a friend and to either call them for a name (so you can send the person their own invitation) or add "and Guest" to their invitation.

□   If the woman plans to retain her birth name or if the couple is adopting a hyphenated or an altogether new surname, a small printed or engraved card (matching the wedding stationery) can be inserted in the wedding invitation or announcement: "After their marriage, Clarissa Graham and Charles Belton will use the surname Belton-Graham," or "Clarissa Graham wishes to announce that following her marriage she will retain her birth name."

□   When either the bride or the groom is a member of the military, it is customary to use their rank on invitations and announcements unless they are a noncommissioned officer or enlisted personnel, in which case it may be omitted if desired. The title is listed before the name for higher ranks ("Major Barbara Lambert, United States Air Force"), after the name for other ranks ("Peter Locksley-Jones, Lieutenant, United States Army").

Format

□   Wedding invitations and announcements may be engraved, printed, or handwritten. A bewildering variety of papers, type styles, inks, and designs are available at printers, stationery stores, and large department stores. Ecru remains the most popular color for invitations and social stationery. Your choice will have a great deal to do with the type of wedding you are having— the more formal the wedding, the more formal the invitations and announcements. You may want to order matching name cards, thank you notes, informals, notepaper, or other stationery at the same time.

□   Note that envelopes (for example, for reply cards and thank you notes) must be at least 5 inches wide by $3\frac{1}{2}$ inches high to comply with postal regulations. Also, check your invitations and announcements very carefully for the correct postage; if they are oversized or if they are over an ounce (which can happen with high-quality paper and two envelopes) they will need extra postage.

□   Formal wedding invitations have two envelopes: the outer envelope can be sealed for mailing, carries your return address, and is hand-addressed; the inner envelope, which contains the invitation (face up as you open the envelope), is unsealed (the flap does not have any glue) and carries the names of the invitees on the front. There may also be a loose piece of tissue paper to protect the engraving and enclosures such as at-home cards or reception cards. Reply cards are inserted in envelopes addressed to you (printed or engraved) and stamped, and then placed in the inner envelope. The inner envelope can be omitted; growing concern about our use of paper prompts many people to do this or to use recycled paper for their invitations.

☐   Wedding announcement notices to newspapers should be typed, double-spaced. If a photograph accompanies it, identify it on the back in case it gets separated from the announcement (use a return-address label or taped-on piece of paper; do not write directly on the back of the photo).

☐   If there are no reply cards in a wedding invitation, use formal notepaper or foldovers. If you have a card with your name on it, you may write underneath your name "accepts with pleasure" or "declines with regret" and then repeat the information about the event and the date.

WORDS

acknowledge   marriage   union
announcement   matrimony   vows
celebrate   nuptials   wedding
ceremony   ritual

PHRASES

acknowledges with thanks the receipt of   joined in holy matrimony
conjugal joy/bliss   marital union
happy couple   request the honour of your presence
happy to announce/to invite you to   at/the pleasure of your company at
have the honour to announce the   united in wedlock
   marriage of   wedding party
help us celebrate our wedding   wedding vows
holy wedlock/matrimony   we would be honored to
invite you to celebrate/share in the   wish to acknowledge the receipt of
   joy/attend the wedding of

SENTENCES

After marriage, Leonora and Daniel will use the surname Halm-Eberstein.
Best wishes on your wedding day!
Jane Vallens and Andrew Satchel gratefully acknowledge the receipt of your beautiful wedding gift and look forward to writing you a personal note of thanks at an early date.
Mary Llewellyn and Martin Hallam request the pleasure of your company at the marriage of their daughter Mary Frances.
Please join us for this happy occasion.

Please join us in celebrating the marriage of our daughter Sally to William Carter.

Stella Halliday will retain her birth name after her marriage to Frank Ashurst.

Thank you for your very generous check, which will go a long ways toward helping us buy the piano we have our eye on—we know you'll approve!

The ceremony will take place at 1:30 p.m., and a reception at the house will follow.

We're sorry, but we can only have so many guests at the reception and we've decided to make it adults only.

We share in your happiness and wish you all the best.

We wish you every happiness as you celebrate the love you share.

PARAGRAPHS

▷ Christina Hossett and Albert Edward Preemby were married June 18, 1992, at Wells First Christian Church. The Reverend Wilfred Devizes performed the ceremony. Parents are Mr. and Mrs. H.G. Hossett of Wells and Mr. and Mrs. A.E. Preemby, Sr., of Waynesville. Christina and Albert want to thank all the guests who celebrated with them. Both are employed at Stephens Insurance.

▷ Bernice and I are absolutely delighted with the electric blanket. You must have been poor students yourselves once, living on the third floor of an old brownstone, hoping that perhaps today the heat might make it all the way upstairs. It's a beautiful, thoughtful, practical gift, and we're grateful.

▷ Julia and I are going to be married at our apartment on Saturday, June eighteenth at 5:30 p.m. It would mean a great deal to us if you would join us for the ceremony and for a reception afterwards.

▷ Mr. and Mrs. Solomon Darke accept with pleasure Mr. and Mrs. Charles Heath's invitation to the marriage of their daughter Margaret to Rupert Johnson on Saturday, the twelfth of June.

▷ We would like to make an appointment with you to discuss the music for our wedding, which is scheduled for June 16 at 1:00 p.m. We have some ideas (and will bring some music with us), but would appreciate some suggestions from you.

—————————————— SAMPLE LETTERS ——————————————

The honour of your presence
is requested at the marriage of
Sybil Anstey Herbert
to
Harry Jardine
on Saturday, the tenth of October
at one o'clock
Lehmann Methodist Church
and afterward at
The New Lehmann Inn

R.S.V.P.
Sybil Anstey Herbert
20 Ianthe Court
Lehmann, OH 45042

. . . .

Mr. Edmund Roundelay
regrets that owing to
the recent death of
Evelyn Ferguson Roundelay
the invitations to the marriage
of their daughter Crystal
to Maxwell Dunston
must be recalled.

. . . .

Roseanne Gargano

and Jerome A. DePalma

request the honour of your presence

at their marriage

on Friday, the second of June

nineteen hundred and eighty-nine

at half after seven o'clock in the evening

Sunset Gardens

3931 East Sunset Road

Las Vegas, Nevada

Reception immediately following

. . . .

Dear Lucy and Fred,

Christopher and I are so pleased you will be able to attend our wedding celebration. I'm afraid there's been a misunderstanding, however. You know how much we enjoy Freddy, Elsa, and Charles, but we are not planning on having any children at the reception. I hope you can find a babysitter so you can still come. Thanks for understanding.

Love,

. . . .

Miss Laetitia Prism

regrets that she is unable to accept

the kind invitation of

Mr. and Mrs. Oscar Fairfax

to the marriage of their daughter

Gwendolyn Fairfax

Saturday, the sixth of June

nineteen hundred ninety-two

at 7:30 p.m.

. . . .

Christina Allaby and Theobald Pontifex

announce with great pleasure

their marriage on

Saturday, the twenty-third of June

Nineteen hundred ninety-three

Butler, Maine

. . . .

Dear Marjorie,

Will and I have finally made the great decision—we're going to be married next August 19! And the really important question is: will you be my attendant? I can't imagine having anyone but you. However, if you can't get away—and what with your job, Richard's new business, and the children's activities, I know it will take some doing—I will certainly understand.

Enclosed is a sketch of the dress you'd wear. I want to pay for it, so don't worry about that. And of course you'll stay at the house, but unfortunately my budget won't run to your airfare. Will that be a problem?

I'll call next week after you've had time to think about this. In the meantime, Will sends his love along with mine.

. . . .

Mr. and Mrs. Orville Jones

accept with pleasure

the kind invitation of

Belinda Jorricks

and

Charles Stobbs

to their marriage on

Friday, the tenth of May

Nineteen hundred ninety-three

at 7:00 p.m.

St. James A.M.E. Zion Church

Reception following

Surtees Country Club

1838 Plains Highway

. . . .

Dear Grace and Harold,

Our dear Stella and Stanley Kowalski are being married on Saturday, September 4, at 3:00 p.m. in an informal ceremony at our house.

We would love to have you celebrate with us, and to stay after the ceremony for a small reception. Let me know if you can join us.

Fondly,

. . . .

Mimi Wynant and Christian Jorgensen

announce that their marriage

has been postponed from

Saturday, the third of June

until

Saturday, the sixth of August

at 2:00 o'clock

St. Anselm's Church

Webster City.

Reception to follow

Webster City Country Club.

. . . .

We have experienced love . . .
in our parents, our families and friends
and now a new love in each other
With sincere joy and a firm desire
to give love its fullest expression
we will be joined in marriage
on Friday, the seventeenth of November

nineteen hundred and eighty-nine
at six o'clock in the evening
St. Luke's Catholic Church
Lexington and Summit
Saint Paul, Minnesota
Cathryn Carolyn O'Sullivan Steffes
and
Keith Ryan Jonn

Dinner Reception following
Fort Snelling Officers Club
Located: 494 (5) and Fort Road

. . . .

Mr. and Mrs. David Herries
announce that the marriage of
their daughter Dorothy
to Arthur Bellairs
on Saturday, the tenth of May
will not take place.

See also: ACCEPTANCES, ACKNOWLEDGMENTS, CONGRATULATIONS, IN-VITATIONS, REFUSALS, REQUESTS, THANK YOU.

40

Letters of Welcome

Because they are always optional, letters of welcome leave the recipient feeling very positive toward the sender. They can be a powerful sales tool for businesses and a charming approach to smoothing and cementing interpersonal relations among neighbors, co-workers, and people with whom we have frequent dealings. For the naturally hospitable among us, they are a way of life and a great pleasure to write.

Write Letters of Welcome To

- new businesses in the neighborhood
- new business contacts/customers/clients
- new co-workers/employees
- new members of club/organization/temple/church
- new neighbors
- new students/teachers
- potential customers/clients
- prospective in-laws

How to Say It

□ Welcome the person, saying how glad you are to have them join your firm, family, group, neighborhood.

□ Offer to help the person get settled in, find things, learn the routine.

□ Mention a possible future meeting, if appropriate.

☐   When welcoming new employees, include detailed terms of employment to avoid later misunderstandings: hours, duties, salary, title, starting date, supervisor, personnel contact.

What Not to Say

☐   Avoid a strong selling message when welcoming new or potential customers.

☐   Keep the tone positive; do not introduce bad news, negative ideas, or hints of trouble ahead (for example, hoping that the new owners have better luck than the previous ones).

Tips on Writing

☐   The welcome letter is most appreciated when it is sent promptly, when "the new kid on the block" still feels insecure. It doesn't have nearly the impact weeks later when the individual feels settled and confident.

Special Situations

☐   In late August, many teachers send out postcards with a brief welcoming message to their new students. This is effective in helping students feel good about returning to school in the fall. There is usually a mention of some project that the class will enjoy or sometimes a vague statement, such as "I think we're going to have a great year."

☐   If you have certain expectations of the soon-to-be-established relationship between you and the new party, the welcome letter is a good place to state them tactfully before unwelcome patterns of behavior take over. (If you want a new neighbor to know that you don't relish casual drop-in visits, you could say, "We look forward to seeing you once you're settled in—but do give us a call first.")

☐   Welcome letters to new employees are highly recommended. They inspire a sense of loyalty, good will, and enthusiasm about the position and the firm.

☐   When welcoming a new business or new family to your market area, focus on establishing name-recognition and product-association in their minds. You may want to offer a free service or product to introduce the potential customer to your goods and services and to encourage them to visit your office or store.

◻   In the long run, a personal letter of welcome to potential customers over the manager's or president's signature will be more cost-effective than mass-produced flyers stuck between a door.

◻   Whenever you know that a customer or client is making a first visit to your place of business, follow up with a letter of welcome. If you have not done so earlier, you might now offer some sort of discount or coupon to encourage the customer to return a second time—the possible beginnings of a habit.

◻   To invite prospective customers to an open house or to visit your new store or offices at their convenience, see INVITATIONS.

Format

◻   Welcome letters that carry a sales message and letters to new employees, colleagues, and organization members are typed on letterhead or business-personal stationery.

◻   Letters to new neighbors, prospective in-laws, and new students or teachers can be handwritten on foldovers or personal stationery.

◻   Postcards are often successfully used to welcome new customers with a special offer or discount.

─────────────────── WORDS ───────────────────

community	group	organization
congregation	hope	pleased
delighted	hospitality	receive
future	introduce	reception
glad	meet	visit
greetings	neighborhood	welcome

─────────────────── PHRASES ───────────────────

bid a cordial welcome	look forward to meeting/seeing you
delighted to make your acquaintance	look us up
eager to serve you	make yourself at home
expect long and fruitful years of association	open arms/door/house
extend a welcome	pleasure to welcome you
family circle	so happy you can join
gladly received	take great pleasure in
good place to pitch your tent	to help you get acquainted
happy to hear	warm reception waiting
help you get established	welcome aboard/back
	welcome mat

———————————————— SENTENCES ————————————————

I feel sure you'll like it here.

If I can be of any help, I'll be glad to do what I can.

I look forward to a mutually satisfying business relationship.

It is a pleasure to welcome you as a new customer.

It is with the greatest pleasure that I welcome you to Paragon Pictures.

It will be a pleasure to serve you.

Let us know how we can help you feel quickly at home.

The door is always open to you.

We believe you will enjoy meeting this challenge with us.

We hope you will enjoy this neighborhood and its friendly inhabitants as much as
    we have.

Welcome to the team!

Welcome to the neighborhood!

We're glad to have you aboard!

We're looking forward to a long, productive association with you.

We want to welcome you to the store and to thank you for doing business with us.

You've made a wonderful choice (in my opinion)!

———————————————— PARAGRAPHS ————————————————

▷   It is my great pleasure to welcome you to the Rivermouth Centipedes. The
enclosed preapproved membership card entitles you to all benefits and privileges of
club membership.

▷   Welcome to Plattsville! All of us here at The Tarkington Gift and Card Shop
hope that you soon feel at home in your new surroundings and that you find much
to enjoy and appreciate in Plattsville. To help acquaint you with your new town, we
have put together a packet of information in conjunction with the chamber of commerce that we hope you will find helpful. Also enclosed is a coupon for 25% off your
first purchase with us.

▷   Nothing pleases us more than to be able to say "welcome back" when an inactive
account is revived. We appreciate your return to our list of active accounts and look
forward to serving you again.

▷   On behalf of the staff, I'd like to welcome you to the best sports fiction published today! If you haven't already received your first issue, you will shortly. We're
very pleased to have you as a *SportStory* subscriber.

▷   Welcome to Clyde Episcopal Church. I hope you felt "at home" with us at your
first service last Sunday. On February 16 at 7:00 p.m. we are having a welcome party
for new parishioners in the church hall. Newcomers have found it helpful to meet
some of their neighbors and to hear about the programs we offer. We hope that the
whole family will be able to come.

▷   Thank you for your first purchase at Eyvind Hardware, and welcome to our
store! We are "more than just a hardware store," and you can ask any one of us for
advice and information on a wide range of topics—whether it's the most appropriate
floor finish for your home, the differences between grades of sandpaper and steel

wool, how to use our rental products, or the advantages and disadvantages of various grout cleaners. Don't hesitate to bring us all your home maintenance questions. To show our appreciation for your business, we are enclosing a coupon good for a free pair of gardening gloves. Visit us again soon!

▷   Welcome to the Guest & Company family of shoppers! It is always a pleasure to greet a new customer. Customer satisfaction has had the highest priority at Guest & Company since 1860. Although the value, variety, and dependability of our products probably inspired your first order, it is only great service that will keep you coming back. If you are not satisfied with your purchase for any reason, just return it for a refund, exchange, or credit—no questions asked! Thank you for shopping with us, and we hope you are pleased with your first order.

SAMPLE LETTERS

Dear Ms. Spenser-Smith:

It is with the greatest pleasure that we welcome you to the E.H. Young Literary Society. Enclosed please find a copy of our by-laws, a schedule of this year's meetings, and minutes from the last meeting.

Your mentor—to make your introduction into the Society as pleasant as possible—will be Ms. Hannah Mole. If you have any questions, please feel free to direct them to her or to me.

I am looking forward to visiting with you after the next meeting. With very best wishes, I am

Sincerely yours,

. . . .

Dear Mr. Jellyband:

The Dover Business Association welcomes you to one of the busiest and most successful retail areas on the south coast. Those of us who own or manage businesses here have been working together to bring new business in and to promote the area for the past eleven years. Enclosed is a description of the group's purpose and activities.

As the new owner of The Fisherman's Rest, you are cordially invited to join the Association. The next meeting will be held June 15 at The Crown and Feather. We hope you will enjoy doing business in Dover as much as we have.

Feel free to contact any of the listed members for information or assistance.

Sincerely,

. . . .

Dear Emma,

Welcome to the sixth grade! I am looking forward to meeting you when school starts. We have some exciting, challenging projects in store for us this year, and I am eager to get started. See you next week!

Sincerely,

. . . .

Dear Mr. Harness,

I am pleased to tell you that your six-month review shows that your work is more than satisfactory, your sales record is exceptional, and your relationships with managers, co-workers, and customers are all very cordial and productive. As of today, you are being upgraded from temporary to permanent employee status. Welcome to Trengartha Tin Plate Works.

With best wishes,

. . . .

Dear Dr. and Mrs. Townshend-Mahony,

Welcome to Buddlecombe! We're having a neighborhood barbecue/potluck dinner on August 3 at our place, and we would love to have you come. Most of the neighbors will be there, and we think you'll enjoy meeting them. If you'd like to bring something, a cold salad would be perfect.

Yours truly,

. . . .

Dear Sidney,

Welcome to Lorry, Darnay, and Manette. We were all very impressed with your qualifications and are looking forward to a long and happy association.

If I can be of any help in your first few months here, please let me know.

Sincerely,

. . . .

Dear Mr. and Mrs. Webb,

Welcome to Groves Corners. We sincerely hope you'll enjoy living in this friendly community. We at Thornton Furniture offer you a special welcome and invite you to come in and say hello to our friendly, courteous salespeople who are eager to serve you. To make your shopping even more convenient and enjoyable, we are pleased to extend credit privileges to you. Just fill out an application form the next time you are in the store.

We are always happy to answer questions, help you find what you need, or place special orders. Don't hesitate to ask. We pride ourselves on satisfying our customers!

Yours truly,

. . . .

Dear Godfrey,

Nancy just told us the good news, and we are both so happy that she has chosen to spend the rest of her life with you, and you with her. I can't say we were entirely surprised, as we have been hearing about you quite a bit lately! You already feel like part of the family, and we're looking forward to seeing you both at the end of the month. Welcome to the family!

With best wishes,

. . . .

Dear Rose Lorimer:

Welcome back! We're very pleased you have decided to renew your membership in the Medieval History Round Table, and we know you'll continue to be pleased with the many benefits that are yours to enjoy in the next year.

You are entitled to tuition discounts at the University, admission discounts at all conferences, workshops, and special lectures, and a subscription to the monthly newsletter. A less tangible benefit is the opportunity to meet people with interests and pursuits very like your own.

Your membership dollars help support our programming, and your participation helps make the Round Table more responsive to the people it serves.

Sincerely,

See also: EMPLOYMENT, SALES.

APPENDIX I
Letters: The Mechanics

> "'The horror of that moment,' the King went on, 'I shall
> never, never forget!' 'You will, though,' the Queen said,
> 'if you don't make a memorandum of it,'" (Lewis Carroll)

This appendix deals with the concrete aspects of letterwriting: how to select stationery, decide what goes on your letterhead, address an envelope, fold and insert a letter into an envelope, and get the best postage rates. For information on the other aspects of letterwriting (tone, style, language, grammar and usage), see APPENDIX II.

Types of Stationery

Business stationery

Size: 8-½ by 11 inches is the standard size. There is a practical as well as a traditional reason for staying with this size: odd-sized stationery is difficult to file.

Color: White, off-white, cream, light gray, or other neutral shades are acceptable.

Paper: Twenty-pound rag bond paper is popular and of good quality. For higher quality, go to a higher-weight paper, for example, thirty-pound paper. At different weights, you'll have a choice of textures and finishes: flat, matte, smooth, woven, linen-look, watermarked. Note that many businesses are choosing to use recyclable paper, which is a good public relations choice as well as a laudable and well-received statement of corporate values. Erasable bond is not recommended for business use since it invariably smudges.

Letterhead: Although the arrangements of the elements on the page can vary somewhat, essential information should include: firm name; address including zip code; area code and telephone number; telex and fax number if these are used. Optional elements include: a logo; the executive's name and title; a list of board of directors or other governing bodies (if very long, this is often placed along the left edge of the page). A good letterhead will be readable, informative, attractive, and not too insistent. For help in selecting appropriate letterhead stationery, visit a reliable printer who can show you many styles of type, formats, inks, papers, and samples of different engraving and printing methods. The more formal and conservative choice is black ink on white or off-white high-quality paper.

Second sheets: These should be of the same quality as the letterhead paper. They can either have no printing on them or be printed or engraved with the company's name. The print is smaller than it is on the letterhead, and the address is not included.

Envelopes: Envelopes should match your stationery in color, weight, general style, and letterhead. By eliminating the extra printing or typing of an address, window envelopes are convenient and popular. The best choice is a simple window (with no glassine), because the plastic is not biodegradable. Many people take note of which companies use which. Be sure to have your return address imprinted in the upper left corner of the front of the envelope. The United States Postal Service discourages return addresses on the back flap, because mail is sorted by machines that cannot flip envelopes over to check for a return address on the back.

When to use: Business stationery is never wrong when writing about business matters to those outside the company. Sometimes its in-house use is also appropriate. Business letterhead stationery should be used only for business-related matters.

Personal-business stationery

Size: 7 or 7-1/2 by 10 inches is a common size, often referred to as executive, Monarch, or personal-business size.

Color: White, off-white, neutral, or very pale shades are acceptable.

Paper: Use good-quality bond paper; many choices are available.

Letterhead: Include the company name and address with the person's name or name and title set underneath or off to one side.

When to use: Use personal-business stationery for brief notes; when you are writing to someone as individual to individual rather than as company representative to employee or customer; when the information is casual; for matters that have a hint of the social or personal about them (congratulating a business acquaintance on the birth of a baby, for example).

Memos

Size: Memos range from 8-1/2-by-11-inch business-sized stationery to 3-by-5-inch pads of printed memo sheets.

Color: Use white, off-white, or pastels.

Printing: Companies may have their own memo stationery printed with only the company name at the top, or, if memos are sent outside the company to longtime customers, suppliers, or colleagues, with the name, address, and telephone number. Memo stationery generally matches the firm's regular business stationery. Some memos may be labeled with something like "Internal Correspondence" and will also have preprinted "TO: FROM: DATE: SUBJECT:" with a space after each at the top. Office supply stores carry commercial memo paper to fill almost any need; these can have the company's name imprinted on them.

When to use: Originally intended for inter-office or in-house communication, the memo now also travels outside the company—for orders, for brief communications with regular customers or suppliers, for transmitting material, and for such routine messages as acknowledgments, confirmations, and inquiries. It is estimated that as many as one in four business hours are spent reading and writing memos. Dean Acheson said, "A memorandum is written not to inform the reader but to protect the writer." Although providing written documentation of what has been done or suggested is certainly one purpose of a memo, its main purpose is to communicate quickly, directly, and succinctly. It rarely contains anything personal and lacks the sort of slow and courteous opening and closing sentences that a regular business letter might have. Although memos are generally typewritten or machine-produced, brief, casual inter-office memos may be handwritten, at a great savings of time and effort.

Personal letter stationery

Size: You may need 8-½-by-11-inch paper for some personal uses (complaints, household business matters), but personal stationery is generally 7-½ by 10-½ inches, 7 or 8 by 10 inches, 5-½ by 6-½ or 7-½ inches. It usually comes with matching envelopes.

Color: Stationery used formally (handwritten invitations, condolences, thank yous) should be white, off-white, cream, eggshell, straw, beige, gray, or some other neutral color. It may have a self border or contrasting border. For informal use, almost anything is acceptable, although some authorities warn against stationery that is perfumed, decorated, ruled, oddly shaped, or otherwise says too loudly, "Look at me!"

Envelopes: Buy matching envelopes whenever possible. Those with a paper lining glued inside are expensive but elegant. If you are using letterhead or other printed stationery, you may want to have a matching imprint for your envelopes.

Second sheets: If you use a letterhead, monograms, or other printing, your second sheets will be plain but should be the same color and quality as your first sheets.

<u>Personal notes or foldovers:</u> One-page notecards and foldovers (at least 3-1/2 by 5 inches when folded) are a heavier weight paper than stationery and are very popular for writing thank you notes, handwritten invitations, replies to invitations, condolences, and other formal and informal messages. They usually come with matching envelopes and may be engraved or printed. If your name, address, initials, or other printing appear on the front panel, write on the inside—beginning at the top of the two panels for a long letter or using the bottom panel only for a short note. Otherwise, you may begin your note on the front panel.

<u>Printing/engraving:</u> Larger sizes of personal stationery can be engraved or printed with a letterhead that includes your name, address, telephone number, and, if you wish, a logo of some sort. Smaller stationery, note cards, and foldovers may be engraved or printed with your name only, your name and address, your address only (for use by anyone in the household), your initials, a monogram, or a family crest or coat of arms. A company name is never included on personal stationery. There used to be many distinctions between men's stationery and women's stationery (sizes, colors, types of printing, name usage), but these may all be safely ignored today. Cities and states are written out (no abbreviations), and numbers may be written out if not too long. The zip code is always included. When deciding whether to include social titles ("Ms.," "Miss," "Dr.") on your printed or engraved stationery, follow personal preference and local custom. There used to be a number of rules governing such usage, but there is no longer a right and wrong where social titles are concerned. The trend seems to be to omit them altogether.

Note that the United States Postal Service frowns upon the practice of printing or engraving the return address on the envelope's flap. Letter-Sorting Machines (LSMs) cannot flip a letter to check its back when it fails to find the return address on the front.

Miscellaneous

Postcards are increasingly popular and versatile. In the home, they make it easy to keep in touch with family and friends. In the business setting, they are used for billing purposes, to announce sales and open houses, to send brief inquiries, acknowledgments, reminders, confirmations, and even orders. They can be printed with your logo and return address in the upper left corner of the front, and the back can carry a printed form message, perhaps with fill-in blanks.

Commercial greeting cards are useful—especially if you keep on hand a selection of the cards you use most often (congratulations, "get well," birthday, sympathy) and do not have to make a trip to the store each time you need one. A handwritten message is always added to greeting cards.

Addressing the Envelope

Business

The United States Postal Service says you will get the best service if you use the optical-character-reader (OCR) format for your envelopes—a machine-readable style for rapid sorting. Type or machine-print all address information in capital letters, using black ink on white paper and sharp, clear print with no overlapping or touching letters (avoid italic or script type). Type addresses flush left style, that is, the first letter of each line in the address should be directly under the first letter of the line above. Include as much address information as possible: apartment, floor, suite number, zip code or zip + 4. Omit all punctuation (except the hyphen in the zip + 4). Use the two-letter state abbreviations approved and preferred by the United State Postal Service (see list at the end of this Appendix). Use the common abbreviations listed in the zip code directory (AVE, ST, APT). Leave at least one space between words and two spaces between word groups. Leave the bar code area free of any writing. Allow for a bottom margin of at least 5/8 inch and a left margin of at least 1 inch. If you have an attention line ("ATTN: Tom Bowling"), it goes on the second line (under the company name). If the address contains both a post office box and a street address, it will be delivered to whichever appears directly above the city and state. Hand-stamp or type mailing directions ("Airmail," "Third Class," "Special Delivery") under the area where the postage will go. When necessary, indicate "Personal" or "Confidential" just to the left and about one space above the address.

Personal

For all formal and many informal personal letters, handwrite your own return address (upper left corner) as well as the addressee's (lower right). For less formal personal correspondence the envelope may be typed (single-spaced). All envelopes should be sealed except for those that are hand-delivered (sealing optional). Although formal personal stationery is often engraved or printed with the person's name and address on the back flap, the United States Postal Service prefers the return address on the front. For the recipient's address, you may use either block style, where each line's left edge lines up, or indented style, where each successive line is indented one or two spaces. In formal correspondence, do not use abbreviations for "Street," "Avenue," "Parkway," or "Road." Personal letters generally bear postage stamps, especially colorful commemoratives, rather than postage-meter tape or preprinted postage.

Zip codes

For both personal and business letters, using zip codes is the best thing you can do to ensure that your mail arrives quickly at the proper destination. When you know it, use the zip + 4 number, which indicates local routes and can speed your letter even more. The United States Postal Service publishes an annual zip code directory; get a copy for your home or office.

Folding and inserting

When inserting a sheet of 8-1/2-by-11-inch stationery into a number ten envelope, fold it in horizontal thirds, and insert it with the back of the top third facing the flap so that when the recipient pulls out the letter and flips up that third, they are ready to begin reading. When you are using window envelopes, the letters will need to be folded so that the name and address appear in the window.

When inserting a full-size sheet into an envelope smaller than a number ten, fold it in half horizontally and then again in thirds and insert it so that the open end is on the left and the top fold faces the flap. The recipient pulls it out, rotates it a quarter turn to the right, opens it, and is ready to read.

Personal stationery is folded once with the writing inside and inserted into its matching envelope, open edges down. The recipient removes the letter and flips up the top half to read.

No matter what stationery you're using, the salutation (which will be inside the folds) faces the flap of the envelope.

Enclosures

Small enclosures (checks, folded flyers, business cards) are placed inside the folds of the letter. To safeguard against overlooking them include an enclosure line in your letter ("Enc.: subscription blank"). When your enclosures are bulkier, use an appropriately sized manila envelope (many businesses have their own imprinted larger envelopes). When your package is bulky, perhaps it ought not be going as first class mail. Send the letter first class, and advise your correspondent of the separate third-class or fourth-class package. Note that if a package contains a letter, the entire package must go first class.

Writing, Typing, Printing

Handwritten

Never use pencil; black or blue ink is preferred to other colors. Certain types of correspondence are almost always written by hand: thank you notes, messages of sympathy, replies to invitations, invitations that are not engraved or printed. Write by hand any time you want to convey personal feeling or informality or, in the case of an interoffice memo, when you have a one- or two-line message.

Typewritten or computer-generated

With very few exceptions, business correspondence is handled by machine, and anywhere from half to all of it is being word processed in most places of business.

Engraved/printed

Acknowledgments, announcements, invitations, and response cards are commonly engraved or printed (engraving is more expensive). A reputable printer can explain the differences between the various types of engraving and printing, show you dozens of samples, and offer you a wide variety of papers, formats, type styles, and inks as well as advice on how to word your message.

Other

Machines and methods that help in reproducing or transmitting letters include: electronic mail, teleprinters (telexes), facsimile machines, the printing press, and the photocopier.

Letter Formats

Personal letters

Date: The date is placed near the top of the right side of the page. If the person is not familiar with your address, however, and you are not using stationery with your address printed on it, the date should be preceded by your address. (These three lines are block style, their left edges flush with each other.)

Salutation: Begin the salutation a few spaces down and flush left. It is followed by a comma ("Dear Jean,"). No inside address is used.

Body of the letter: Begin the body of your letter by indenting the first paragraph—five spaces if you are typing the letter, about three-quarters of an inch if you are handwriting it. Indent all other paragraphs the same way.

Closing: The complimentary close ("Love," "Sincerely,") is set about one line below your last sentence and to the right, its left edge approximately underneath the left edge of your date. Your signature is on the line below the complimentary close.

If your letter is more than one page long, generally write only on one side of your stationery.

For examples of special formats used in personal announcements and invitations, see the appropriate chapters. If you are writing a personal-business letter (to the contractor about work on your garage, for example), follow the guidelines under business letters.

Memos

The memo has three main parts: the to/from/date/subject lines, which replace the letter's salutation; the message or body of the memo; and notation lines, which list the names of people receiving copies or which list enclosures or attachments.

The three most common ways of arranging the headings on the page are:

TO: Paul Rayley   TO: Rowena Ravenstock
FROM: Minta Doyle   FROM: Max Tryte
DATE: April 23, 1992   DATE: November 1, 1992
RE: Lighthouse repairs   SUBJECT: Gouache supplies

TO: Martin Fenner   DATE: July 14, 1992
FROM: Owen Kettle   SUBJECT: Series on tuberculosis

There is no rigid format for spacing in a memo, but you may want to leave two or three blank lines between the headings and the text, which is usually single-spaced. Most commonly each paragraph begins flush left and is separated from others by a single line of space.

No signature is necessary on a memo (sender's name is indicated in one of the headings), but people often initial it at the bottom.

Notations such as "Enc.:" or "cc:" are placed flush left at the bottom as in a letter.

Some memos are structured in two parts so that the recipient can respond on and return the bottom half.

Business letters

Each business letter contains most of the following elements: letterhead or return address; date line; personal or confidential notation; inside address; attention line; salutation; subject or reference line; body or text; complimentary close; signature; name and title lines; identification line; postscript; enclosure line; copies line; mailing notation; postscript.

Return address: If you are not using letterhead stationery, you will need to include your address—use the two lines immediately preceding the date line. Unless the letter is extremely formal, you may use abbreviations ("Rd.," "Apt.," "NY"). Include your zip code.

Date: The most common form for the date is "October 2, 1992." The month is never abbreviated, the day is never spelled out, and endings for numbers ("16th," "2nd") are never used. You will also see "2 October 1992," particularly for international or government business. If you are typing your return address, the date line goes directly beneath it. Otherwise, it is placed two to six lines below the printed address. If you use the shortened date form ("11/6/92," for example) in a casual memo, remember that for virtually all non-Americans the first number is the day, the second the month.

Confidential or personal notation: Indicate "Confidential" or "Personal" between the date line and the inside address.

Inside address: The number of spaces between the date line and the inside address depends on the length of your letter. The idea is to balance the various elements of the letter so that there is not too much white space above the inside address or below the last printed line. The inside address is always flush left and single spaced. If one of the lines is very long, put half of it on the next line, indenting two or three spaces. Guidelines for the address itself: The person's name goes on the first line. If there is a brief title, it can follow the name, preceded by a comma. Otherwise the title goes on the second line or, if you need the space, can be omitted. If you're writing to two or more people, list them one to a line in alphabetical order. The company's name, carefully spelled, is on the next line, and the department or division is on the following line (unless space is a problem, in which case you omit it). Information such as suite, room, floor, and apartment usually has its own line, unless it and the street address are short enough to fit on one line. It used to be standard practice to spell out all words of the inside address, but the use of two-letter state abbreviations has spread from the envelopes (where the United States Postal Service wants to see them) to the inside address, and if the letter is not very formal, other abbreviations ("Ave.") may appear as well. Spell out compass directions that precede a street name but abbreviate those that follow it ("14 North Cedar," "14 Cedar N.W.").

Attention line: Used when you don't know the name of the individual you are writing to, the attention line ("ATTN: Customer Service Representative") is placed below the inside address, leaving one line of space between them. You can also include an attention line as part of the inside address on either the first or second line (after the company name).

Subject line: Beginning with "Subject:" or "Re:" state in less than one line, preferably in a word or two, the subject of your letter. The subject line may be situated between the salutation and the body of the letter or between the inside address and the salutation (one line of space before and after). It also very often replaces the salutation entirely when writing an impersonal letter to an anonymous recipient (your credit card statement was incorrect, for example). The subject line is gaining in popularity as people handle stacks of incoming letters, trying to quickly identify the purpose of each;

the subject line's brisk, memo-like flavor is more of a plus than a minus. It is not recommended when your letter deals with several different subjects.

Reference line: When you need to refer to an order number or to a reference number used either by your correspondent or by your own firm, it can be handled like a subject line and placed between the inside address and the salutation or between the salutation and the body of the letter (leave one line of space on both sides in each case). It may also be placed between the date line and the inside address.

Salutation: Leave one line of space between the inside address (or the subject line) and the salutation. The salutation is followed by a colon (more formal) or a comma.

Body of the letter: Leave one line of space between the salutation (or the subject line) and the body of the letter. In general, single space within paragraphs and leave a line of space between paragraphs. If your letter is very brief, however, double-spacing (or even 1-1/2 spacing) will give it a better look on the page. Wide margins will also balance brief letters on the page just as narrow margins (but not less than 1-1/4 inches) balance long letters. If you indent paragraphs, start in five to ten spaces. If your letter runs to a second page, indicate the name of the recipient, the page number, and the date across the top of the page (about six lines below the paper's edge). If you're writing two individuals, put both names on the left, one under the other, and on the right indicate the date with the page number under it. Then leave three to five lines before resuming the body of the text. There should be a minimum of three lines of type in addition to the signature block to justify a second page.

Complimentary close: Leave one line between the body of the text and the complimentary close.

Signature: Your handwritten signature goes between the complimentary close and your typed name and title.

Name and title lines: Four spaces (or more, if your signature is large) below the complimentary close, type your name with the first letter directly beneath the first letter of the complimentary close. If you are using a title, it is typed on the line beneath your name, and also lined up with the left edge of your name and the complimentary close. Omit the title if it appears on the letterhead.

Identification line: Leave one line of space between the name or title line and the identification line. Type the letter-signer's initials in capital letters flush left, followed by a slash or colon and the typist's initials in lowercase letters ("GTM/rc," "PW:bn"). Or, since it is obvious who has signed the letter, the typist's initials appear alone. The identification line may be going the way of the dodo, however; before automatically including it, ask if it is truly necessary. If you need to know who typed or machine-produced a letter, records can be kept on hard copies or computer files.

Enclosure line: Leave one line of space between the identification line or the name/title line and the enclosure line. Set flush left, this line begins with "Enc.:" and lists any enclosures in the order in which they are found in the envelope, one to a line. You may also use "Encl." or "Enclosures" followed by the number of items enclosed: "Enclosures (4)."

Copies line: Leave one line of space between previous material and the copy line. After "cc:" or "Copy(ies) to" list those individuals receiving copies of the letter in alphabetical order, one to a line, either by their full name, initials and last name, or title and last name only. The person's address may also be included. If you do not want the recipient of the original letter to know about copies being sent, indicate "bcc:" (blind carbon copy) with the names of those receiving copies on the office copy of the letter.

Mailing notation: Instructions for mailing (Special Delivery, Overnight Express) are noted on copies of the letter, but not on the original.

Postscript: A postscript can be typed flush left two spaces below the last typed line. It is most often preceded by "P.S."

The above elements can be placed on the page in different ways to give your letter an overall look or format. The final choice is always up to you, and there is no "right" or "wrong" way. When choosing a format from the ones commonly used today or when designing your own, keep two things in mind: Does it help the reader quickly grasp the message? Does it look like your organization? Formats can make a letter feel personal or impersonal, formal or informal, brisk or low-key. Develop a format that conveys information clearly and logically and that reflects your organization's style.

Full-block letter: The easiest format for the typist, full block style means that every line begins at the left margin—no exceptions. If you have a second page, the name of the recipient, the page number, and the date are typed flush left, one under the other.

Block letter: The block letter is identical to the full-block with two exceptions: the date line and reference line are typed flush right and the signature block (complimentary close plus signature plus name line and title line) are also set flush right or at least to the right of center. Otherwise, everything is flush left and there are no indentations. This format has a more traditional look than the full-block format.

Modified-block: Also known as the semi-block, this format is identical to the block format with one exception: it has indentations. All paragraphs are indented five to ten spaces. The subject line may also be indented. As in the block style, the date line, the reference line, and the signature block are all set flush right or at least to the right of center.

Simplified: With its streamlined contemporary look, the simplified format is easily identified. Like the full-block style, all lines begin at the left margin. But it also has a subject line (typed in capital letters) instead of a salutation, and there is no complimentary close. The letterwriter's name and title are typed in all capital letters.

Official: This style is the same as the semi-block except that the inside address appears two to five lines below the signature block. If an identification line or enclosure line is used, it is placed below the address, leaving one line of space. This format is used by some government agencies.

United States Postal Service Guidelines

The United States Postal Service is your single most important asset in getting your letters where they need to go as quickly and as efficiently as possible. In the past decade or so, the Postal Service has leaped into the future with a precision and vigor that many people still fail to appreciate.

If you are taking advantage of all that the United States Postal Service has to offer, read no further. However, if you do not have ready access to some of the many USPS publications, have not visited your nearest post office to ask how your particular business can benefit from certain postal strategies, have not looked into preparing your mail for automated handling, have not seen the United States Postal Service video "From Cave to Computer: A Short History of Mail Preparation" (or others on more specific subjects), you are not doing all you can do to achieve first-rate mail service for your business—or to cut down on postage costs. As the USPS says, "Your business mail is a resource well worth managing."

Following are some suggestions to improve mail handling:

□ The number-one favor you can do yourself is to ensure that your mail is readable by the Optical Character Readers (OCRs) used in automated sorting: use envelopes of standard size and shape (first-class mail must be rectangular—a square envelope, for example, will be assessed a surcharge); use only white, ivory, or pastels; avoid unusual features like odd papers or bright graphics; type the address IN CAPITAL LETTERS with no punctuation (except for the hyphen in zip + 4 codes), with one or two spaces between words, and with nothing but the address in the lower right part of the envelope.

□ Do not use paperclips to fasten letters or papers; they often jam the Letter-Sorting Machines (LSMs).

□ A surprising number of people still fail to put their return address on envelopes, causing problems for the Postal Service and themselves.

□ Zip code and zip + 4 state directories are published annually and can be obtained in post office lobbies. Use the two-letter state abbreviations, the zip code, and the zip + 4 when known. Their effectiveness in speeding your mail along cannot be overstated.

□ If you include both a street address and a box number in an address, the Postal Service will deliver it to whichever appears in the line immediately above the city and state.

□   Set up a home postal center. Obtain copies of USPS brochures listing postage rates, fees, and information. Invest in a small postage scale, and buy stamps of different denominations to keep in small nine- or fifteen-drawer organizers.

□   Attend USPS workshops on such subjects as marketing with direct mail, professional mailroom management, and organizing your mail for optimum service. The seminars are designed to help cut costs and improve efficiency and will try to match USPS programs to your company's needs. There is usually a small registration fee.

□   Businesses may want to subscribe to *Domestic Mail Manual* and *International Mail Manual*. At upwards of $76 per year, they may be too expensive (and unnecessary) for individual letter writers, but some businesses find them indispensable.

□   Write to: Memo to Mailers, U.S. Postal Service, Post Office Box 999, Springfield, VA 22150-0999 for a free subscription to "Memo to Mailers." Someone in your mailroom should keep track of current United States Postal Service information, and this is one way of doing it.

□   The USPS has a number of helpful videos available for viewing or reproduction. If you are interested in second-class mailings, for example, a video covers requirements for presorting, packaging, sorting and labeling, mailing list preparation, size standards, postage payment and acceptance procedures.

□   The Business Reply Mail Accounting System (BRMAS) is available to customers who use Business Reply Mail, and there are no volume requirements.

□   Look into the possibilities of bar coding your mail; using both zip + 4 and bar codes gives you the largest postal discount available, and the bar coding equipment eventually pays for itself. The USPS expects to bar code virtually all mail by 1995, although not all of it will be done by customers. Automated mail processing (using Optical Character Readers and a bar code sorter) is five times less expensive than mechanical handling (where the LSMs are handled by employees who key in the numbers) and more than nine times less expensive than manual sorting. If you are interested in bar coding your mail, contact an account representative at your local USPS Marketing and Communications office.

□   Check frequently with your local post office about publications, programs, rates, and services as the USPS seems to update old services and introduce new ones all the time. One recent program alerts associate postal offices in advance of the expected arrival and delivery dates of large business mailings entering the mail stream.

□   The USPS is your best source of information on the requirements of first-class mail, the differences between first-class and priority mail, between third-class and fourth-class mail, between Certified Mail, Registered Mail, Insured Mail, and COD mail. It can also tell you about such programs as Stamps by Mail, International Surface Air Lift™ (ISAL), Express Mail Military Service, and the National Change of Address (NCOA) system. Ask for their kit on saving money and for brochures such as "Creative Solutions for Your Business Needs," "A Consumer's Directory of Postal Services and Products," "Addressing for Success," "Directory of AIS [Address Information System] Products and Services," "How to Prepare and Wrap Packages," "Postal Answer Line" (information on postal services using a touch-tone telephone), "Postage Rates, Fees, and Information" (Notice 59 or Poster 103), "International Postal Rates and Fees," "U.S. Postal Service Official Zone Chart," and an impressive number of other pamphlets and brochures explaining every aspect of mailing.

State Abbreviations

Alabama	AL		Montana	MT
Alaska	AK		Nebraska	NE
Arizona	AZ		Nevada	NV
Arkansas	AR		New Hampshire	NH
California	CA		New Jersey	NJ
Colorado	CO		New Mexico	NM
Connecticut	CT		New York	NY
Delaware	DE		North Carolina	NC
Dist. of Col.	DC		North Dakota	ND
Florida	FL		Ohio	OH
Georgia	GA		Oklahoma	OK
Guam	GU		Oregon	OR
Hawaii	HI		Pennsylvania	PA
Idaho	ID		Puerto Rico	PR
Illinois	IL		Rhode Island	RI
Indiana	IN		South Carolina	SC
Iowa	IA		South Dakota	SD
Kansas	KS		Tennessee	TN
Kentucky	KY		Texas	TX
Louisiana	LA		Utah	UT
Maine	ME		Vermont	VT
Maryland	MD		Virgin Islands	VI
Massachusetts	MA		Virginia	VA
Michigan	MI		Washington	WA
Minnesota	MN		West Virginia	WV
Mississippi	MS		Wisconsin	WI
Missouri	MO		Wyoming	WY

APPENDIX II
Letters: The Content

Appendix I tells you *how* to put your letter on the page (and what kind of a page to put it on). Appendix II offers guidelines on *what* to put on the page: principles of good letterwriting; tips on effective form letters; grammar and usage; avoiding exclusive (sexist, racist, ageist) language; how to deal with people's names and titles; special help with salutations, complimentary closes, and signatures; lists of frequently misspelled words; redundant words and phrases; and forms of address.

General Guidelines on Letter Content

The following guidelines apply primarily to business letters. For example, where brevity is a virtue in a business letter, it may not be so well appreciated in a personal letter. And you do not have to state your main idea (if indeed you have one) in the first sentence of a newsy letter to a friend. However, most of these sensible tips will improve all your letterwriting.

□ Use (don't overuse) the word "you" throughout your letter, and particularly in the opening sentences. Being conscious of "you" will reinforce that most important letterwriting rule, "Keep your reader in mind." "You" helps you phrase your message in terms of your reader's interests, needs, and expectations. It also involves the reader in the letter. The exception to the use of "you" is the letter of complaint or disagreement, in which "you"-statements are perceived as (and often are) accusing and hostile. It is better to phrase your message in terms of "I" statements. (It is always "I"—not "we"— unless you are speaking on behalf of your company or a group of people.)

□ Be brief. George Burns's advice on a good sermon applies equally well to letters: "a good beginning and a good ending . . . as close together as possible." Augustus J.C. Hare received an invitation that read: "Will you be so very kind as to allow me to take the liberty of entreating you to have the kindness to confer the favour upon me of giving me the happiness of your

393

company on Friday?" Although we can feel virtuous for not having written that, many letters could be pared down to greater effect. Give brief explanations, instructions, reasons. Overexplaining always appears weak. If your reader needs to know more, they can ask.

☐ State the main idea in the first or second sentence.

☐ Avoid slang, jargon, buzz words, legalese, elitist language, and stilted usage like "I shall." Choose the familiar word over the unfamiliar. Also avoid clichés, gimmicks, rhetorical questions, jokes, and "clever" remarks. The problem is that we are so used to our own manner of writing that we are often unaware of these problems. In a place of business where people are supportive of each other and employees have fairly healthy egos, you might want to schedule a one- or two-hour workshop where a few letterwriting principles are given and then have participants critique each other's letters (a packet of sample letters can be photocopied and distributed).

☐ Be pleasant, courteous, positive, and encouraging. For being so inexpensive, upbeat attitudes are amazingly effective. Watch for hidden insults, threats, argumentative or antagonistic postures, bullying, patronizing expressions, or messages that may be subtly humiliating. The momentary satisfaction you get from expressing your feelings will generally cost you the correspondent's cooperation or satisfaction.

☐ Be factual. Avoid emotion in business letters. Your readers do not care about your feelings; they want the facts, they want to know what's going to happen next, they want to know why something happened. Feelings are not persuasive, facts are. Also avoid exaggerating or dramatizing your message. You will lose credibility with your reader. It is better to mildly understate your case and let the reader take credit for seeing how wonderful it really is.

☐ Use the active instead of the passive voice ("I received your letter last week," not "Your letter was received last week"). Use strong, direct, action-filled verbs ("is/are," "do," and "make" are not some of them). Think of the subtle difference between the verbs "arrange" and "organize." Which sounds more powerful? Get in the habit of using a thesaurus to find dynamic (but not unusual, unfamiliar, or unpronounceable) substitutes for your most overused words.

☐ Be specific. Nothing gives writing more power than details—not unnecessary details, but details that replace vague words and phrases. Instead of saying "a powerful motor," tell *how* powerful: 18 h.p.? a motor powerful enough to pull three adult water-skiers? a motor so powerful that cold, heat, damp, and rust cannot prevail against it? Readers love details: how much, what color, what date, what time, how big, how little. Go back through your letters and question every adjective—is it pulling its weight? Could it be more specific?

☐ Use a lively, conversational tone. Reading your letters out loud for several weeks will help you spot awkwardnesses.

 □ Choose a tone for your letter and stick to it. A letter that starts off friendly, grows indignant in the middle, and winds up with a demand will confuse the reader. A letter might be formal or informal, cool or warm, serious or light-hearted, brisk or relaxed, simple or complex, elegant or down home.

 □ Avoid overused words such as "very" and "basically." Basically, neither of them means very much, and they become annoying to the reader.

 □ When writing to people from other countries, keep your sentences and syntax as simple as possible. Avoid slang, jargon, figures of speech, references to facets of American culture, the passive voice, and complex verb constructions. Keep to the present and simple past tenses. Instead of "If we had only known . . . ," say "We did not know . . ." If using numerals for the date, use day/month/year instead of month/day/year. If you know them, use social titles from the reader's own language ("Madame," "Signore," "Herr," "Señora"). Use the address exactly as given; it is most deliverable in that form. Letters from other countries often have ritualized closing sentences that express the writer's respect and good wishes; take your cue from your correspondent's letter and reply in kind.

 □ Make it easy for your correspondent to reply to you: enclose a postage-paid reply envelope or a self-addressed stamped envelope.

Form Letters

Form letters have been one of the most wildly successful innovations in business letterwriting. They have done away with the numbing and time-consuming chore of typing the same letter thousands of times. With the use of word processing and mail merge capabilities, letters can be printed, individually addressed and dated, and mailed out in a fraction of the time it used to take to do half as many. Form letters have been worth their weight in gold in direct sales marketing and in the processing of many routine business letters (confirmations, acknowledgments, cover letters, rejections).

Form letters have a negative side. Joseph Heller poked fun at them in *Catch 22:* "Dear Mrs, Mr, Miss, or Mr and Mrs Daneeka: Words cannot express the deep personal grief I experienced when your husband, son, father or brother was killed, wounded or reported missing in action."

To make the most of form letters, your message should appear to be directed solely at the person who is reading it. Inserting the person's name at intervals is not the way to do this; too many spelling errors can creep in, and it appears that people do not mistake this cheery and obviously phony friendship for real intimacy. Make your letter personal by using "you," by tailoring your letter to the individual. It will help if you are using mailing lists of specific market targets. Then, if you are writing to members of a list who are all gardeners or who have all contributed to a charity within the past six months, you know how to frame your letter. For important mailings, you can achieve the personal look by using a high-quality paper, signing each letter individually (there are people who look first to see if the signature is "real" or not and then either read the letter or toss it), and mailing the letter first class.

In addition to form letters, you may want to keep boilerplate material in a special computer file—paragraphs, signature blocks, addresses, and other bits and pieces of letters that you use over and over. Most word processing systems have a "phrase library" or similar construct so that by typing two keys you can insert whole paragraphs any time you need them.

Grammar and Usage

The following tips cover a few of the most common grammar and usage problems that crop up in letterwriting.

□ Use **periods** at the end of sentences. Or sentence fragments. Always leave two spaces between a period and the next sentence. A period also follows an abbrev. Ellipsis points are used to replace missing words: three dots in the middle of the sentence, four at the end.

□ **Commas** separate items or lists of things. It is correct either to use or not to use a comma before "and" in a series ("Milk, butter and eggs" or "Milk, butter, and eggs")—the only rule is to do it one way or the other *consistently.* If you don't know when to use a comma, read the sentence aloud dramatically. The places where you pause to group thought phrases together may need commas. However, when in doubt, you may do well to err on the side of no comma; people tend to overuse them.

□ Don't use **question marks** after indirect questions or requests ("He asked what went wrong" or "Please sweep up here after yourself"). Omit the comma after the question mark in cases like "Do you like it?" she asked.

□ Except perhaps for sales letters, business correspondence does not require **exclamation marks.** It is well to be stingy with them in personal correspondence as well. J.L. Basford believed that "One who uses many periods is a philosopher; many interrogations, a student; many exclamations, a fanatic." Exclamations give your letters a certain manic look, like a person laughing at their own jokes. At first, it will tear at your heart to remove them; by and by, you will be well pleased to find that you can get along quite nicely without most of them.

□ **Quotation marks** are used for quoted words and for the titles of magazine articles and TV and radio shows. All punctuation goes inside the quotation marks ("What?" "Egads!" "I won't," he said). Common sense ought to indicate the rare exceptions. If the punctuation in no way belongs to the quotation, you can leave it outside, as in the following sentence: How many times have you heard a child say "But I'm not tired"?

□ **Parentheses** are used to enclose asides to your main train of thought. When the aside is an incomplete thought (incomplete sentence) it is placed in the middle of a regular sentence; the first word inside does not begin with a capital, nor is there any punctuation. (Sometimes, however, your thought is a complete thought, or complete sentence, in which case it is set inside parentheses and has its own initial capital letter and final punctuation.) When using parentheses within a sentence, all punctuation goes after the parentheses: Please order more ribbons, paper (30#), and file folders.

□ In general, **hyphens** are used to help word pairs or groups form one easy-to-read thought group. Traditional exceptions are words ending in -ly ("newly appointed") and adjective groups that *follow* a noun ("well-known telecaster" but "she was well known for . . ."). The trend is to one word rather than a hyphenated word or two separate words ("headlight," not "head-light" or "head light"). There are a number of rules on hyphenation, but a quick check with a dictionary will give you the correct form for most words.

□ Use **apostrophes** to replace missing letters ("isn't") and to show possession ("Simon's"). The apostrophe most commonly shows up in the wrong place in "its" and "it's." If you can write "it is" in place of your word, it needs the apostrophe. If you have trouble with this pair, write only "it is" or "its" until you are comfortable with the difference. When more than one person is involved, show the plural possessive by placing the apostrophe after the "s" ("union members' votes" or "the parents' recommendations"). Omit the apostrophe when making plurals of number and letter combinations: Ph.D.s, the 1990s, the '50s, three 100s, IBMs.

□ **Colons** often precede a list or a long quotation ("We carry the following brand names: . . ." or "The hospital issued the following apology: . . ."). Do not use a colon when it unnecessarily breaks up a sentence (remove the colon in "Your kit contains: a lifetime supply of glue, four colors of paint, and a set of two brushes"). The colon is also used after a business or formal salutation ("Mr. President:").

□ **Semicolons** tend to give a stuffy, old-fashioned look to a letter. However, they are still useful on occasion. When writing a long list that has internal punctuation, separate each element with a semicolon ("New members for January: Rachel and Darke Solomon of Velindre, their children Peter, Jasper, Ruby, and Amber; . . ."). You may also separate two independent clauses of a sentence with a semicolon ("In prosperity our friends know us; in adversity we know our friends."—J. Churton Collins).

□ The widespread overuse of **dashes** is questionable and indicates a rather slapdash (you see where it comes from?) style. If you are a regular dash-user, check to see if other punctuation might not do as well. Once the dash habit takes hold, dashes proliferate on the page, giving a letter a rather forward-leaning, breathless quality.

□ One of the most common grammar errors involves **noun-verb agreement.** In complicated sentences, where the noun and verb become separated from each other, it is easy to make a mistake. When proofreading your letters, pick out long sentences, find your noun and verb, put them together, and see if they still make sense. Some nouns that look singular ("data") take a plural verb; some that look plural take a singular verb ("a series of books is scheduled for"; "the board of directors is investigating"). What do you do with "None of them has/have voted yet"? When in doubt, re-word the sentence ("Nobody has voted yet"; "Not one of them has voted yet") or ask what the sense of the phrase is. If you are indeed speaking of only one person, use "has"; if the sense of the phrase means a lot of people, use "have." "A number of accountants are signing up for . . ." but "The number of accountants is decreasing."

□ **Underline** titles of books and movies; other titles go in quotation marks.

□ One of the best things you can do for your writing is to become aware of **parallel structures**—from little things like capitalizing or not capitalizing all the words in a list to making sure each word in the list is the same part of speech. In long sentences, writers often forget that they started one phrase with "to interview . . ." but started the next with "calling the candidate" and the final one with "and, finally, you could meet with . . ." A parallel form would have "to interview . . . to call . . . to meet with . . ." Parallel constructions are used throughout this book; if you are interested in finding other examples, most pages offer some.

□ Good **paragraphing** can do a lot for your letter. Keep paragraphs short. Let each one develop a single idea. You can either start with your broadest idea and then support it with detailed refinements. Or you can start with details and lead the reader to your final, topic sentence.

□ Learn the difference between "that" and "which." In general, the easiest way to remember is to see if you need commas or not. Commas and "which" go together: "The file, which eventually turned up on Frank's desk, had been missing for a week." "The file that had been missing eventually turned up on Frank's desk." *Do not* set off a phrase beginning with "that" with commas, and *do* set off a "which" clause with commas.

□ "Howard and Paul had lunch together before he left." Which "he" left? A common error is forgetting to check pronouns ("who," "she," "they") to be sure the **antecedents** (the persons they refer to) are obvious.

□ **Dangling modifiers** are another common error. A group of words are tacked onto a sentence, front or back (sometimes even in the middle), in such a way that the reader doesn't know what it modifies. In *Watch Your Language*, Theodore M. Bernstein gives several examples, among them: "Although definitely extinct, Professor Daevey said it had not been too long ago that the moa was floundering around his deathtrap swamps." "As reconstructed by the police, Pfeffer at first denied any knowledge of the Byrd murder."

    □   "Between" is generally between two people, no more. (And the correct expression is always "between you and me," "between Florrie and me.") "Among" is generally for three or more: "We should have the necessary know-how among the four of us."

    □   Watch the placement of "only" and "not only"; they should go right next to the word they modify. Instead of "I am only buying one," write "I am buying only one."

    □   "Whom" and "whomever" do not occur nearly as often as people suppose they do. Use them only when you can show they are the object of a verb. The most common misuse of "whomever" occurs in a situation like this: "Please mail this file to whoever is elected secretary." "Whoever" is correct; it is the subject of the clause. If you are troubled by this construction, see a good grammar; until then, it is perhaps enough to alert you to the problem.

Exclusive Language

Exclusive language *excludes* certain people or groups of people. When writing to another company and beginning the letter "Gentlemen:" you have excluded all women who work there. When you invite customers to an open house and neglect to make arrangements for handicapped accessibility or fail to indicate on your invitation that the event is accessible, you exclude people with disabilities from attending. When you refer to the "Christian ethic" or the "Judeo-Christian ethic," you exclude large numbers of highly ethical people who are not included in that description. People are also excluded linguistically on the basis of age, race, and socioeconomic class.

The rationale for using inclusive language is well established: (1) Research has shown that how we think, how we speak, and how we act are inextricably linked. Changing how we speak will not of itself change society; however, society cannot change as long as we continue to use exclusive language. (2) Exclusive language is damaging. Many studies have shown that where words like "man" and "mankind" are used, readers and viewers do not picture all people, but primarily men; these are *not* generic terms. Whenever people are consistently excluded linguistically, they have a much smaller share in society's goods and services. (3) People from all walks of life want to be represented in the language; too many groups have been invisible for too long. This is grass-roots change. At the same time, government agencies, legislatures, religious bodies, businesses, educational institutions, and many other groups are setting language standards, asking that all correspondence be inclusive. This is change from the top down. (4) Businesses that fail to include all customers in their letters and other writings may have a death wish; customers are increasingly sensitive to and active against insensitive and exclusive language.

The following guidelines will help keep your correspondence inclusive:

□ An old psychology maxim states that "labels are disabling." Avoid labels whenever possible. Labels are by their very nature stereotypes: senior citizens, Asian-Americans, unmarried women, cancer patients, teenagers, Methodists, second-generation Italians. When you begin talking about a class of people, you skate on thin ground because psychologically all of us think of ourselves as individuals. No two "young mothers" are alike. Nor are any two "Roman Catholic priests" or "lawyers" or "blue-collar workers." Write to individuals and write of people as individuals.

□ When asked what labels offended them, young people listed "teens," "teenagers," "youth," "kids," "girls and boys," "adolescents," "minors," and "juveniles." What's left? "People" or "young people," they said. Nobody likes labels.

□ Although they didn't know it, those young people were supporting the "people first" rule. People are always people first, and only secondarily people who have disabilities, people who are over sixty-five, people who are Baptists, people who are Finnish-Americans. In all your writing, ask first if you truly need to mention classifications such as sex, age, race, religion, economic class, or disability. Very often it is not necessary at all. When in doubt, omit it. Beware of identifying the whole person by a part of the person. Madeline is a person who happens to have paraplegia. Referring to her as "a paraplegic" identifies the whole Madeline by one part of her. Another common error is speaking about someone as being passively "confined to a wheelchair." The correct and active phrase is "uses a wheelchair."

□ Avoid the derogatory use of the word "old" as it contributes to stereotypes about our later years. Likewise, avoid the word "black" (a good word in itself) as it is used in too many negative expressions: the bad guy wearing the black hat, blackening someone's name, a black sheep, blackguard, black-balling someone, the black market. Particularly pernicious is the expression "black and white" meaning very sharply divided into good and bad groups, sides, or ideas, or evaluating things as either all good or all bad. Many people no longer use this expression. It is too easy to sigh at this point, and ask if there's *any*thing left one can say. If it is your ox that is being gored, you would be sensitive indeed to the power of language. And once people become committed to the idea of respecting all of us as individuals, it becomes fairly easy to use language that supports it. Two other good reasons for being vigilant about exclusive language are that you will soon be out of the mainstream if you don't and that customers will eventually make their wishes known to you.

□ Some language implies strongly that people of lower socioeconomic classes somehow deserve their position in society. This is offensive and excludes the great majority who live at poverty level or who are homeless despite their own best efforts. There are few vocal representatives of this group asking not to be excluded, so it may take a little extra effort to remember them.

❑   The most visible problem today is that of sexism in language. Here is a short course on keeping your letters free of sexism.

Eliminate all mention of gender unless there is a good reason for including it. Usually there isn't. More and more frequently social titles are being dropped. "Chris Parish" is a good sales rep whether it turns out to be "Mr. Chris Parish" or "Ms. Chris Parish." If you think you can't write a business letter to "Chris Parish" without knowing whether you're writing to a woman or a man, ask yourself why you can't. Do not use words with so-called feminine endings: both women and men are poets, actors, hosts, directors, adventurers, authors, deacons, and patrons. There is no justification for keeping words like "poetess," "directress," "deaconness." Any word that specifies sex should trigger a query: Why does it? Who wants to know? There are only a handful of necessary and biological sex-linked words; "sperm donor" and "surrogate mother" are two.

Use parallel constructions when speaking of women and men in your letters. If she is Ms. Maria Gostrey, he is Mr. Ray Parker (not Ray Parker, Ray, or Mr. Parker). If he is Parker, she is Gostrey (not Ms. Gostrey or Maria). If he is a man, she is a woman (not a wife); when she is a wife, he is a husband (not a man). Watch out for inequal or nonparallel constructions: college man and college girl; three lawyers, one of whom was a woman [why single her out?]; the high-flying company director and the beautiful assistant director [guess which sex is which]. A radio news item illustrates how a message can be extremely sexist without having a sexist word in it: "More women than ever before are living with men without being married to them. And more unmarried women than ever before are having babies." Rewriting this for parallel treatment of men and women would have been simple: "More men and women than ever before are living together without being married. And more unmarried couples than ever before are having babies."

Never use "man" or "mankind" to represent everyone. Neither word is a true generic. Use instead: humanity, people, we, us, humankind, persons, individuals, souls, creatures, society, human society, nature, folks, the general public, planet earth, the world, adults, citizens, taxpayers, the general population.

Never use "he" when you mean "he or she." When "he" does not refer to a specific boy or man, but instead is meant to convey "someone," change it. The best solution is to make the sentence plural ("A mailcarrier has his work cut out for him today" is "Mailcarriers have their work cut out for them today"). A second good solution is to rewrite the sentence so that the pronoun is "you" or "we." Depending on the material, this will work very well or not at all. Sometimes the pronouns "he," "his," or "him" can simply be omitted or replaced with a noun. Only as a last resort and very infrequently should you use "his or her," "she or he." The construction is awkward and too

many of them are annoying and distracting. In addition, it is rarely necessary. A growing trend today is to return to earlier days and use the singular
"they" ("To each their own"). This construction, found throughout this
book, was very commonly used (Shakespeare used it) until eighteenth-
century male grammarians decided that number was more important than
gender and voted down the singular "they" (error of number) in favor of the
"generic" he (error in gender).

Watch out for sex stereotypes. There are too many of these to list (for
example, women gossip while men shoot the bull), but the danger signal is
any statement that is actually saying, "All men are like this" or "All women
are like this." This is another version of labeling. Cultural stereotypes,
which say that women behave one way (are not aggressive, for example) and
men behave another way (do not cry, for example), keep all of us from being
whoever we are. Including cultural stereotypes in your letters will mark
you as sexist. We cannot assume that "all women" or "all men" will come in
any predetermined style. There are two ways to guard against subtle stereotypes slipping into your letter: First, if you're talking about either men or
women, substitute the other gender to see if it reads as well. This little test
works well unless you are writing about some sex-specific issue (pregnancy,
for example). Second, reread your letter as though it were addressed to you.
Do you feel patronized or narrowly labeled?

Identify women as their own people. In addition to using the names
women use for themselves, avoid identifying women as somebody's wife,
mother, or sister.

Avoid words ending in "-person." With a few exceptions ("layperson," for
example), these words are fairly new, contrived, and awkward. They served a
good purpose in the beginning when people were eager to be inclusive, but
didn't have time to find better words. However, alternatives exist for almost
all "-person" words. The problem with "-person" is that it signals rather self-
consciously that we are trying to be inclusive. Why use "spokesperson" when
the word "representative" is so much punchier and accurate? Why use
"chairperson" when "chair" is actually the older word of the two and quite
respectable today? People who object to being called a piece of furniture forget that we use the analogous word "head," which borders on the gruesome,
without a second thought. In general, "chairperson," "spokesperson," and
their ilk end up being reserved for women while men continue to be
"chairmen" and "spokesmen." "Chair" should be your first choice.

Names

Today there are very few hard and fast rules about names. The most
general and compelling principle is to use whatever form of their name your
correspondents prefer. When deciding which form of your own name to use,

be guided not so much by rules (many of which were laid down in earlier times and by means of less congenial points of reference), but by common sense and your own preferences. Research shows that naming has great power, and the power of saying who we are belongs to us alone. Some broad guidelines may nonetheless be useful:

□ Spell your correspondent's name correctly. It is worth the few minutes and the forty cents or so to call long distance to get the correct spelling and current title.

□ Although in some fields and in some parts of the country, people are quick to call each other by their first names, you may do well to write "Dear Ms. Medinger" rather than "Dear Mary Kaye" and "Dear Mr. Wall" rather than "Dear John" until you are sure that the more intimate form is welcome. Miss Manners, the ineffably correct etiquette maven, says that in order to prevent the unauthorized use of her first name, she took the precaution of not having one at all. When you have any doubts about the degree of formality or informality that exists between you and a correspondent, the more formal approach is always the correct choice.

□ When ordering business cards or personal calling cards, spell out your full name. Social titles (Mr., Mrs., Miss) used to precede the name, although they are largely omitted today. Medical specialists use "Dr." or "Doctor" on social cards ("Doctor Christopher Bembridge"), but use "M.D.," "D.O.," "D.D.S.," "O.D.," etc., on business cards ("Muriel Eden, D.D.S."). Either "Joseph Farr, Jr." or "Joseph Farr, junior" is correct. When using "Esq." (short for Esquire) after lawyers' names ("Marian Beltham, Esq."), omit all other titles (Mr., Ms., Mrs., Miss) before it.

□ Which social titles (also called courtesy titles or honorifics) to use for women is not the difficult problem it is thought to be. The first solution is to use whatever name and social title she uses (see her last letter or call her home or office to check on the spelling of her name and to ask "Do you prefer Miss, Mrs., or Ms. with that?"). If there is no clue to her marital status (and remember that you have been addressing men for years without worrying about this), use her full name without a social title ("Dear Florence Churchill") or (and this is especially a safe choice in most business contexts) use "Ms." and her last name. The worst that can happen is that the letter you receive in return has a "(Mrs.)" or a "Dr." or some other large clue on the typed signature line before her name. Now you know. In business, women invariably use their own first names. This used to indicate that a woman was single, divorced, or possibly widowed. Today it just means that that is her first name. Socially, some women use their husbands' names. They may sign a letter "Nelly Christie" but type underneath "Mrs. John Christie." Traditionally, married or widowed women used their husbands' names ("Mrs. Philip Halliday"), while divorced women used their own first name and either their family-of-origin name, their married name, or both. Single women were to use "Miss" or not, as they pleased. This marital coding system is no longer as reliable or as popular as it once was.

□ Naming couples also requires common sense and sensitivity. Use the form they use themselves. A few possibilities are: "Mr. and Mrs. Walter Evson"; "Adela and George Norrington"; "Dr. Guy and Mrs. Elizabeth Phillips"; "Katherine Halstead and Frank Luttrell"; "Dr. Linda and Mr. Arnaud Hallet." When addressing envelopes or typing the inside address, and each name is fairly long, put one to a line in alphabetic order.

□ When addressing more than one person, use each person's full name or use a social title plus last name for each. For single-sex groups, you may use "Mesdames" ("Mmes.") for women and "Messieurs" ("Messrs.") for men, although these terms have an old-fashioned ring to them. These titles are followed by the individuals' last names only. When addressing both women and men, use an inclusive salutation such as "Dear Friends," "Dear Co-chairs," "Dear Committee Members," or "To: (list names, one to a line in alphabetical order)."

Salutations, Complimentary Closes, and Signatures

Salutations: The salutation is almost always set flush left. The first letter of the first word is capitalized but other modifying words are not ("My very dear Joanna"). All titles and names are capitalized. Use abbreviations for Ms., Mr., Mrs., Dr., but spell out religious, military, and professional titles such as Father, Major, Professor, Sister, Colonel. The salutation generally ends in a comma for personal or informal letters, and in a colon or a comma for business letters.

Traditionally, the most formal and official salutation was "My dear Dr. Hernon," with the less formal being "Dear Dr. Hernon." However, unless you receive this type of mail and want to reciprocate, this somewhat affected style is better abandoned in favor of the more simple and contemporary "Dear Dr. Hernon."

Whenever possible, obtain the name of the person who is best suited to receive your letter; call the company if necessary. Equally important, spell the name correctly.

When you know the person's name, write: "Dear Neil A. McTodd" or "Dear Agnes Bailey" (full name with no social title) or "Dear Ms. Lee," "Dear Captain Crowe," "Dear Inspector Hopkins," "Dear Senator Burnside" (social title plus last name). The first convention is useful when you don't know the person's sex ("Audley Egerton") or which social title (Ms., Mrs., Miss) the person uses. Professional or academic titles (Dr., Representative) are always used instead of social titles (Mr., Miss).

When you are writing a form letter or you don't know your correspondent's name, you can still write "Dear . . ." with nouns like: Neighbor, Subscriber, Friend, Motorist, Reader, Colleague, Student, Customer, Gardener, Client, Employee, Parishioner, Collector, Cardholder, Concerned

Parent, Initiate-Elect, Handgun Control Supporter, Member, Homeowner, Supplier, Executive, Aquarist, Equestrian, Do-It-Yourselfer. Or try job titles: Dentist, Copywriter, Electrician, Metallurgist, Customer Service Manager. Or use the company's name: Poulengay Upholsterers, Elliot-Lewis Stationers, Handford Lawn Care. You can also use an impersonal salutation like Good morning! Hello! Greetings! The best solution may be to replace the salutation with a subject line.

Complimentary close: The complimentary close follows the body of your letter, with one line of space between them. It always begins with a capital letter and ends with a comma. Words in between are not capitalized.

The most everyday, acceptable, and all-purpose complimentary closes are: Sincerely, Sincerely yours, Very sincerely yours, Very sincerely, Yours truly, Very truly yours. You cannot go wrong with one of these.

For a highly formal letter involving White House, diplomatic, judicial, or ecclesiastical correspondence, use: Respectfully yours or Respectfully. An informal letter in the same instances uses: Very respectfully yours, Yours respectfully, or Sincerely yours. In formal letters to members of Congress, senators, high-ranking politicians and government figures, priests, rabbis, and ministers use: Yours very truly. The informal form is: Sincerely yours.

For most formal letters—regular business and personal—choose from among: Sincerely, Sincerely yours, Yours sincerely, Very sincerely yours, Very sincerely, Truly yours, Yours truly, Very truly yours, Yours very truly, Very cordially yours.

Informal closes include: Love, With all my love, Lovingly, Lovingly yours, Fondly, Affectionately, Yours affectionately, Sincerely, Sincerely yours, Cordially, Cordially yours, Yours cordially, Faithfully, Faithfully yours, Yours faithfully, As ever, As always, Devotedly, Yours, Best regards, Kindest regards, Warmest regards, Cheers, Your friend, Be well, Until next time.

Complimentary closes somewhere between formal and informal include: With all kind regards, Warm regards, Best regards, Best, Best wishes, With best wishes, With all best wishes, Cordially, Sincerely, All the very best, With every good wish, Warm personal regards.

After studying the above lists, choose one or two complimentary closes that reflect your letterwriting style and use them for most of your correspondence. It's not worth the trouble to fit a special complimentary close to each letter. As the foregoing lists indicate, the ubiquitous "Sincerely," for example, can be used as a formal, informal, or in-between close. Few people pay any attention to the complimentary close as it is in most cases a meaningless convention. There is no "right" or "wrong" complimentary close. Some types of letters do not use it at all (the simplified block form, for example) and there will certainly be no outcries if you omit it even from standard letter formats.

Shakespeare might as well have been writing of the complimentary close when he said, "Stand not upon the order of your going, / But go at once." A quickly written "Yours truly" does the job as well as anything more elaborate or time-consuming.

Signature: Although there used to be many rules governing signatures, it's fairly simple today: use the version of your name that you want the person to use for you. If there is any ambiguity (for example, the person knows you only under your pen name, birth name, married name, or business name), put the name that might be more easily recognized in parentheses under your signature. Signatures rarely include social titles, so omit the "Dr.," "Mrs.," or "Ms." (They may be typed on the name line, however.) In personal letters, your signature stands alone. In business letters, it is followed by your name and title (on one or two lines, depending on length). The name and title lines are typed four lines below the complimentary close, or more if you have a particularly sweeping signature. If your name and title are given on the letterhead, omit them under your signature. When signing a letter for someone else, put your initials just below and to the right of the signature, often after a slash. When you write a letter on someone else's behalf, sign your own name above a name line that identifies you: "Son of Walter Haversham" or "Secretary to Ada Herbert."

If your salutation uses the person's first name, sign the letter with your first name. Nonparallel salutations and signatures can be insulting and off-putting. If you write "Dear Fred," and sign it "Dr. Francis Etherington," you have assumed a superior position; writing it the other way around presumes an intimacy that may not exist. Except in very rare cases, the salutation and signature should be strictly parallel: "Dear Rosa, . . . Love, Judy"; "Dear Thomas Eustick, . . . Sincerely, Margaret Kraft."

FREQUENTLY MISSPELLED WORDS

abscess	appalled	Brittany
accommodate	appalling	Caribbean
acknowledge	apparatus	category
acknowledging	aquarium	cemetery
acknowledgment	barracks	colossal
acquaintance	barrage	colossus
all right (no such word	beneficiary	consensus
as "alright")	Britannica	concur

concurred
concurrence
consistency
correspondence
correspondent
desperate
discernible
drunkenness
elegance
elegant
embarrass
embarrassment
exhaustible
exhilarate
fluorescence
fulfilled
fulfillment
genealogy
grievance
harass
harassment

hemorrhage
hitchhiker
hypocrisy
indispensable
inoculate
iridescent
iridescence
irresistible
jewel
jeweled
jeweler
jewelry
knowledge
knowledgeable
lieutenant
liqueur
liquor
maintenance
mischievous
missile
misspell

niece
occasion
occur
occurred
occurrence
parallel
paraphernalia
perennial
permissible
Pharaoh
precede
proceed
receive
realtor
sacrilegious
seize
siege
sieve
threshold
vengeance

Word Weeds

The words listed below to the left of the equal sign often make up the fatty deposits of letterwriting, the weeds in our garden of words. Read through the list several times to get a sense of those constructions that are awkward and cumbersome. Mark any that appear often in your writing and try to eliminate them. To find out which ones you've made a habit of, check your letters against the list for a week or so.

above-mentioned = OMIT
absolutely essential/
   necessary = essential/necessary
accompanied by = with
according to our records = we find, our
   records show, or OMIT
acknowledge receipt of = thank you for
acquaint = tell/inform/let know
activate = begin/start
active consideration = consideration
actual experience/truth = experience/
   truth
advance forward = advance

advance planning/preparation/
   warning = planning/warning/
   preparation
advise = tell/inform
afford an opportunity = allow/permit
aforementioned = OMIT
aggregate/aggregation = total
a great deal of = much
all of = all
almost similar = similar
along the lines of = like
already exists = exists

a majority of = most
and etc. = etc.
an early date = soon
anent = about/concerning/regarding
a number of = about
a number of cases = some
any and all = any/all, but not both
applicable to = suitable for, relevant,
    appropriate, apply to
appreciate in value = appreciate
appreciate your informing me = please
    write/tell me
approximately = about
are of the opinion that = think that
around about [number] = about [number]
as a matter of fact = in fact, or OMIT
ascertain = learn/find out
as far as I am concerned = as for me
as I am sure you know = as you know,
    or OMIT
as per = according to
as regards = regarding/concerning/about
assist/assistance = help
as the case may be = OMIT
as to = about
at about = at
at all times = always
at an early/later date = soon/later
at a time when = when
at hand = OMIT
at present = now
attached please find/attached herewith/
    attached hereto = attached/I am
    attaching/I em enclosing
attach together = attach
at that/this point in time = then/now
at the earliest possible
    moment = immediately/very soon
at the moment = now/just now
at the present writing = now
at this (point in) time = now/just now
at your earliest convenience = soon
awaiting your instructions = please let
    me know
baby puppies = puppies
balance of equilibrium = balance/
    equilibrium, not both
based on the fact that = because

basic fundamentals/
    essentials = fundamentals/essentials
be dependent on = depend on
beg to [state/differ/advise] = OMIT
be in possession of = possess
be the recipient of = receive
beyond a shadow of a
    doubt = undoubtedly
big in size = big
bona fide = genuine
brief moment = moment
but even so = but/even so, not both
but in any case = but/in any case,
    not both
but however/nevertheless/nonetheless
    = one or the other, not both
but on the other hand = but/on the other
    hand, not both
by means of = by/with
call your attention to = please note
cancel out = cancel
circle around = circle
classify into groups = classify
climb up = climb
close proximity = proximity/nearby/
    close by
co-equal = equal
cognizant = aware
collaborate together = collaborate
come to the realization = realize
commence = begin/start
commendation = praise
communicate/communication = write,
    telephone/letter, telegram
commute back and forth = commute
completely filled = filled
completely accurate/compatible/
    finished/unanimous = accurate/
    compatible/finished/unanimous
conclude = close/end
conclusion = closing
conclusive proof = proof
consensus of opinion = consensus
construct = make
cooperate together = cooperate
could care less = couldn't care less (if
    you use this at all)
crucial/critical = important

current news = news
customary channels = usual
   way/regular procedure
deeds and actions = deeds or actions, not
   both
deem = consider, think
deem it advisable = suggest
definite decision = decision
demonstrate = show
deserving of = deserve
despite the fact that = although
different [two different dresses/several
   different movies] = OMIT
direct confrontation = confrontation
discontinue = stop
disincentive = penalty
doctorate degree = doctorate
do not hesitate to = please
drop down = drop
due consideration = consideration
due to the fact that = because
duly = OMIT
during the course of = during
during the time that = while
effectuate = effect
either one of the two = either one/either
   of the two/either
empty space = space
enclosed herewith is/enclosed please
   find = enclosed is/I enclose
encounter = meet
endeavor = try
endeavor to ascertain = try to find out
end result = result
engineer by profession = engineer
equivalent = equal
essentially = OMIT
etc. = avoid whenever possible
eventuate = result
exactly identical = identical
exactly the same = the same
exact replica = replica
exact same = exact or same, not both
exhibit/show/have a tendency to =
   tend to
existing condition = condition
expedite = hurry
extreme hazard = hazard

facilitate = ease/simplify/chair the
   meeting
fearful of = fear
feedback = comments/advice/reactions/
   opinions/thoughts
feel free to call/write = please call/write
fellow colleague = colleague
few in number = few
field of anthropology/politics,
   etc. = anthropology/politics, etc.
filled to capacity = filled
final conclusion/outcome =
   conclusion/outcome
finalize = end/conclude/complete
first and foremost = first or foremost,
   not both
first created = created
foot pedal = pedal
foreign imports = imports
formulate = form
for the period of a week/month/
   year = for a week/month/year
for the purpose of = for
for the reason that = because/
   since/as/for
frankly = OMIT
free gift = gift
fullest possible extent = fully
full satisfaction = satisfaction
furnish = give
future plans = plans
gather together = gather
get more for your money's
   worth = more for your money/get
   your money's worth
give an answer = answer
give encouragement to = encourage
give this matter your attention = OMIT
good benefit = benefit
grand total = total
grateful thanks = thanks
great majority = majority
have a belief in = believe
heir apparent = heir
herein = in this
hereinafter = from now on
herewith = enclosed/attached
homologous = alike

honestly = OMIT
hopefully = it is to be hoped, we
  hope, etc.
hopeful that = hope
if and when = if or when, not both
if it meets with your approval = if
  you approve
if at all possible = if possible
if you desire = if you wish/want
immediately adjoining = adjoining
I myself personally = I myself
in accordance with = with/as/by
in addition to = besides
inadvertent oversight = oversight
in all honesty = OMIT
in a matter of seconds/minutes/
  hours/days = in seconds/minutes/
  hours/days
in a number of cases = sometimes
in a satisfactory manner = satisfactorily
inasmuch as = as/since/because
inaugurate = begin/start
in back of = behind
in close proximity = near
in compliance with your request = as
  you requested/as you asked
in connection with = in/on/to, or OMIT
increase by a factor of two = double
indicate = show
individual person = individual or
  person, not both
initial = first
initiate = begin/start
in lieu of = instead of
in order that = so that
in order to = to
input = advice/opinions/thoughts/
  reactions
in re = about
in receipt of = received
in reference to = about
in regard to = about/concerning
in relation to = toward/to/about
in respect of = about/concerning
inside of = inside
integral part = part
interface with = meet with
in terms of = in

in the amount of = for
in the case of = of/in, or OMIT
in the course of = during
in the event of/that = if
in the final analysis = OMIT
in the majority of instances =
  usually/often
in the matter of = about/in/of
in the meantime = meanwhile
in the near future = soon
in the neighborhood of = about
in the time of = during
in the vast majority of cases = in most
  cases
in this connection = OMIT
intrinsically = OMIT
in view of = because/since
in view of the fact that = as
invited guest = guest
irregardless = regardless/irrespective
I share your concern = like you, I believe
is indicative of = indicates
is of the opinion = thinks
is when/is where = is the day/is the
  place
it goes without saying = OMIT
it is clear/obvious that = clearly/
  obviously
it is my intention = I intend
it would not be unreasonable to
  believe/think/assume = I
  believe/think/assume
I would hope = I hope
I would like to express my
  appreciation = I appreciate
joint collaboration = collaboration
join together = join
kindly = please
kind of/sort of = OMIT
kneel down = kneel
lift up = lift
literally = OMIT 99% of the time
literally and figuratively = OMIT 99%
  of the time
little baby = baby
lot/lots/a whole lot = OMIT
major breakthrough = breakthrough
make a decision = decide

make a mention of = mention
make inquiry regarding = inquire
mandatory requirements =
   requirements
meet with approval = approve
merge together = merge
meet up with = meet
mental telepathy = telepathy
modification = change
modus operandi = method
month of December = December
more importantly = more important
mutual agreement/cooperation
   = agreement/cooperation
my personal opinion = my opinion/I
   believe that
native habitat = habitat
necessary prerequisite = prerequisite
needless to say = OMIT
never before = never
new initiative/record/recruit =
   initiative/record/recruit
none at all = none
not in a position to = unable to
not to mention = OMIT
notwithstanding the fact
   that = although/even though
obviate = do away with
official business = business
off of = off
old adage = adage
on a continuing basis = constantly/
   continually
on a daily/monthly/weekly
   basis = daily/monthly/weekly
on a few occasions = occasionally
on a regular basis = regularly
on behalf of = for
one and the same = the same
only other alternative = alternative
on the grounds that = because
on the order of = about
on the part of = for/among
open up/close up/fold up/settle
   up = open, close, fold, settle
original source = source
other alternative = alternative
overall = OMIT

overexaggerate = exaggerate
owing to = because of
over with = over
past experience = experience
past history = history
per = a
per annum = a year
per diem = a day
perfectly clear = clear
perform an examination = examine
permeate throughout = permeate
permit me to say = OMIT
per se = as such
personal friend/opinion = friend/
   opinion
pervasive = widespread
pervasively = throughout
place emphasis on = emphasize
positive identification = identification
postponed until later = postponed
predicated on = based on
preparatory to = before
prepared to offer = able to offer
preplanned = planned
present a conclusion = conclude
present status = status
preventative/orientated =
   preventive/oriented
previous to = before
previous experience = experience
prioritize = list/rank/rate (in order of
   importance)
prior to = before
pursuant to = according to
quite a = OMIT
quite unique = unique
radically new = new or radical, not
   both
raison d'être = reason for
rarely ever/seldom ever = rarely/seldom
reach an agreement = agree
rectangular in shape = rectangular
reduce to a minimum = minimize
red/yellow/blue in
   color = red/yellow/blue
refer back to = refer to
reiterate again = reiterate
relating to = about

relative to = about/regarding/
  concerning
remuneration = pay
repeat again = repeat
reside = live
return back = return
revert back = revert
root cause = cause
round in shape/round circles = round or
  circles, not both
same (as in "will send
  same") = it/them/the items, or OMIT
same identical = same or identical, not
  both
seldom ever = seldom
separate entities = entities
serious crisis/danger = crisis/danger
shuttle back and forth = shuttle
sine qua non = essential
sink down = sink
six in number = six
small in size = small
so advise us = advise us
so consequently/therefore = so
  consequently or therefore, but
  not both
square in shape = square
state of Minnesota = Minnesota
steamlined in appearance = streamlined
still persists = persists
string together = string
subject matter = subject or matter, not
  both
subsequent to = after/following
successful achievement = achievement
sudden impulse = impulse
take and (e.g., "take and read
  this") = OMIT
take the liberty of/take this opportunity
  to = OMIT
technical jargon = jargon
terminate = end
the above = OMIT
the better part of = most of/nearly all of
the bulk of = most/nearly all of
the earliest possible moment = soon/
  immediately
the party = (replace with specific noun)

therein = in
the undersigned/this writer = I
this is to inform you = OMIT
this is to thank you = thank you
thusly = in this way/as follows
too numerous to mention = numerous
total destruction = destruction
to tell the truth = OMIT
true facts = facts
ubiquitous = widespread
undergraduate student = undergraduate
under separate cover = separately
unexpected emergency = emergency
unintentional mistake = mistake
unless and until = unless or until,
  not both
until such time as = until
untimely death = death
up to this writing = until now
usual custom = custom
utilization/utilize = use
vacillating back and forth = vacillating
various different = various or different,
  not both
verbal discussion = discussion
very = OMIT
visible to the eye = visible
wall mural = mural
we are writing to tell you = OMIT
we beg to advise = OMIT
wish to advise/state = OMIT
wish to apologize = we apologize
with all due regard = OMIT
with a view to = to
without further delay = now/
  immediately
with reference/regard/respect
  to = about/concerning/on
with the exception of = except for
with the result that = so that
with this in mind, it is certainly clear
  that = therefore
words cannot describe = OMIT
worthy of merit = worthy or merits, but
  not both
would appreciate your informing/
  advising us = let us know

Forms of Address

No letter has ever been returned stamped, "Incorrect form of address." However, using the correct form says that you are interested in accuracy and respectful of the person's position. On the other hand, our democratic under-pinnings and common sense indicate that a respectful letter addressed to the person by name and beginning "Dear . . ." would be equally effective and acceptable.

The list below will help you compose the inside address and the address on the envelope. At the end of each entry are appropriate salutations. If more than one is given, the first is always the formal salutation, the second the informal. Where addresses are known and permanent, they are given. Any job title not listed is handled in the usual way.

Government Officials

President of the United States
The President
The White House
Washington, DC 20500
Mr./Madam President: / Dear Mr./Madam President:

Vice-President of the United States
The Vice-President
The White House
Washington, DC 20500
The Vice-President: / Dear Madam/Mr. Vice-President: or Madam/Sir:

Spouse of the President of the United States
Mrs. Helen Eliot/Mr. Richard Lockridge
The White House
Washington, DC 20500
Dear Mrs. Eliot/Mr. Lockridge:

Former President of the United States
The Honorable William Eybe
Sir: / Dear Mr. Eybe:

Governor (state or territory)
The Honorable Eustace Kinnit/Kate Hardcastle
Governor of California
Sir:/Madam: / Dear Governor Kinnit/Hardcastle: or Dear Governor:

> Note that instead of "The Honorable . . ." the correct form in Massa-chusetts is "His/Her Excellency, the Governor of Massachusetts." This form can be used for other governors, too.

Lieutenant Governor/Acting Governor (state or territory)
The Honorable James Mardley/Diana Fagan
Lieutenant Governor/Acting Governor of Texas
Madam/Sir: / Dear Ms. Fagan/Mr. Mardley:

United States Senator
The Honorable Gideon Forsyth/Nancy Dolour
United States Senate
Washington, DC 20510
or
The Honorable Nancy Dolour/Gideon Forsyth
United States Senator
(local address)
Madam/Sir: / Dear Senator Forsyth/Dolour:

United States Representative
The Honorable Emily Crowthorne/John Brough
United States House of Representatives
Washington, DC 20515
or
The Honorable John Brough/Emily Crowthorne
Representative in Congress
(local address)
Sir/Madam: / Dear Ms. Crowthorne/Mr. Brough: or Dear Representative
    Brough/Crowthorne:

Senate/House Committee/Subcommittee Chair
The Honorable Janet Lownie/Matthew Ligne
Chair, Committee/Subcommittee on Foreign Affairs
United States Senate/United States House of Representatives
Washington, DC 20515
Dear Senator/Representative Lownie/Ligne:

> Members of Congress-elect and former members of Congress are also
> addressed as "The Honorable . . ." and "Dear Madam/Sir:" or "Dear
> Mr./Ms. . . ." Members of Congress holding special positions are ad-
> dressed as "The Honorable . . . ," followed by their title ("Speaker of
> the House of Representatives," "President of the United States Senate"),
> with a salutation of "Sir:/Madam:"/"Dear Madam/Mr. Speaker:" or
> "Dear Ms./Mr.:"

Mayor
The Honorable Rosa Emerson/Edward Kipps
Mayor of Caldwell
City Hall
Dear Madam/Sir: / Dear Mayor Emerson/Kipps: / Dear Mr./Ms. Mayor:

Chief Justice of the United States Supreme Court
The Chief Justice
The Supreme Court of the United States
or
The Honorable Alvin Belknap/Constance Neville
Chief Justice of the United States Supreme Court
The Supreme Court
Washington, DC 20543
Sir:/Madam: / Dear Mr./Madam Chief Justice:

Associate Justice of the United States Supreme Court
Mr. Justice Dempster/Madam Justice Sherston
The Supreme Court of the United States
Washington, DC 20543
Madam/Sir: / Dear Madam/Mr. Justice: or Dear Justice Dempster/Sherston:

Honorables

The following government positions—and others like them—are treated similarly. "The Honorable" precedes the person's name ("The Honorable Matthew Northmore" or "The Honorable Donna Clara D'Almanza"). On the next line is their complete title ("Attorney General of the United States") followed on subsequent lines by the address. The formal salutation is "Madam/Sir:" Informal salutations include using the title ("Dear Mr./Ms. [or Madam] Under Secretary of Labor:"); using the title plus a last name ("Dear Chief Justice Claverton:"); using a social title plus their last name ("Dear Ms. Fielding:" or "Dear Mr. Dale:"); or simply "Dear Madam:"/"Dear Sir:" If the use of "The Honorable" seems pretentious in some cases, you may omit it without undue anxiety; the trend today is toward less formality.

Secretary, Under Secretary, or Assistant Secretary of State, the Treasury, Defense, the Interior, Agriculture, Commerce, Labor, Health and Human Services, Housing and Urban Development, Transportation, Energy, Education (address the Secretary as "Dear Mr./Ms. Secretary" omitting the department).
Postmaster General of the United States
Attorney General of the United States
Comptroller General
Public Printer
directors/heads of independent federal agencies, commissions, offices, and organizations
Press Secretary to the President
Secretary to the President
Assistant to the President
state senator or representative, delegate, member of the assembly

president of a state senate or state house speaker (speaker of the state assembly,
   state house of delegates, state house of representatives, state general
   assembly)
state secretary ("Secretary of the State of Kentucky")
state attorney general ("Attorney General of the State of Iowa")
state auditor, treasurer, comptroller, and other state officials
district attorney, county attorney
county supervisor
president of a city board of commissioners
city attorney, city commissioner
city councillors
state supreme court chief justice, presiding justice, associate justice, and
   justices
judges—federal, state, local (excluding U.S. Supreme Court)
resident commissioners
territorial delegates

Heads of State

President of a Republic
His/Her Excellency Abdou Diouf/L. Sédar-Senghor
President of the Republic of Senegal
Excellency: / Dear Madam/Mr. President:

Prime Minister
His/Her Excellency Lt. Colonel Ramahatra Victor/Gabrielle Ranavalona
Prime Minister of Madagascar
Excellency: / Dear Mr./Madam Prime Minister:

Prime Minister of Great Britain/Canada
The Right Honorable Julia Lancester/John James Ridley
Prime Minister of Great Britain/the Dominion of Canada
Sir:/Madam: / Dear Madam/Mr. Prime Minister: or Dear Mr. Ridley/
   Madam Lancester:

Premier
His/Her Excellency Major Pedro Pires/Luzia Sotavento
Premier of the Republic of Cape Verde
Excellency: / Dear Mr./Madam Premier:

> When writing to officials of another country, check the country's exact
> name (a desk almanac will help) and the correct spelling of the official's
> name. Country leaders include queens, kings, rulers, co-regents, presi-
> dents, prime ministers, premiers, governor-generals, chancellors, emirs,
> episcopal co-princes, and sultans; verify the correct title. For example, in
> Mauritania, you write to the Chief of State and Head of Government, The
> Islamic Republic of Mauritania.

Diplomats

Ambassador to the United States
Her/His Excellency Elizabeth Tenbruggen/Kristian Koppig
Ambassador of The Netherlands or His/Her Excellency the Ambassador
from The Netherlands
Excellency: / Dear Mr./Madam Ambassador:

> Use full name of country except for Great Britain; address British representatives as British Ambassador or British Minister. If an ambassador has a personal title, use it before the name ("Her Excellency Lady Catherine De Bourgh"). For an ambassador with a military title, substitute that title for "The Honorable" ("Colonel Jean Albert De Charleu").

U.S. Ambassador
The Honorable Millicent Chyne/Lambert Strether
The United States Ambassador/Ambassador from the United States
The United States Embassy
Madam/Sir: / Dear Madam/Sir: or Dear Madam/Mr. Ambassador: or Dear
   Ambassador Chyne/Strether:

U.S. Consul-General, Consul, Vice-Consul, Chargé d'Affaires
Mr./Ms. Christopher Pumphrey/Margaret Hart
Consul-General/Consul/Vice-Consul/Chargé d'Affaires of the United States
   of America
Madam: / Sir: / Dear Ms. Hart/Mr. Pumphrey: or Dear Madam/Sir:

Foreign Chargé d'Affaires
Mr. Raoul de Castro/Ms. H.G. Nuñez
Chargé d'Affaires of Spain
Sir/Madam: / Dear Mr. de Castro/Ms. Nuñez:

U.S. or Foreign Ministers
The Honorable Nathan Rosenstein/Adèle Rossignol
United States Minister to Pakistan/Minister of France
Madam/Sir: Dear Sir/Madam: or Dear Mr./Madam Minister:

High Commissioner
The Honorable Basil Fane/Julia Norman
United States High Commissioner to Argentina
Madam/Sir: / Dear Mr. Fane/Ms. Norman:

Secretary General of the United Nations
Her/His Excellency Anne Menzies/Peter Levi
Secretary General of the United Nations
The Secretariat
United Nations

United Nations Plaza
New York, NY 10017/10021
Excellency: / Dear Ms./Mr. Secretary General: or Dear Ms. Menzies/
    Mr. Levi:

Under Secretary of the United Nations
The Honorable Rose Mei-Hua/Thomas Henry Fould
Under Secretary of the United Nations
Sir/Madam: / Dear Mr./Ms. Under Secretary or Dear Ms. Mei-Hua/
    Mr. Fould:

U.S. Delegate to the United Nations
Mr./Ms. Napier Harpenden/Elizabeth Randall
Chief of/Delegate from the United States Mission to the United Nations
Dear Mr. Harpenden/Ms. Randall:

U.S. Representative to the U.N. with Rank of Ambassador
The Honorable Isabella Tarry/Gilleis Otley
United States Representative to the United Nations
Sir/Madam: / Dear Mr./Madam Ambassador:

Foreign Representative to the U.N. with Rank of Ambassador
His/Her Excellency Pietro Spina/Eline Vere
Representative of Italy to the United Nations
Excellency: / Dear Mr./Madam Ambassador:

Academics

College/University President
Dr. Angusina Mackenzie/Philip Winter
President, Alexander College of the Arts
Madam/Sir: / Dear Dr./President Winter/Mackenzie:

> In the case of a member of the clergy, use the religious title first and put
> affiliations and degrees after the name ("The Reverend Malachi Bren-
> nan, S.J., Ph.D." or "Sister Mary Beatrice Fitzclare, B.V.M., Ph.D.") and
> use either "Dear Dr. Brennan/Fitzclare:" or "Dear Father Brennan/Sister
> Fitzclare:").

Professor/Associate Professor/Assistant Professor
Professor/Dr./Ms./Mr. Godfrey St. Peter/Kate Fansler or Kate Fansler,
    Ph.D./Godfrey St. Peter, Ph.D.
Department of English
Reed Amhearst University
Dear Professor/Dr./Ms./Mr. Fansler/St. Peter: or Dear Madam/Sir:

> "Dr." meaning someone who has received a doctoral degree and "Ph.D."
> do not appear together; use one or the other. If the instructor does not

have a doctoral degree, use a social title (Mr., Ms., Mrs., Miss) instead of "Dr." Address instructors by social titles if they do not have a doctoral degree, otherwise by "Dr." Do not use "Professor."

Dean/Assistant Dean
Dean/Assistant Dean/Dr. Andrea Fitch/Rupert Birkin
Dean/Assistant, School of Dentistry
Brangwen University
Dear Madam/Sir: / Dear Dean/Dr. Fitch/Birkin:

Chancellor
Dr. Jane Geoghegan/Edward Bronckhorst
Chancellor
Robinson University
Sir/Madam: / Dear Dr. Geoghegan/Bronckhorst:

Chaplain
Chaplain/The Reverend Sarah Brockett/Martin Whitelaw, D.D., Ph.D.
Crowther United College
Dear Chaplain/Dr. Brockett/Whitelaw:

Members of the Clergy

Rabbi
Rabbi Miriam Ephraim/Benjamin Ezra
    or Rabbi Miriam Ephraim, D.D./Benjamin Ezra, D.D.
Temple of Mount Zion
Madam/Sir: / Dear Rabbi/Dr. Ephraim/Rosedale:

Cantor
Cantor Simon Rosedale/Leah Dvoshe
Temple Ben Aaron
Sir/Madam: / Dear Cantor Rosedale/Dvoshe:

Canon
The Reverend/The Very Reverend Esmé Howe-Nevinson, D.D.
Canon of St. Elizabeth's
Reverend Sir: / Dear Canon Howe-Nevinson:

Nun/Sister
Sister Donna Agnes Rebura, C.N.D.
Dear Sister Donna Agnes: / Dear Sister: or Dear Sister Rebura:

Brother
Brother Casimir Lypiatt, O.S.B.
Dear Brother: / Dear Brother Casimir: or Dear Brother Lypiatt:

Minister, Priest, or Member of the Clergy
The Reverend George B. Callender, Ph.D./Martha Rodd, Ph.D.
      or The Reverend Martha Rodd/George B. Callender
      or The Reverend George B. Callender, D.D.
      or The Reverend Dr. Martha Dodd
Reverend Sir/Madam: or Dear Reverend Madam/Sir: / Dear Dr./Father/Ms./
      Mr./Reverend Callender/Rodd:

      An Eastern Orthodox priest's title is "Reverend Father Kostes Palamas"
      and the salutation is "Dear Father Palamas:"

Dean (Cathedral/Seminary)
The Very Reverend Andrew Montfitchet, D.D.
Dean of St. Philip's Seminary
Very Reverend Sir: / Dear Dean Montfitchet:

Monsignor
The Right Reverend Monsignor John Woodley
Reverend Monsignor: / Dear Monsignor Woodley: or Dear Monsignor:

Abbot
The Right Reverend Gilbert Belling Torpenhow, O.S.B.
Abbot of Heldar Abbey
Right Reverend Abbot: / Dear Father Abbot: or Dear Father Torpenhow:

Father/Brother Superior
The Very Reverend Richard Crosland, M.M.
Director/Superior of The Mission Fathers/Brothers
Dear Father/Brother Superior: / Dear Father Crosland/Brother Richard:

      See the *Official Catholic Directory* if you are unsure whether the indi-
      vidual is a priest or a brother or if he has other titles.

Mother/Sister Superior
The Reverend Mother/Sister Superior Ellen Mary Montgomery, A.C.M.
Convent of St. Joseph
      or Mother Ellen Mary Montgomery
      Superior of St. Joseph's Convent
      or Mother Ellen Mary Montgomery, Superior
      Convent of St. Joseph
Reverend Mother/Sister: / Dear Reverend Sister/Mother: or Dear Mother/
      Sister Superior: or Dear Mother Ellen Mary Montgomery: or Dear
      Mother Ellen Mary: or Dear Madam:

      There are also titles such as Regional Superior, Provincial Superior, and
      President, and salutations like "Dear Religious Leader" are used when
      writing to large or international orders. Someone within the order
      might write simply "Dear Sister." For the correct title, check the *Offi-
      cial Catholic Directory*.

Anglican Bishop
The Right Reverend James Crowther
The Lord Bishop of Oxford
Right Reverend Sir: / Dear Bishop Crowther:

Anglican Archbishop
The Most Reverend Reginald Kershaw
Archbishop of Salisbury
    or The Most Reverend Archbishop of Salisbury
    or The Lord Archbishop of Salisbury
Your Grace: / Dear Archbishop Kershaw: or Dear Archbishop:

Episcopal Bishop
The Right Reverend Dinah Morris
Bishop of New York
Right Reverend Bishop: / Dear Bishop:

    The Presiding Bishop of the Protestant Episcopal Church in the United
    States has that title in place of "Bishop of New York." You can also
    replace "The Right Reverend" with "The Most Reverend" and address
    him as "Most Reverend Sir:"

Protestant Bishop
The Reverend George Cassilis
Bishop of Los Angeles
Dear Bishop:

Methodist Bishop
Bishop Richard Feverel of the Miami Area
    or The Reverend Richard Feverel
    Methodist Bishop of Miami
Reverend Sir: / Dear Bishop Feverel:

Mormon Bishop
Bishop Roger Dainton
The Church of Jesus Christ of the Latter-Day Saints.
Dear Bishop Dainton: / Sir:

Roman Catholic Archbishop/Bishop
The Most Reverend Jean Latour
Archbishop/Bishop of Santa Fe
Your Excellency: / Dear Archbishop/Bishop Latour: or Most
Reverend Sir:

Eastern Orthodox Archbishop
The Most Reverend George, Archbishop of Philadelphia
    or His Eminence George, Archbishop of Philadelphia
Your Excellency:

Episcopal Archdeacon
The Venerable Nicholas Broune
Archdeacon of San Francisco
Venerable Sir: / Dear Archdeacon:

Cardinal
His Eminence James Cardinal Wickham
Archbishop of New York
Your Eminence: / Dear Cardinal Wickham:

Roman Catholic Pope
His Holiness, Pope John Paul II
    or His Holiness, the Pope
Vatican City
00187 Rome, Italy
Your Holiness or Most Holy Father:

> There is no informal salutation; the complimentary close is always
> "Respectfully yours,."

Apostolic Pro-Nuncio
His Excellency, The Most Reverend John Sylvester Clayton
Titular Archbishop of Greece
The Apostolic Pro-Nuncio
Your Excellency: / Dear Archbishop Clayton:

Greek Orthodox Patriarch
His All Holiness Patriarch George
Your All Holiness:

Russian Orthodox Patriarch
His Holiness the Patriarch of Chicago
Your Holiness:

Military Personnel

When writing to officers and enlisted personnel use: full rank (may be
abbreviated), full name, comma, initials for the branch of service ("Captain
Molly Cuthbertson, U.S.A."). For retired personnel, add "(Ret.)" after the
service affiliation. Abbreviations for the service branches are:

Air Force, U.S.A.F.
Army, U.S.A.
Army Reserve, U.S.A.R.
Coast Guard, U.S.C.G.
Coast Guard Reserve, U.S.C.G.R.
Marine Corps, U.S.M.C.
Marine Corps Reserve, U.S.M.C.R.

Naval Reserve, U.S.N.R.
Navy, U.S.N.

Salutations include the rank and last name ("Dear Commander Culverin:") or rank only ("Dear Commander:"). You may write simply "Dear General:" when addressing a general, lieutenant general, major general, or brigadier general. "Dear Admiral:" includes fleet, vice, rear, and ordinary admirals. The salutation for junior officers, petty officers, warrant officers, enlisted personnel, ensigns, and noncommissioned officers is "Dear Ms./Mr. Kirker:"

For chaplains use: "Chaplain," full name, comma, rank, comma, initials of their branch of service ("Chaplain Michael Sabrov, Captain, U.S.A."). In the Navy, the order is reversed: "Captain Michael Sabrov (Ch.C.), U.S.N."). The salutation is "Dear Chaplain:"

Index

A